A–Z of Policing Law

Roger Lorton LL B, M.Phil.

London: The Stationery Office

Applications for reproduction should be made in writing to The Stationery Office Limited, St Crispins, Duke Street, Norwich NR3 1PD.

Roger Lorton has asserted his moral rights under the Copyright, Designs and Patents Act 1988, to be identified as the author of this work.

A CIP catalogue record for this book is available from the British Library
A Library of Congress CIP catalogue record has been applied for

First edition© Roger Lorton 2000
ISBN 0 11 702812 6
First published 2001

Published by The Stationery Office and available from:
The Stationery Office
(mail, telephone and fax orders only)
PO Box 29, Norwich, NR3 1GN
Telephone orders/ General enquiries 0870 600 5522
Fax orders 0870 600 5533

www.clicktso.com
www.thestationeryoffice.com

The Stationery Office Bookshops
123 Kingsway, London WC2B 6PQ
0207 242 6393 Fax 0207 242 6394
68–69 Bull Street, Birmingham B4 6AD
0121 236 9696 Fax 0121 236 9699
33 Wine Street, Bristol BS1 2BQ
0117 926 4306 Fax 0117 929 4515
9–21 Princess Street, Manchester M60 8AS
0161 834 7201 Fax 0161 833 0634
16 Arthur Street, Belfast BT1 4GD
028 9023 8451 Fax 028 9023 5401
The Stationery Office Oriel Bookshop
18–19, High Street, Cardiff CF1 2BZ
029 2039 5548 Fax 029 2038 4347
71 Lothian Road, Edinburgh EH3 9AZ
0870 606 5566 Fax 0870 606 5588

The Stationery Office's Accredited Agents
(see Yellow Pages)

and through good booksellers

Printed in the United Kingdom by the Stationery Office, London
TJ005181   C20   11/01   651552   19585

CONTENTS

PREFACE TO THE 1ST EDITION

The criminal law is a large and complex subject which few publications have successfully compiled in a form useful to practising police officers. In attempting to write a book of manageable proportions focusing on the areas of criminal law that may be encountered by police officers during their normal working day, I have considered nearly 1,000 offences from which some criminal liability arises. The result is a book detailing offences from more than 100 statutes, regulations and orders.

I have adopted a standard form in the presentation of these offences while attempting to restate the law as it was written, without embellishment. This has not always been possible however and in such cases the wording of the statute has been adapted to suit the format used throughout this book. Where necessary I have added definitions, general information and notes which may be of use to the reader. Each section also includes the relevant powers available to a police officer. I have included the maximum punishments applicable to each offence as these have a bearing on the powers available to a constable and will identify in which court an offence may be dealt with.

Legislation has been recorded chronologically in each section and where no section is specified, the offences stated are a compilation of a number of subsections under that Act.

In this work I have attempted to use the language of the various statutes and it has not been possible to meet fully the needs of political correctness. Rather I have relied upon the Interpretation Act 1978 which states that in any Act, unless the contrary intention appears:

(a)   words importing the masculine gender include the feminine;

(b)   words importing the feminine gender include the masculine;

(c)   words in the singular include the plural; and

(d)   words in the plural include the singular.

To those whose knowledge of the law is limited this book offers an easy to use work of reference which may act as a base for developing their understanding. For those with a working knowledge of policing law it offers a concise reference identifying a range of different offences and the legislation from which they arise. It is intended as a 'ready reckoner' of law applicable to operational officers and offers, in a single volume, the principal policing offences, from A to Z.

Roger Lorton, *January 1998*

PREFACE TO THE 2ND EDITION

The first edition has been fully updated and now includes nearly 800 offences pertinent to police duties, together with the associated powers of arrest, search and seizure. The law is as it stands in August 2001. In an effort to assist those officers studying for their promotion examinations I have used a grey bar to indicate the subject areas that they should have a working knowledge of. The work will be kept updated at www.policelaw.co.uk. While the politics of policing are ever-changing, the job on the ground remains largely as it has always been. This book is aimed at those with their feet on the ground.

Roger Lorton, *August 2001*

For Jack – welcome to the world.

TABLE OF LEGISLATION

xiv

XV

xviii

xix

xxi

xxii

XXV

xxviii

ABANDONED VEHICLES

See also Highways and Roads, Litter, PACE – Arrest, Parking

Offence: It is an offence for any person, without lawful authority, to abandon on any land in the open air, or on any other land forming part of a highway:

(a) a motor vehicle; or

(b) anything which formed part of a motor vehicle and was removed from it in the course of dismantling the vehicle on the land.

Contrary to: Refuse Disposal (Amenity) Act 1978 s.2(1)(a)

Max. sentence: Magistrates' Court: 3 months' imprisonment/ £2,500 fine.[1]

Power: Report / s.25 PACE

Offence: It is an offence to fail to remove a vehicle as soon as practicable on being required to do so by a police constable.

Contrary to: Removal and Disposal of Vehicles Regulations 1986 r.3

Max. sentence: Magistrates' Court: 3 months' imprisonment/ £2,500 fine.

Power: Report / s.25 PACE

General Powers

A constable may require a vehicle to be removed by its owner, driver or the person in charge or control of the vehicle, if such is in a position, condition or circumstances as to cause an obstruction, or be likely to cause a danger to other road users.[2]

If the driver refuses to remove the motor vehicle or is not available, a police officer may remove it or cause it to be removed.[3]

Definitions

Motor vehicle: a mechanically propelled vehicle intended or adapted for use on roads, whether or not it is in a fit state for such use, and includes any trailer intended or adapted for use as an attachment to such a vehicle, any chassis or body, with or without wheels, appearing to have formed part of such a vehicle or trailer and anything attached to such a vehicle or trailer.[4]

General Information

For the purposes of the offence under s.2 of the Refuse Disposal (Amenity) Act 1978, a person who leaves any thing on any land in such circumstances or for such a period that he may reasonably be assumed to have abandoned it or to have brought it to the land for the purpose of abandoning it there shall be deemed to have done so unless the contrary is shown.

Notes

1   Following conviction, any removal costs may be recovered from the offender following an application to the court from the local authority.

2   Removal and Disposal of Vehicles Regulations 1986 r.3. This power includes vehicles parked in contravention of no-waiting signs, traffic regulation orders, motorway regulations and pedestrian crossing regulations. See page 287.

3   See r.4

4   Refuse Disposal (Amenity) Act 1978 s.11.

ABSCONDERS AND ESCAPEES

See also Armed Forces, Attempts, Bail, Children and Young Persons, Criminal Justice, Mental Health, PACE – Arrest, Police

Offence: It is an offence for a person to escape from legal custody.

Contrary to: Common Law

Max. sentence: Crown Court: 10 years' imprisonment/unlimited fine.

Power: Arrestable Offence

Offence: It is an offence for any person to aid any prisoner in escaping or attempting to escape from a prison or who, with intent to facilitate the escape of any prisoner:

(a) conveys any thing into a prison or to a prisoner;

(b) sends any thing (by post or otherwise) into a prison or to a prisoner; or

(c) places any thing anywhere outside a prison with a view to its coming into the possession of a prisoner.

Contrary to: Prison Act 1952 s.39

Max. sentence: Crown Court: 10 years' imprisonment / unlimited fine.

Power: Arrestable Offence[1]

Offence: It is an offence for any person to:

(a) knowingly harbour a person who has escaped from prison or other institution, or who having been sentenced in any part of the United Kingdom or in any of the Channel Islands or the Isle of Man to imprisonment or detention, is otherwise unlawfully at large; or

(b) give to any such person any assistance with intent to prevent, hinder or interfere with his being taken into custody.

Contrary to: Criminal Justice Act 1961 s.22(2)

Max. sentence: Magistrates' Court: 6 months' imprisonment / £5,000 fine.

Crown Court: 10 years' imprisonment / unlimited fine.

Power: Arrestable Offence

Offence: It is an offence, where a person has committed an arrestable offence,[2] for any other person, knowing or believing him to be guilty of the offence or of some other arrestable offence, without lawful authority or reasonable excuse, to do any act with intent to impede his apprehension or prosecution.

Contrary to: Criminal Law Act 1967 s.4

Max. sentence: Magistrates' Court: 6 months' imprisonment / £5,000 fine.

Crown Court: 10 years' imprisonment[3] / unlimited fine.

Power: Arrestable Offence[4]

Offence: It is an offence[5] for a person who has been temporarily released under rules made under the Prison Act 1952, to:

(a) without reasonable excuse, remain unlawfully at large beyond the expiry of the period for which he was temporarily released; or

(b) knowing or believing an order recalling him to have been made, and while unlawfully at large by virtue of such an order, fails, without reasonable excuse, to take all necessary steps for complying as soon as reasonably practicable with that order.

Contrary to: Prisoners (Return to Custody) Act 1995 s.1(1)

Max. sentence: Magistrates' Court: 6 months' imprisonment / £5,000 fine.

Power: Arrest without warrant.[6]

General Powers

Any person who, having been sentenced to imprisonment,[7] custody for life or detention in a young offender institution or ordered to be detained in a young offender institution or secure training centre, or having been committed to a prison or remand centre, is unlawfully at large, may be arrested by a constable without warrant and taken to the

place in which he is required in accordance with law to be detained.[8]
If a child or young person is absent without the consent of the responsible person:

(a) from a place of safety to which he has been taken under s.16(3) of the Children and Young Persons Act 1969; or

(b) from local authority accommodation

   (i) in which he is required to live under s.12AA;

   (ii) to which he has been remanded under s.16(3A); or

   (iii) to which he has been remanded or committed under s.23(1)

he may be arrested by a constable and conducted to the place of safety, the local authority accommodation or such other place as the responsible person may direct.[9]

A constable may enter and search any premises for the purposes of recapturing any person who is unlawfully at large while liable to be detained in a prison, remand centre, young offender institution or secure training centre.[10]

Notes

1 Police and Criminal Evidence Act 1984 s.24.

2 See page 282.

3 The sentence is dependent upon the offence originally committed and is generally half of the maximum for that offence; e.g. where the original offender is liable to a term of 10 years' imprisonment a person found guilty of assisting him is liable to 5 years. In any case where the original punishment is less than 10 years the potential maximum is 3 years. Proceedings require the consent of the Director of Public Prosecutions.

4 But see note 2 above.

5 This offence does not apply in the case of a person temporarily released from a secure training unit.

6 A person shall be deemed for the purposes of the Prisoners (Return to Custody) Act 1995 s.1, to be unlawfully at large for the purposes of the Prison Act 1952 s.49. See General Powers.

7 Includes children and young persons detained under a direction of the Secretary of State [Criminal Justice Act 1967 s.67].

8 Prison Act 1952 s.49.

9 Children and Young Persons Act 1969 s.32(1A) and (1B). This power is

concerned with the apprehension of children and young persons who have been committed to the care of the local authority. A power of entry is available under s.17 of the Police and Criminal Evidence Act 1984.

10   Police and Criminal Evidence Act 1984 s.17(ca) and (cb).

ABSTRACTING ELECTRICITY

See also Computers and the Internet, Deception, PACE – Arrest, Telecommunications, Theft

Offence: It is an offence for a person to dishonestly[1]

(a)   use without due authority; or

(b)   cause to be wasted or diverted, any electricity.

Contrary to: Theft Act 1968 s.13

Max. sentence: Magistrates' Court: 6 months' imprisonment / £5,000 fine.

Crown Court: 5 years' imprisonment / unlimited fine.

Power: Arrestable Offence[2]

Offence: It is an offence to dishonestly obtain a service[3] with intent to avoid payment of any charge applicable to the provision of that service.

Contrary to: Telecommunications Act 1984 s.42

Max. sentence: Magistrates' Court: 6 months' imprisonment / £5,000 fine.

Crown Court: 5 years' imprisonment / unlimited fine.

Power: Arrestable Offence

Offence: It is an offence for any person[4] intentionally or by culpable negligence:

(a)   to alter the register of any meter used for measuring the quantity of electricity supplied to any premises by an electricity supplier; or

    (b) to prevent any such meter from duly registering the quantity of electricity supplied.

Contrary to: Electricity Act 1989 Sch.7(11)

Max. sentence: Magistrates' Court: £1,000 fine.

Power: Report / s.25 PACE

General Information

A person's appropriation of property belonging to another may be dishonest notwithstanding that he is willing to pay for the property.[5]

Notes

1   See page 402 for the definitions relevant to offences under the Theft Act 1968.

2   See page 281.

3   This applies to any service provided by means of a telecommunication service, which is authorised by licence.

4   The possession of artificial means for causing an alteration of the register of the meter or, as the case may be, the prevention of the meter from duly registering shall, if the meter was in his custody or under his control, be *prima facie* evidence that the alteration or prevention was intentionally caused by him.

5   See page 403.

AGGRAVATED VEHICLE-TAKING

See also Dangerous and Careless Driving / Riding, PACE – Arrest, Taking a Conveyance, Theft, Vehicle Interference

Offence: It is an offence[1] for a person, without having the consent of the owner or other lawful authority,

    (a) to take any conveyance for his own or another's use; or

    (b) knowing that any conveyance has been taken without such authority, to drive it or allow himself to be carried in or on it[2]

and, if the conveyance is a mechanically propelled

vehicle, at any time after the vehicle was unlawfully taken[3] and before it was recovered, the vehicle was driven, and injury or damage was caused in one or more of the following circumstances:

    (i) that the vehicle was driven dangerously on a road or other public place;

    (ii) that, owing to the driving of the vehicle, an accident occurred by which injury was caused to any person;[4]

    (iii) that, owing to the driving of the vehicle, an accident occurred by which damage was caused to any property, other than the vehicle;

    (iv) that damage was caused to the vehicle.

Contrary to: Theft Act 1968 s.12A

Max. sentence: Magistrates' Court: 6 months' imprisonment / £5,000 fine.

Crown Court: 5 years' imprisonment / unlimited fine.[5]

Power: Arrestable Offence[6]

Definitions

Recovered: a vehicle is 'recovered' when it is restored to its owner or to other lawful possession or custody; for example, a police officer has taken charge of the vehicle.[7]

Dangerous: a vehicle is driven 'dangerously' if it is driven in such a way as to fall far below that which would be expected of a competent and careful driver and where it would be obvious to a competent and careful driver that such driving would be dangerous.[8]

Notes

1   A person is not guilty of an offence under this section if he proves that, as regards any such proven driving, injury or damage either the driving, accident or damage occurred before he committed the basic offence of taking a

conveyance without authority or he was neither in, on or in the immediate vicinity of the vehicle when that driving, accident or damage occurred.

2   Referred to as the 'basic offence'. See also page 386.

3   By him, or another.

4   In *R* v *Marsh* (1997) it was held that the words '... owing to the driving of the vehicle ...' were plain and simple and there was no requirement of fault in the driving of the vehicle.

5   The maximum is applicable where a death occurs. In other cases the maximum is 2 years' imprisonment. 12 months' disqualification for this offence is mandatory.

6   Either under the Police and Criminal Evidence Act 1984 s.24(1) where death occurs or under s.24(2)(d). See page 282.

7   Theft Act 1968 s.12A(8).

8   Ibid., s.12A(7).

AIDING AND ABETTING

See also Attempts, Conspiracy and Incitement

Offence: Any person who aids, abets, counsels or procures the commission of an indictable offence shall be punished as a principal.

Contrary to: Accessories and Abettors Act 1861 s.8

Max. sentence: An offender is liable to the same penalty as that which may be imposed on a principal.

Offence: Any person who aids, abets, counsels or procures the commission of a summary offence, shall be guilty of a like offence.

Contrary to: Magistrates' Courts Act 1980 s.44

Max. sentence: An offender is liable to the same penalty as that which may be imposed on a principal.

General Powers

Where a power of arrest would apply to a principal, then such a power also applies to any person aiding, abetting, counselling or procuring the commission of that offence.

Definitions

Abet: to abet is to be present and assisting or encouraging another at a time when that other is committing an offence.[1]

Counsel: to counsel is to be knowingly involved in advising or assisting a person at a time before that other commits an offence.[2]

Principal: the person who directly commits an offence.

General Information

A person cannot be convicted on a charge of 'aiding and abetting' unless he was present at the commission of the offence[3] and passive acquiescence does not constitute aiding and abetting. An offender must be active in providing assistance or encouragement to another to commit these offences; however, where a duty to act lies on a person, then he may still be guilty of an offence if he fails to act.[4]

In cases where there is any doubt as to whether the *actus reus* is aiding, abetting, counselling or procuring, then a suspect should be charged with all four.

Notes

1   *R* v *Betts and Ridley* (1930), *Smith* v *Baker* (1971), *R* v *Clarkson* (1971).

2   *National Coal Board* v *Gamble* (1959), *R* v *Bainbridge* (1960).

3   *Bowker* v *Premier Drug Company* (1928).

4   *Rubie* v *Faulkner* (1940), *Taylor's Central Garages Ltd* v *Roper* (1951), *Smith* v *Reynolds* (1986).

AIR WEAPONS

See also Burglary, Explosives, Firearms – Criminal Use, Firearms – Licensing, Offensive Weapons, PACE – Arrest

Offence: It is an offence for a person under the age of 17 to purchase or hire any firearm[1] or ammunition.

Contrary to: Firearms Act 1968 s.22(1)

Max. sentence: Magistrates' Court: 6 months' imprisonment / £5,000 fine.

Power: Report / s.25 PACE

Offence: It is an offence[2] for a person under the age of 14 to have with him[3] an air weapon or ammunition for an air weapon.

Contrary to: Firearms Act 1968 s.22(4)

Max. sentence: Magistrates' Court: £1,000 fine.

Power: Report / s.25 PACE

Offence: It is an offence for a person under the age of 17 to have an air weapon with him in a public place, except an air gun or air rifle which is so covered with a securely fastened gun cover that it cannot be fired.[4]

Contrary to: Firearms Act 1968 s.22(5)

Max. sentence: Magistrates' Court: £1,000 fine.

Power: Report / s.25 PACE

Offence: It is an offence for a person aged under 14, where an air weapon is being used on any premises, to use it to fire any missile beyond those premises.

Contrary to: Firearms Act 1968 s.23(1)(a)

Max. sentence: Magistrates' Court: £1,000 fine.

Power: Report / s.25 PACE

Offence: It is an offence for the supervisor of a person aged under 14, where an air weapon is being used on any premises, to allow him to use the air weapon for firing any missile beyond those premises.

Contrary to: Firearms Act 1968 s.23(1)(b)

Max. sentence: Magistrates' Court: £1,000 fine.

Power: Report / s.25 PACE

Offence: It is an offence to make a gift of an air weapon or ammunition for an air weapon to a person under the age of 14 or to part with the possession of an air weapon or ammunition for an air weapon to a person under that age.[5]

Contrary to: Firearms Act 1968 s.24(4)

Max. sentence: Magistrates' Court: £1,000 fine.

Power: Report / s.25 PACE

Offence: It is an offence for a person having a firearm or ammunition with him to fail to hand it over when required to do so by a constable.

Contrary to: Firearms Act 1968 s.47(2)

Max. sentence: Magistrates' Court: 3 months' imprisonment / £2,500 fine.

Power: Report / s.25 PACE

General Powers

A constable may require any person whom he has reasonable cause to suspect:

(a) of having a firearm, with or without ammunition, with him in a public place; or

(b) to be committing or about to commit, elsewhere than in a public place, an offence under s.18(1), (2) or s.20[6] of the Firearms Act 1968,

to hand over the firearm or any ammunition for examination by the constable.[7]

The constable may search that person and detain him for the purposes of doing so. The constable may also search any vehicle where he has reasonable cause to believe that there is a firearm and require the person driving or in charge of it, to stop it for that purpose. In order to exercise these powers a constable may enter any place.[8]

Definitions

Air weapon: an air rifle, air gun or air pistol of a type which has not been declared especially dangerous by the Home Secretary under the Firearms (Dangerous Air Weapons) Rules 1969.

Premises: includes any land.

Public place: includes any highway and any other premises or place to which at the material time the public have or are permitted to have access, whether on payment or otherwise.

General Information

Air weapons are 'firearms' for the purposes of any criminal use[9] and an offence of robbery with an air gun is just as serious as that with a shotgun. Currently limited to a muzzle velocity of 12 ft.lbs for air rifles and 6 ft.lbs for air pistols, these weapons are of relatively low power but are still potentially lethal. If an air weapon's muzzle velocity exceeds these limits then it becomes a s.1 firearm subject to the certification process of those guns.[10]

The Firearms (Amendment) Act 1997 amended the Firearms Act 1968 to include within its definition of 'air weapons', guns for which the propellant is compressed carbon dioxide gas; for example, those used in paint-ball games.

Air weapons are not currently subject to control by licensing.

Proceedings initiated more than 6 months after the commission of the offence require the permission of the Director of Public Prosecutions.

Notes

1 Including an air weapon. See page 156 for the definition of 'firearm' under s.57 of the 1968 Act.

2 This is not an offence where the person under 14 is supervised by someone aged 21 or over *and* the air weapon is not used to fire any missile beyond the premises in which it is being used.

3 This is more than mere possession and requires a close physical link and control although the term would not necessarily require the weapon to be carried by that person.

4   It is not an offence under either s.22(4) or (5) for a person to have an air
    weapon or ammunition with them whilst, as a member, they are engaged
    in rifle club activities or in connection with target practice or at a shooting
    gallery where the air weapons do not exceed .23 inch calibre; for example,
    the type of gallery found at a fairground.

5   It is a defence for the accused to prove that he believed the other person to
    be of or over the age mentioned and that he had reasonable cause for that
    belief.

6   These offences refer to the use of firearms for indictable offences, resisting
    arrest and trespassing with a firearm. See page153.

7   Firearms Act 1968 s.47(1) and (6)

8   Ibid., s.47(3) and (4).

9   See page 151.

10 See page 157.

ALIENS AND IMMIGRATION

See also PACE – Arrest; Racial Hatred

Offence: It is an offence for a person, who is not a British
               citizen, to:

               (a) knowingly enter the United Kingdom in
                    breach of a deportation order or without
                    leave;[1]

               (aa) obtain or seek to obtain leave to enter or
                    remain in the United Kingdom by means
                    which include deception;

               (b) knowingly remain beyond the time limited by
                    the leave or fail to observe a condition of the
                    leave;

               (c) remain without leave beyond the time limit
                    allowed by s.8(1), having lawfully entered the
                    United Kingdom without leave;[2]

               (d) ....[3]

    (e)   fail to observe any restriction imposed on him as to residence, employment or occupation or as to reporting to the police or immigration officer, without reasonable excuse.

Contrary to: Immigration Act 1971 s.24(1)

Max. sentence: Magistrates' Court: 6 months' imprisonment / £5,000 fine.

Power: A constable may arrest without warrant anyone who has committed or attempted to commit these offences or whom he has reasonable grounds for suspecting has committed or attempted to commit such an offence.[4]

Offence:

It is an offence for a person who is not a British citizen if, by means which include deception by him:

(a)   he obtains or seeks to obtain leave to enter or remain in the United Kingdom; or

(b)   he secures or seeks to secure the avoidance, postponement or revocation of enforcement action[5] against him.

Contrary to: Immigration Act 1971 s.24A[6]

Max. sentence: Magistrates' Court: 6 months' imprisonment / £5,000 fine.

Crown Court: 2 years' imprisonment / unlimited fine.

Power: A constable may arrest without warrant anyone who has, or whom he with reasonable cause suspects to have, committed or attempted to commit this offence.[7]

Offence:

It is an offence for a person to knowingly concern himself in making or carrying out arrangements for securing or facilitating:

(a) the entry into the United Kingdom of anyone whom he knows or has reasonable cause to believe to be an illegal entrant;

(b) the entry into the United Kingdom of anyone whom he knows or has reasonable cause to believe to be an asylum claimant;[8] or

(c) the obtaining by anyone of leave to remain in the United Kingdom by means of which he knows or has reasonable cause for believing to include deception.

Contrary to: Immigration Act 1971 s.25(1)

Max. sentence: Magistrates' Court: 6 months' imprisonment / £5,000 fine.

Crown Court: 10 years' imprisonment / unlimited fine.

Power: Arrestable Offence

Offence:

It is an offence for a person to knowingly harbour[9] anyone whom he knows or has reasonable cause for believing to be either an illegal entrant or a person who has committed an offence under s. 24(1)(b) or (c).

Contrary to: Immigration Act 1971 s.25(2)

Max. sentence: Magistrates' Court: 6 months' imprisonment / £5,000 fine.

Power: Report / s.25 PACE

Offence:

It is an offence for a person, as the keeper of premises to which the Immigration (Hotel Records) Order 1972 applies, to fail without reasonable excuse to require all persons of or over the age of 16 to comply with their obligations under the Order.

Contrary to: Immigration (Hotel Records) Order 1972 art.5(a)

| **Max. sentence:** | Magistrates' Court: 6 months' imprisonment / £5,000 fine. |
| **Power:** | Report / s.25 PACE |

Offence:

It is an offence for a person, as the keeper of premises to which the Immigration (Hotel Records) Order 1972 applies, to fail without reasonable excuse to keep for a period of at least 12 months a written record of:

    (a)   the date of arrival of all persons of or over the age of 16 who stayed at the premises; or

    (b)   all information provided by such persons in compliance with their obligations.[10]

Contrary to:	Immigration (Hotel Records) Order 1972 art.5(b)
Max. sentence:	Magistrates' Court: 6 months' imprisonment / £5,000 fine.
Power:	Report / s.25 PACE

Notes

1   As a result of the Immigration and Asylum Act 1999, clandestine entrants arriving in the United Kingdom concealed in a vehicle, ship or aircraft leave the owner, operator or carrier liable to a penalty payable to the Secretary of State.

2   The exceptions under s.8(1) allow for seamen and airmen to enter the United Kingdom until their craft's departure.

3   Subsection (d) concerns attendance and submission to medical tests.

4   This does not apply in relation to an offence under s.24(1)(d). Immigration officers also have a power of arrest under this legislation [Immigration Act 1971 s.28A as amended by the Immigration and Asylum Act 1999].

5   For example, the making of a deportation order or directions for removal from the United Kingdom.

6   As amended by the Immigration and Asylum Act 1999.

7   Immigration Act 1971 s.28A.

8   This does not include anything which is done otherwise than for gain or in the course of employment by a *bona fide* organisation whose purpose is assisting refugees.

9   That is, 'to give shelter' [*R* v *Mistry* (1980)].

10   These are made out in art.4 of the Order.

ANIMALS

See also Dogs, Drunkenness, Footpaths, Footways and Bridleways, Metropolitan Police Act, Poaching, Road Traffic Collisions, Straying Animals, Theft, Town Police Clauses, Wildlife

Offence: It is an offence to:

(a)   cruelly beat, kick, ill-treat, override, overdrive, overload, torture, infuriate or terrify any animal, or to cause or procure, or, being the owner, permit[1] any animal[2] to be so used, or, by wantonly or unreasonably doing or omitting to do any act, to cause or procure the commission or omission of any act, cause any unnecessary suffering, or, being the owner, permit any unnecessary[3] suffering to be so caused to any animal;

(b)   convey or carry, or cause or procure, or, being the owner, permit to be conveyed or carried, any animal in such manner or position as to cause that animal any unnecessary suffering;

(c)   cause, procure, or assist at the fighting or baiting of any animal;

(d)   willfully, without any reasonable cause or excuse, administer, or cause or procure, or, being the owner, permit such administration of, any poisonous or injurious drug or substance to any animal;

(e)   subject, or cause or procure, or, being the owner, permit to be subjected, any animal to any operation which is performed without due care and humanity; or

(f) tether any horse, ass or mule under such conditions or in such manner as to cause that animal unnecessary suffering.

Contrary to: Protection of Animals Act 1911 s.1(1)

Max. sentence: Magistrates' Court: 6 months' imprisonment / £5,000 fine.

Power: A police constable may arrest without warrant any person[4] whom he has reason to believe is guilty of an offence under the Protection of Animals Act 1911 s.1.[5]

Offence:

It is an offence for a person, without reasonable excuse, to be present when animals are placed together for the purposes of their fighting each other.

Contrary to: Protection of Animals Act 1911 s.5A

Max. sentence: Magistrates' Court: £2,500 fine.

Power: Report / s.25 PACE

Offence:

It is an offence for a person to promote, or cause or knowingly permit to take place, or take part in, any public performance that includes any episode consisting or involving:

(a) throwing or casting, with ropes or other appliances, any unbroken horse or untrained bull;

(b) wrestling, fighting or struggling with any untrained bull; or

(c) riding, or attempting to ride, any horse or bull which, by the use of any appliance or treatment involving cruelty is, or has been, stimulated with the intention of making it buck during the performance.

Contrary to:	Protection of Animals Act 1934 s.1
Max. sentence:	Magistrates' Court: 3 months' imprisonment / £2,500 fine.
Power:	Report / s.25 PACE

Offence:

It is an offence for a person to sell an animal as a pet in any part of a street or public place, or at a stall or barrow in a market.

Contrary to:	Pet Animals Act 1951 s.2
Max. sentence:	Magistrates' Court: 3 months' imprisonment / £500 fine.
Power:	Report / s.25 PACE

Offence:

It is an offence for a person to sell an animal as a pet to a person whom he has reasonable cause to believe to be under the age of 12 years.

Contrary to:	Pet Animals Act 1951 s.3
Max. sentence:	Magistrates' Court: 3 months' imprisonment / £500 fine.
Power:	Report / s.25 PACE

Offence:

It is an offence for a person to have in his possession any instrument or appliance designed or adapted for use in connection with the fighting of any domestic fowl.

Contrary to:	Cock Fighting Act 1952 s.1
Max. sentence:	Magistrates' Court: 3 months' imprisonment / £1,000 fine.
Power:	Report / s.25 PACE

Offence:

It is an offence for a person to have custody of any animal in contravention of an order disqualifying him from having that animal.[6]

Contrary to:	Protection of Animals (Amendment) Act 1954 s.2
Max. sentence:	Magistrates' Court: 3 months' imprisonment / £1,000 fine.
Power:	Report / s.25 PACE

Offence: It is an offence of cruelty[7] for a person, being the owner or having charge or control of any animal and without reasonable cause or excuse, to abandon it[8] in circumstances likely to cause the animal any unnecessary suffering.

Contrary to: Abandonment of Animals Act 1960 s.1

Max. sentence: Magistrates' Court: 6 months' imprisonment / £5,000 fine.

Power: A police constable may arrest without warrant any person whom he has reason to believe is guilty of an offence.[9]

Offence: It is an offence[10] for any person to land or attempt to land an animal[11] in Great Britain,[12] the landing of which is prohibited, or cause or permit the landing or attempted landing of any such animal.

Contrary to: Rabies (Importation of Dogs, Cats etc.) Order 1974 art.16

Max. sentence: Magistrates' Court: £5,000 fine.

Power: A constable may arrest without warrant any person whom he suspects to be in the act of committing or to have committed an offence under this Order.[13]

General Powers

If a police constable finds any animal[14] so diseased or so severely injured or in such a physical condition that, in his opinion and having regard to the means available for removing the animal, there is no possibility of removing it without cruelty, he shall at once[15] summon a registered veterinary surgeon. If it appears by the certificate of such veterinary surgeon that the animal is so injured, diseased or in such a condition that it would be cruel to keep it alive, it shall be lawful for the constable, without the consent of the owner, to slaughter the animal, or cause or procure it to be slaughtered, so as to inflict as little suffering as practicable. If the slaughter takes place on a highway, the constable is empowered to remove the carcase or cause or procure its removal.[16]

If a veterinary surgeon certifies that the injured animal can be removed without cruelty, it shall be the duty of the person in charge of the animal to cause it to be removed with as little suffering as possible. If that person fails to do so, then the constable may, without the consent of that person, cause the animal to be removed.[17]

Notes

1   That is, failing to exercise reasonable care and supervision [s.1(2)].

2   That is, any domestic or captive animal. A domestic animal is any horse, ass, mule, bull, sheep, pig, goat, dog, cat or fowl or any other animal that is tame or is being tamed.

3   The suffering becomes unnecessary in circumstances where it is not inevitable but can be terminated or alleviated by some reasonable measure [*RSPCA* v *Issacs* (1994)].

4   There is an exception with regard to owners who are convicted by reason only of having failed to exercise care and supervision. Such a person is not liable to imprisonment without the option of a fine and may not be arrested.

5   Protection of Animals Act 1911 s.12.

6   Under s.1 of the Protection of Animals (Amendment) Act 1954, a court may impose an order disqualifying a person from having custody of an animal for a set period following a conviction for cruelty.

7   Within the provisions of the Protection of Animals Act 1911.

8   Or cause or procure it to be abandoned or, being the owner, permit it to be so abandoned. The term 'abandon' implies more than merely leaving the animal unattended, there must be some disregard for the duty to care for the animal [*Hunt v Duckering* (1993)].

9   The provisions of the Protection of Animals Acts shall apply to an offence under this section as they apply to an offence under s.1(1) of the 1911 Act.

10 No offence is committed if the landing is under the authority of a licence. Pet passports are now possible allowing the entry of animals carried by

specified carriers from specified foreign countries. See *A–Z of Countryside Law second edition*.

11　These are detailed in Sch.1 to the Order and include dogs, cats, rabbits, gerbils, guinea-pigs, goats and sheep together with a wide range of more exotic species.

12　No offence is committed if the animal is being brought from Northern Ireland, the Republic of Ireland, the Channel Islands or the Isle of Man.

13　Animal Health Act 1981 s.61.

14　For the purposes of these powers, 'animal' means any horse, mule, ass, bull, sheep, goat or pig.

15　If the owner is absent or refuses to consent to the destruction of the animal.

16　Protection of Animals Act 1911 s.11(1).

17　See s.11(2). Any reasonable expenses incurred in the exercise of these powers may be recovered from the animal's owner as a civil debt.

ANTI-SOCIAL BEHAVIOUR

See also Children and Young Persons, Damage, Harassment and Intimidation, Nuisance, Public Order

Offence:　It is an offence for a person, without reasonable excuse, to do anything that he is prohibited from doing by an anti-social behaviour order.[1]

Contrary to:　Crime and Disorder Act 1998 s.1(10)

Max. sentence:　Magistrates' Court: 6 months' imprisonment / £5,000.

Crown Court: 5 years' imprisonment / unlimited fine.

Power:　Arrestable Offence[2]

General Information

Anti-social behaviour orders may be made by a court in respect of any person aged 10 or over where it is proved that the person:

(a)　has acted in an anti-social manner, that is to say, in a manner that caused or was likely to cause harassment, alarm or distress to one or more persons not of the same household as himself; and

(b)   that the order is necessary to protect persons in the area in which the harassment, alarm or distress was caused or was likely to be caused from further anti-social acts by him.

Notes

1   An anti-social behaviour order has effect for a period specified within the order, which will be not less than 2 years.

2   See page 281.

ARMED FORCES

See also Absconders and Escapees, Handling Stolen Goods, Theft

Offence: It is an offence for any person to personate the holder of a certificate of service or discharge.

Contrary to: Seamen's and Soldier's False Characters Act 1906 s.1

Max. sentence: Magistrates' Court: 3 months' imprisonment / £500 fine.

Power: Report / s.25 PACE

Offence: It is an offence for a person to maliciously and advisedly endeavour to seduce any member of Her Majesty's forces from his duty or allegiance to Her Majesty.

Contrary to: Incitement to Disaffection Act 1934 s.1[1]

Max. sentence: Magistrates' Court: 4 months' imprisonment / £5,000 fine.

Crown Court: 2 years' imprisonment / unlimited fine.

Power: Report / s.25 PACE

Offence: It is an offence for any person, with intent to commit, or to aid, abet, counsel or procure the commission of an offence under s.1 of this Act, to have in his possession or under his control any document of such a nature that the dissemination of copies thereof among members of Her Majesty's forces would constitute such an offence.

Contrary to: Incitement to Disaffection Act 1934 s.2(1)

Max. sentence: Magistrates' Court: 4 months' imprisonment / £5,000 fine.

Crown Court: 2 years' imprisonment / unlimited fine.

Power: Report / s.25 PACE

Offence:

It is an offence for a member of the armed forces to absent themselves, without leave, or to desert.

Contrary to: Army and Air Force Acts 1955 s.37 and s.38,[2] Naval Discipline Act 1957 s.17

Power: A constable[3] may arrest any person whom he has reasonable cause to suspect of being an officer, warrant officer, non-commissioned officer or soldier of the regular forces who has deserted or is absent without leave.[4]

Offence:

It is an offence for a person to falsely represent himself to any military, naval, air force or civil authority to be a deserter from the regular forces.

Contrary to: Army and Air Force Acts 1955 s.191, Naval Discipline Act 1957 s.96[5]

Power: Report / s.25 PACE

Offence:

It is an offence for a person to assist a member of the armed forces to absent themselves without leave or to desert.

Contrary to: Army and Air Force Acts 1955 s.192, Naval Discipline Act 1957 s.97

Power: Report / s.25 PACE

Offence:

It is an offence for any person:

(a) to procure or persuade any officer, warrant officer, non-commissioned officer or soldier of the regular forces to desert or to absent himself without leave;

(b) knowing that any such officer, warrant officer, non-commissioned officer or soldier is about to desert or absent himself without leave, to assist him in doing so; or

(c) knowing any person to be a deserter or absentee without leave from the regular forces, to procure or persuade or assist him to remain such a deserter or absentee.

Contrary to: Army and Air Force Acts 1955 s.192, Naval Discipline Act 1957 s.97[6]

Max. sentence: Magistrates' Court: 3 months' imprisonment / £5,000 fine.

Crown Court: 2 years' imprisonment / unlimited fine.

Power: Report / s.25 PACE

Offence:

It is an offence for any person to wilfully obstruct or otherwise interfere with any officer, warrant officer, non-commissioned officer or soldier of the regular forces acting in the execution of his duty.

Contrary to: Army and Air Force Acts 1955 s.193

Max. sentence: Magistrates' Court: 3 months' imprisonment / £1,000 fine.

Power: Report / s.25 PACE

Offence: It is an offence for any person to:

a)   produce in any officer, warrant officer, non-commissioned officer or soldier of the regular forces any sickness or disability; or

b)   supply to or for him any drug or preparation calculated or likely to render him, or lead to the belief that he is, permanently or temporarily unfit for service with a view to enabling him to avoid military service.

Contrary to: Army and Air Force Acts 1955 s.194

Max. sentence: Magistrates' Court: 3 months' imprisonment / £5,000 fine.

Crown Court: 2 years' imprisonment / unlimited fine.

Power: Report / s.25 PACE

Offence: It is an offence for any person to acquire any military stores or naval property or solicit or procure any person to dispose of any such stores, or act for any person in the disposing of any such stores.

Contrary to: Army and Air Force Acts 1955 s.195, Naval Discipline Act 1957 s.98

Max. sentence: Magistrates' Court: 3 months' imprisonment / £5,000 fine.

Crown Court: 2 years' imprisonment / unlimited fine.

Power: Report / s.25 PACE

Definitions

Absentee: a person who is absent from his unit without leave (permission) but who intends to return.

Deserter: a person who is absent without leave and who does not intend to return to his unit.

General Information

Generally, absentees and deserters who are arrested without a warrant should be taken before a court in order that they may be remanded in custody to await an escort. Absentees or deserters arrested on a naval warrant should be delivered into naval custody as soon as practicable.

Absentees or deserters who surrender themselves should be handed over to a suitable escort as soon as practicable, and without the need for them to appear before a court unless the person so requests. In cases of surrender it may be appropriate for the absentee or deserter to be allowed to return to their unit unaccompanied. A rail warrant may be issued for this purpose.

Notes

1   Consent of the Director of Public Prosecutions required for offences under this Act.

2   Also Reserve Forces Act 1996 s.98. The maximum punishment for reserve forces for this offence is 6 months' imprisonment / £5,000 fine.

3   Where no constable is available, any other person may arrest.

4   Army and Air Force Acts 1955 s.186(1), Naval Discipline Act 1957 s.105(1). There is no associated power of entry.

5   Also Reserve Forces Act 1996 s.99.

6   Ibid., s.101.

ASSAULTS

See also Children and Young Persons, Firearms – Criminal Use, Indecent and Obscene Behaviour, PACE – Arrest, Police, Public Order, Racial Hatred, Robbery, Wounding and Grievous Bodily Harm

Offence: It is an offence for a person, without lawful excuse, to make to another a threat intending that that other would fear it would be carried out, to kill that other or a third person.

Contrary to: Offences Against the Person Act 1861 s.16

| Max. sentence: | Crown Court: 10 years' imprisonment / unlimited fine. |
| Power: | Arrestable Offence |

Offence:

It is an offence for a person, by any means whatsoever, to:

(a) attempt to choke, suffocate, or strangle any other person; or

(b) by any means calculated to choke, suffocate or strangle, attempt to render any other person insensible, unconscious, or incapable of resistance,

with intent to enable himself or any other person to commit any indictable offence.[1]

Contrary to:	Offences Against the Person Act 1861 s.21
Max. sentence:	Crown Court: life imprisonment.
Power:	Arrestable Offence

Offence:

It is an offence for a person to unlawfully apply or administer to or cause to be taken by,[2] any person, any chloroform, laudanum, or other stupefying or overpowering drug, matter or thing, with intent to enable himself or any other person to commit any indictable offence.[3]

Contrary to:	Offences Against the Person Act 1861 s.22
Max. sentence:	Crown Court: life imprisonment.
Power:	Arrestable Offence

Offence:

It is an offence to unlawfully and maliciously administer to, or cause to be administered to, or taken by, any other person, any poison, or other destructive or noxious thing, with intent to injure,[4] aggrieve, or annoy.

Contrary to: Offences Against the Person Act 1861 s.24

Max. sentence: Crown Court: 5 years' imprisonment / unlimited fine.

Power: Arrestable Offence

Offence:

It is an offence to assault any person with intent to resist or prevent the lawful apprehension or detainer[5] of himself or of any other person for any offence.

Contrary to: Offences Against the Person Act 1861 s.38

Max. sentence: Crown Court: 2 years' imprisonment / unlimited fine.

Power: Report / s.25 PACE / Breach of the Peace[6]

Offence:

It is an offence to assault any person thereby occasioning them actual bodily harm.[7]

Contrary to: Offences Against the Person Act 1861 s.47

Max. sentence: Crown Court: 5 years' imprisonment / unlimited fine.

Power: Arrestable Offence

Offence:

It is an offence for a person to assault another with intent to rob.[8]

Contrary to: Theft Act 1968 s.8(2)

Max. sentence: Crown Court: life imprisonment / unlimited fine.

Power: Arrestable Offence

Offence:

It is an offence for a person to assault or batter another person.

Contrary to: Criminal Justice Act 1988 s.39[9]

Max. sentence: Magistrates' Court: 6 months' imprisonment / £5,000 fine.

Power: Report / s.25 PACE / Breach of the Peace

Offence:

It is an offence[10] for any public official or person acting in an official capacity,[11] whatever his nationality, to intentionally inflict severe pain or suffering[12] on another in the performance or purported performance of his official duties.

Contrary to: Criminal Justice Act 1988 s.134 (1)

Max. sentence: Crown Court: life imprisonment / unlimited fine.

Power: Arrestable Offence

Offence:

It is an offence for any person to assault a constable[13] in the execution of his duty, or a person assisting a constable in the execution of his duty.

Contrary to: Police Act 1996 s.89(1)

Max. sentence: Magistrates' Court: 6 months' imprisonment / £5,000 fine.

Power: Report / s.25 PACE / Breach of the Peace[14]

Definitions

Assault: any intentional or reckless act, which causes a person to apprehend immediate unlawful force or personal violence.

Battery: any intentional or reckless infliction of unlawful force or personal violence.

General Information

An assault does not necessarily involve any physical contact. It may merely be a threatening gesture, although the circumstances need to be such that the victim is reasonably able to apprehend force or violence; for example, if a blow is thrown by a person too far away to be able to connect, then such an action is not an assault. Words alone are unlikely to be sufficient, however abusive or insulting they may be.

A battery requires some physical contact, although this may be only the slightest of touches if applied in anger.[15] A battery may include an assault but this is not necessary; for example, a blow struck from behind of which the victim was never aware. There needs to be some hostile intention and any accidental touching will not constitute a battery nor will any reasonable action; for example touching a person in order to attract their attention or force reasonably inflicted as part of a tackle in a game of football.

The test of recklessness requires the prosecution to establish that a defendant had foreseen the risk and yet continued with his actions.[16]

Consent is capable of negating an allegation of assault or battery unless it is held not to be in the public interest; for example, the sado-masochistic infliction of pain.[17] Moderate and reasonable chastisement, such as a parent may inflict on their child, would not constitute either 'assault' or 'battery' although attitudes to this are changing in light of decisions by the European Court of Human Rights. Players in a lawful sport consent to a degree of force but only within the acceptable limits of the rules. Any excessive breach of such rules may negate that consent.

A person is entitled to use reasonable force in defence of themselves, their property or another person, or to prevent a crime.[18] Police officers acting within their powers or on an order of the court are generally empowered to use such reasonable force as is necessary to carry out their duty, although if unreasonable force is used or they are acting outside of their duty then they may leave themselves liable. The question of whether a police officer was acting in the execution of his duty is often unclear and is a matter of fact for the court to decide.

A charge alleging both 'assault' and 'battery' is bad for duplicity and a clear distinction should be made between the two, although in common usage the term 'assault' is now generally taken to incorporate 'battery'. Where there is both an apprehension, and infliction, of force the proper charge should be 'assault by beating'.[19]

Notes

1   Includes an intention to assist another person to commit an indictable offence, for example, rape.

2   Or attempt any of these.

3   Includes an intention to assist another person.

4 That is, physical harm [*R* v *Hill* (1986)].

5 That is, arrest.

6 But see the offence under the Police Act 1996 below.

7 This means any harm capable of interfering with the health or comfort of the victim and is capable of including psychiatric injury. It would not include emotions such as fear, distress or panic although silent telephone calls which made the victim apprehensive and caused psychological damage may be sufficient [*R* v *Ireland* (1997)].

8 See page 357.

9 This section restates common assault and battery as separate statutory offences.

10 To be known as 'Torture'. It will be a defence to show that the conduct had lawful authority, justification or excuse. Proceedings require the Attorney General's consent.

11 Or a person acting at the instigation, or with the consent or acquiescence of a public official or person acting in an official capacity.

12 Physical or mental.

13 This includes a 'Special Constable'.

14 In circumstances where a Breach of the Peace is likely to occur, a Common Law power of arrest exists for this offence.

15 *Cole* v *Turner* (1704).

16 *R* v *Cunningham* (1959).

17 *R* v *Brown* (1993).

18 Criminal Law Act 1967 s.3.

19 *DPP* v *Taylor and Little* (1992).

ATTEMPTS

See also Aiding and Abetting, Conspiracy and Incitement, Vehicle Interference

Offence: If, with intent to commit an offence to which this section applies,[1] a person does an act which is more than merely preparatory to the commission of the offence, he is guilty of attempting to commit the offence.

Contrary to: Criminal Attempts Act 1981 s.1

| **Max. sentence:** | An offender is liable to the same penalty as that which may be imposed on the principal for a completed offence.[2] |
| **Power:** | Determined by the nature of the offence attempted.[3] |

General Information

Section 1 of the Criminal Attempts Act 1981 only applies to indictable or either-way offences. To be an 'attempt' the act which is the subject of a charge must be 'more than merely preparatory' to the commission of a full offence.[4] This will be a matter of fact for a jury to decide although any act that would be the last one necessary before an offence is complete is always likely to be an attempt, even where completion of the intended offence is actually impossible[5] or where the facts are not as the offender considered them to be.[6]

Notes

1 This applies to any offence that would be triable as an indictable offence other than conspiracy, aiding and abetting, counselling and procuring, assisting offenders and accepting a consideration not to disclose information about an arrestable offence.

2 Criminal Attempts Act 1981 s.4.

3 Ibid., s.4.

4 Ibid., s.3.

5 For example, a thief attempts to steal from a handbag which is, in reality, empty. The attempt is still complete [*R* v *Smith and Smith* (1986)].

6 For example, a person believes he is in possession of a controlled drug but in fact the substance is harmless. The attempt is still complete [*R* v *Shivpuri* (1987)].

AUDIBLE WARNING INSTRUMENTS

See also Construction and Use, Noise

| **Offence:** | It is an offence: |
| | (a)   for a motor vehicle which has a maximum |

speed of more than 20 mph not to be fitted with a horn;[1]

(b)   for the sound emitted by any horn fitted to a wheeled vehicle[2] not to be continuous and uniform or to be strident;

(c)   for a reversing alarm fitted to a wheeled vehicle to be strident;

(d)   for a motor vehicle to be fitted with a gong, siren or two-tone[3] horn; or

(e)   for:

(i)   any bell, gong or siren fitted to a vehicle for the purpose of preventing theft or attempted theft of the vehicle or its contents, or

(ii)   any device fitted to a motor vehicle so as to cause a horn to sound for those purposes,

not to be fitted with a device designed to stop the bell, gong or siren emitting noise for a continuous period of more than 5 minutes; and every such device shall at all times be maintained in good working order.

Contrary to: Road Vehicles (Construction and Use) Regulations 1986 r.37[4]

Max. sentence: Magistrates' Court: £1,000 fine.[5]

Power: Report / s.25 PACE

Offence:

It is an offence for a person to sound, or cause or permit to be sounded, any horn, gong, bell or siren fitted to or carried on a vehicle which is:

(a)   stationary on a road, at any time, other than at times of danger due to another moving vehicle on or near the road;[6] or

(b) in motion on a restricted road, between 23.30 hours and 07.00 hours in the following morning.

Contrary to: Road Vehicles (Construction and Use) Regulations 1986 r.99(1)

Max. sentence: Magistrates' Court: £1,000 fine.

Power: Report / s.25 PACE

Offence:

It is an offence for a person to sound, or cause or permit to be sounded, any gong, bell, siren or two-tone horn fitted to or carried on a vehicle.[7]

Contrary to: Road Vehicles (Construction and Use) Regulations 1986 r.99(4)

Max. sentence: Magistrates' Court: £1,000 fine.

Power: Report / s.25 PACE

Notes

1 Not being a reversing alarm or two-tone horn. 'Horn' means an instrument, not being a gong, bell or siren, capable of giving audible and sufficient warning of the approach or position of the vehicle to which it is fitted.

2 First used on or after 1 August 1973.

3 A two-tone horn is defined as an instrument that automatically produces a sound, which alternates at regular intervals between two fixed notes. Exceptions to this offence are detailed in note 7 below.

4 This regulation does not apply to an agricultural motor vehicle, unless it is being driven at more than 20 mph.

5 Rising to £2,500 in the case of goods vehicles and vehicles adapted to carry more than 8 passengers.

6 This does not apply in respect of the sounding of a reversing alarm when the vehicle to which it is fitted is about to move backwards and its engine is running.

7 This does not prevent the sounding of:

(a) an instrument or apparatus fitted to, or otherwise carried on, a vehicle at a time when the vehicle is being used for emergencies and it is necessary and desirable to do so to indicate to other road users the urgency of the purpose for which the vehicle is being used, or to warn other road users of the vehicle's presence; or

(b) a horn (not being a two-tone horn), bell, gong or siren to raise the alarm as to the theft or the attempted theft of the vehicle or its contents or, in the case of a bus, to summon help.

BAIL

See also Absconders and Escapees, Criminal Justice, Forgery, PACE – Arrest

Offence: It is an offence for a person who has been released on bail in criminal proceedings to fail without reasonable cause[1] to surrender to custody.

Contrary to: Bail Act 1976 s.6(1)

Max. sentence: Magistrates' Court: 3 months' imprisonment / £5,000 fine.

Crown Court: 12 months' imprisonment / unlimited fine.

Power: Arrest[2]

Offence: It is an offence for a person who:

(a) has been released on bail in criminal proceedings; and

(b) has failed with reasonable cause to surrender to custody,

to fail to surrender to custody at the appointed place as soon after the appointed time as is reasonably practicable.

Contrary to: Bail Act 1976 s.6(2)

Max. sentence: Magistrates' Court: 3 months' imprisonment / £5,000 fine.

Crown Court: 12 months' imprisonment / unlimited fine.

Power: Arrest

General Powers

A constable may arrest without warrant where there are reasonable grounds for believing that a bailed person:

(a)   is not likely to surrender to custody;

(b)   is likely to break any of the conditions of his bail; or

(c)   has broken any of those conditions.[3]

A constable may arrest without warrant a bailed person where a surety notifies the constable, in writing, that the bailed person is unlikely to surrender to custody and that the surety wishes to be relieved of his obligation.[4]

A constable may arrest without warrant any person who, having been released on bail subject to a duty to attend a police station, fails to do so at the time appointed.[5]

Definitions

Bail in criminal proceedings: means:

(a)   bail grantable in or in connection with proceedings for an offence to a person who is accused or convicted of the offence; or

(b)   bail grantable in connection with an offence to a person who is under arrest for the offence or for whose arrest for the offence a warrant (endorsed for bail) is being issued.[6]

Notes

1   It shall be for the accused to prove that he had reasonable cause for his failure to surrender to custody [Bail Act 1976 s.6(3)].

2   See *General Powers*.

3   Bail Act 1976 s.7(3).

4   Ibid., s.7(3)(c).

5   Police and Criminal Evidence Act 1984 s.46A.

6   Bail Act 1976 s.1(1).

BEGGING

See also Children and Young Persons, PACE – Arrest, Street Trading, Vagrancy

Offence: It is an offence for a person wandering abroad to:

(a) place themselves in any public place,[1] street, highway, court or passage, to beg or gather alms; or

(b) cause or procure or encourage any child or children to do so.

Contrary to: Vagrancy Act 1824 s.3

Max. sentence: Magistrates' Court: 1 month imprisonment / £1,000 fine.

Power: Any person may arrest an offender found committing.[2]

Offence: It is an offence for a person to:

(a) wander abroad and endeavour by the exposure of wounds or deformities to obtain or gather alms; or

(b) go about as a gatherer or collector of alms, endeavouring to procure charitable contributions of any nature or kind, under any false or fraudulent pretence.

Contrary to: Vagrancy Act 1824 s.4

Max. sentence: Magistrates' Court: 3 months' imprisonment / £1,000 fine.

Power: Any person may arrest an offender found committing.[3]

Offence: It is an offence for a person to:

(a) cause or procure any child or young person under the age of 16 years; or

(b)   having responsibility for such a child or young person, to allow him to be in any street, premises, or place,

for the purpose of begging or receiving alms, or of inducing the giving of alms (whether or not there is any pretence of singing, playing, performing, offering anything for sale or otherwise).

Contrary to: Children and Young Persons Act 1933 s.4

Max. sentence: Magistrates' Court: 3 months' imprisonment / £500 fine.

Power: Report / s.25 PACE[4]

General Information

Children and young persons found begging may be removed to a place of safety.[5]

Notes

1   For the purposes of this Act a 'public place' is determined as any place of public resort or recreation grounds belonging to or under the control of a local authority and any unfenced ground adjoining or abutting any street in an urban district.
2   Vagrancy Act 1824 s.6. This includes police officers [*Gapper* v *CC Avon & Somerset Constabulary* (1998)]. If not found committing, then proceedings are by way of summons unless any of the conditions of s.25 of the Police and Criminal Evidence Act 1984 apply.
3   Vagrancy Act 1824 s.6.
4   The power under the Vagrancy Act 1824 may also apply.
5   See page 51.

BLACKMAIL

See also Deception, Harassment and Intimidation, PACE – Arrest, Robbery, Theft

Offence: It is an offence for a person, with a view to gain for himself or another or with intent to cause loss to another, to make any unwarranted demand with menaces.

Contrary to: Theft Act 1968 s.21

Max. sentence: Crown Court: 14 years' imprisonment / unlimited fine.

Power: Arrestable Offence.

Definitions

'Gain' and 'loss' are to be construed as extending only to money or other property, whether temporary or permanent and :

Gain: includes a gain by keeping what one has, as well as a gain by getting what one has not.

Loss: includes a loss by not getting what one might get, as well as a loss by parting with what one has.[1]

General Information

A demand with menaces is unwarranted unless the person making it does so in the belief:

(a) that he had reasonable grounds for making the demand; and

(b) that the use of the menaces is a proper means of reinforcing the demand.

The menace need not be limited to violence alone but can include a range of threats, which the person receiving the demand would perceive as unpleasant or adverse; for example, damage to property. However the victim does not need actually to feel threatened provided the words or conduct used are such that they would operate on a person of reasonable courage.[2]

Notes

1   Theft Act 1968 s.34 (2).

2   *R* v *Clear* (1968).

BRAKES

See also Construction and Use, Drivers and Riders, Driving Documents

Offence: It is an offence for a person to fail to maintain every part of every braking system and of the means of operation thereof fitted to a vehicle, in good and efficient working order and properly adjusted.

Contrary to: Road Vehicles (Construction and Use) Regulations 1986 r.18(1)

Max. sentence: Magistrates' Court: £2,500 fine.

Power: Report / s.25 PACE

Offence:

It is an offence for the driver of a motor vehicle drawing a trailer to fail to be in a position readily to operate the brakes fitted to the trailer as well as the brakes fitted to the motor vehicle.[1]

Contrary to: Road Vehicles (Construction and Use) Regulations 1986 r.19

Max. sentence: Magistrates' Court: £2,500 fine.

Power: Report / s.25 PACE

Offence:

It is an offence for a person to:

(a) contravene or fail to comply with a construction and use requirement as to brakes;

(b) use on a road a motor vehicle or trailer which does not comply with such a requirement; or

(c) cause or permit a motor vehicle or trailer to be so used.

Contrary to: Road Traffic Act 1988 s.41A

Max. sentence: Magistrates' Court: £2,500 fine.[2]

Power: Report / s.25 PACE

Notes

1   No offence is committed if a person other than the driver is in a position and competent efficiently to apply the brakes of a trailer. Nor does this regulation apply to a trailer which is a broken down vehicle being drawn, whether or not in consequence of a breakdown, in such a manner that it cannot be steered by its own steering gear.

2   Rising to £5,000 in the case of goods vehicles or passenger vehicles adapted to carry more than 8 passengers under the Road Traffic Offenders Act 1988 Sch.2. Punishment includes discretionary disqualification and obligatory endorsement.

BREACH OF THE PEACE

See also Bail, Highways and Roads, Noise, Nuisance, PACE– Arrest, Police, Public Order

Complaint: The peace is the normal state of society and a Breach of the Peace occurs when harm is done or is likely to be done to a person, or in his presence to his property, or a person is in fear of such harm.[1]

Contrary to: Common Law

Max. sentence: Magistrates' Court: Order.[2]

Power:

(a)   Any person[3] may arrest any person who is committing[4] a Breach of the Peace.

(b)   Any person may arrest any person where a Breach of the Peace has been committed and it is reasonably believed that a renewal is threatened.

(c)   Any person may arrest any person when it is reasonably believed that a Breach of the Peace is about to be committed.[5]

(d)   Any person may enter any premises where a Breach of the Peace is being committed, or for the purpose of preventing such a Breach of the Peace.

General Information

A Breach of the Peace is not an 'offence' for which an information is laid before a court. It is a 'complaint'. This has its origins in both Common Law and statute. The Justice of the Peace Act 1361 allows courts to take 'all them that be [not] of good fame, where they shall be found, sufficient surety and main prise them of their good behaviour towards the King and his people, and the other duly to punish; to the intent that the people be not by such rioters or rebels troubled or endamaged, nor the peace blemished.' This Act is still in force.

A Breach of the Peace can occur in public or in private.

Notes

1 *R* v *Howell* (1982).

2 Being bound over to keep the peace is not a punishment, but is imposed to prevent any further danger of a Breach of the Peace occurring. The courts have the power to bind a person to keep the peace and to be of good behaviour, either on his own recognisance or with sureties and with the option of committing to prison if he does not comply. Before a court can order a person to enter into a recognisance to keep the peace and be of good behaviour there has to be some grounds for believing that there is the possibility of a future Breach of the Peace by that person [Justice of the Peace Act 1968 s.7; Magistrates' Courts Act 1980 s.115]. The ability of the courts to bind people over 'to be of good behaviour' is now being questioned following *Hashman and Harrap* v *United Kingdom* (1999). This human rights case held the term 'good behaviour' to be too vague.

3 This includes a police constable.

4 The key question is 'from whom is the threat coming?'. A person acting lawfully and reasonably cannot be in Breach of the Peace even where their actions inflame others provided that they do not tend to provoke violence. Free speech extends to the irritating, the contentious, the eccentric, the heretical, the unwelcome and the provocative [*Redmond-Bate* v *DPP* (1999)] and even the lawfully intimidating [*Bibby* v *CC Essex Constabulary* (2000)].

5 This requires the threat of an immediate Breach of the Peace [*Foulkes* v *CC Merseyside Police* (1998)].

BURGLARY

See also Attempts, Offensive Weapons, PACE – Arrest, Theft, Trespass

Offence: It is an offence for a person:

(a)   to enter[1] a building or part of a building as a trespasser and with intent[2] to commit theft, grievous bodily harm, rape or unlawful damage; or

(b) having entered a building or part of a building[3] as a trespasser to steal or attempt to steal anything in the building or that part of it or to inflict, or attempt to inflict, on any person therein any grievous bodily harm.

Contrary to: Theft Act 1968 s.9(1)

Max. sentence: Magistrates' Court: 6 months' imprisonment / £5,000 fine[4].

Crown Court: 14 years' imprisonment[5] / unlimited fine.

Power: Arrestable Offence

Offence:

It is an aggravated offence of burglary if a person commits any burglary and at the time has with him any firearm, imitation firearm, any weapon of offence or any explosive.

Contrary to: Theft Act 1968 s.10(1)

Max. sentence: Crown Court: life imprisonment.

Power: Arrestable Offence

Definitions

Building: this term also applies to an inhabited[6] vehicle or vessel, and shall apply to any such vehicle or vessel at times when the person having a habitation in it is not there as well as at times when he is.[7]

Trespass: any unauthorised entry into or on to property, which takes place intentionally or recklessly.

Firearm: includes an air gun or air pistol.[8]

Imitation firearm: anything which has the appearance of being a firearm, whether capable of being discharged or not.[9]

Weapon of offence: anything made, or adapted for use for causing injury to or incapacitating a person, or intended by the person having it with him for that purpose.[10]

Explosive: any article manufactured for the purpose of producing a practical effect by explosion, or intended by the person having it with him for that purpose.[11]

General Information

A trespass in civil law would include an entry by mistake; however, the need for *mens rea* or recklessness in criminal law, means that such a trespass would be insufficient for the offences above.[12] Impossibility does not mean that the intention at the point of entry will be insufficient for the offence under s.9(1)(a) to be complete.[13]

Notes

1   Any degree of entry is sufficient, for example, a person's hand going through a broken window.

2   That is, at the time of the entry.

3   For example, going from being lawfully in one part of a building, to being a trespasser in another part.

4   A burglary involving an intention to rape or commit grievous bodily harm is triable only on indictment.

5   A maximum sentence of 14 years applies to the burglary of a dwelling. In any other case the maximum sentence is 10 years. Burglary in a dwelling where someone inside was subjected to, or threatened with, violence, is triable only on indictment, Magistrates' Courts Act 1980. A minimum 3 year imprisonment should be imposed following a third conviction for domestic burglary under the provisions of the Crime (Sentences) Act 1997 s.4.

6   That is, lived in.

7   Theft Act 1968 s.9(4).

8   Ibid., s.10(1)(a). See page 10.

9   Ibid., s.10(1)(a).

10   Ibid., s.10(1)(b). See page 276.

11   Ibid., s.10(1)(c). See page 145.

12   *R* v *Collins* (1972).

13   See also page 34.

CHILDREN AND YOUNG PERSONS

See also Begging, Drunkenness, Firearms – Licensing, Hostages, Kidnapping and False Imprisonment, Indecent and Obscene Behaviour, PACE – Arrest, Licensed Premises, Sexual Offences

Offence: It is an offence for any person to unlawfully abandon, or expose any child, being under the age of 2 years, whereby the life of such child shall be endangered, or the health of such child shall have been or shall likely to be permanently injured.

Contrary to: Offences Against the Person Act 1861 s.27

Max. sentence: Magistrates' Court: 6 months' imprisonment / £5,000 fine.

Crown Court: 5 years' imprisonment / unlimited fine.

Power: Arrestable Offence

Offence:

It is an offence for any person to be found drunk:

(a)   in any highway or other public place, whether a building or not; or

(b)   on any licensed premises,

while having the charge of a child apparently under the age of 7 years.

Contrary to: Licensing Act 1902 s.2

Max. sentence: Magistrates' Court: 1 month imprisonment / £500 fine.

Power: Report / s.25 PACE

Offence:

It is an offence for a person who has attained the age of 16 years and has responsibility[1] for any child or young person under that age to:

(a)   wilfully[2] assault;

(b)   ill-treat;

(c)   neglect;[3]

(d)   abandon; or

(e)   expose,

that child or young person in a manner likely to cause him unnecessary suffering or injury to health.[4]

Contrary to: Children and Young Persons Act 1933 s.1(1)

Max. sentence: Magistrates' Court: 6 months' imprisonment / £5,000 fine.

Crown Court: 10 years' imprisonment / unlimited fine.

Power: Arrestable Offence

Offence:

It is an offence for any person to give, or cause to be given, to any child under the age of 5 years any intoxicating liquor except upon the order of a duly qualified medical practitioner, or in a case of sickness, apprehended sickness or other urgent cause.

Contrary to: Children and Young Persons Act 1933 s.5

Max. sentence: Magistrates' Court: £200 fine.

Power: Report / s.25 PACE

Offence:

It is an offence for a person to sell to a person under the age of 16 years any tobacco[5] or cigarette papers, whether for his own use or not.[6]

Contrary to: Children and Young Persons Act 1933 s.7

Max. sentence: Magistrates' Court: £2,500 fine.

Power: Report / s.25 PACE

Offence:

It is an offence for a person who has attained the age of 16 years, having responsibility for any child under the age of 12 years, to allow the child to be in any room containing an open fire grate or heating appliance[7] not sufficiently protected to guard against the risk of burning or scalding, and by reason thereof the child is killed or suffers serious injury.

Contrary to: Children and Young Persons Act 1933 s. 11

Max. sentence: Magistrates' Court: £200 fine.

Power: Report / s.25 PACE

Offence: It is an offence for any person, where there is provided an entertainment for children[8] in any building,[9] to fail to station sufficient adult attendants[10] to control the children, their movement and to take all reasonable precautions for their safety.

Contrary to: Children and Young Persons Act 1933 s.12

Max. sentence: Magistrates' Court: £1,000 fine.

Power: Report / s.25 PACE[11]

Offence: It is an offence for a child[12] to engage or be employed in street trading.[13]

Contrary to: Children and Young Persons Act 1933 s.20

Max. sentence: Magistrates' Court: £200 fine.

Power: Report / s.25 PACE

Offence: It is an offence[14] for a person to employ a child:

(a)   under the age of 13 years;[15]

(aa)   to do any work other than light work;

(b)   before the close of school hours on any day on which he is required to attend school;

(c)   before 07.00 hours or after 19.00 hours on any day;

(d)   for more than 2 hours on any day on which he is required to attend school;

(e)   for more than 2 hours on any Sunday;

(f)   ... *repealed* ...

(g)   for more than 8 hours or, if he is under 15 years, for more than 5 hours in any day:

(i)   on which he is not required to attend school, and

(ii)   which is not a Sunday;

(h)   for more than 35 hours or, if he is under the age of 15 years, for more than 25 hours in any

CHILDREN AND YOUNG PERSONS   49

week in which he is not required to attend school;

(i) for more than 4 hours in any day without a rest break of 1 hour;

(j) at any time in a year unless at that time he has had, or could still have, during a period in the year in which he is not required to attend school, at least 2 consecutive weeks without employment.

Contrary to: Children and Young Persons Act 1933 s.21

Max. sentence: Magistrates' Court: £1,000 fine.

Power: Report / s.25 PACE

Offence:
It is an offence[16] to tattoo a person under the age of 18 except where the tattoo is performed for medical reasons by a qualified medical practitioner or by a person working under his direction.

Contrary to: Tattooing of Minors Act 1969 s.1

Max. sentence: Magistrates' Court: £1,000 fine.

Power: Report / s.25 PACE

Offence:
It is an offence for a person, knowingly and without lawful authority or reasonable excuse, to:

(a) take a child who is in care, subject of an emergency protection order or in police protection, away from the responsible person;[17]

(b) keep such a child away from the responsible person; or

(c) induce, assist or incite such a child to run away or stay away from the responsible person.

Contrary to: Children Act 1989 s.49

Max. sentence: Magistrates' Court: 6 months' imprisonment / £5,000 fine.

Power: Report / s.25 PACE

Offence:
It is an offence for any person[18] to cause or permit a child under the age of 14 years to ride a horse on a road[19] unless the child is wearing protective headgear.[20]

Contrary to: Horses (Protective Headgear for Young Riders) Act 1990 s.1

Max. sentence: Magistrates' Court: £200 fine.

Power: Report / s.25 PACE

Offence:
It is an offence for a person carrying on a retail business to sell cigarettes to any person other than in pre-packed quantities of 10 or more cigarettes in their original package.

Contrary to: Children and Young Persons (Protection from Tobacco) Act 1991 s.3

Max. sentence: Magistrates' Court: £1,000 fine.

Power: Report / s.25 PACE

Offence:
It is an offence[21] for a person to supply any cigarette lighter refill canister containing butane or a substance with butane as a constituent part to any person under the age of 18.

Contrary to: Cigarette Lighter Refill (Safety) Regulations 1999 r.2

Max. sentence: Magistrates' Court: 6 months' imprisonment/ £1,000 fine.

Power: Report / s.25 PACE

General Powers

Where a constable has reasonable cause to believe that a child would otherwise be likely to suffer significant harm, he may:[22]

(a) remove the child to suitable accommodation and keep him there; or

(b) take such steps as are reasonable to ensure that the child's removal from any hospital, or other place, in which he is then being accommodated is prevented.

If a child or young person is absent without the consent of the responsible person:

(a) from a place of safety to which he has been taken under the Children and Young Persons Act 1969 s.16(3); or

(b) from local authority accommodation:

    (i) in which he is required to live under s.12AA; or

    (ii) to which he has been remanded under s.16(3A); or

    (iii) to which he has been remanded or committed under s.23(1),

he may be arrested by a constable and conducted to the place of safety, the local authority accommodation or such other place as the responsible person may direct.[23]

A constable in uniform may seize any tobacco or cigarette papers in the possession of any person apparently under the age of 16 years who he finds smoking in any street or public place and any tobacco or cigarette papers so seized shall be disposed of in such manner as the police authority may direct.[24]

Definitions

Child: a person under the age of 14 years.

Young person: a person between 14 and 17 years of age.

General Information

For the purposes of the offence under the Children and Young Persons Act 1933 s.1, a parent or other person legally liable to maintain a child or young person, or the legal guardian, shall be deemed to have neglected him in a manner likely to cause injury to his health if he has failed to provide adequate food, clothing, medical aid or lodging.[25] Where it is proved that the death of an infant under 3 years of age was caused by suffocation while the infant was in bed with a person of or over 16, that person shall, if under the influence of drink at the time he went to bed, be deemed to have neglected the infant in a manner likely to cause injury to its health.[26]

Notes

1   Means anyone with parental responsibility, who is legally liable to maintain the child as well as any person who has the care of the child. [Children and Young Persons Act 1933 s.17].

2   That is deliberately or recklessly.

3   See *General Information*.

4   For these purposes a parent or guardian shall be deemed to have neglected him if he has failed to provide adequate food, clothing, medical aid or lodgings. If an infant under 3 years of age suffocates as a result of being in the same bed as a person who has attained the age of 16, and that person was under the influence of drink, it shall be deemed that the infant was neglected.

5   This includes any cigarette and any product containing tobacco which is intended for oral or nasal use (for example, snuff).

6   It shall be a defence to prove that all reasonable precautions were taken and all due diligence exercised to avoid the commission of the offence.

7   Liable to cause injury to a person by contact therewith.

8   100 or more.

9   The institution of proceedings falls to the local authority in the case of buildings licensed under the Cinemas Act 1985 or licensed for entertainment or for music, singing and dancing. In any other case proceedings may be instituted by the police.

10   Properly instructed.

11   This section includes a specific power of entry whereby a constable may enter any building in which he has reason to believe that such an entertainment is being, or about to be, provided, with a view to seeing whether the provisions of the section are being carried out.

12   Local authorities may make byelaws allowing children of 14 years to be employed by their parents.

13   Includes the hawking of newspapers, matches, flowers and other articles, playing, singing or performing for profit, shoe-blacking and other like occupations carried on in streets or public places.

14   A local authority may make byelaws with respect to the employment of children authorising some limited employment.

15   Children (Protection at Work) Regulations 2000.

16   It shall be a defence to show that at the time the tattoo was performed he had reasonable cause to believe that the person tattooed was of or over 18 and that he did in fact so believe.

17   This means any person who for the time being has care of him by virtue of such an order.

18 This offence may be committed by any person who has responsibility for the child for the purposes of Part I of the Children and Young Persons Act 1933; any owner of the horse; any person who has custody or is in charge of the horse immediately before the child rides it or, if the child is employed, his employer and any other person to whose orders the child is subject in the course of his employment.

19 For the purposes of this Act, 'road' does not include a footpath or bridleway.

20 No offence will be committed where the child is a Sikh whilst wearing a turban, where the riding is within 30 metres of the high water mark or ordinary spring tides and the horse is being led on a leading rein by the owner or other person over 18 years and no more than 2 horses are being led at any one time.

21 It is a defence to show that all reasonable steps were taken, and all due diligence exercised to avoid the commission of the offence.

22 Police protection is for a maximum of 72 hours. Children Act 1989, s.46.

23 Children and Young Persons Act 1969 s.32(1A) and (1B). This power is concerned with the apprehension of children and young persons who have been committed to the care of the local authority. A power of entry is available under s.17 of the Police and Criminal Evidence Act 1984. See page 5.

24 Children and Young Persons Act 1933 s.7.

25 This includes failing to procure any of these through enactments provided for that purpose; for example, social welfare. [Children and Young Persons Act 1933 s.1(2)(a)].

26 Ibid., s.1(2)(b).

COMPUTERS AND THE INTERNET

See also Abstracting Electricity, Deception, Indecent and Obscene Behaviour, Post and Mail, Telecommunications, Theft

Offence: It is an offence for a person to cause a computer to perform any function with intent to secure access to any program or data held in any computer and the access he intends to secure is unauthorised and he knows at the time when he causes the computer to perform the function that that is the case.

Contrary to: Computer Misuse Act 1990 s.1(1)

| Max. sentence: | Magistrates' Court: 6 months' imprisonment / £5,000 fine.[1] |
| Power: | Report / s.25 PACE[2] |

Offence: It is an offence[3] for a person to do any act which causes an unauthorised modification of the contents of any computer and at the time when he does the act he intends to:

(a)   impair the operation of any computer;

(b)   prevent or hinder access to any program or data held in any computer; or

(c)   impair the operation of any such program or the reliability of any such data.

Contrary to:	Computer Misuse Act 1990 s.3(1)
Max. sentence:	Magistrates' Court: 6 months' imprisonment / £5,000 fine
	Crown Court: 5 years' imprisonment / unlimited fine.
Power:	Arrestable Offence

Offence: It is an offence for a person to whom a s. 49 notice has been given to knowingly fail to make the disclosure required by the notice.[4]

Contrary to:	Regulation of Investigatory Powers Act 2000., s. 53
Max. sentence:	Magistrates' Court: 6 months' imprisonment / £5,000 fine.
	Crown Court: 2 years' imprisonment / unlimited fine.
Power:	Report / s.25 PACE

Notes

1   A person who commits this offence with intent to commit a criminal offence for which the sentence is fixed by law or is liable to a term of 5 years' imprisonment on first conviction becomes liable to an increased penalty on indictment of 5 years' imprisonment and/or an unlimited fine.

2   But see note 1 above.

3   For the purposes of the Criminal Damage Act 1971 a modification of the contents of a computer shall not be regarded as damaging any computer or computer storage medium unless its effect on that computer or computer storage medium impairs its physical condition [s.3(6)].

4   Section 49 notices are concerned with the keys (codes) to encrypted information. A notice demanding the key may be made where necessary on the grounds of national security, for the purpose of preventing or detecting crime or in the interests of the economic well-being of the United Kingdom. Any failure to comply is an offence.

CONSPIRACY AND INCITEMENT

See also Aiding and Abetting, Attempts, Noise, Nuisance, PACE – Arrest

Offence: It is an offence for a person to conspire to defraud another.

Contrary to: Common Law

Max. sentence: Crown Court: 10 years' imprisonment / unlimited fine.[1]

Power: Arrestable Offence

Offence: It is an offence for a person to incite[2] another to commit an offence, even though an offence is not committed.

Contrary to: Common Law

Max. sentence: An offender is liable to the same penalty as that which may be imposed on a principal.[3]

Power: Dependent upon those powers applicable to the offence concerned.[4]

Offence: It is an offence[5] for a person to agree with any other person or persons that a course of conduct shall be pursued which, if the agreement is carried out in accordance with their intentions either:

(a)   will necessarily amount to or involve the commission of any offence or offences by one or more of the parties to the agreement; or

(b)   would do so but for the existence of facts which render the commission of the offence or any of the offences impossible.

Contrary to: Criminal Law Act 1977 s.1(1)[6]

Max. sentence: An offender is liable to the same penalty as that which may be imposed on a principal.[7]

Power: Dependent upon those powers applicable to the offence concerned.[8]

Notes

1   Criminal Justice Act 1987 s.12.

2   That is, urge on to action, stir up. An incitement, however, cannot be committed where it is impossible to commit the offence [*R* v *Fitzmaurice* (1983)].

3   Where the offence has actually been committed, then the person inciting will be liable as an accessory.

4   Where the offence being incited, is an Arrestable Offence, then the incitement is also an Arrestable Offence.

5   A person is not guilty of conspiracy to commit any offence if he is an intended victim of that offence. A person shall not be guilty of conspiracy to commit any offence if the only other person or persons with whom he agrees are (both initially and at all times during the currency of the agreement) persons who are:

    (a)   his spouse;

    (b)   under the age of criminal responsibility;

    (c)   an intended victim.

6   If the elements of this section are satisfied, then the person is guilty of conspiracy to commit the offence or offences in question.

7   The institution of proceedings requires the consent of the Director of Public Prosecutions, or in some limited cases, the Attorney General.

8   Where the offence subject of the conspiracy is an Arrestable Offence, then the conspiracy is also an Arrestable Offence.

See also Brakes, Drivers and Riders, Goods Vehicles Operators, Lights on Vehicles, Seat Belts, Speeding, Steering, Tyres

Offence: It is an offence[1] for a motor vehicle, every trailer drawn thereby and all parts and accessories of such vehicle and trailer, not to be at all times in such condition, and:

(a)   the number of passengers carried by such vehicle or trailer,

(b)   the manner in which any passengers are carried in or on such vehicle or trailer, and

(c)   the weight, distribution, packing and adjustment of the load of such vehicle or trailer shall at all times be such, that no danger is caused or is likely to be caused to any person in or on the vehicle or trailer or on a road.

Contrary to: Road Vehicles (Construction and Use) Regulations 1986 r.100(1)

Max. sentence: Magistrates' Court: £1,000 fine.

Power: Report / s.25 PACE

Offence: It is an offence for the load carried by a motor vehicle or trailer not to be at all times so secured, if need be by physical restraint other than its own weight, and be in such a position, that neither danger or nuisance is likely to be caused to any person or property by reason of the load or any part thereof falling or being blown from the vehicle or by reason of any other movement of the load or part thereof in relation to the vehicle.

Contrary to: Road Vehicles (Construction and Use) Regulations 1986 r.100(2)

Max. sentence:	Magistrates' Court: £1,000 fine.
Power:	Report / s.25 PACE

Offence:

It is an offence for a motor vehicle or trailer to be used for any purpose for which it is so unsuitable[2] as to cause or be likely to cause danger or nuisance to any person in or on the vehicle or trailer or on a road.

Contrary to:	Road Vehicles (Construction and Use) Regulations 1986 r.100(3)
Max. sentence:	Magistrates' Court: £1,000 fine.
Power:	Report / s.25 PACE

Offence:

It is an offence for a vehicle fitted with any apparatus or appliance designed for lifting where part of the apparatus or appliance consists of a suspended implement, not to secure the appliance or apparatus so that no danger is caused or is likely to be caused to any person on the vehicle or on the road when the vehicle is in motion on a road and when the implement is not attached to any load supported by the appliance or apparatus.

Contrary to:	Road Vehicles (Construction and Use) Regulations 1986 r.108
Max. sentence:	Magistrates' Court: £1,000 fine.
Power:	Report / s.25 PACE

Offence:

It is an offence to use, or cause or permit another to use a motor vehicle or trailer on a road when:

(a) the condition of the motor vehicle or trailer, or of its accessories or equipment;

(b) the purpose for which it is used;

(c) the number of passengers carried by it, or the manner in which they are carried; or

(d)   the weight, position or distribution of its load, or the manner in which it is secured,

is such that the use of the motor vehicle or trailer involves a danger of injury to any person.

Contrary to: Road Traffic Act 1988 s.40A

Max. sentence: Magistrates' Court: £5,000 fine.[3]

Power: Report / s.25 PACE

Offence:

It is an offence for a person:

(a)   to contravene or fail to comply with any construction and use requirement as to brakes, steering gear or tyres; or

(b)   to use on a road a motor vehicle or trailer which does not comply with such a requirement, or causes or permits a motor vehicle or trailer to be so used.

Contrary to: Road Traffic Act 1988 s.41A

Max. sentence: Magistrates' Court: £5,000 fine.[4]

Power: Report / s.25 PACE

Offence:

It is an offence for a person:

(a)   to contravene or fail to comply with any construction and use requirement as to any description of weight applicable to a goods vehicle, or a motor vehicle or trailer adapted to carry more than 8 passengers; or

(b)   to use on a road a vehicle which does not comply with such requirement, or causes or permits a vehicle to be so used.

Contrary to: Road Traffic Act 1988 s.41B

Max. sentence: Magistrates' Court: £5,000 fine.

Power: Report / s.25 PACE

Offence:

It is an offence for a person:

(a) to contravene or fail to comply with any construction and use requirement other than brakes, steering gear or tyres; or

(b) to use on a road a motor vehicle or trailer which does not comply with such a requirement, or causes or permits a motor vehicle or trailer to be so used.

Contrary to: Road Traffic Act 1988 s.42

Max. sentence: Magistrates' Court: £2,500 fine.[5]

Power: Report / s.25 PACE

Offence:

It is an offence for a person[6] to sell, offer to sell or to supply or expose for sale a motor vehicle or trailer:

(a) in an unroadworthy condition as respects brakes, steering gear, construction, weight or tyres; or

(b) in such a condition that its use on a road would involve a danger of injury to any person.

Contrary to: Road Traffic Act 1988 s.75

Max. sentence: Magistrates' Court: £5,000 fine.

Power: Report / s.25 PACE

General Powers:

A person driving a mechanically propelled vehicle on a road must stop the vehicle on being required to do so by a constable in uniform.[7]

A constable in uniform, authorised to act as an examiner by or on behalf of a chief constable, may test or inspect a motor vehicle or trailer on a road[8] for the purpose of:

(a) ascertaining whether the following requirements are complied with as respects the vehicle, namely:

(i) the construction and use requirements, and

(ii) the requirement that the condition of the vehicle is not such that its use on a road would involve danger or injury to any person;

(b)   bringing to the notice of the driver any failure to comply with those requirements.[9]

If on any inspection of a motor vehicle it appears to an authorised constable that owing to any defects in the vehicle it is, or is likely to become, unfit for service, he may prohibit the driving of the vehicle on a road.[10]

If on any inspection of a motor vehicle it appears to an authorised constable that owing to any defects in the vehicle driving it would involve a danger of injury to any person, he may prohibit the driving of the vehicle on a road.[11]

A constable in uniform is empowered to test and inspect the brakes, silencers, steering gear and tyres of any vehicle and on any premises where that vehicle is located provided that, if required to do so, he shall produce his authorisation.[12]

A constable who is an authorised vehicle examiner:

(a)   may at any time, on production if so required of his authority, inspect[13] any relevant vehicle[14] and for that purpose detain the vehicle during such time as is required for the inspection, and

(b)   may at any time which is reasonable having regard to the circumstances of the case, enter any premises on which he has reason to believe that such a vehicle is kept.[15]

A constable in uniform or vehicle examiner may at any time require any person in charge of a relevant vehicle[16] which is stationary on a road, to proceed with the vehicle for the purpose of having it inspected, to any place where the inspection can suitably be carried out, not being more than 5 miles from the place where the requirement was made.[17]

Definitions

Motor vehicle: a mechanically propelled vehicle intended or adapted for use on roads.

Notes

1   Does not apply to tramcars or trolley vehicles.

2   For example, a vehicle too high to pass under a bridge [*British Road Services Ltd* v *Owen* (1971)].

3   In the case of a goods vehicle or one designed for the carrying of more than 8 passengers. £2,500 in other cases.

4   As note 1 above.

5   In the case of a goods vehicle or one designed for the carrying of more than 8 passengers. £1,000 in other cases.

6   An 'auctioneer' does not 'offer to sell' for these purposes [*British Car Auctions* v *Wright* (1972)].

7   Road Traffic Act 1988 s.163.

8   This may be done immediately if:

   (a) an accident has occurred, owing to the presence of the motor vehicle on a road and it is requisite that a test be carried out forthwith;

   (b) in the opinion of a constable the vehicle is apparently so defective that it ought not to be allowed to proceed without a test being carried out.

   In any other case the driver of the vehicle may elect that the test be deferred to a time and place fixed in accordance with Sch. 2 to the 1988 Act. [Road Traffic Act 1988 s.67].

9   Road Traffic Act 1988 s.67(1). See also page 199. Where a constable, who is not an authorised examiner, carries out any tests on a motor vehicle with the defendant's co-operation, then such evidence is admissible in any proceedings [*Stoneley* v *Richardson* (1973)].

10 Road Traffic Act 1988 s.69(1).

11 Ibid., s.69(2).

12 Road Vehicles (Construction and Use) Regulations 1986 r.74. Conditions placed on this power include:

   (a) no entry to premises without the consent of the owner of the premises;

   (b) no test or inspection may take place on any premises without the consent of the vehicle's owner unless such owner has been given prior notice or the test takes place within 48 hours of an accident.

13 Includes testing it and driving the vehicle for the purpose of testing it.

14 That is, goods vehicles, public service vehicles and motor vehicles which are not public service vehicles but are adapted to carry more than 8 passengers.

15 Road Traffic Act 1988 s.68(1). Does not apply in the case of passenger carrying motor vehicles (8 or more passengers) operating under permits authorising educational or community bus service purposes.

16 See note 14.

17 Road Traffic Act 1988 s. 68(4). A person in charge of such a vehicle who refuses or neglects to comply commits an offence.

CRIMINAL JUSTICE

See also Absconders and Escapees, Assaults, Bail, Conspiracy and Incitement, Forgery, Harassment and Intimidation, Police

Offence: It is an offence for a person to do any act tending and intended to pervert the course of public justice.

Contrary to: Common Law

Max. sentence: Crown Court: unlimited fine.

Power: Arrestable Offence

Offence: It is an offence for any person, lawfully sworn as a witness or as an interpreter in judicial proceedings,[1] wilfully to make a statement which he knows to be false, or does not believe to be true.[2]

Contrary to: Perjury Act 1911 s.1

Max. sentence: Crown Court: 7 years' imprisonment / unlimited fine

Power: Arrestable Offence

Offence: It is an offence for any person, in giving testimony (either orally or in writing) otherwise than on oath, where required to do so by an order under s. 2 of the Evidence (Proceedings in Other Jurisdictions) Act 1975, to make a statement:

(a) which he knows to be false in a material particular; or

(b) which is false in a material particular and which he does not believe to be true.

Contrary to: Perjury Act 1911 s.1A

Max. sentence: Magistrates' Court: 6 months' imprisonment / £5,000 fine.

Crown Court: 2 years' imprisonment / unlimited fine.

Power: Report / s.25 PACE

Offence: It is an offence for any person, being required or authorised by law to make any statement on oath for any purpose, and being lawfully sworn[3] to wilfully make a material statement which he knows to be false or does not believe to be true.

Contrary to: Perjury Act 1911 s.2

Max. sentence: Crown Court: 7 years' imprisonment / unlimited fine.

Power: Arrestable Offence

Offence: It is an offence for any person to aid, abet, counsel or procure, or suborn or incite another person to commit an offence of perjury.

Contrary to: Perjury Act 1911 s.7.

Max. sentence: Crown Court: 7 years' imprisonment / unlimited fine.

Power: Arrestable Offence

Offence: It is an offence for a person in a written statement[4] tendered in evidence in criminal proceedings to wilfully make a material statement which he knows to be false or does not believe to be true.

Contrary to: Criminal Justice Act 1967 s.89

Max. sentence: Crown Court: 2 years' imprisonment / unlimited fine.

Power: Report / s.25 PACE

Offence: It is an offence for a person, where a person has committed an arrestable offence, and knowing or believing him to be guilty of that or some other arrestable offence, without lawful authority or reasonable excuse, to do any act with intent to impede his apprehension or prosecution.

Contrary to: Criminal Law Act 1967 s.4(1)

Max. sentence:	Crown Court: 10 years' imprisonment / unlimited fine.[5]
Power:	Arrestable Offence[6]

Offence:

It is an offence for a person, knowing or believing that an arrestable offence has been committed, and that he has information that might be of material assistance in securing the prosecution or conviction of an offender for it, to accept or agree to accept for not disclosing that information any consideration.[7]

Contrary to:	Criminal Law Act 1967 s.5(1)
Max. sentence:	Crown Court: 2 years' imprisonment / unlimited fine.
Power:	Report / s.25 PACE

Offence:

It is an offence for a person to cause any wasteful employment of the police by knowingly making to any person a false report tending:

(a) to show that an offence has been committed;

(b) to give rise to apprehension for the safety of any persons or property; or

(c) to tend to show that he has information material to a police inquiry.

Contrary to:	Criminal Law Act 1967 s.5(2)
Max. sentence:	Magistrates' Court: 6 months' imprisonment / £5,000 fine.
Power:	Report / s.25 PACE

Offence:

It is an offence for any person in a written statement[8] admitted in evidence in criminal proceedings to wilfully make a material statement which he knows to be false or does not believe to be true.

Contrary to:	Magistrates' Courts Act 1980 s. 106

| Max. sentence: | Crown Court: 2 years' imprisonment / unlimited fine. |
| Power: | Report / s.25 PACE |

Offence: It is an offence for a person to assault a court security officer acting in the execution of his duty.

Contrary to:	Criminal Justice Act 1991 s.78(1)
Max. sentence:	Magistrates' Court: 6 months' imprisonment / £5,000 fine.
Power:	Report / s.25 PACE

Offence: It is an offence for a person to resist or wilfully obstruct a court security officer acting in the execution of his duty.

Contrary to:	Criminal Justice Act 1991 s.78(2)
Max. sentence:	Magistrates' Court: £1,000 fine.
Power:	Report / s.25 PACE

Offence: It is an offence for a person to assault a prisoner custody officer:

(a) acting in pursuance of prisoner escort arrangements;

(b) performing custodial duties at a contracted out prison; or

(c) performing contracted out functions at a directly managed prison.

Contrary to:	Criminal Justice Act 1991 s.90(1)
Max. sentence:	Magistrates' Court: 6 months' imprisonment / £5,000 fine.
Power:	Report / s.25 PACE

Offence: It is an offence for a person to resist or wilfully obstruct a prisoner custody officer:

(d) acting in pursuance of prisoner escort arrangements;

(e)　performing custodial duties at a contracted out prison; or

(f)　performing contracted out functions at a directly managed prison.

Contrary to:　Criminal Justice Act 1991 s.90(3)

Max. sentence:　Magistrates' Court: £1,000 fine.

Power:　Report / s.25 PACE

Offence:

It is an offence for a person to do to another any act[9] which intimidates, and is intended to intimidate, that other person knowing or believing that the other is assisting in the investigation of an offence or is a witness or potential witness or a juror or potential juror in proceedings for an offence, intending thereby to cause the investigation or the course of justice to be obstructed, perverted or interfered with.

Contrary to:　Criminal Justice and Public Order Act 1994 s.51(1)

Max. sentence:　Magistrates' Court: 6 months' imprisonment / £5,000 fine.

Crown Court: 5 years' imprisonment / unlimited fine.

Power:　Arrestable Offence

Offence:

It is an offence for a person to do or threaten to do to another person any act which harms or would harm, and is intended to harm that other knowing or believing that the other, or some other person, has assisted in an investigation into an offence, or has given evidence or particular evidence in proceedings for an offence or has acted as a juror or concurred to a particular verdict in proceedings for an offence.

Contrary to:　Criminal Justice and Public Order Act 1994 s.51(2)

Max. sentence:	Magistrates' Court: 6 months' imprisonment / £5,000 fine.
	Crown Court: 5 years' imprisonment / unlimited fine.
Power:	Arrestable Offence

Offence:

It is an offence for a person to:

(a) do an act[10] which intimidates, and is intended to intimidate, another person; and

(b) do the act:

(i) knowing or believing that the victim is or may be a witness in any relevant proceedings;[11] and

(ii) intending, by his act, to cause the course of justice to be obstructed, perverted or interfered with; and

(c) the act is done after the commencement of those proceedings.

Contrary to:	Criminal Justice and Police Act 2001 s.39(1)[12]
Max. sentence:	Magistrates' Court: 6 months' imprisonment / £5,000 fine.
	Crown Court: 5 years' imprisonment / unlimited fine.
Power:	Arrestable Offence

Offence:

It is an offence for a person, knowing or believing that some person has been a witness in relevant proceedings,[13] to:

(a) do an act[14] which harms, and is intended to harm, another person; or

(b) intending to cause another person to fear harm, threaten to do an act which would harm that other person.

| **Contrary to:** | Criminal Justice and Police Act 2001 s.40(1)[15] |

Max. sentence: Magistrates' Court: 6 months' imprisonment / £5,000 fine.

Crown Court: 5 years' imprisonment / unlimited fine.

Power: Arrestable Offence

Notes

1   Includes any proceedings before any court, tribunal or before any person having power under the law to hear, receive and examine evidence on oath.

2   Corroboration is required for perjury offences.

3   Otherwise than in judicial proceedings.

4   Section 9 statements.

5   The penalty is dependent upon the gravity of the other person's offence. Where the sentence for that other is fixed by law then the offender under this section would be liable to a penalty of 10 years. If it is one for which a person may be sentenced to 14 years, the liability is 7 years; where the sentence may be 10 years the liability is 5 years and in any other case the liability will be 3 years.

6   See note 5 above. In the case of the lower liability this is not an arrestable offence.

7   Other than the making good of any loss or injury caused by the offence, or the making of reasonable compensation for that loss or injury.

8   Which complies with the Magistrates' Courts Act 1980 s.5B.

9   A person does an act 'to' another person not only where the act is done in the presence of that other and directed at him but also where the act is done to a third party and is intended, in the circumstances, to intimidate or (as the case may be) harm the person at whom the act is directed. Harm may be financial as well as physical.

10 Includes threats. It is immaterial whether or not the act is done in the presence of the victim; whether the act is done to the victim or another person; and whether or not the intention to cause the course of justice to be obstructed, perverted or interfered with is the predominating intention of the person doing the act.

11 Relevant proceedings include proceedings before the Court of Appeal, High Court, Crown Court or any county or magistrates' court which are not proceedings for an offence.

12 In Force from 1.8.01.

13 This offence may be committed up to 1 year after the proceedings. Relevant proceedings include proceedings before the Court of Appeal,

High Court, Crown Court or any county or magistrates' court which are not proceedings for an offence.

14 See note 10. The harm threatened can be physical or financial or aimed at property.

15 In force from 1.8.01.

CROSSBOWS

See also Air Weapons, Assaults, Damage, Firearms – Criminal Use, Offensive Weapons

Offence: It is an offence[1] for a person to sell or let on hire a crossbow or part of a crossbow to a person under the age of 17.

Contrary to: Crossbows Act 1987 s.1

Max. sentence: Magistrates' Court: 6 months' imprisonment / £5,000 fine.

Power: Report / s.25 PACE

Offence: It is an offence for any person under the age of 17 to buy or hire a crossbow or part of a crossbow.

Contrary to: Crossbows Act 1987 s.2

Max. sentence: Magistrates' Court: £1,000 fine.

Power: Report / s.25 PACE

Offence: It is an offence[2] for a person under the age of 17 to have with him a crossbow which is capable of discharging a missile, or parts of a crossbow which together can be assembled to form a crossbow capable of discharging a missile.

Contrary to: Crossbows Act 1987 s.3

Max. sentence: Magistrates' Court: £1,000 fine.

Power: Report / s.25 PACE

General Powers

If a constable suspects, with reasonable cause, that a person is committing or has committed an offence under s.3 of the Crossbows Act 1987, he may:

(a) search that person for a crossbow or part of a crossbow; or

(b) search any vehicle, or anything in or on a vehicle, in or on which the constable suspects with reasonable cause there is a crossbow or part of a crossbow connected with the offence.[3]

A constable may detain a person or vehicle for the purposes of a search.[4]

A constable may seize and retain anything discovered by him in the course of a search which appears to him to be a crossbow or part of a crossbow.[5]

For the purposes of exercising these powers a constable may enter any land other than a dwelling-house.[6]

Definitions

Crossbow: for the purposes of this Act a crossbow is defined as having a draw weight exceeding 1.4 kg.

Notes

1 It is a defence for an accused to show that he believed the other person to be of or over the age of 17 and had a reasonable cause for such a belief.

2 No offence is committed where the person under 17 is being supervised by a person aged 21 or older.

3 Crossbows Act 1987 s.4(1).

4 Ibid., s.4(2)

5 Ibid., s.4(3).

6 Ibid., s.4(4).

DAMAGE

See also Air Weapons, Burglary, Computers and the Internet, Firearms – Criminal Use, Litter, PACE – Arrest, Racial Hatred, Railways, Taxis and Private Hire, Theft

Offence: It is an offence for a person to wilfully cause any injury or damage to any fence of a town or village green.[1]

Contrary to: Inclosure Act 1857 s.12

Max. sentence: Magistrates' Court: £200 fine.

Power: Report / s.25 PACE[2]

Offence:

It is an offence for a person to unlawfully mask, alter or remove any light or signal, or unlawfully exhibit any false light or signal, with intent to bring any ship, vessel or boat into danger, or unlawfully and maliciously do anything tending to the immediate loss or destruction of any ship, vessel or boat.

Contrary to: Malicious Damage Act 1861 s.47

Max. sentence: Crown Court: life imprisonment.

Power: Arrestable Offence

Offence:

It is an offence for a person to unlawfully and maliciously cut away, cast adrift, remove, alter, deface, sink or destroy, or unlawfully and maliciously do any act with such intent, or in any other manner unlawfully and maliciously injure or conceal any boat, buoy, buoy-rope or mark, used or intended for the guidance of seamen or for the purpose of navigation.

Contrary to: Malicious Damage Act 1861 s.48

Max. sentence: Crown Court: 7 years' imprisonment / unlimited fine

Power: Arrestable Offence

Offence:

It is an offence for a person, without lawful excuse, to destroy or damage[3] any property belonging to another[4] intending to destroy or damage any such property or being reckless as to whether any such property would be destroyed or damaged.

Contrary to:	Criminal Damage Act 1971 s.1(1)
Max. sentence:	Magistrates' Court: 6 months' imprisonment / £5,000 fine.
	Crown Court: 10 years' imprisonment.
Power:	Arrestable Offence

Offence:

It is an offence for a person, without lawful excuse, to destroy or damage any property, whether belonging to himself or another:

(a) intending to destroy or damage any property or being reckless as to whether any property would be destroyed or damaged; and

(b) intending by the destruction or damage to endanger the life of another[5] or being reckless as to whether the life of another would be thereby endangered.

Contrary to:	Criminal Damage Act 1971 s.1(2)
Max. sentence:	Crown Court: life imprisonment.
Power:	Arrestable Offence

Offence:

It is an offence for a person, without lawful excuse, to make to another a threat, intending that that other would fear it would be carried out:

(a) to destroy or damage any property belonging to that other or a third person; or

(b) to destroy or damage his own property in a way which he knows is likely to endanger the life of that other or a third person.

Contrary to:	Criminal Damage Act 1971 s.2
Max. sentence:	Magistrates' Court: 6 months' imprisonment / £5,000 fine.
	Crown Court: 10 years' imprisonment / unlimited fine.
Power:	Arrestable Offence

Offence: It is an offence for a person, without lawful excuse, to have anything in his custody or under his control intending to use it or cause or permit another to use it:

  (a) to destroy or damage any property belonging to some other person; or

  (b) to destroy or damage his own or the user's property in a way which he knows is likely to endanger the life of some other person.

Contrary to: Criminal Damage Act 1971 s.3

Max. sentence: Magistrates' Court: 6 months' imprisonment / £5,000 fine.

Crown Court: 10 years' imprisonment / unlimited fine.

Power: Arrestable Offence

Offence: It is an offence for any person, without lawful excuse to destroy or damage any protected monument,[6] knowing that it is a protected monument and intending to destroy or damage the monument or being reckless as to whether the monument would be destroyed or damaged.

Contrary to: Ancient Monuments and Archaeological Areas Act 1979 s.28

Max. sentence: Magistrates' Court: 6 months' imprisonment / £5,000 fine.

Crown Court: 2 years' imprisonment / unlimited fine.

Power: Report / s.25 PACE[7]

Offence: It is an offence for any person unlawfully and intentionally:

  (a) to destroy an aircraft in service or to so damage such an aircraft as to render it incapable of flight or as to be likely to endanger its safety in flight; or

(b) to commit on board an aircraft in flight any act of violence[8] which is likely to endanger the safety of the aircraft.

Contrary to:	Aviation Security Act 1982 s.2(1)
Max. sentence:	Crown Court: life imprisonment / unlimited fine.
Power:	Arrestable Offence

Offence: It is an offence for a person, with intent:

(a) to cause public alarm or anxiety;

(b) to cause injury to members of the public consuming or using the goods;

(c) to cause economic loss to any person by reason of their goods being shunned by members of the public;

(d) to cause economic loss to any person by reason of steps taken to avoid injury, alarm, anxiety or loss,

to contaminate or interfere with goods, or make it appear that goods have been contaminated or interfered with, or which appear to have been interfered with or contaminated in a place where goods of that description are sold, consumed or otherwise supplied.[9]

Contrary to:	Public Order Act 1986 s.38(1)
Max. sentence:	Magistrates' Court: 6 months' imprisonment / £5,000 fine.
	Crown Court: 10 years' imprisonment / unlimited fine.
Power:	Arrestable Offence

General Powers

Where a constable has reasonable cause to suspect that a person about to embark on an aircraft, or a person on board an aircraft, intends to commit an offence against s.2 of the Aviation Security Act 1982, the constable may prohibit him from travelling on board the aircraft, and for the purpose of enforcing that prohibition may prevent him from embarking, may remove him from the aircraft and may arrest without warrant and detain for as long as may be necessary.[10]

Definitions

Lawful excuse: the Criminal Damage Act 1971 identifies two occasions where it will be deemed that a 'lawful excuse' was present:

(a) where the person charged believed that consent had been given by a person having the power to consent to the destruction or damage or that consent would have been given, had the circumstances been known;

(b) that the destruction or damage was necessary to protect other property and the person charged believed that such property was in immediate need of protection and that the means of protection were reasonable.[11]

Destroy or damage: this includes damage caused by dismantling,[12] erasure[13] and preventing something from performing its normal function.[14] Damage will have been caused where subsequent cleaning involves some expense.[15] Tangible property may be damaged even where the damage itself is intangible, for example where changes are made to a computer program.[16]

Reckless: the test for recklessness is that outlined in *Rv Caldwell* (1982); that is, that, having committed an act which creates an obvious risk of destruction or damage, the person either gives no thought to the possibility of there being such a risk, or, having recognised the risk, nevertheless goes on to commit the act.

Property: means property of a tangible nature whether real or personal, including money, and:

(a) including wild creatures which have been tamed or are ordinarily kept in captivity and any other wild creatures or their carcasses if, but only if, they have been reduced into possession which has not been lost or abandoned or are in the course of being reduced into possession; but

(b) not including mushrooms growing wild on any land or flowers, fruit or foliage of a plant growing wild on any land.[17]

Belonging to another: property shall be treated as belonging to any person:

(a) having custody or control of it;

(b) having in it any proprietary right or interest (not being an equitable interest arising only from an agreement to transfer or grant an interest); or

(c) having a charge on it.

Where property is subject to a trust, the persons to whom it belongs shall be so treated as including any person having a right to enforce the trust.

Property of a corporation sole shall be regarded as belonging to the corporation notwithstanding a vacancy in the corporation.

General Information

An offence committed under s.1 of the Criminal Damage Act 1971, by destroying or damaging property by fire shall be charged as arson.[18]

The value of the damage caused has an effect on sentencing under the 1971 Act. Where the value is £2,000 or less the offence is triable only summarily with a maximum sentence of 3 months' imprisonment and a fine of £2,500. Damage exceeding £2,000 is triable either way. This is not the case where the charge alleges that there was an intention to endanger life[19] or the accused was reckless as to whether life would be endangered. Such a charge is triable only on indictment.

In any case compensation up to £5,000 may be ordered in addition, or in preference, to any fine.

Notes

1   These areas are registered by the local authority for an area.

2   But consider the offence under the Criminal Damage Act 1971 s.1(1).

3   It is a matter for the court to decide what constitutes 'damage'. The

damage need not be permanent [*Roe* v *Kingerlee* (1986)] and may include
a permanent or temporary reduction in value or usefulness [*Morphitis* v
Salmon (1989)]. Alterations impairing a computer system, albeit
imperceptible until the computer is used, is criminal damage. Impairment
does not require breaking [*R* v *Whiteley* (1991)].

4   See page 78

5   It is not required to be shown that some life was actually endangered
    [*R* v *Parker* (1993)].

6   This means any monument scheduled under the Act or under the
    ownership and control of the Secretary of State, Commission or local
    authority.

7   But consider the offence under the Criminal Damage Act 1971 s.1(1).

8   This means any act which constitutes the offence of murder, attempted
    murder, manslaughter or assault or an offence under ss. 18, 20, 21, 22, 23,
    24, 28 or 29 of the Offences Against the Person Act 1861.

9   Or to threaten to do so. [Public Order Act 1986 s.38(2)].

10 Aviation Security Act 1982 s.7. Obstruction of a constable is an offence
    subject to 2 years' imprisonment on indictment.

11 Criminal Damage Act 1971 s.5.

12 *Morphitis* v *Salmon* (1990).

13 *Cox* v *Riley* (1986).

14 *Samuel* v *Stubbs* (1972).

15 *Hardmans* v *CC Avon & Somerset Constabulary* (1986).

16 *R* v *Whiteley* (1999).

17 Criminal Damage Act 1971, s.10(1). For the purposes of this subsection
    'mushroom' includes any fungus and 'plant' includes any shrub or tree.

18 Punishable by life imprisonment.

19 Criminal Damage Act 1971, s.1(2).

DANGEROUS AND CARELESS DRIVING/ RIDING

See also Aggravated Vehicle-Taking, Drink and Drive / Ride, Driving
Documents, Road Traffic Collisions, Taxis and Private Hire, Vehicle
Interference

Offence: It is an offence for any person, within the limits of
the   metropolitan   police   district,   in   any

thoroughfare or public place, to ride or drive furiously so as to endanger the life or limb of any person, or to the common danger of the passengers in any thoroughfare.

Contrary to: Metropolitan Police Act 1839 s.54

Max. sentence: Magistrates' Court: £500 fine.

Power: Report / s.25 PACE

Offence:

It is an offence for any person, in any street to the obstruction, annoyance or danger of the residents or passengers, to ride or drive furiously any horse or carriage.

Contrary to: Town Police Clauses Act 1847 s.28

Max. sentence: Magistrates' Court: 14 days' imprisonment / £1,000 fine.

Power: Report / s.25 PACE

Offence:

It is an offence for any person, having the charge of any carriage or vehicle,[1] by wanton or furious driving or racing, or other wilful misconduct, or by wilful negligence, to do or cause to be done any bodily harm to any person whatsoever.

Contrary to: Offences Against the Person Act 1861 s.35

Max. sentence: Crown Court: 2 years' imprisonment / unlimited fine.

Power: Report / s.25 PACE

Offence:

It is an offence for a person to cause the death of another person by driving a mechanically propelled vehicle dangerously on a road or other public place.

Contrary to: Road Traffic Act 1988 s.1

Max. sentence: Crown Court: 10 years' imprisonment / unlimited fine.[2]

Power: Arrestable Offence.

Offence: It is an offence for a person to drive a mechanically propelled vehicle dangerously on a road or other public place.

Contrary to: Road Traffic Act 1988 s.2

Max. sentence: Magistrates' Court: 6 months' imprisonment / £5,000 fine.

Crown Court: 2 years' imprisonment / unlimited fine.

Power: Report / s.25 PACE

Offence: It is an offence for a person to drive a mechanically propelled vehicle on a road or other public place:

(a)   without due care and attention; or

(b)   without reasonable consideration for other persons using the road or public place.

Contrary to: Road Traffic Act 1988 s.3

Max. sentence: Magistrates' Court: £2,500 fine.

Power: Report / s.25 PACE

Offence: It is an offence for a person to ride a cycle on a road dangerously.[3]

Contrary to: Road Traffic Act 1988 s.28

Max. sentence: Magistrates' Court: £2,500 fine.

Power: Report / s.25 PACE

Offence: It is an offence for a person to ride a cycle on a road without due care and attention, or without reasonable consideration for other persons using the road.

Contrary to: Road Traffic Act 1988 s.29

Max. sentence: Magistrates' Court: £1,000 fine.

Power: Report / s.25 PACE

Offence: It is an offence for a person who is:

(a)　the driver of a mechanically propelled vehicle who is alleged to have committed an offence under s.2 or s.3 of the Road Traffic Act 1988; or

(b)　the rider of a cycle who is alleged to have committed an offence under s.28 or s.29,

to refuse, on being required by any person having reasonable grounds for so requiring, to give his name and address, or give a false name or address.[4]

Contrary to:　Road Traffic Act 1988 s.168

Max. sentence:　Magistrates' Court: £1,000 fine.

Power:　Report / s.25 PACE

General Powers

A person driving a mechanically propelled vehicle on a road must stop the vehicle on being required to do so by a constable in uniform.[5]

Definitions

Driving: a person is driving if he is in the driving seat or in control of the steering wheel and has something to do with the propulsion of the vehicle. A passenger who grabs the wheel is not 'driving' it nor is a person who walks alongside and steers without pushing the vehicle; for example, it is moving under the effects of gravity.[6] A motor cyclist sitting on the vehicle and propelling it with his feet has been held to be 'driving'.[7]

Dangerously: a person is to be regarded as driving dangerously if the way he drives falls far below what would be expected of a competent and careful driver and it would be obvious to a competent and careful driver that the driving in that way would be dangerous. A person is also to be regarded as driving dangerously if it would be obvious to a competent and careful driver that driving the vehicle in its current state would be dangerous.[8]

General Information

A Notice of Intended Prosecution is applicable in relation to the offences of dangerous and careless driving.[9]

Notes

1   Includes pedal cycles.

2   Plus disqualification until a driving test is re-taken.

3   A person is to be regarded as riding dangerously if the way he rides falls far below what would be expected of a competent and careful cyclist and it would be obvious to a competent and careful cyclist that riding in that way would be dangerous.

4   See also page 284 and s.25 of the Police and Criminal Evidence Act 1984.

5   Road Traffic Act 1988 s.163.

6   *R* v *MacDonagh* (1974).

7   *Gunnel* v *DPP* (1994).

8   Road Traffic Act 1988 s.2A.

9   That is, a person shall not be convicted of an offence to which this section applies unless:

   (a) he was warned at the time the offence was committed that the question of prosecuting him would be taken into consideration;

   (b) within 14 days of the commission of the offence a summons for the offence was served on him, or

   (c) within 14 days of the commission of the offence a Notice of Intended Prosecution specifying the nature of the alleged offence and the time and place where it is alleged to have been committed was served on him or the registered keeper of the vehicle [Road Traffic Offenders Act 1988 s.1].

This requirement applies to dangerous, careless and inconsiderate driving, exceeding the speed limit, failing to comply with the directions given by a traffic sign, failing to comply with the directions given by a constable concerned with the direction of traffic and leaving a vehicle in a dangerous position.

DECEPTION

See also Blackmail, Burglary, Forgery, PACE – Arrest, Police, Theft

Offence: It is an offence for a person to win from any other person any sum of money or valuable thing by any fraud or unlawful device or ill practice in playing with cards, dice, tables or other game, or in bearing a part in stakes, wagers or adventures, or in betting on the sides or hands of them that do play, or in wagering on the event of any game, sport, pastime or exercise.

Contrary to: Gaming Act 1845 s.17

Max. sentence: Magistrates' Court: 6 months' imprisonment / £5,000 fine.

Crown Court: 2 years' imprisonment / unlimited fine.

Power: Report / s.25 PACE

Offence:
It is an offence for a person, by any deception, to dishonestly obtain property belonging to another with the intention of permanently depriving the other of it.[1]

Contrary to: Theft Act 1968 s.15(1)

Max. sentence: Magistrates' Court: 6 months' imprisonment / £5,000 fine.

Crown Court: 10 years' imprisonment / unlimited fine.

Power: Arrestable Offence

Offence:
It is an offence for a person, by any deception, to dishonestly obtain a money transfer[2] for himself or another.

Contrary to: Theft Act 1968 s.15A

Max. sentence: Magistrates' Court: 6 months' imprisonment / £5,000 fine.

Crown Court: 10 years' imprisonment / unlimited fine.

Power: Arrestable Offence

Offence:
It is an offence for a person, by any deception, to dishonestly obtain for himself or another any pecuniary advantage.

Contrary to:	Theft Act 1968 s.16
Max. sentence:	Magistrates' Court: 6 months' imprisonment / £5,000 fine.
	Crown Court: 5 years' imprisonment / unlimited fine.
Power:	Arrestable Offence

Offence:

It is an offence for a person, by any deception, to dishonestly obtain services from another.

Contrary to:	Theft Act 1978 s.1(1)
Max. sentence:	Magistrates' Court: 6 months' imprisonment / £5,000 fine.
	Crown Court: 5 years' imprisonment / unlimited fine.
Power:	Arrestable Offence

Offence:

It is an offence for a person, by any deception, to:

(a) dishonestly secure the remission of the whole or part of any existing liability to make a payment, whether his own liability[3] or another's;

(b) with intent to make permanent default in whole or in part of any existing liability to make a payment, or with intent to let another do so, dishonestly induces the creditor or any person claiming payment on behalf of the creditor to wait for payment or to forego payment;[4] or

(c) dishonestly obtain[5] any exemption from, or abatement of, liability to make a payment.

Contrary to:	Theft Act 1978 s.2(1)
Max. sentence:	Magistrates' Court: 6 months' imprisonment / £5,000 fine.

Crown Court: 5 years' imprisonment / unlimited fine.

Power: Arrestable Offence

Offence:

It is an offence for a person, with intent to deceive to falsely represent himself to possess qualifications in nursing, midwifery or health visiting or to falsely represent himself to be registered in the register, or in a particular part of it.

Contrary to: Nurses, Midwives and Health Visitors Act 1997 s.13

Max. sentence: Magistrates' Court: £2,500 fine.

Power: Report / s.25 PACE

Definitions

Deception: any deception (whether deliberate or reckless[6]) by words or conduct as to fact or as to law, including a deception as to the present intentions of the person using the deception or any other person.[7]

Dishonest: the court must decide whether the act was 'dishonest' according to the ordinary standards of reasonable and honest people and, if so, whether the accused must have realised that he was being dishonest by those standards.[8]

Obtain property: a person is to be treated as obtaining property if he obtains ownership, possession or control of it – and 'obtain' includes obtaining for another or enabling another to obtain or to retain.[9]

Pecuniary advantage: occurs where a person is allowed to borrow by way of overdraft, or to take out any policy of insurance or annuity contract, or obtains an improvement of the terms on which he is allowed to do so; or he is given the opportunity to earn remuneration or greater remuneration in an office or employment, or to win money by betting.[10]

General Information

The prosecution must prove that the deception acted upon the mind of the victim.

It is an obtaining of services where the other is induced to confer a benefit by doing some act, or causing or permitting some act to be done, on the understanding that the benefit has been or will be paid for. This includes where the other is induced to make a loan, or to cause or permit a loan to be made, on the understanding that any payment (whether by way of interest or otherwise) will be or has been made in respect of the loan.[11]

Notes

1   For the definitions of 'property' and 'belonging to another' see Theft.

2   A money transfer occurs when a debit is made to one account or a credit is made to another and the credit results from the debit or the debit results from the credit.

3   That is, a legally enforceable liability [Theft Act 1978 s.2(2)].

4   For the purposes of s.2(1)(b), a person induced to take in payment a cheque or other security for money by way of conditional satisfaction of a pre-existing liability is to be treated not as being paid but as being induced to wait for payment.

5   Includes obtaining for another or enabling another to obtain.

6   This is more than careless or negligent and can include an indifference as to whether a statement is true or false [*R* v *Staines* (1974)].

7   Theft Act 1968 s.15(4).

8   *R* v *Ghosh* (1982).

9   Theft Act 1968 s.15(2).

10   Ibid., s.16(2).

11   Theft Act 1978 s.1(2) and (3).

DISQUALIFIED DRIVING

See also Dangerous and Careless Driving / Riding, Drivers and Riders, Driving Documents, Road Traffic Collisions

Offence: It is an offence for a person who is disqualified from holding or obtaining a licence to:

(a)   obtain a licence; or

(b)   drive a motor vehicle on a road.

Contrary to: Road Traffic Act 1988 s.103

Max. sentence: Magistrates' Court: 6 months' imprisonment / £5,000 fine.[1]

Power: A constable in uniform may arrest without warrant any person driving a motor vehicle on a road whom he has reasonable cause to suspect of being disqualified by order of a court.[2]

General Information

In addition to being disqualified by a court, a person will be disqualified from holding or obtaining a licence to drive a motor vehicle of a class specified, if he is under the age specified in relation to that vehicle.

A person is also disqualified from obtaining a licence authorising him to drive a motor vehicle of any class so long as he is the holder of another licence authorising him to drive a motor vehicle of that class, whether the licence is suspended or not.[3]

Evidence of a conviction resulting in disqualification may be provided by admission, fingerprints or through the testimony of someone present at the time.[4]

At the end of a period of disqualification the return of licensed status is not automatic and a licence must be applied for before a disqualified person can resume driving.

Notes

1   Offence (a) is subject to a maximum fine of £1,000. The courts also have discretion to disqualify or endorse the offender's licence.

2   Road Traffic Act 1988 s.103(3). 'Disqualified' for this power does not include being disqualified by reason of age. In any other circumstances proceedings are by way of summons only unless any of the conditions of s.25 of the Police and Criminal Evidence Act 1984 are satisfied.

3   Road Traffic Act 1988 s.102.

4   *R* v *Derwentside Magistrates' Court, ex. parte Heaviside* (1995); *R* v *DPP, ex. parte Monsfield* (1997).

DOGS

See also Animals, Poaching, Straying Animals, Wildlife

Offence: It is an offence for any person, within the limits of the metropolitan police district, in any thoroughfare or public place, to suffer to be at large any unmuzzled ferocious dog, or to set on, or urge, any dog or other animal to attack, worry or put in fear any person, horse or other animal.

Contrary to: Metropolitan Police Act 1839 s.54

Max. sentence: Magistrates' Court: £500 fine.

Power: Report / s.25 PACE

Offence: It is an offence for any person in any street and to the obstruction, annoyance or danger of the residents or passengers to suffer to be at large any unmuzzled ferocious dog, or to set on, or urge, any dog or other animal to attack, worry or put in fear any person or animal.

Contrary to: Town Police Clauses Act 1847 s.28

Max. sentence: Magistrates' Court: 14 days' imprisonment / £200 fine.

Power: Report / s.25 PACE

Complaint: Any court of summary jurisdiction may take cognisance of a complaint that a dog is dangerous[2] and not kept under proper control, and if it appears to the court that such a dog is dangerous, the court may make an order directing the dog to be kept by the owner under proper control or destroyed.

Contrary to: Dogs Act 1871 s.2

Max. sentence: Magistrates' Court: Order.[3]

Power: Report

Offence: It is an offence for a person to knowingly and without reasonable excuse permit the carcass of any head of cattle[4] belonging to him, or under his control, to remain unburied in a field or other place to which dogs can gain access.

Contrary to: Dogs Act 1906 s.6

Max. sentence: Magistrates' Court: £200 fine.

Power: Report / s.25 PACE

Offence: It is an offence[5] for a dog to worry[6] livestock on any agricultural land[7] and the owner of the dog or the person in charge, if other than its owner, shall be liable.[8]

Contrary to: Dogs (Protection of Livestock) Act 1953 s.1

Max. sentence: Magistrates' Court: £1,000 fine.

Power: Report / s.25 PACE

Offence: It is an offence to use or permit the use of a guard dog at any premises unless a person (the handler) who is capable of controlling the dog is present[9] on the premises and the dog is under the control of the handler at all times while it is being so used except while it is secured so that it is not at liberty to go freely about the premises.

Contrary to: Guard Dogs Act 1975 s.1(1)

Max. sentence: Magistrates' Court: £5,000 fine.

Power: Report / s.25 PACE

Offence: It is an offence for the handler of a guard dog not to keep the dog under his control at all times while it is being used as a guard dog at any premises except while another handler has control over the dog, or while the dog is secured so that it is not at liberty to go freely about the premises.

Contrary to:	Guard Dogs Act 1975 s.1(2)
Max. sentence:	Magistrates' Court: £5,000 fine.
Power:	Report / s.25 PACE

Offence: It is an offence for a person to use or permit the use of a guard dog at any premises unless a notice containing a warning that a guard dog is present is clearly exhibited at each entrance to the premises.

Contrary to:	Guard Dogs Act 1975 s.1(3)
Max. sentence:	Magistrates' Court: £5,000 fine.
Power:	Report / s.25 PACE

Offence: It is an offence for the owner of a dog or the person in charge of a dog, without lawful authority or excuse, proof of which shall lie on him, to cause or permit the dog to be in a highway or in a place of public resort not wearing a collar with the name and address of the owner thereon.[10]

Contrary to:	Animal Health Act 1981 s.13(2)(a)[11]
Max. sentence:	Magistrates' Court: 6 months' imprisonment / £5,000 fine.
Power:	Report / s.25 PACE

Offence: It is an offence for a person to cause or permit a dog to be on a designated road[12] without the dog being held on a lead.

Contrary to:	Road Traffic Act 1988 s.27
Max. sentence:	Magistrates' Court: £200 fine.
Power:	Report / s.25 PACE

Offence: It is an offence for a person who takes possession of a stray dog to fail to:

(a) return it to its owner;

(b) take the dog to the local authority officer for the area or to the police station nearest to where it was found;

(c) inform the local authority or police as to where it was found; or

(d) if keeping the dog, to fail to keep it for at least 1 calendar month.

Contrary to: Environmental Protection Act 1990 s.150(5)

Max. sentence: Magistrates' Court: £500 fine.

Power: Report / s.25 PACE

Offence:

It is an offence for a person[13] to:

(a) breed, or breed from, a dog to which this section applies;14

(b) sell or exchange such a dog or offer, advertise or expose such a dog for sale or exchange;

(c) make or offer to make a gift of such a dog or advertise or expose such a dog as a gift;

(d) allow such a dog of which he is the owner or of which he is for the time being in charge to be in a public place15 without being muzzled and kept on a lead; or

(e) abandon such a dog of which he is the owner or, being the owner or for the time being in charge of such a dog, allow it to stray.

Contrary to: Dangerous Dogs Act 1991 s.1(2)

Max. sentence: Magistrates' Court: 6 months' imprisonment / £5,000 fine.

Crown Court: 2 years' imprisonment / unlimited fine.[16]

Power: Report / s.25 PACE

Offence:

It is an offence for a person to have any dog to which this section applies[17] in his possession or custody after 30 November 1991.

Contrary to: Dangerous Dogs Act 1991 s.1(3)

Max. sentence: Magistrates' Court: 6 months' imprisonment /
£5,000 fine.

Power: Report / s.25 PACE

Offence: It is an offence[18] for a dog to be dangerously out of
control[19] in a public place.[20]

Contrary to: Dangerous Dogs Act 1991 s.3(1)

Max. sentence: Magistrates' Court: 6 months' imprisonment /
£5,000 fine.

Crown Court: 2 years' imprisonment / unlimited
fine.[21]

Power: Report / s.25 PACE

Offence: It is an offence for the owner or, if different, the
person for the time being in charge of a dog to allow
it to enter a place which is not a public place[22] but
where it is not permitted to be and while it is
there it injures any person or there are grounds
for reasonable apprehension that it will do
so.

Contrary to: Dangerous Dogs Act 1991 s.3(3)

Max. sentence: Magistrates' Court: 6 months' imprisonment /
£5,000 fine.[23]

Crown Court: 2 years' imprisonment / unlimited
fine.

Power: Report / s.25 PACE

Offence: It is an offence[24] for a person in charge of a dog
which defecates at any time on designated land[25] to
fail to remove the faeces from the land forthwith
unless he has a reasonable excuse for failing to do
so or the owner, occupier or other person or
authority having control of the land has consented
(generally or specifically) to his failing to do so.

Contrary to:	Dogs (Fouling of Land) Act 1996 s.1
Max. sentence:	Magistrates' Court: £1,000 fine.
Power:	Report / s.25 PACE

General Powers

Where a police officer has reason to believe that any dog found on a highway or in a place of public resort is a stray dog, he may seize the dog and may detain it until the owner has claimed it and paid all expenses incurred by reason of its detention.[26]

 A constable may seize any dog which appears to be of a type known as a pit bull terrier or Japanese tosa and which is in a public place and unmuzzled or not on a lead.[27]

A constable may seize any dog in a public place which appears to him to be dangerously out of control.[28]

Notes

1. See *Breach of the Peace*.

2. If a dog is shown to have injured cattle or poultry or chased sheep, it may be dealt with as being dangerous under the Dogs Act 1906 s.1. Danger is not restricted to mankind.

3. That is, an order either to keep the dog under control, to destroy the dog or to disqualify a person from having custody of any dog for a specified period under the Dangerous Dogs Acts 1989 and 1991. Any failure to comply is itself an offence subject to a maximum fine of £1,000.

4. Horses, mules, asses, sheep, goats and pigs.

5. The owner and person in charge of the dog are both liable unless the owner can show that the person in charge was a fit and proper person.

6. Attack or chase in a way as may reasonably be expected to cause injury or suffering, or abortion or loss or diminution in the produce. Worry also includes to be at large (not on a lead or under close control) in a field or enclosure containing sheep. Where a dog is shown to have injured cattle or poultry, or chased sheep, it may be dealt with under s.2 of the Dogs Act 1871.

7. Arable, meadow or grazing land or land used for the purposes of poultry farming, pig farming, market gardens, allotments, nursery grounds and orchards.

8. Exceptions apply to police dogs, guide dogs, trained sheep dogs, working gun dogs and pack hounds.

9. Unless the dog is secured [*Hobson* v *Gledhill* (1978)].

10 Exceptions include packs of hounds, dogs being used for sporting purposes, dogs driving cattle or sheep, police dogs and guide dogs. Any dog contravening this section may be treated as a stray under s.3 of the Dogs Act 1906.

11 Control of Dogs Order 1992.

12 This is a length of road specified by an order of a local authority. The exceptions to this section are dogs proved to be kept for driving or tending sheep or cattle in the course of trade or business and dogs being used for sporting purposes which are under proper control.

13 If the owner is under 16 years, then liability will extend to the head of that person's household.

14 This section applies to any dog of the type known as the pit bull terrier, the Japanese tosa or any other dog designated by an order of the Home Secretary. The Dangerous Dogs (Designated Types) Order 1991 has now added the Dogo argentino and the Fila braziliero.

15 See note 20.

16 In a case where someone is bitten.

17 See note 14.

18 The owner, or any person for the time being in charge, will be liable. If the dog injures any person, then the offence is aggravated and the maximum sentence increases to 2 years' imprisonment on indictment.

19 A dog will be regarded as dangerously out of control on any occasion on which there are grounds for reasonable apprehension that it will injure any person, whether or not it actually does so. This does not include a dog being lawfully used by a constable or a person in the service of the Crown. The term 'dangerous' will include a dog being dangerous to other dogs [*Brisco* v *Shattock* (1998)].

20 Public place means any street, road or other place (whether or not enclosed) to which the public have or are permitted to have access whether for payment or otherwise and includes the common parts of a building containing 2 or more separate dwellings. N.B. a garden path is not a public place for the purposes of this section, [*DPP* v *Fellows* (1993)], although an enclosed common area may be, [*Cummins* v *DPP* (1999)]. A car which is in a public place is a public place for the purposes of this Act, [*Bates* v *DPP* (1993)].

21 As note 16.

22 As note 20.

23 See note 11.

24 No offence under this section is committed by a person who is registered blind.

25 This section applies to any land in the open air to which the public are entitled or permitted to have access (with or without payment) and which

is 'designated' by an order of the local authority but does not apply to any land comprised in or running alongside a highway which comprises a carriageway unless subject to a speed limit of less than 40 mph. The 1996 Act similarly does not apply to agricultural land, woodland, marshland, moor or heath or to common land.

26 Dogs Act 1906 s.3.

27 Dangerous Dogs Act 1991 s.5(1)(a).

28 Ibid., s.5(1)(c).

DRINK AND DRIVE / RIDE

See also Dangerous and Careless Driving / Riding, Drivers and Riders, Drunkenness, PACE – Arrest, Pedal Cycles, Railways, Taxis and Private Hire

Offence: It is an offence for a person to be drunk whilst in charge on any highway or other public place of any carriage,[1] horse, cattle, or steam engine.

Contrary to: Licensing Act 1872 s.12

Max. sentence: Magistrates' Court: 1 month imprisonment / £200 fine.

Power: Report / s.25 PACE

Offence: It is an offence[2] for a person to cause the death of another person by driving a mechanically propelled vehicle on a road or other public place without due care and attention, or without reasonable consideration for other persons using the road, and:

(a) he is, at the time when he is driving, unfit to drive through drink or drugs;

(b) he has consumed so much alcohol that the proportion of it in his breath, blood or urine at that time exceeds the prescribed limit; or

(c) he is, within 18 hours after that time, required to provide a specimen in pursuance of s.7, but without reasonable excuse fails to provide it.

Contrary to: Road Traffic Act 1988 s.3A

Max. sentence: Crown Court: 10 years' imprisonment / unlimited fine.

Power: Arrestable Offence

Offence:

It is an offence for a person, when driving or attempting to drive a mechanically propelled vehicle on a road or other public place, to be unfit to drive through drink or drugs.[3]

Contrary to: Road Traffic Act 1988 s.4(1)

Max. sentence: Magistrates' Court: 6 months' imprisonment / £5,000 fine.

Power: A constable may arrest without warrant any person he has reasonable cause to suspect is, or has been, committing this offence and for the purpose of making such an arrest a constable may enter (if need be by force) any place where that person is or where the constable, with reasonable cause, suspects him to be.[4]

Offence:

It is an offence for a person, when in charge[5] of a mechanically propelled vehicle on a road or other public place, to be unfit to drive through drink or drugs.

Contrary to: Road Traffic Act 1988 s.4(2)

Max. sentence: Magistrates' Court: 3 months' imprisonment / £2,500 fine.

Power: A constable may arrest without warrant any person he has reasonable cause to suspect is, or has been, committing this offence and for the purpose of making such an arrest a constable may enter (if need be by force) any place where that person is or where the constable, with reasonable cause, suspects him to be.

Offence: It is an offence for a person to drive, or attempt to drive, a motor vehicle on a road or other public place after consuming so much alcohol that the proportion of it in his breath, blood or urine exceeds the prescribed limit.

Contrary to: Road Traffic Act 1988 s.5(1)(a)

Max. sentence: Magistrates' Court: 6 months' imprisonment / £5,000 fine.

Power: A constable may arrest without warrant any person if as a result of a breath test he has reasonable cause to suspect that the proportion of alcohol in that person's breath, blood or urine exceeds the prescribed limit.[6]

Offence: It is an offence for a person to be in charge[7] of a motor vehicle on a road or other public place, after consuming so much alcohol that the proportion of it in his breath, blood or urine exceeds the prescribed limit.

Contrary to: Road Traffic Act 1988 s.5(1)(b)

Max. sentence: Magistrates' Court: 3 months' imprisonment / £2,500 fine.

Power: A constable may arrest without warrant any person if as a result of a breath test he has reasonable cause to suspect that the proportion of alcohol in that person's breath, blood or urine exceeds the prescribed limit.[8]

Offence: It is an offence for a person, without reasonable excuse, to fail to provide a specimen of breath

having been required to do so in pursuance of the
Road Traffic Act 1988 s.6.[9]

Contrary to: Road Traffic Act 1988 s.6(4)

Max. sentence: Magistrates' Court: £1,000 fine.

Power: A constable may arrest without warrant any person
if that person has failed[10] to provide a specimen of
breath for a breath test when required to do so and
the constable has reasonable cause to suspect that
he has alcohol in his body.

Offence:

It is an offence for a person, without reasonable
excuse, to fail to provide two specimens of breath
for analysis by an approved device, or a specimen of
blood or a specimen of urine for a laboratory test
having been required to do so in pursuance of the
Road Traffic Act 1988 s.7.[11]

Contrary to: Road Traffic Act 1988 s.7(6)

Max. sentence: Magistrates' Court: 6 months' imprisonment /
£5,000 fine.

Power: Report / Charge

Offence:

It is an offence for a person to ride a cycle on a road
or other public place, whilst unfit[12] through drink
or drugs.

Contrary to: Road Traffic Act 1988 s.30

Max. sentence: Magistrates' Court: £1,000 fine.

Power: Report / s.25 PACE

General Powers

Where a constable in uniform has reasonable cause to suspect:[13]

(a)   that a person driving or attempting to drive or in charge of a
motor vehicle on a road, or other public place, has alcohol in his
body or has committed a traffic offence whilst the vehicle was in
motion;

(b)   that a person has been driving or attempting to drive or been in charge of a motor vehicle on a road, or other public place with alcohol in his body and that that person still has alcohol in his body; or

(c)   that a person has been driving or attempting to drive or been in charge of a motor vehicle on a road, or other public place, and has committed a traffic offence whilst the vehicle was in motion;

He may, subject to s.9 of the Road Traffic Act 1988,[14] require him to provide a specimen of breath for a breath test.[15]

If an accident occurs owing to the presence of a motor vehicle on a road or other public place, a constable[16] may, subject to s.9 of the 1988 Act,[17] require any person who he has reasonable cause to believe was driving or attempting to drive or in charge of the vehicle at the time of the accident to provide a specimen of breath for a breath test.[18]

A constable may, for the purpose of requiring a person to provide a specimen of breath following a road traffic accident where he has reasonable cause to suspect that the accident involved injury to another person, or of arresting him following a positive breath test or a failure to provide a breath test, enter (if need be by force) any place where that person is or is, with reasonable cause, suspected to be.[19]

In the course of an investigation into whether a person has committed an offence under s.4 or s.5 a constable may require him to provide two specimens of breath for analysis[20] or to provide two specimens of blood or urine for a laboratory test.[21]

Definitions

Breath test: means a preliminary test for the purpose of obtaining, by means of an approved device, an indication whether the proportion of alcohol in a person's breath is likely to exceed the prescribed limit.

Drug: includes any intoxicant other than alcohol.

Prescribed limit: These are:[22]

Breath:	35 µg of alcohol in 100 ml of breath.
Blood:	80 mg of alcohol in 100 ml of blood.
Urine:	107 mg of alcohol in 100 ml of urine.

Public place: a place where the public have access.[23]

General Information

A person may be required under either s.6(1) or s.6(2), to provide a specimen either at, or near, the place where the requirement is made or, if the requirement is made under s.6(2) following an accident and the constable making the requirement thinks fit, at a police station specified by that constable.

The roadside test is merely an indication of the likelihood of a person exceeding the prescribed limit and has no evidential value. Evidence is gained from the 'specimen of breath' that is required at a police station. Two specimens of breath are taken but only the one with the lowest proportion of alcohol will be used for evidential purposes.

Notes

1   Includes motor vehicles and trailers.

2   Section 3A(1)(b) and (c) of the 1998 Act shall not apply to a person driving a mechanically propelled vehicle other than a motor vehicle.

3   Includes solvents and in particular the chemical elements of an adhesives [*Bradford* v *Wilson* (1983)].

4   Road Traffic Act 1988 s.4(6) and (7).

5   A person shall not have been in charge if he can show that at the material times the circumstances were such that there was no likelihood of his driving so long as he remained unfit: ibid, s.4(3).

6   Road Traffic Act 1988 s.6(5). But a person shall not be arrested by virtue of this when he is at a hospital as a patient.

7   It is a defence for a person charged under this section to show that, at the time he is alleged to have committed the offence, the circumstances were such that there was no likelihood of his driving the vehicle whilst the proportion of alcohol remained likely to exceed the prescribed limit.

8   See note 6.

9   This refers to the screening test taken at the roadside. A requirement is not lawful if the constable is a trespasser [*R* v *Fox* (1986)].

10 'Fail' includes 'refuse'. A person does not provide a specimen of breath for a breath test, or for analysis, unless the specimen is sufficient to enable the test or the analysis to be carried out and is provided in such a way as to enable the objective of the test, or analysis, to be satisfactorily achieved.

11 This refers to the sample for analysis taken at a police station. A constable must warn that a failure to provide a specimen may render the offender liable to prosecution. The warning must be understood. Any failure to give such a warning will render the specimen result inadmissible [*Murray* v *DPP* (1993)].

12 To such an extent as to be incapable of having proper control of the cycle.

13 Reasonable suspicion may arise as a result of information, anonymous or otherwise [*DPP* v *Wilson* 1991].

14 This section sets out protection for hospital patients and only allows the provision of breath specimens if the medical practitioner in charge of that case has been informed and does not object on the basis of the provision being prejudicial to the proper care and treatment of the patient.

15 Road Traffic Act 1988 s.6(1).

16 There is no requirement for a constable to be in uniform under s.6(2) of the 1988 Act.

17 See note 14.

18 Road Traffic Act 1988 s.6(2).

19 Ibid., s.6(6).

20 By a device approved by the Secretary of State. This requirement can only be made at a police station.

21 Road Trafffic Act 1988 s.7(1).

22 These may be varied by regulations made by the Secretary of State.

23 This may include a car park but not at times where the owner does not permit parking; for example, outside licensing hours.

DRIVERS AND RIDERS

See also Brakes, Construction and Use, Dangerous and Careless Driving / Riding, Drink and Drive / Ride, Driving Documents, Metropolitan Police Act, Speeding, Town Police Clauses

Offence: It is an offence for a person to drive, or cause or permit any other person to drive, a motor vehicle on a road if he is in such a position that he cannot have proper control of the vehicle or have a full view of the road and traffic ahead.[1]

Contrary to: Road Vehicles (Construction and Use) Regulations 1986 r.104

| Max. sentence: | Magistrates' Court: £1,000 fine. |
| Power: | Report / s.25 PACE |

Offence:

It is an offence for a person to open, or cause or permit to be opened, any door of a vehicle on a road so as to injure or endanger any person.

Contrary to:	Road Vehicles (Construction and Use) Regulations 1986 r.105
Max. sentence:	Magistrates' Court: £1,000 fine.
Power:	Report / s.25 PACE

Offence:

It is an offence for a person to drive, or cause or permit to be driven, a motor vehicle backwards on a road further than may be requisite for the safety or reasonable convenience of the occupants of the vehicle or other traffic, unless it is a road roller or is engaged in the construction, maintenance or repair of the road.

Contrary to:	Road Vehicles (Construction and Use) Regulations 1986 r.106
Max. sentence:	Magistrates' Court: £1,000 fine.
Power:	Report / s.25 PACE

Offence:

It is an offence[2] for a person to leave, or cause or permit to be left, on a road a motor vehicle which is not attended by a person licensed to drive it unless the engine is stopped and any parking brake with which the vehicle is required to be equipped is effectively set.

Contrary to:	Road Vehicles (Construction and Use) Regulations 1986 r.107
Max. sentence:	Magistrates' Court: £1,000 fine.
Power:	Report / s.25 PACE

Offence: It is an offence for a person to drive, or cause or permit to be driven, a motor vehicle on a road if the driver is in such a position as to be able to see, whether directly or by reflection, any television receiving apparatus[3] or other cinematographic apparatus used to display anything other than information:

(a) about the state of the vehicle or its equipment;

(b) about the location of the vehicle and the road on which it is located;

(c) to assist the driver to see the road adjacent to the vehicle; or

(d) to assist the driver to reach his destination.

Contrary to: Road Vehicles (Construction and Use) Regulations 1986 r.109

Max. sentence: Magistrates' Court: £1,000 fine.

Power: Report / s.25 PACE

Offence: It is an offence for a person to promote or take part in an unauthorised competition or trial[4] (other than a race or trial of speed) involving the use of motor vehicles on a public way.[5]

Contrary to: Road Traffic Act 1988 s.13(1)

Max. sentence: Magistrates' Court: £1,000 fine.

Power: Report / s.25 PACE

Offence: It is an offence for a person to drive a motor vehicle on a road while his eyesight is such[6] that he cannot comply with any requirement as to eyesight prescribed by this Act.[7]

Contrary to: Road Traffic Act 1988 s.96(1)

Max. sentence: Magistrates' Court: £1,000 fine.[8]

Power: Report / s.25 PACE

Offence: It is an offence for a person to give paid instruction in the driving of a motor car unless:

    (a)   the name of the person giving the instruction is in the register of approved instructors; or

    (b)   the person giving the instruction is the holder of a current licence granted under Part V of the Road Traffic Act 1988 authorising him to give such instruction.[9]

Contrary to: Road Traffic Act 1988 s.123(4)

Max. sentence: Magistrates' Court: £2,500 fine.

Power: Report / s.25 PACE

Offence: It is an offence for a person driving a mechanically propelled vehicle on a road to fail to stop on being required to do so by a constable in uniform.

Contrary to: Road Traffic Act 1988 s.163(3)

Max. sentence: Magistrates' Court: £1,000 fine.

Power: Report / s.25 PACE

Offence: It is an offence, where the driver of a vehicle is alleged to be guilty of an offence to which this section applies:[10]

    (a)   for a person who is the keeper of the vehicle to fail to give such information as to the identity of the driver as he may be required to give by or on behalf of a chief officer of police; or

    (b)   for any other person to fail to give any information which it is in his power to give and may lead to the identification of the driver, when required to do so as above.

Contrary to: Road Traffic Act 1988 s.172(3)

Max. sentence: Magistrates' Court: £1,000 fine.

Power: Report / s.25 PACE

General Powers

A person driving a mechanically propelled vehicle on a road must stop the vehicle on being required to do so by a constable in uniform.[11]

A constable who is an authorised examiner[12] may test a motor vehicle on a road for the purposes of:

(a) ascertaining whether the construction and use requirements, and the requirement that the condition of the vehicle is not such that its use on a road would involve danger or injury to any person, are complied with as respects the vehicle; or

(b) bringing to the notice of the driver any failure to comply with those requirements.[13]

For the purpose of testing a vehicle the examiner may require the driver to comply with any reasonable instruction and the examiner may drive the vehicle.[14]

Where it appears to a constable that, by reason of an accident having occurred owing to the presence of the vehicle on a road, it is requisite that a test should be carried out forthwith, he may require it to be carried out and, if he is not to carry it out himself, may require that the vehicle shall not be taken away until the test has been carried out.[15]

A constable having reason to suspect that a person driving a motor vehicle may be committing an offence under s.96 of the Road Traffic Act 1988 may require him to submit to a test for the purpose of ascertaining whether, using no other means of correction than he used at the time of driving, he can comply with the requirement.[16]

Definitions

Driving: a person is driving if he is in the driving seat or in control of the steering wheel and has something to do with the propulsion of the vehicle. A passenger who grabs the wheel is not 'driving' it nor is a person who walks alongside and steers without pushing the vehicle; for example, it is moving under the effects of gravity.[17] A motor cyclist sitting on the vehicle and propelling it with his feet has been held to be 'driving'.[18]

Using: a person is using a motor vehicle if he has the use of the vehicle on a road regardless of whether the vehicle is capable of moving or of the owner's intentions for the vehicle. A person will also use if they gain an advantage from the use of the vehicle; for example, a temporary disabled person being driven in their own vehicle.

Causing: this requires some position of authority and requires an express or positive mandate.

Permitting: this is a permission where no position of authority exists. A permission may be implied by the circumstances in which a vehicle is made available; for example, the vehicle is left at another's disposal with no particular permission being given for a specific journey. Such permission can only come from a person in a position to refuse.

General Information

Mens rea is still a requisite for the offences of 'causing' and 'permitting'.

Notes

1 See also the Road Traffic Act 1988 s.42 on page 61.

2 The requirement as to the stopping of the engine shall not apply in respect of a vehicle being used for ambulance, fire brigade or police purposes or in such conditions where the engine is being used for purposes other than driving.

3 This means any cathode ray tube carried on a vehicle and on which there can be displayed an image derived from a television broadcast, a recording or a camera or computer.

4 Except as authorised by the Secretary of State.

5 That is, a highway. See also page 379.

6 Whether through a defect which cannot be, or one which is not for the time being, sufficiently corrected.

7 That is, read in good daylight (with the aid of corrective lenses if worn) a registration mark from a distance of 20.5 m.

8 Plus obligatory penalty points. Disqualification is at the discretion of the court.

9 These must be fixed to and exhibited on that motor vehicle, [Road Traffic Act 1988 s.123(2)]. An exception applies in the case of police instructors.

10 This section applies to all offences under the Road Traffic Act 1988, except ss.13, 16, 51(2)], 61(4), s.67(9), 68(4), 96, 120 and ss.123 to 142 (driving instruction); to any offence under ss.25, 26 and 27 of the Road Traffic Offenders Act 1988 and to any offence under any other enactment relating to the use of vehicles on roads.

11 Road Traffic Act 1988 s.163.

12 That is, authorised by a chief constable.

13 Road Traffic Act 1988 s.67(1).

14 Ibid., s.67(2). The driver may elect to defer the test to a specified time, date and place. See Sch. 2 to the Road Traffic Act 1988.

15 Ibid., s.67(7).

16 Ibid., s.96(2). If that person refuses to submit to the test, he is guilty of a separate offence [Ibid., s.96(3)].

17 *R* v *MacDonagh* (1974).

18 *Gunnel* v *DPP* (1994).

DRIVERS' RECORDS

See also Drivers and Riders, Driving Documents, Excise Licences, Goods Vehicles Operators

Offence: It is an offence for the requirements of the domestic drivers' code as to hours of work to be contravened and a driver or any other person (being that driver's employer or a person to whose orders that driver was subject) who caused or permitted the contravention will be liable.[1]

Contrary to: Transport Act 1968 s.96(11)

Max. sentence: Magistrates' Court: £2,500 fine.

Power: Report / s.25 PACE

Offence: It is an offence for any requirement of the applicable Community rules as to periods of driving, or distance driven, or periods on or off duty, to be contravened and the driver and any other person (being that driver's employer or a person to whose orders that driver was subject) who caused or permitted the contravention will be liable.[2]

Contrary to: Transport Act 1968 s.96(11A)

Max. sentence: Magistrates' Court: £2,500 fine.

Power: Report / s.25 PACE

Offence:

It is an offence for a person to use, or cause or permit to be used, a vehicle to which this section applies[3] unless:

(a) there is recording equipment[4] in the vehicle which complies with the Community Recording Equipment Regulation;[5] and

(b) the equipment is being used as provided by that Regulation.

Contrary to: Transport Act 1968 s.97(1)

Max. sentence: Magistrates' Court: £5,000 fine.

Power: Report / s.25 PACE

Offence:

It is an offence for an employed driver to fail:

(a) without reasonable excuse to return any record sheet which relates to him to his employer within 21 days of completing it; or

(b) where he has two or more employers by whom he is employed as a driver of such a vehicle, to notify each of them of the name and address of the other or others of them.

Contrary to: Transport Act 1968 s.97A(1)

Max. sentence: Magistrates' Court: £2,500 fine.

Power: Report / s.25 PACE

Offence:

It is an offence for an employer of drivers of a vehicle to which s.97 applies, to fail without reasonable excuse to secure that they comply with the provisions of s.97(1)(a).

Contrary to:	Transport Act 1968 s.97A(2)
Max. sentence:	Magistrates' Court: £2,500 fine.
Power:	Report / s.25 PACE

Offence:

It is an offence for a person, with intent to deceive, to forge, alter or use any seal on recording equipment installed in, or designed for installation in, a vehicle to which s.97 applies.

Contrary to:	Transport Act 1968 s.97AA(1)
Max. sentence:	Magistrates' Court: 6 months' imprisonment / £5,000 fine.
	Crown Court: 2 years' imprisonment / unlimited fine.
Power:	Report / s.25 PACE

Offence:

It is an offence for any person to contravene any regulations made or any requirements as to books, records or documents.[6]

Contrary to:	Transport Act 1968 s.98(4)
Max. sentence:	Magistrates' Court: £2,500 fine.
Power:	Report / s.25 PACE

Offence:

It is an offence for any person to fail to comply with any requirement to allow the inspection of records or to obstruct an officer in the exercise of his powers under s.99.

Contrary to:	Transport Act 1968 s.99(4)
Max. sentence:	Magistrates' Court: £1,000 fine.
Power:	Report / s.25 PACE

Offence:

It is an offence for any person to make, or cause to be made, any record or entry on a record sheet kept or carried for the purposes of the Community Recording Equipment Regulation, or s.97 of the 1968 Act, or any entry in any book, register or document kept or carried for the purposes of regulation under s.98 thereof or the applicable Community rules, which he knows to be false or, with intent to deceive, alters or causes to be altered any such record or entry.

Contrary to: Transport Act 1968 s.99(5)

Max. sentence: Magistrates' Court: £5,000 fine.

Crown Court: 2 years' imprisonment / unlimited fine.

Power: Report / s.25 PACE

Offence:

It is an offence for any person to:

(a)   drive a vehicle on a road in contravention of a prohibition imposed under s.99A(1)[7] of the 1968 Act;

(b)   cause or permit a vehicle to be driven on a road in contravention of such a prohibition; or

(c)   refuse or fail to comply within a reasonable time with a direction given under s.99A(2) of the 1968 Act.

Contrary to: Transport Act 1968 s.99C

Max. sentence: Magistrates' Court: £5,000 fine.

Power: Report / s.25 PACE

General Powers

A constable[8] may require any person to produce and permit him to inspect and copy:

(a)   any book or register which the person is required by regulations under s.98 of the Transport Act 1968 to carry or have in his possession for the purpose of making in it any entry required by those regulations or which is required to be carried on any vehicle of which that person is the driver;

(b)   any book or register which that person is required to preserve;

(bb) any record sheet which that person is required by Article 14(2) of the Community Recording Equipment Regulation to retain or to be able to produce (Article 15(7) of the Regulation);

(c) if that person is the owner of a vehicle to which the Transport Act 1968 applies, any other document of that person which the officer may reasonably require to inspect for the purpose of ascertaining whether the provisions of the Act, or of regulations made thereunder, have been complied with; or

(d) any book, register or document required by the applicable Community rules or which the officer may reasonably require to inspect for the purpose of ascertaining whether the requirements of the applicable Community rules have been complied with;

and that record sheet, book, register or document shall, if the officer so requires by notice in writing served on that person, be produced at the office of the traffic commissioner specified not less than 10 days from the service of the notice.[9]

For the purpose of exercising these powers an officer may detain the vehicle in question during such time as is required for the exercise of that power, [10] if:

(a) the driver of a United Kingdom vehicle obstructs an authorised person[11] in the exercise of his powers under subsection (2) or (3) of s.99 of the Transport Act 1968 or fails to comply with any requirement made by an authorised person under subsection (1) of that section;

(b) it appears to an authorised person that, in relation to a United Kingdom vehicle or its driver, there has been a contravention of any of the provisions of:

   (i) ss.96 to 98[12] of the 1968 Act and any orders or regulations made under those sections, or

   (ii) the applicable Community rules, or that there will be such a contravention if the vehicle is driven on a road, or

(c) it appears to an authorised person that an offence under s.99(5) of the 1968 Act has been committed in respect of a United Kingdom vehicle or its driver,

the authorised person may prohibit the driving of the vehicle on a road either for a specified period or without limitation of time.[13]

Where an authorised person prohibits the driving of a vehicle under this section, he may also direct the driver to remove the vehicle[14] to such place and subject to such conditions as specified in the direction.[15]

General Information

Article 6 of the Community Drivers' Hours Regulation restricts the time periods during which a driver can continue to drive a vehicle without resting. In general terms these include:

(a) the daily driving period (that is, between any two daily rest periods or between a daily rest period and a weekly rest period) shall not exceed 9 hours;[16]

(b) a driver must take a weekly rest period after a maximum of 6 daily driving periods;[17]

(c) the total period of driving within any one fortnight will not exceed 90 hours;

(d) after 4½ hours driving there shall be a break of at least 45 minutes;

(e) in each period of 24 hours the driver shall have a rest period of at least 11 consecutive hours which may be reduced to 9 consecutive hours not more than 3 times in any one week; and

(f) in the course of each week one of the rest periods will be extended, by way of weekly rest, to a total of 45 consecutive hours.

To ensure compliance with these restrictions records are required to be kept. Tachographs and other records are employed for this purpose and detail a driver's work and rest periods.

Notes

1   A person shall not be liable if he proves to the court:

(a) that the contravention was due to an unavoidable delay in the completion of a journey arising out of circumstances which he could not have reasonably foreseen; or

(b) that the contravention was due to the fact that the driver had driven or been on duty otherwise than in the employment of that person and that the person charged was not, and could not reasonably have become, aware of that fact.

2   As note 1 above.

3   This section applies at any time to any vehicle engaged in the carriage of passengers or goods by road and to which the Community Drivers' Hours and Recording Equipment (Exemptions and Supplementary Provisions) Regulations 1986 apply. Generally this includes goods vehicles exceeding 3.5 tonnes maximum weight and all passenger vehicles constructed to carry more than 9 passengers (including the driver). There are many exceptions to this however.

4   That is, a tachograph.

5   Defences include not knowing that the equipment had not been installed, being en route to have such equipment installed or that it was not reasonably practicable to have the equipment repaired.

6   This is concerned with the keeping of records of work in relation to drivers as per the Drivers' Hours (Goods Vehicles) (Keeping of Records) Regulations 1987.

7   See *General Powers*.

8   If not in uniform must produce authority.

9   Transport Act 1968 s.99(1).

10 Ibid., s.99(3).

11 For example, a constable authorised by his chief constable.

12 These relate to permissible drivers' hours.

13 Transport Act 1968 s.99A(1), as amended by the Transport Act 2000.

14 Together with any trailer.

15 Transport Act 1968, s.99A(2).

16 May be extended twice a week to 10 hours.

17 This may be postponed until the end of the sixth day if the total driving time over the 6 days does not exceed 56 hours.

DRIVING DOCUMENTS

See also Construction and Use, Disqualified Driving, Drivers and Riders, Excise Licences, Forgery, Goods Vehicles Operators, Motor Cycles, Public Service Vehicles, Road Traffic Collisions

Offence: It is an offence for a person to use on a road at any time, or to cause or permit to be so used, a motor vehicle as respects which no test certificate has been issued within the preceding 12 months.[1]

Contrary to: Road Traffic Act 1988 s.47(1)

Max. sentence: Magistrates' Court: £1,000 fine.[2]

Power: Report / s.25 PACE

Offence: It is an offence for a person to use on a road a goods vehicle required by the Goods Vehicles (Plating and Testing) Regulations 1988 to have been submitted for examination for plating, or to cause or permit to be used on a road a goods vehicle of such a class, and at the time there is no plating certificate in force for the vehicle.

Contrary to: Road Traffic Act 1988 s.53(1)

Max. sentence: Magistrates' Court: £1,000 fine.

Power: Report / s.25 PACE

Offence: It is an offence for a person to use on a road a goods vehicle required by the Goods Vehicles (Plating and Testing) Regulations 1988 to have been submitted for examination for a goods vehicle test, or to cause or permit to be used on a road a goods vehicle of such a class, and at the time there is no goods vehicle test certificate in force for the vehicle.

Contrary to: Road Traffic Act 1988 s.53(2)

Max. sentence: Magistrates' Court: £2,500 fine.

Power: Report / s.25 PACE

Offence: It is an offence for a person to drive on a road a motor vehicle of any class otherwise than in accordance[3] with a licence authorising him to drive a motor vehicle of that class.

Contrary to: Road Traffic Act 1988 s.87(1)

Max. sentence: Magistrates' Court: £1,000 fine.

Power: Report / s.25 PACE

Offence: It is an offence for a person to cause or permit another person to drive on a road a motor vehicle of any class otherwise than in accordance with a licence authorising that other person to drive a motor vehicle of that class.

Contrary to: Road Traffic Act 1988 s.87(2)

Max. sentence: Magistrates' Court: £1,000 fine.

Power: Report / s.25 PACE

Offence: It is an offence for a person to use a motor vehicle on a road or other public place[4] unless there is in force in relation to the use of the vehicle by that person such a policy of insurance or such a security in respect of third party risks as complies with the requirements of the Road Traffic Act 1988.[5]

Contrary to: Road Traffic Act 1988 s.143(1)(a)

Max. sentence: Magistrates' Court: £5,000 fine.

Power: Report / s.25 PACE

Offence: It is an offence for a person to cause or permit any other person to use a motor vehicle on a road or other public place unless there is in force in relation to the use of the vehicle by that other person such a policy of insurance or such a security in respect of third party risks as complies with the requirements of the Road Traffic Act 1988.

Contrary to:	Road Traffic Act 1988 s.143(1)(b)
Max. sentence:	Magistrates' Court: £5,000 fine.
Power:	Report / s.25 PACE

Offence: It is an offence[6] for a person required by a constable to produce a licence and its counterpart or state his date of birth or to produce his certificate of completion of a training course for motor cyclists to fail to do so.

Contrary to:	Road Traffic Act 1988 s.164(6)
Max. sentence:	Magistrates' Court: £1,000 fine.
Power:	Report / s.25 PACE

Offence: It is an offence for a person to fail to produce:

(a) a certificate of insurance or certificate of security;

(b) test certificate;

(c) goods vehicle plating certificate;

(d) goods vehicle test certificate; or

to state his name and address and the name and address of the owner of the vehicle on being required to do so by a constable.

Contrary to:	Road Traffic Act 1988 s.165(3)
Max. sentence:	Magistrates' Court: £1,000 fine.
Power:	Report / s.25 PACE

Offence: It is an offence for the supervisor of a provisional licence holder to fail to comply with a requirement by a constable to provide his name and address in prescribed circumstances.[7]

Contrary to:	Road Traffic Act 1988 s.165(6)
Max. sentence:	Magistrates' Court: £1,000 fine.
Power:	Report / s.25 PACE

Offence: It is an offence for a person, with intent to deceive, to:

(a) forge,[8] alter or use a document or other thing to which this section applies;[9]

(b) lend, or allow to be used by, any other person a document or other thing to which this section applies; or

(c) make or have in his possession any document or other thing so closely resembling a document or other thing to which this section applies as to be calculated to deceive.[10]

Contrary to: Road Traffic Act 1988 s.173(1)(a)

Max. sentence: Magistrates' Court: 6 months' imprisonment/£5,000 fine.

Crown Court: 2 years' imprisonment/unlimited fine.

Power: Report / s.25 PACE

Offence: It is an offence for a person to knowingly make a false statement for the purpose of:

(a) obtaining the grant of a licence to himself or any other person;

(b) preventing the grant of a licence;

(c) procuring the imposition of a condition or limitation in relation to any licence;

(d) securing the entry or retention of the name of any person in the register of approved instructors;

(e) obtaining the grant to any person of a certificate under s.133A;[11] or

(f) obtaining the grant of an international road haulage permit to himself or any other person.

Contrary to: Road Traffic Act 1988 s.174(1)

Max. sentence: Magistrates' Court: £2,500 fine.

Power: Report / s.25 PACE

Offence: It is an offence for a person to make a false statement or withhold any material information for the purpose of obtaining the issue of a certificate of insurance or certificate of security or of any document issued to prescribe evidence which may be produced in lieu of a certificate of insurance or security.

Contrary to: Road Traffic Act 1988 s.174(5)

Max. sentence: Magistrates' Court: £2,500 fine.

Power: Report / s.25 PACE

General Powers

A person driving a mechanically propelled vehicle on a road must stop the vehicle on being required to do so by a constable in uniform.[12] A constable may require:

(a)   a person driving a motor vehicle on a road;

(b)   a person whom he has reasonable cause to believe to have been the driver of a motor vehicle at a time when an accident occurred owing to its presence on a road;

(c)   a person whom he has reasonable cause to believe to have committed an offence in relation to the use of a motor vehicle on a road; or

(d)   a person

(i)   who supervises the holder of a provisional licence while the holder is driving a motor vehicle on a road, or

(ii)   whom he has reasonable cause to believe was supervising the holder of a provisional licence while driving, at a time when an accident occurred owing to the presence of the vehicle on a road or at a time when an offence is suspected of having been committed by the holder of the provisional licence in relation to the use of the vehicle on a road, to produce his licence and its counterpart for examination, so as to enable the constable to ascertain the name and address of the holder of the licence, the date of issue and the authority by which they were issued, and the person so required must, in prescribed circumstances,[13] state his date of birth.[14]

If the Secretary of State has revoked a licence or served a notice requiring the delivery of a licence to him and the holder of the licence fails to deliver it and its counterpart, a constable may require him to produce the licence and its counterpart, and upon their being produced may seize them and deliver them to the Secretary of State.[15]

Where a constable has reasonable cause to believe that the holder of a licence, or any other person, has knowingly made a false statement for the purpose of obtaining the grant of the licence, the constable may require the holder of the licence to produce it and its counterpart to him.[16]

Where a constable to whom a provisional licence has been produced by a person driving a motor bicycle has reasonable cause to believe that the holder was not driving it as a part of the training being provided on a training course for motor cyclists, the constable may require him to produce the prescribed certificate of completion of a training course for motor cyclists.[17]

A constable may require:

(a)   a person driving a motor vehicle[18] on a road;

(b)   a person whom he has reasonable cause to believe to have been the driver of a motor vehicle at a time when an accident occurred owing to its presence on a road other public place; or

(c)   a person whom he has reasonable cause to believe to have committed an offence in relation to the use on a road of a motor vehicle,

to give his name and address and the name and address of the owner of the vehicle and produce the relevant certificate of insurance or certificate of security, test certificate, goods vehicle plating certificate or goods vehicle test certificate.[19]

A constable may require a person:

(a) who supervises the holder of a provisional licence while the holder is driving on a road a motor vehicle,[20] or

(b) whom he has reasonable cause to believe was supervising the holder of such a licence while driving, at a time when an accident occurred owing to the presence of the vehicle on a road or at a time when an offence is suspected of having been committed by the holder of the provisional licence in relation to the use of the vehicle on a road;

to give his name and address and the name and address of the owner of the vehicle.[21]

When required for the purpose of determining whether a motor vehicle was or was not being driven without insurance, the owner of a motor vehicle must give such information as he may be required, by or on behalf of the chief officer of police, to give.[22]

If a constable has reasonable cause to believe that a document produced to him is a document in relation, to which an offence has been committed under s.173 or 174 of the Road Traffic Act 1988, he may seize the document.[23]

General Information

The conditions attached to a provisional licence holder are that he shall not drive:

(a) otherwise than under the supervision of a qualified driver[24] who is present with him in or on the vehicle;[25]

(b) unless a distinguishing mark[26] is displayed on the vehicle in such a manner as to be clearly visible to other persons using the road from within a reasonable distance from the front and the back of the vehicle; or

(c) while it is being used to draw a trailer.[27]

While it is an offence to fail to produce a driving licence, certificate of insurance or test certificate on demand to a constable, it will be a defence to show that:

(a) the items were produced within 7 days of the requirement;[28]

(b) the items were produced as soon as was reasonably practicable; or

(c) it was not reasonably practicable to produce the items before proceedings were commenced.[29]

Driving licences may only be produced by their holders.[30]

The owner of a mechanically propelled vehicle in respect of which a registration book has been issued shall produce it for inspection if he is at any reasonable time required to do so by a police officer.[31]

Notes

1   Passenger vehicles with more than 8 seats excluding that of the driver, taxis, ambulances and goods vehicles require a Ministry of Transport test certificate every year. Otherwise a yearly certificate is only required after the first 3 years following first registration.

2   Rising to £2,500 in the case of a vehicle adapted to carry more than 8 passengers.

3   For example, every person to whom a licence is granted shall forthwith sign it in ink with his usual signature. [Motor Vehicles (Driving Licences) Regulations 1999 r.20] See *General Information* for the conditions attached to a provisional driving licence.

4   Added by the Motor Vehicles (Compulsory Insurance) Regulations 2000.

5   These include issue by an authorised insurer and insurance against the death of, or bodily injury to, any person and any damage arising from the use of the vehicle. See further Road Traffic Act 1988 ss.145 and 146.

6   It shall be a defence to show that the item required was produced within 7 days.

7   See *General Powers*.

8   'Forge' means to make a false document or other thing in order that it may be used as genuine.

9   This includes driving licences and their counterparts, Community licence counterparts, test certificates, goods vehicle test certificates, plating certificates, certificates of conformity, type approval certificates, seals plates, any document evidencing the appointment of an examiner, operator's records, motor cycle training course certificates, disabled driver's badges, insurance certificates and certificates of security as well as any other document produced as evidence of compulsory insurance and international road haulage permits.

10 This means 'likely to deceive' rather than 'intended to deceive'.

11 This refers to the grant of certificates and badges to disabled drivers.

12 Road Traffic Act 1988 s.163(1). It is an offence to fail to do so.

13 The prescribed circumstances are contained in the Motor Vehicles (Driving Licences) Regulations 1999; that is, the person so required fails to produce forthwith his licence or the constable has reason to suspect that the licence was not granted to that person, was granted in error or contains an alteration in the particulars entered on it.

14 Road Traffic Act 1988 s.164(1) and (2).

15 The Secretary of State is represented by the DVLA in these matters.

16 Road Traffic Act 1988., s.164(4).

17 Ibid., s.164(4A).

18 For the purposes of this section a 'motor vehicle' does not include an invalid carriage.

19 Road Traffic Act 1988 s.165(1).

20 This section does not apply to invalid carriages.

21 Road Traffic Act 1988 s.165(5).

22 Ibid., s.171. It is an offence for the owner of a motor vehicle to fail to provide the information required, punishable by a £2,500 fine on summary conviction.

23 Road Traffic Act 1988 s.176(1).

24 That is, is 21 years or older and holds a full licence for the vehicle concerned, (and in the case of categories C, C+E and D+E has held such a licence for 3 years and also has held a B category licence for at least 3 years).

25 This condition does not apply to mopeds or motor bicycles as a condition of a provisional licence for these exclude the carrying of any other person.

26 That is, an 'L' plate. In Wales the distinguishing mark is a 'D' plate.

27 Motor Vehicles (Driving Licences) Regulations 1999 r.16.

28 At a police station specified by him at the time that production was required.

29 Road Traffic Act 1988 s.164(8) and s.165(4).

30 Ibid., s.164(8).

31 Road Vehicles (Registration and Licensing) Regulations 1971 r.8.

See also Drivers and Riders, Highways and Roads, Parking, Trespass

Offence: It is an offence[1] for a person, without lawful authority, to drive or park a mechanically propelled[2] vehicle wholly or partly on a cycle track.

Contrary to: Road Traffic Act 1988 s.21(1)
Max. sentence: Magistrates' Court: £1,000 fine.
Power: Report / s.25 PACE

Offence: It is an offence[3] for a person, without lawful authority, to drive a mechanically propelled vehicle:

(a) on to or upon any common land, moorland or land of any other description, not being land forming part of a road`; or

(b) on any road being a footpath, bridleway or restricted byway.[4]

Contrary to: Road Traffic Act 1988 s.34(1)[5]
Max. sentence: Magistrates' Court: £1,000 fine.
Power: Report / s.25 PACE

Notes

1 Exceptions include driving or parking for the purposes of saving life, extinguishing fires or meeting like emergencies. Other exceptions allow for cleaning and repair by highways authority vehicles and statutory undertakers.

2 Does not include pedestrian controlled mowing machines or other vehicles or electrically assisted pedal cycles.

3 It is not an offence under this section to drive a mechanically propelled vehicle on any land within 15 yards of a road, being a road on which a motor vehicle may lawfully be driven, for the purpose only of parking the vehicle on that land. It will be a defence to show that the vehicle was driven in contravention of this section for the purpose of saving life or extinguishing fire or meeting other like emergency.

4   Currently shown on definitive maps as Roads used as Public Paths. See also *A–Z of Countryside Law second edition*.

5   As amended by the Countryside and Rights of Way Act 2000.

DRUGS

See also Attempts, Conspiracy and Incitement, PACE – Arrest, Substance Abuse

Offence: It is an offence[1] for any person to import or to export a controlled drug.

Contrary to: Misuse of Drugs Act 1971 s.3

Max. sentence: Magistrates' Court: 6 months' imprisonment / £5,000 fine.

Crown Court: life imprisonment / unlimited fine.[2]

Power: Arrestable Offence

Offence: It is an offence for a person to produce[3] a controlled drug, or to be concerned in the production of a controlled drug by another.

Contrary to: Misuse of Drugs Act 1971 s.4(2)

Max. sentence: Magistrates' Court: 6 months' imprisonment / £5,000 fine.

Crown Court: life imprisonment / unlimited fine.[4]

Power: Arrestable Offence[5]

Offence: It is an offence for a person:

(a) to supply [6] or offer [7] to supply a controlled drug to another;

(b) to be concerned in the supplying of such a drug to another; or

(c) to be concerned in the making to another of an offer to supply such a drug.

Contrary to: Misuse of Drugs Act 1971 s.4(3)

Max. sentence: Magistrates' Court: 6 months' imprisonment / £5,000 fine.

Crown Court: life imprisonment / unlimited fine.[8]

Power: Arrestable Offence

Offence:

It is an offence [9] for a person to have a controlled drug[10] in his possession.[11]

Contrary to: Misuse of Drugs Act 1971 s.5(2)

Max. sentence: Magistrates' Court: 6 months' imprisonment / £5,000 fine.

Crown Court: 7 years' imprisonment / £5000 fine[12].

Power: Arrestable Offence[13]

Offence:

It is an offence for a person to have a controlled drug in his possession, whether lawful or not, with intent to supply it to another.[14]

Contrary to: Misuse of Drugs Act 1971 s.5(3)

Max. sentence: Magistrates' Court: 6 months' imprisonment / £5,000 fine.

Crown Court: life imprisonment / unlimited fine.[15]

Power: Arrestable Offence

Offence:

It is an offence for a person to cultivate any plant of the genus *Cannabis*.

Contrary to: Misuse of Drugs Act 1971 s.6

Max. sentence: Magistrates' Court: 6 months' imprisonment / £5,000 fine.

Crown Court: 14 years' imprisonment / £5000 fine.

Power: Arrestable Offence

Offence:

It is an offence for a person, being the occupier or concerned in the management of any premises,[16] to knowingly[17] permit of suffer any:

(a) production or attempted production of a controlled drug;

(b) supply, attempt to supply or offer to supply, of a controlled drug;

(c) preparation of opium for smoking;

(d) smoking of cannabis, cannabis resin or prepared opium.[18]

Contrary to: Misuse of Drugs Act 1971 s.8

Max. sentence: Magistrates' Court: 6 months' imprisonment / £5,000 fine.

Crown Court: 14 years imprisonment / unlimited fine.[19]

Power: Arrestable Offence

Offence:

It is an offence for a person:

(a) to smoke or otherwise use prepared opium;

(b) to frequent a place used for the purpose of opium smoking; or

(c) to have in his possession:

(i) any pipes or other utensils made or adapted for use in connection with the smoking of opium, being pipes or utensils which have been used by him or with his knowledge and permission in that connection or which he intends to use or permit another to use in that connection; or

(ii) any utensils which have been used by him or with his knowledge and permission in connection with the preparation of opium for smoking.

Contrary to: Misuse of Drugs Act 1971 s.9

Max. sentence: Magistrates' Court: 6 months' imprisonment / £5,000 fine.

Crown Court: 14 years' imprisonment / unlimited fine.

Power: Arrestable Offence

Offence:

It is an offence for a person to supply or offer to supply any article[20] which may be used or adapted to be used[21] in the administration by any person of a controlled drug to himself or another, or which may be used to prepare a controlled drug for administration by any person to himself or another, believing that the article is to be so used in circumstances where the administration is unlawful.

Contrary to: Misuse of Drugs Act 1971 s.9A

Max. sentence: Magistrates' Court: 6 months' imprisonment / £5,000 fine.

Power: Report / s.25 PACE

Offence:

It is an offence for a person in the United Kingdom, to assist in or induce the commission in any place outside the United Kingdom of an offence punishable under the provisions of a corresponding law in force in that place.

Contrary to: Misuse of Drugs Act 1971 s.20

Max. sentence: Magistrates' Court: 6 months' imprisonment / £5,000 fine.

Crown Court: 14 years' imprisonment / unlimited fine.

Power: Arrestable Offence

Offence:

It is an offence for a person to:

(a)   intentionally obstruct a person in the exercise of his powers under this section;[22]

(b) conceal from any person exercising his powers under s.23(1) any books, documents, stocks or drugs; or

(c) fail to produce, without reasonable excuse, any such books or documents where their production is demanded by a person in the exercise of his powers under s.23(1).

Contrary to: Misuse of Drugs Act 1971 s.23(4)

Max. sentence: Magistrates' Court: 6 months' imprisonment / £5,000 fine.

Crown Court: 2 years' imprisonment / unlimited fine.

Power: Report / s.25 PACE

Offence:

It is an offence for a person to:

(a) conceal or disguise any property which is, or in whole or part, directly or indirectly representative of his proceeds of drug trafficking; or

(b) convert or transfer that property or remove it from the jurisdiction,

for the purpose of avoiding prosecution for a drug trafficking offence or the making or enforcement in his case of a confiscation order.

Contrary to: Drug Trafficking Act 1994 s. 49(1)

Max. sentence: Magistrates' Court: 6 months' imprisonment / £5,000 fine.

Crown Court: 14 years' imprisonment / unlimited fine.

Power: Arrestable Offence

Offence:

It is an offence for a person, knowing or having reasonable grounds to suspect that any property is, in whole or part, directly or indirectly, representative of another's proceeds of drug trafficking, to:

(a) conceal or disguise that property; or

(b) convert or transfer that property or remove it from the jurisdiction,

for the purpose of assisting any person to avoid prosecution for a drug trafficking offence or the making or enforcement of a confiscation order.

Contrary to: Drug Trafficking Act 1994 s. 49(2)

Max. sentence: Magistrates' Court: 6 months' imprisonment / £5,000 fine.

Crown Court: 14 years' imprisonment / unlimited fine.

Power: Arrestable Offence

Offence:

It is an offence[23] for a person to enter into or otherwise be concerned in an arrangement whereby:

(a) the retention or control of another person's proceeds of drug trafficking is facilitated,[24] or

(b) that other's proceeds of drug trafficking are used to secure funds that are placed at that other person's disposal or are used for his benefit to acquire property by way of investment,

and knowing or suspecting that the other is a person who carries on or has carried on drug trafficking or has benefited from drug trafficking.

Contrary to: Drug Trafficking Act 1994 s. 50(1)

Max. sentence: Magistrates' Court: 6 months' imprisonment / £5,000 fine.

Crown Court: 14 years' imprisonment / unlimited fine.

Power: Arrestable Offence

Offence: It is an offence[25] for a person, knowing that any property is, in whole or part directly or indirectly representative of another person's proceeds of drug trafficking, to acquire or use that property or have possession of it.

Contrary to: Drug Trafficking Act 1994 s. 51 (1)

Max. sentence: Magistrates' Court: 6 months' imprisonment / £5,000 fine.

Crown Court: 14 years' imprisonment / unlimited fine.

Power: Arrestable Offence

Offence: It is an offence[26] for a person, knowing or suspecting that another person is engaged in drug money laundering, and the information, or other matter, on which that knowledge or suspicion is based came to his attention in the course of his trade, profession, business or employment, to fail to disclose the information or other matter to a constable as soon as is reasonably practicable after it came to his attention.

Contrary to: Drug Trafficking Act 1994 s. 52 (1)

Max. sentence: Magistrates' Court: 6 months' imprisonment / £5,000 fine.

Crown Court: 5 years' imprisonment / unlimited fine.

Power: Arrestable Offence

Offence: It is an offence for a person, knowing or suspecting that a constable is acting, or is proposing to act, in connection with an investigation which is being, or is about to be, conducted into drug money laundering, to disclose to any other person information or any other matter which is likely to prejudice that investigation or proposed investigation.

Contrary to: Drug Trafficking Act 1994 s. 53 (1)

Max. sentence: Magistrates' Court: 6 months' imprisonment / £5,000 fine.

Crown Court: 5 years' imprisonment / unlimited fine.

Power: Arrestable Offence

General Powers

A constable has the power to enter the premises of a person carrying on business as a producer or supplier of any controlled drug and to demand the production of, and to inspect, any books or documents relating to dealings in any such drugs and to inspect any stocks of any such drugs.[27]

If a constable has reasonable grounds to suspect that any person is in possession of a controlled drug, he may:

(a) search that person, and detain him for the purpose of searching him;

(b) search any vehicle or vessel in which the constable suspects that the drug may be found, and for that purpose require the person in control of the vehicle or vessel to stop it; or

(c) seize and detain anything found in the course of the search which appears to the constable to be evidence of an offence under the Misuse of Drugs Act 1971.[28]

Definitions

Cannabis: (except in the expression 'cannabis resin') means any plant of the genus *Cannabis* or any part of any such plant (by whatever name designated) except that it does not include cannabis resin or any of the following products after separation from the rest of the plant, namely:

(a)   the mature stalk of any such plant,

(b)   fibre produced from the mature stalk of any such plant; and

(c)   the seed of any such plant.

Cannabis resin: means the separated resin, whether crude or purified, obtained from any plant of the genus *Cannabis.*

Controlled drug: these are specified in Sch. 2 to the 1971 Act although the list can be varied by an Order in Council. Examples of controlled drugs include:

Class A = Cocaine, heroin, LSD, morphine and opium.

Class B = Amphetamines, cannabis, cannabis resin, codeine, dexedrine, methadrine, some derivatives of morphine, and preludin.

Class C = Diazepam, mandrax, temazepam, testosterone.

Prepared opium: means opium prepared for smoking and includes dross and any other residues remaining after the opium has been smoked.

Produce: where the reference is to producing a controlled drug, means producing it by manufacture, cultivation or any other method.

General Information

It shall be a defence in any proceedings for an offence under s. 5(2) in which it is proved that the accused had a controlled drug in his possession, to prove that:

(a)   knowing or suspecting it to be a controlled drug, he took possession of it for the purpose of preventing another from committing or continuing to commit an offence in connection with that drug and that as soon as possible after taking possession of it he took all such steps as were reasonably open to him to destroy the drug or to deliver it into the custody of a person lawfully entitled to take custody of it; or

(b)   knowing or suspecting it to be a controlled drug, he took possession of it for the purpose of delivering it into the custody of a person lawfully entitled to take possession of it and that as soon as possible after taking possession of it he took all such steps as were reasonably open to him to deliver it into the custody of such a person.[29]

It shall be a defence in any proceeding for an offence under s.4(2) and (3), s.5(2) and (3) and s.6 for the accused to prove that he neither knew of nor suspected nor had reason to suspect the existence of some fact alleged by the prosecution which it is necessary for the prosecution to prove if he is to be convicted of the offence charged. However it is necessary, if the accused is to be convicted of the offence charged, for the prosecution to prove that some substance or product involved in the alleged offence was the controlled drug which the prosecution alleges it to have been, and if it is proved that the substance or product in question was that controlled drug, the accused:

(a) shall not be acquitted of the offence charged by reason only of proving that he neither knew or suspected nor had reason to suspect that the substance or product in question was the particular controlled drug alleged; but

(b) shall be acquitted:

(i) if he proves that he neither believed nor suspected nor had reason to suspect that the substance or product in question was a controlled drug; or

(ii) if he proves that he believed the substance or product in question to be a controlled drug, or a controlled drug of a description, such that, if it had in fact been that controlled drug or a controlled drug of that description, he would not at the material time have been committing any offence.[30]

Any charge should state the amounts involved.

Notes

1 The Home Secretary has the power to make exceptions to the prohibitions contained in this legislation and to issue licences. It is also an offence for a person to incite another to commit any of these offences, see page 56.

2 Indictable under the Customs and Excise Management Act 1979.

3 This means production by manufacture, cultivation or any other method

and includes the conversion of one drug into another [Misuse of Drugs Act 1971 s.37].

4   This penalty is for a Class A drug. Class B is a maximum of 14 years while Class C is 5 years.

5   Maximum penalties for all the offences under the 1971 Act are determined by the class of drug involved in the offences. This only affects the power of arrest in the case of an offence of possessing a Class C drug under s.5(2).

6   Misuse of Drugs Act 1971, s.37. Includes distribution.

7   This offence may be complete although the drug possessed was not a controlled drug, [*Haggard* v *Mason* (1976)]. The offence is committed when the offer is made, regardless of the offender's real intention [*R* v *Goddard* (1992)].

8   This penalty is for a Class A drug. Class B is a maximum of 14 years while Class C is 5 years.

9   For defences, see *General Information*.

10 The quantity needs to be sufficient for a court to identify that it amounts to something. However, if its character has been changed by consumption, then it is no longer a controlled drug.

11 This will include a drug that was in somebody else's custody but under the control of the accused.

12 This penalty is for a Class A drug. Class B is a maximum of 5 years on indictment (3 months and/or £2,500 summarily) while Class C is 2 years (3 months and/or £1,000 summarily).

13 The maximum sentence may be imposed for possession of a Class A drug while a Class B drug may attract a term of imprisonment of 5 years. The maximum penalty for a Class C drug however is only 2 years' imprisonment and is not therefore an Arrestable Offence.

14 Who is not authorised to possess.

15 This penalty is for a Class A drug. Class B is a maximum of 14 years while Class C is 5 years.

16 This includes persons exercising control over premises regardless of whether they are in lawful possession.

17 Mere suspicion is not enough, [*R* v *Thomas* (1976)]. It is not necessary to prove that the defendant knew which particular drug was being supplied, [*R* v *Bett* (1999)].

18 The wording of (d) is to be changed to 'administering or using a controlled drug which is unlawfully in any person's possession at or immediately before the time when it is administered or used'. This change is introduced by the Criminal Justice and Police Act 2001 s.38, when in force.

19 This penalty is for a Class A drug. Class B is a maximum of 14 years while Class C is 5 years.

20 This does not include a hypodermic syringe, or any part of one.

21 Whether by itself or in combination with another article or other articles.

22 See *General Powers*.

23 It is a defence to prove that he did not know or suspect that the arrangement related to any person's proceeds of drug trafficking; that he did not know or suspect that by the arrangement the retention or control by or on behalf of the other of any property was facilitated or that he intended to disclose to a constable such a suspicion, belief or matter.

24 Whether by concealment, removal from the jurisdiction, transfer to nominees or otherwise.

25 It is a defence to show that the property was acquired, used or possessed for adequate consideration.

26 But not in the case of a professional legal advisor who has gained the information or other matter in privileged circumstances.

27 Misuse of Drugs Act 1971 s.23(1).

28 Ibid., s.23(2).

29 Ibid., s.4(4).

30 Ibid., s.28.

DRUNKENNESS

See also Breach of the Peace, Children and Young Persons, Drink and Drive / Ride, Firearms – Criminal Use, Licensed Premises, PACE – Arrest Public Order

Offence: It is an offence for a person to be found[1] drunk[2] in any highway or other public place,[3] whether a building or not, or on any licensed premises[4] or to be drunk whilst in charge on any highway or other public place of any carriage, horse, cattle, or steam engine or to be drunk when in possession of a loaded firearm.

Contrary to: Licensing Act 1872 s.12

Max. sentence: Magistrates' Court: 1 month's imprisonment / £200 fine.

Power: If a person is found drunk on any highway or in other public place, whether a building or not, or on any licensed premises, and appears to be incapable of taking care of himself, he may be apprehended.[5]

Offence: It is an offence for a person to be found drunk on any highway or in other public place,[6] whether a building or not, or on any licensed premises, while having the charge of a child apparently under the age of 7 years.

Contrary to: Licensing Act 1902 s.2

Max. sentence: Magistrates' Court: 1 month's imprisonment / £500 fine.

Power: If a person is found drunk on any highway or in other public place, whether a building or not, or on any licensed premises, and appears to be incapable of taking care of himself, he may be apprehended.[7]

Offence: It is an offence for a person in any public place, while drunk to be guilty of disorderly behaviour.[8]

Contrary to: Criminal Justice Act 1967 s.91

Max. sentence: Magistrates' Court: £1,000 fine.

Power: Arrest[9]

Offence: It is an offence for a person to sell or transfer any firearm or ammunition to, or to repair, prove or test any firearm or ammunition for, another person whom he knows or has reasonable cause for believing to be drunk or of unsound mind.

Contrary to: Firearms Act 1968 s.25

Max. sentence: Magistrates' Court: 3 months' imprisonment / £1,000 fine.

Power: Report / s.25 PACE

Offence: It is an offence for the skipper of, or a seaman employed or engaged in a United Kingdom fishing vessel to be, while on board the vessel, under the influence of drink or a drug to such an extent that his capacity to fulfil his responsibility for the vessel or, as the case may be, to carry out the duties of his employment or engagement is impaired.

Contrary to: Merchant Shipping Act 1995 s.117(1)

Max. sentence: Magistrates' Court: 6 months' imprisonment / £5,000 fine.

Crown Court: 2 years' imprisonment / unlimited fine.

Power: Report / s.25 PACE

Offence:

It is an offence for a person to:

(a)   refuse to surrender intoxicating liquor; or

(b)   refuse to state his name and address,

when required by a constable exercising his powers under this Act.

Contrary to: Confiscation of Alcohol (Young Persons) Act 1997 s.1(3)

Max. sentence: Magistrates' Court: £500 fine.

Power: A constable may arrest without warrant any person who fails to comply with a requirement imposed under s.1(1).[10]

Offence:

It is an offence for a person to fail, without reasonable excuse, to comply with a requirement imposed on him by a constable exercising his powers under s. 12(2).

Contrary to: Criminal Justice and Police Act 2001 s.12(4)[11]

Max. sentence: Magistrates' Court: £500 fine.

Power: Arrestable Offence[12]

General Powers

Where a constable reasonably suspects that a person in a relevant place[13] is in possession of intoxicating liquor and that either:

(a)   he is under the age of 18;

(b)   he intends that any of the liquor should be consumed by a person under the age of 18 in that or any other relevant place; or

(c)   a person under the age of 18 who is, or has recently been, with him has recently consumed intoxicating liquor in that or any other relevant place,

the constable may require him to surrender anything in his possession which is, or which the constable reasonably believes to be, intoxicating liquor or a container for such liquor (other than a sealed container) and to state his name and address.[14]

A constable may dispose of anything surrendered to him under s.1(1) in such manner as he considers appropriate.[15]

Under the Criminal Justice and Police Act 2001,[16] if a constable believes that a person is, or has been, consuming intoxicating liquor in a designated public place or intends to consume intoxicating liquor in such a place, he may require the person concerned:

(a)   not to consume in that place anything which is, or which the constable reasonably believes to be, intoxicating liquor;

(b)   to surrender anything in his possession which is, or which the constable reasonably believes to be, intoxicating liquor or a container for such liquor (other than a sealed container).[17]

A constable may dispose of anything surrendered to him under s.12(2) in such manner as he considers appropriate.

Definitions

Designated public place: a place is a designated public place if it is a public place[18] in the area of a local authority, and is identified as such by an order made by that authority.

General Information

A police officer may provide a court with 'expert' evidence of drunkenness. In every case this is a subjective test based on the officer's observations and typically such evidence will include the smell of alcohol, glazing of the eyes, slurred speech and unsteadiness.

Notes

1 This can include cases where the drunken offender is only there momentarily or is carried into a public place against his own will, [*Winzar* v. *CC of Kent* (1983)].

2 This state cannot be induced by anything other than alcohol, [*Neale* v. *E (a minor)* (1983)].

3 'Public place' will also include vehicles which are on highways or in public places. However, the communal reception to a block of flats controlled by a key coded entrance will not be a public place, [*Williams* v. *DPP* (1992)].

4 This will include premises where intoxicating liquor is sold under an occasional licence.

5 Licensing Act 1902 s.1.

6 That is, any place to which the public have access, whether on payment or otherwise.

7 Licensing Act 1902 s.1.

8 This would include being excessively noisy, aggressive or violent.

9 Where a person is drunk and disorderly in a public place there is a power of arrest [Criminal Justice Act 1967 s.91]. A person arrested under s.12 of the Licensing Act 1872, or s.91 of the Criminal Justice Act 1967, may be taken to a treatment centre if one is available [(Criminal Justice Act 1972 s.34.].

10 Prior to arrest the person shall be informed of the constable's suspicion and be warned that failing without reasonable excuse to comply is an offence.

11 In Force from 1.9.01.

12 Police and Criminal Evidence Act 1984 s.24(2)(qa).

13 This means, in relation to a person:

   (a) any public place, other than licensed premises; or

   (b) any place, other than a public place, to which the person has unlawfully gained access;

   and for this purpose a place is a public place if at the material times the public or any section of the public has access to it, on payment or otherwise, as of right or by virtue of express or implied permission.

14 Confiscation of Alcohol (Young Persons) Act 1997 s.1(1).

15 Ibid., s.1(2).

16 When in force. This is being done section by section.

17 Criminal Justice and Police Act 2001 s.12(1) and (2). This section will override any local byelaws which create similar offences.

18 But will not include licensed premises or registered clubs or their curtilages, or places where the sale of liquor is authorised by an occasional licence.

EXCISE LICENCES

See also Driving Documents, Forgery, Goods Vehicles Operators, Registration and Licensing, PACE – Arrest

Offence: It is an offence for a person to alter, deface, mutilate, or add anything to any licence for any mechanically propelled vehicle or to exhibit upon any mechanically propelled vehicle any licence which has been altered, defaced, mutilated or added to or upon which any of the figures or particulars have become illegible or the colour has become altered by fading or otherwise.

Contrary to: Road Vehicles (Registration and Licensing) Regulations 1971 r.7(1)

Max. sentence: Magistrates' Court: £1,000.

Power: Report / s.25 PACE

Offence: It is an offence for a person to use or keep, on a public road[1] a vehicle (not being an exempt vehicle) which is unlicensed.[2]

Contrary to: Vehicle Excise and Registration Act 1994 s.29(1)

Max. sentence: Magistrates' Court: £1,000.[3]

Power: Report / s.25 PACE

Offence: It is an offence for a person to use or keep, on a public road a vehicle in respect of which vehicle excise duty is chargeable, and there is not fixed to and exhibited on the vehicle in the manner prescribed a licence for, or in respect of, the vehicle which is for the time being in force.

Contrary to:	Vehicle Excise and Registration Act 1994 s.33(1)
Max. sentence:	Magistrates' Court: £200 fine.
Power:	Report / s.25 PACE

Offence: It is an offence for a person holding a trade licence or licences to:

(a) use at any one time on a public road a greater number of vehicles[4] than he is authorised to use;

(b) use a vehicle[5] on a public road for any purpose other than a prescribed purpose;[6] or

(c) use a trade licence for the purpose of keeping on a public road in circumstances other than those prescribed, a vehicle which is not being used on that road.

Contrary to:	Vehicle Excise and Registration Act 1994 s.34(1)
Max. sentence:	Magistrates' Court: £200 fine.
Power:	Report / s.25 PACE

Offence: It is an offence where:

(a) a vehicle licence has been taken out for a vehicle at any rate of vehicle excise duty;

(b) at any time while the licence is in force the vehicle is so used that duty at a higher rate becomes chargeable in respect of the licence for the vehicle; and

(c) duty at that higher rate is not paid before the vehicle was so used.

Contrary to:	Vehicle Excise and Registration Act 1994 s.37(1)
Max. sentence:	Magistrates' Court: £1,000.[7]
Power:	Report / s.25 PACE

Offence: It is an offence for a person to forge, fraudulently[8] alter, fraudulently use,[9] fraudulently lend or fraudulently allow to be used by another person a vehicle licence.

Contrary to:	Vehicle Excise and Registration Act 1994 s.44(1)
Max. sentence:	Magistrates' Court: 6 months' imprisonment / £5,000 fine.
	Crown Court: 2 years' imprisonment / unlimited fine.
Power:	Report / s.25 PACE

Offence:

It is an offence for a person in connection with an application for a vehicle licence or a claim for a rebate to make any declaration which to his knowledge is either false or in any material respect misleading.

Contrary to:	Vehicle Excise and Registration Act 1994 s.45(1)
Max. sentence:	Magistrates' Court: 6 months' imprisonment / £5,000 fine.
	Crown Court: 2 years' imprisonment / unlimited fine.
Power:	Report / s.25 PACE

Definitions

Public road: means a road repairable at public expense.

General Information

The vehicle excise licence must be fixed to the vehicle in a holder sufficient to protect it from any effects of the weather to which it would otherwise be exposed and shall be exhibited on the vehicle:

(a) in the case of an invalid vehicle, tricycle, or bicycle (other than in (b) or (c) below), on the near side of the vehicle in front of the driving seat so that all the particulars thereon are clearly visible by daylight from the near side of the road;

(b) in the case of a bicycle drawing a side-car or to which a side-car is attached when the bicycle is being kept on a public road, on the near side of the handlebars of the bicycle or on the near side of the side-car in front of the driving seat so that all the particulars thereon are clearly visible by daylight from the near side of the road;

(c) in the case of any vehicles fitted with a glass windscreen in front of the driver extending across the vehicle to its near side, on or adjacent to the near side of the windscreen, so that all the particulars thereon are clearly visible by daylight from the near side of the road;

(d) in the case of any other vehicle, if the vehicle is fitted with a driver's cab containing a near side window, on such window, or on the near side of the vehicle in front of the driver's seat or towards the front of the vehicle in the case of a pedestrian controlled vehicle and not less than 2 ft 6 in and not more than 6 ft above the surface of the road, so that all the particulars thereon are clearly visible by daylight from the near side of the road.[10]

The burden of proving an exemption lies on the accused.

Notes

1 No offence is committed while the vehicle is on any private road.

2 A vehicle is unlicensed if no vehicle excise licence or trade licence is in force for or in respect of the vehicle.

3 Five times the amount of the vehicle excise duty chargeable in respect of the vehicle or £1,000, whichever is the greater.

4 Not being a vehicle for which a vehicle excise licence is in force.

5 As note 4.

6 As prescribed in the Road Vehicles (Registration and Licensing) Regulations 1971.

7 As note 3 above.

8 'Fraudulently' includes for the purpose of deceiving a police officer.

9 'Use' is use on a public road.

10 Road Vehicles (Registration and Licensing) Regulations 1971 r.16.

EXPLOSIVES

See also Burglary, Firearms – Criminal Use, Fireworks, PACE – Arrest, Post and Mail, Railways

Offence:	It is an offence for a person to unlawfully and maliciously, by the explosion of gunpowder or other explosive substance, burn, maim, disfigure, disable, or do any grievous bodily harm to any person.
Contrary to:	Offences Against the Person Act 1861 s.28
Max. sentence:	Crown Court: life imprisonment.
Power:	Arrestable Offence

Offence:	It is an offence for a person to unlawfully and maliciously cause any gunpowder or other explosive substance to explode, or send or deliver to, or cause to be taken or received by, any person any explosive substance, or any other dangerous or noxious thing, or put or lay at any place, or cast or throw at or upon, or otherwise apply to any person, any corrosive fluid or any destructive or explosive substance with intent to burn, maim, disfigure or disable any person, or to do some grievous bodily harm, to any person, whether any bodily injury be effected or not.
Contrary to:	Offences Against the Person Act 1861 s.29
Max. sentence:	Crown Court: life imprisonment.
Power:	Arrestable Offence

Offence:	It is an offence to unlawfully and maliciously place or throw in, into, upon against or near any building, ship or vessel, any gunpowder, or other explosive substance, with intent to do any bodily injury to any

person, whether or not any explosion takes place, or whether or not any bodily injury be effected.

Contrary to: Offences Against the Person Act 1861 s.30

Max. sentence: Crown Court: 14 years' imprisonment / unlimited fine.

Power: Arrestable Offence

Offence:

It is an offence for a person to knowingly have in his possession, or make or manufacture any gunpowder, explosive substance, or any dangerous or noxious thing, or any machine, engine, instrument, or thing, with intent, by means thereof, to commit, or for the purpose of enabling any other person to commit any offence mentioned in this Act.

Contrary to: Offences Against the Person Act 1861 s.64

Max. sentence: Crown Court: 2 years' imprisonment / unlimited fine.

Power: Report / s.25 PACE

Offence:

It is an offence for gunpowder[1] to be hawked, sold or exposed for sale upon any highway, street, public thoroughfare or public place.

Contrary to: Explosives Act 1875 s.30

Max. sentence: Magistrates' Court: £5,000 fine.

Power: Report / s.25 PACE

Offence:

It is an offence for a person to sell gunpowder to any person apparently under the age of 16 years.

Contrary to: Explosives Act 1875 s.31

Max. sentence: Magistrates' Court: £5,000 fine.

Power: Report / s.25 PACE

Offence: It is an offence for any person to unlawfully and maliciously cause, by any explosive substance, an explosion of a nature likely to endanger life, or to cause serious injury to property, whether such injury to persons or property has been caused or not.

Contrary to: Explosive Substances Act 1883 s.2

Max. sentence: Crown Court: life imprisonment / unlimited fine.

Power: Arrestable Offence

Offence: It is an offence for any person, unlawfully and maliciously, to do any act with intent to cause, or to conspire to cause, by an explosive substance, an explosion of a nature likely to endanger life or to cause serious injury to property; or to make or have in his possession or under his control, an explosive substance with intent by means thereof to endanger life or to cause serious injury to property.[2]

Contrary to: Explosive Substances Act 1883 s.3(1)

Max. sentence: Crown Court: life imprisonment / unlimited fine.

Power: Arrestable Offence

Offence: It is an offence for any person to make, or knowingly have in his possession or under his control any explosive substance,[3] under such circumstances as to give rise to a reasonable suspicion that he is not making it or does not have it in his possession or under his control for a lawful object.

Contrary to: Explosive Substances Act 1883 s.4(1)

Max. sentence: Crown Court: 14 years' imprisonment / unlimited fine.

Power: Arrestable Offence

Offence: It is an offence[4] for a person to use in or near any waters[5] any explosive substance with intent thereby to take or destroy fish.

Contrary to: Salmon and Freshwater Fisheries Act 1975 s.5(4)

Max. sentence: Magistrates' Court: £5,000 fine.

Crown Court: 2 years' imprisonment / unlimited fine.

Power: Report / s.25 PACE

Offence: It is an offence for a person to

(a)   place any article[6] in any place whatever; or

(b)   dispatch any article by post, rail or other means whatever of sending things from one place to another,

with the intention (in either case) of inducing in some other person[7] a belief that it is likely to explode or ignite and thereby cause personal injury or damage to property.

Contrary to: Criminal Law Act 1977 s.51(1)

Max. sentence: Magistrates' Court: 6 months' imprisonment / £5,000 fine.

Crown Court: 7 years' imprisonment / unlimited fine.

Power: Arrestable Offence

Offence: It is an offence for a person to communicate any information which he knows or believes to be false to another person with the intention of inducing in him or any other person a false belief that a bomb or other thing likely to explode or ignite is present in any place or location[8] whatever.

Contrary to: Criminal Law Act 1977 s.51(2)

Max. sentence: Magistrates' Court: 6 months' imprisonment / £5,000 fine.

Crown Court: 7 years' imprisonment / unlimited fine.

Power: Arrestable Offence

Offence:

It is an offence[9] for a person to use for the purpose of killing or taking[10] any wild bird, any explosive other than ammunition for a firearm.

Contrary to: Wildlife and Countryside Act 1981 s.5

Max. sentence: Magistrates' Court: 6 months' imprisonment / £5,000 fine.

Power: Report / s.25 PACE [11]

Offence:

It is an offence for a person to use for the purpose of killing or taking any wild animal, any explosive other than ammunition for a firearm.

Contrary to: Wildlife and Countryside Act 1981 s.11(1)(b)

Max. sentence: Magistrates' Court: 6 months' imprisonment / £5,000 fine.

Power: Report / s.25 PACE

Offence:

It is an offence for any person, without lawful authority or reasonable excuse to have with him in any aircraft in the United Kingdom or in flight over the United Kingdom or to have with him in any part of an aerodrome or in any air navigation unit which does not form part of an aerodrome:

(a) any explosive;

(b) any article manufactured or adapted so as to have the appearance of being an explosive, whether it is capable of producing a practical effect by explosion or not; or

(c) any article marked or labelled so as to indicate that it is or contains an explosive.

Contrary to: Aviation Security Act 1982 s.4

Max. sentence: Magistrates' Court: 3 months' imprisonment / £5,000 fine.

Crown Court: 5 years' imprisonment / unlimited fine.

Power: Arrestable Offence

General Powers

If a constable suspects with reasonable cause that a person is committing or has committed an offence under s. 5 or s. 11 of the Wildlife and Countryside Act 1981, the constable may without warrant:

(a) stop and search that person if the constable suspects with reasonable cause that evidence of the commission of the offence is to be found on that person;

(b) search or examine any thing which that person may be using or have in his possession if the constable suspects with reasonable cause that evidence of the commission of the offence is to be found on that thing;

(c) *repealed...*

(d) seize and detain for the purposes of proceedings anything which may be evidence of the commission of the offence.[12]

If a constable suspects with reasonable cause that any person is committing an offence under s.5 or s.11 of the Wildlife and Countryside Act 1981, he may, for the purpose of exercising the powers above or to arrest any person under s.25 of the Police and Criminal Evidence Act 1984, for such an offence, enter any land other than a dwelling-house.[13]

Notes

1   The 1875 Act is primarily concerned with the manufacture and storage of explosives and 'gunpowder' is to include every other description of explosive; for example, dynamite, blasting powders, fog-signals, fireworks, fuses, rockets, detonators, cartridges and ammunition of all descriptions [Explosives Act 1875 s.3].

2   This is the case whether or not any explosion actually takes place and regardless of whether any injury to persons or property has been caused or not.

3   'Explosive substance' means any materials for making any explosive substance. It also includes any apparatus, machine, implement or materials used, intended to be used or adapted for causing, or aiding, any explosion.

4   Unless done with the permission of the National Rivers Authority.

5   Including waters adjoining the coast of England and Wales to a distance of 6 nautical miles.

6   The term includes any substance.

7   It is not necessary for an accused to have had any particular person in mind as the person in whom he intends to induce such a belief.

8   This does not need to be specific, [*R* v *Webb* (1995)].

9   It is also an offence to attempt any of these offences under the Wildlife and Countryside Act 1981.

10 That is,capturing.

11   See *General Powers*.

12 Wildlife and Countryside Act 1981 s.19(1).

13 Ibid., s.19(2).

FIREARMS – CRIMINAL USE

See also Air Weapons, Burglary, Crossbows, Drunkenness, Explosives, Firearms – Licensing, Knives and Bladed Articles, Metropolitan Police Act, Offensive Weapons, PACE – Arrest, Robbery, Town Police Clauses

Offence: It is an offence for a person to be drunk when in possession of a loaded firearm.

Contrary to: Licensing Act 1872 s.12

Max. sentence: Magistrates' Court: 1 month imprisonment / £200 fine.

Power: If a person is found drunk in any highway or other public place, whether a building or not, or on any licensed premises, and appears to be incapable of taking care of himself, he may be apprehended.[1]

Offence: It is an offence for a person to have in his possession any firearm or ammunition with intent by means thereof to endanger life, or to enable another person by means thereof to endanger life,[2] whether any injury has been caused or not.

Contrary to: Firearms Act 1968 s.16

Max. sentence: Crown Court: life imprisonment / unlimited fine.

Power: Arrestable Offence

Offence: It is an offence for a person to have in his possession any firearm or imitation firearm with intent by means thereof to cause, or to enable another person by means thereof to cause, any person to believe that unlawful violence will be used against him or another person.

Contrary to: Firearms Act 1968 s.16A

Max. sentence: Crown Court: 10 years' imprisonment / unlimited fine.

Power: Arrestable Offence

Offence: It is an offence for a person to make or attempt to make any use whatsoever of a firearm or imitation firearm with intent to resist or prevent the lawful arrest or detention of himself or another person.

Contrary to: Firearms Act 1968 s.17(1)

Max. sentence: Crown Court: life imprisonment / unlimited fine.

Power: Arrestable Offence

Offence: It is an offence for a person, at the time of his committing or being arrested for an offence specified in Sch. 1 to the Firearms Act 1968[3], to have in his possession a firearm or imitation firearm unless he shows that he had it in his possession for a lawful object.

Contrary to:	Firearms Act 1968 s.17(2)
Max. sentence:	Crown Court: life imprisonment / unlimited fine.
Power:	Arrestable Offence

Offence:

It is an offence for a person to have with him[4] a firearm or imitation firearm with intent to commit an indictable offence,[5] or to resist or prevent the arrest of another, in either case while he has the firearm or imitation firearm with him.

Contrary to:	Firearms Act 1968 s.18(1)
Max. sentence:	Crown Court: life imprisonment / unlimited fine.
Power:	Arrestable Offence

Offence:

It is an offence for a person, without lawful authority or reasonable excuse, to have with him in a public place a loaded shotgun or loaded air weapon or any other firearm, whether loaded or not, together with ammunition suitable for use in that firearm.

Contrary to:	Firearms Act 1968 s.19
Max. sentence:	Magistrates' Court: 6 months' imprisonment / £5,000 fine.
	Crown Court: 7 years' imprisonment / unlimited fine.[6]
Power:	Arrestable Offence[7]

Offence:

It is an offence for a person, while he has a firearm or imitation firearm with him, to enter or be in any building or part of a building as a trespasser without reasonable excuse.

Contrary to:	Firearms Act 1968 s.20(1)
Max. sentence:	Magistrates' Court: 6 months' imprisonment / £5,000 fine.
	Crown Court: 7 years' imprisonment / unlimited fine.[8]

Power:	Arrestable Offence[9]

Offence: It is an offence for a person, while he has a firearm or imitation firearm with him, to enter or be on any land[10] as a trespasser without reasonable excuse.

Contrary to:	Firearms Act 1968 s.20(2)
Max. sentence:	Magistrates' Court: 3 months' imprisonment / £2,500 fine.
Power:	Report / s.25 PACE[11]

Offence: It is an offence for a person having a firearm to fail to hand it over when required to do so by a constable.

Contrary to:	Firearms Act 1968 s.47(2)
Max. sentence:	Magistrates' Court: 3 months' imprisonment / £2,500 fine.
Power:	Report / s.25 PACE[12]

Offence: It is an offence for a person, without lawful authority or excuse, to discharge any firearm within 50 feet of the centre of a highway which consists of or comprises a carriageway, and in consequence thereof the highway is damaged.

Contrary to:	Highways Act 1980 s.131
Max. sentence:	Magistrates' Court: £1,000 fine.
Power:	Report / s.25 PACE

Offence: It is an offence for a person, without lawful authority or excuse, to discharge any firearm within 50 ft of the centre of a highway which consists of or comprises a carriageway, and in consequence thereof a user of the highway is injured, interrupted or endangered.

Contrary to:	Highways Act 1980 s.161

| **Max. sentence:** | Magistrates' Court: £1,000 fine. |
| **Power:** | Report / s.25 PACE |

Offence: It is an offence for any person, without lawful authority or reasonable excuse, to have with him in any aircraft in the United Kingdom or in flight over the United Kingdom or to have with him in any part of an aerodrome or in any air navigation unit which does not form part of an aerodrome:

(a) any firearm; or

(b) any article having the appearance of being a firearm, whether capable of being discharged or not.

Contrary to:	Aviation Security Act 1982 s.4
Max. sentence:	Magistrates' Court: 3 months' imprisonment / £5,000 fine.
	Crown Court: 5 years' imprisonment / unlimited fine.
Power:	Arrestable Offence

General Powers[13]

A constable may require any person whom he has reasonable cause to suspect:

(a) of having a firearm, with or without ammunition, with him in a public place; or

(b) to be committing or about to commit, elsewhere than in a public place, an offence under s.18(1), (2) or s.20 of the Firearms Act 1968, to hand over the firearm or any ammunition for examination by the constable.[14]

If a constable has reasonable cause to suspect a person of having a firearm with him in a public place, or to be committing or about to commit, elsewhere than in a public place, an offence under s.18(1), (2) or s.20, the constable may search that person and may detain him for the purpose of doing so.[15]

If a constable has reasonable cause to suspect that there is a firearm in a vehicle in a public place, or that a vehicle is being or is about to be used in connection with the commission of an offence under s.18(1), (2) or s.20 elsewhere than in a public place, he may search the vehicle and for that purpose require the person driving or in control of it to stop it.[16]

For the purposes of exercising the powers under s.47, a constable may enter any place.

Definitions

Firearm: a lethal barrelled weapon of any description from which any shot, bullet or other missile can be discharged and includes:

(a) any prohibited weapon,[17] whether it is such a lethal weapon as aforesaid or not;

(b) any component part of such a lethal or prohibited weapon; and

(c) any accessory designed or adapted to diminish the noise or flash caused by firing the weapon.[18]

Imitation firearm: a firearm which has the appearance of being a firearm to which s.1 of the 1968 Act applies and is so constructed or adapted as to be readily convertible, without special skill or specialist equipment, into such a firearm.[19]

Ammunition: means ammunition for any firearm and includes grenades, bombs and other like missiles, whether capable of use with a firearm or not, and also includes prohibited ammunition.[20]

Notes

1   Licensing Act 1902 s.1.

2   Does not include suicide of self.

3   That is, criminal damage, laying explosives, assault, causing actual bodily harm [Offences against the Person Act 1861, s.47] assault with intent to resist arrest, child abduction, theft, robbery, burglary, blackmail, taking a motor vehicle, assault on police, rape, abduction of women and aiding, abetting or attempting any of these offences.

4   That is, some close physical link. This will be a matter of fact for the court to decide.

5   It is not necessary that the firearm is used for the crime, [*R* v *Stoddart* (1998)].

6   Not indictable if the firearm is an air weapon.

7   But see note 6 above.

8   As note 6.

9   But not in the case of an imitation firearm or where the firearm is an air weapon.

10   Includes land covered by water.

11   See *General Powers*.

12   But see also page 282.

13   See page 167 for powers in relation to the production of firearms and shotgun certificates.

14   Firearms Act 1968 s.47(2).

15   Ibid.,s.47(3).

16   Ibid., s.47(4).

17   See page 168.

18   Firearms Act 1968., s.57.

19   Firearms Act 1982 s.1.

20   See page 168 for details of prohibited weapons and ammunition.

FIREARMS – LICENSING

See also Air Weapons, Children and Young Persons, Firearms – Criminal Use

Offence: It is an offence[1] for a person to:

(a)   have in his possession,[2] or to purchase or acquire a firearm to which this section applies[3] without holding a firearm certificate[4] in force at the time, or otherwise than as authorised by such a certificate;

(b)   have in his possession, or to purchase or acquire, any ammunition to which this section applies[5] without holding a firearm certificate in force at the time, or otherwise than as authorised by such a certificate, or in quantities in excess of those authorised.

Contrary to: Firearms Act 1968 s.1(1)

Max. sentence: Magistrates' Court: 6 months' imprisonment / £5,000 fine.

Crown Court: 5 years' imprisonment / unlimited fine.

Power: Arrestable Offence

Offence:

It is an offence for a person to fail to comply with a condition subject to which a firearm certificate is held by him.

Contrary to: Firearms Act 1968 s.1(2)

Max. sentence: Magistrates' Court: 6 months' imprisonment / £5,000 fine.

Power: Report / s.25 PACE

Offence:

It is an offence[6] for a person to have in his possession, or to purchase or acquire, a shotgun without holding a certificate authorising him to possess shotguns.

Contrary to: Firearms Act 1968 s.2(1)

Max. sentence: Magistrates' Court: 6 months' imprisonment / £5,000 fine.

Crown Court: 5 years' imprisonment / unlimited fine.

Power: Arrestable Offence

Offence:

It is an offence for a person to fail to comply with a condition subject to which a shotgun certificate is held by him.

Contrary to: Firearms Act 1968 s.2(2)

Max. sentence: Magistrates' Court: 6 months' imprisonment / £5,000 fine.

Power: Report / s.25 PACE

Offence: It is an offence for a person, by way of trade or business, to:

(a) manufacture, sell, transfer, repair, test or prove any firearm[7] or shotgun; or

(b) expose for sale or transfer, or to have in his possession for sale, transfer, repair, test or proof, any such firearm or shotgun,

without being registered as a firearms dealer.

Contrary to: Firearms Act 1968 s.3(1)

Max. sentence: Magistrates' Court: 6 months' imprisonment / £5,000 fine.

Crown Court: 5 years' imprisonment / unlimited fine.

Power: Arrestable Offence

Offence: It is an offence for a person to sell or transfer to any other person in the United Kingdom, other than a registered firearms dealer, any firearm or ammunition to which s.1 applies, or a shotgun, unless that other produces a firearm certificate, authorising him to purchase or acquire it, or, as the case may be, a shotgun certificate, or shows that he is entitled to purchase or acquire it without holding a certificate.

Contrary to: Firearms Act 1968 s.3(2)

Max. sentence: Magistrates' Court: 6 months' imprisonment / £5,000 fine.

Crown Court: 5 years' imprisonment / unlimited fine.

Power: Arrestable Offence

Offence: It is an offence for a person to undertake the

repair, test or proof of any s.1 firearm or ammunition, or of a shotgun, for any other person in the United Kingdom other than a registered firearms dealer as such, unless that other produces or causes to be produced a firearms certificate authorising him to have possession of the firearm or ammunition or, as the case may be, his shotgun certificate, or shows that he is entitled to purchase or acquire it without holding a certificate.

Contrary to: Firearms Act 1968 s.3(3)

Max. sentence: Magistrates' Court: 6 months' imprisonment / £5,000 fine.

Crown Court: 5 years' imprisonment / unlimited fine.

Power: Arrestable Offence

Offence:

It is an offence for a person, with a view to purchasing or acquiring, or procuring the repair, test or proof of any s.1 firearm or ammunition, or a shotgun, to:

(a) produce a false certificate or a certificate in which any false entry has been made;

(b) personate a person to whom a certificate has been granted; or

(c) knowingly or recklessly make a statement false in any material particular.

Contrary to: Firearms Act 1968 s.3(5)

Max. sentence: Magistrates' Court: 6 months' imprisonment / £5,000 fine.

Crown Court: 5 years' imprisonment / unlimited fine.

Power: Arrestable Offence

Offence: It is an offence for a pawnbroker to take in pawn any s.1 firearm or ammunition, or a shotgun.

Contrary to: Firearms Act 1968 s.3(6)

Max. sentence: Magistrates' Court: 3 months' imprisonment / £1,000 fine.

Power: Report / s.25 PACE

Offence: It is an offence[8] for a person to shorten the barrel of a shotgun[9] to a length less than 24 inches.

Contrary to: Firearms Act 1968 s.4(1)

Max. sentence: Magistrates' Court: 6 months' imprisonment / £5,000 fine.

Crown Court: 7 years' imprisonment / unlimited fine.[10]

Power: Arrestable Offence

Offence: It is an offence for a person other than a registered firearms dealer, to convert into a firearm anything which, though having the appearance of being a firearm, is so constructed as to be incapable of discharging any missile through its barrel.

Contrary to: Firearms Act 1968 s.4(3)

Max. sentence: Magistrates' Court: 6 months' imprisonment / £5,000 fine.

Crown Court: 7 years' imprisonment / unlimited fine.[11]

Power: Arrestable Offence

Offence: It is an offence for a person, without the authority of the Home Secretary, to possess, purchase, acquire, manufacture, sell or transfer any prohibited weapon.[12]

Contrary to: Firearms Act 1968 s.5

Max. sentence:	Magistrates' Court: 6 months' imprisonment / £5,000 fine.
	Crown Court: 10 years' imprisonment / unlimited fine.
Power:	Arrestable Offence

Offence:

It is an offence for a person, knowingly or recklessly, to make a statement false in any material particular for the purpose of procuring, whether for himself or another person, the grant of a police permit.[13]

Contrary to:	Firearms Act 1968 s.7(2)
Max. sentence:	Magistrates' Court: 6 months' imprisonment / £5,000 fine.
Power:	Report / s.25 PACE

Offence:

It is an offence for a person who is subject to the restrictions under s.21, to have in his possession any firearm or ammunition.[14]

Contrary to:	Firearms Act 1968 s.21(4)
Max. sentence:	Magistrates' Court: 6 months' imprisonment / £5,000 fine.
	Crown Court: 5 years' imprisonment / unlimited fine.
Power:	Arrestable Offence

Offence:

It is an offence for a person to sell or transfer any firearm or ammunition to, or to repair, test or prove a firearm or ammunition for, a person whom he knows or has reasonable grounds for believing to be prohibited by s.21 from having a firearm or ammunition in his possession.

Contrary to:	Firearms Act 1968 s.21(5)
Max. sentence:	Magistrates' Court: 6 months' imprisonment / £5,000 fine.

	Crown Court: 5 years' imprisonment / unlimited fine.
Power:	Arrestable Offence

Offence: It is an offence for a person under the age of 17 to purchase or hire any firearm or ammunition.

Contrary to: Firearms Act 1968 s.22(1)

Max. sentence: Magistrates' Court: 6 months' imprisonment / £5,000 fine.

Power: Report / s.25 PACE[15]

Offence: It is an offence for a person under the age of 14 to have in his possession any s.1 firearm or ammunition, except in circumstances where he is entitled to have possession without holding a certificate.[16]

Contrary to: Firearms Act 1968 s.22(2)

Max. sentence: Magistrates' Court: 6 months' imprisonment / £5,000 fine.

Power: Report / s.25 PACE

Offence: It is an offence for a person under the age of 15 to have with him an assembled shotgun except while under the supervision of a person of or over the age of 21 or while the gun is so covered with a securely fastened gun cover that it cannot be fired.

Contrary to: Firearms Act 1968 s.22(3)

Max. sentence: Magistrates' Court: £1,000 fine.

Power: Report / s.25 PACE

Offence: It is an offence for a person to sell or let on hire any firearm or ammunition to a person under the age of 17.

Contrary to: Firearms Act 1968 s.24(1)

| Max. sentence: | Magistrates' Court: 6 months' imprisonment / £5,000 fine. |
| Power: | Report / s.25 PACE |

Offence: It is an offence for a person to:

(a) make a gift or lend any s.1 firearm or ammunition to a person under the age of 14; or

(b) part with the possession of any such firearm or ammunition to a person under that age.[17]

Contrary to:	Firearms Act 1968 s.24(2)
Max. sentence:	Magistrates' Court: 6 months' imprisonment / £5,000 fine.
Power:	Report / s.25 PACE

Offence: It is an offence for a person to make a gift of a shotgun or ammunition for a shotgun to a person under the age of 14.

Contrary to:	Firearms Act 1968 s.24(3)
Max. sentence:	Magistrates' Court: £1,000 fine.
Power:	Report / s.25 PACE

Offence: It is an offence for a person to sell or transfer any firearm or ammunition to, or to repair, prove or test any firearm or ammunition for, another person whom he knows or has reasonable cause for believing to be drunk or of unsound mind.

Contrary to:	Firearms Act 1968 s.25
Max. sentence:	Magistrates' Court: 3 months' imprisonment / £1,000 fine.
Power:	Report / s.25 PACE

Offence: It is an offence for a person, knowingly or recklessly to make any statement which is false in any material particular for the purpose of procuring, whether for himself or another, the grant or renewal of a certificate under this Act.

Contrary to: Firearms Act 1968 s.28A(7)

Max. sentence: Magistrates' Court: 6 months' imprisonment / £5,000 fine.

Power: Report / s.25 PACE

Offence:

It is an offence for a person, knowingly or recklessly to make any statement false in any material particular for the purpose of procuring, whether for himself or another, the variation of a firearm certificate.

Contrary to: Firearms Act 1968 s.29(3)

Max. sentence: Magistrates' Court: 6 months' imprisonment / £5,000 fine.

Power: Report / s.25 PACE

Offence:

It is an offence for a person, for the purpose:

(a) of procuring the registration of himself or another person as a firearms dealer; or

(b) of procuring, whether for himself or another person, the entry of any place of business in a register of firearms dealers,

to knowingly or recklessly make a statement false in any material particular.

Contrary to: Firearms Act 1968 s.39(1)

Max. sentence: Magistrates' Court: 6 months' imprisonment / £5,000 fine.

Power: Report / s.25 PACE

Offence:

It is an offence for a registered firearms dealer:

(a) to carry on business as a firearms dealer at any place which is not entered in the register for the area; or

	(b) to fail to comply with any of the conditions of registration imposed on him by the chief officer of police.
Contrary to:	Firearms Act 1968 s.39(2) and (3)
Max. sentence:	Magistrates' Court: 6 months' imprisonment / £5,000 fine.
Power:	Report / s.25 PACE

Offence: It is an offence for a person who by way of trade or business manufactures, sells or transfers firearms or ammunition:

(a) to fail to keep a register of transactions; or

(b) to knowingly make any false entry in such register.

Contrary to:	Firearms Act 1968 s.40(5)
Max. sentence:	Magistrates' Court: 6 months' imprisonment / £5,000 fine.
Power:	Report / s.25 PACE

Offence: It is an offence for a person required under s. 48(2)[18] to declare his name and address to fail or refuse to give his true name and address.

Contrary to:	Firearms Act 1968 s.48(3)
Max. sentence:	Magistrates' Court: £1,000 fine.
Power:	Report / s.25 PACE

Offence: It is an offence for a person to sell ammunition suitable for a shotgun or smooth-bore gun to another person in the United Kingdom who is neither a registered firearms dealer nor a person who sells such ammunition by way of trade or business unless that other person:

(a) produces a certificate authorising him to possess shotguns;

(b) shows that he is entitled to possess a shotgun without holding a certificate; or

(c) produces a certificate authorising another person to possess shotguns, together with that person's written authority to purchase the ammunition on his behalf.

Contrary to: Firearms Act 1988 s.5(1)

Max. sentence: Magistrates' Court: 6 months' imprisonment / £5,000 fine.

Power: Report / s.25 PACE

Offence:

It is an offence for an auctioneer, carrier or warehouseman:

(a) to fail to take reasonable precautions for the safe custody of any firearm or ammunition that he has in his possession without holding a certificate;

(b) to fail to report forthwith to the police the loss or theft of any such firearm or ammunition.

Contrary to: Firearms Act 1988 s.14(1)

Max. sentence: Magistrates' Court: 6 months' imprisonment / £5,000 fine.

Power: Report / s.25 PACE

General Powers

Every person keeping a register of firearms transactions shall, on demand, allow a constable or civilian officer, duly authorised in writing, to enter and inspect all stock in hand and shall on request produce the register for inspection.[19]

A constable may demand, from any person whom he believes to be in possession of a s.1 firearm or ammunition, or of a shotgun, the production of his firearms or shotgun certificate.[20]

If a person to whom a demand is made fails:

(a) to produce the certificate or document;

(b)   to permit the constable to read it; or

(c)   to show that he is entitled to have the firearm, ammunition, or shotgun in his possession without holding a certificate,

the constable may seize and detain the firearm, ammunition or shotgun and may require the person to declare to him immediately his name and address.

Definitions

Section 1 firearm: every firearm[21] except a shotgun within the meaning this Act and an air weapon.[22]

Section 1 ammunition: any ammunition for a firearm except:

(a)   cartridges containing 5 or more shot, none of which exceeds .36 inch in diameter;

(b)   ammunition for an air gun, air rifle or air pistol; and

(c) blank cartridges not more than 1 inch in diameter.

Shotgun: a smooth-bore gun (not being an air gun[23]), which has a barrel not less than 24 inches in length and which does not have any barrel with a bore exceeding 2 inches in diameter and which either has no magazine or has a non-detachable magazine incapable of holding more than 2 cartridges and is not a revolver gun.

Prohibited weapon: includes any:

(a)   firearm which is so designed or adapted that two or more missiles can be successively discharged without repeated pressure on the trigger;

(b)   self-loading rifle or pump-action rifled gun other than one which is chambered for .22 rim-fire cartridges;

(c)   firearm which either has a barrel less than 30 centimetres in length or is less than 60 centimetres in length overall, other than an air weapon, a small-calibre pistol, a muzzle-loading gun or a firearm as signalling apparatus;

(d)   self-loading or pump-action smooth-bore gun which is not an air weapon or chambered for .22 rim-fire cartridges and either has a barrel less than 24 inches in length or is less than 40 inches in length overall;

(e)   smooth-bore revolver gun other than one which is chambered for 9 millimetre rim-fire cartridges or a muzzle loading gun;

(f)   rocket launcher, or any mortar, for projecting a stabilised missile, other than a launcher or mortar designed for line-throwing or pyrotechnic purposes or as signalling apparatus;

(g)   weapon of whatever description designed or adapted[24] for the discharge of any noxious liquid, gas or other thing;

(h)   cartridge with a bullet designed to explode on or immediately before impact, any ammunition containing or designed or adapted to contain any noxious liquid, gas or other thing and, if capable of being used with a firearm of any description, any grenade, bomb (or other like missile), or rocket or shell designed to explode; and

(i)   firearm disguised as another object.[25]

General Information

Section 1 firearms and shotgun certificates are issued by the chief of police for the area in which the applicant resides and are currently renewable every 5 years. Local police chiefs also keep registers of firearms dealers.

Notes

1   This is an offence of strict liability, [R v Howells (1977)]. Exceptions include registered firearms dealers, auctioneers, carriers and warehousemen, licensed slaughtermen, gun-bearers, starters at race meetings and operators of miniature rifle ranges, Other exceptions allow for theatrical performances and the use of signalling equipment on ships and aircraft.

2   This may include constructive possession where the firearm is actually kept elsewhere.

3   See Definitions.

4   Or a police permit.

5   See Definitions.

6   Exceptions include:

   (a)   anyone who borrows a shotgun from the occupier of premises (inc. land) and uses it on those premises in the occupier's presence;

   (b)   shooting at artificial targets on an approved ground;

   (c)   holders of a Northern Ireland certificate; and

(d) people temporarily in Great Britain (not more than 30 days in all the preceding 12 months).

7 To which s.1 applies; that is, not air weapons or shotguns falling within the s.1 definition.

8 It is not an offence for a registered firearms dealer to shorten the barrel of a shotgun for the sole purpose of replacing a defective part of the barrel so as to produce a barrel of not less than 24 inches.

9 Or any other smooth-bore gun by virtue of the Firearms Act 1988 s.6.

10 Possessing, purchasing or acquiring a shotgun with a shortened barrel without holding a s.1 firearm certificate is an aggravated form of the s.1 offence.

11 Possessing, purchasing or acquiring a converted firearm without holding a s.1 firearm certificate is an aggravated form of the section 1 offence.

12 See *Definitions*.

13 A person who has obtained a permit may, without holding a certificate, have in his possession a firearm and ammunition.

14 The Firearms Act 1968 s.21 restricts access to certificates by persons who have been sentenced to a term of imprisonment. If that term exceeded 3 months but was below 3 years, then that person is prohibited from holding a firearm or shotgun certificate for a period of 5 years. If the sentence was for more than 3 years, then the prohibition is for life. Imprisonment includes any form of preventative detention or corrective training, youth custody or detention at a young offender institution.

15 See *General Powers* and also page 284.

16 That is, gun bearers or using on a miniature rifle range or at approved clubs.

17 Except in circumstances where he is entitled to have possession without holding a certificate. See note 16.

18 See *General Powers*.

19 Firearms Act 1968 s.40(4).

20 Ibid., s.48(1). This includes documents issued in other EU Member States; such as European Firearms Passes.

21 For the definition of 'Firearm' see page 156.

22 That is to say, an air rifle, air gun or air pistol not of a type declared specially dangerous. See page 13.

23 See page 11.

24 But not an empty plastic bottle where there is no alteration to it [*R* v *Formosa* (1991)].

25 Further prohibited weapons are those designed for military use. For details see the Firearms Act 1968 s.5(1A).

FIRES AND SMOKE

See also Damage, Explosives, Highways and Roads, Metropolitan Police Act, Town Police Clauses

Offence: It is an offence for any person, in any street and to the obstruction, annoyance or danger of the residents or passengers, to make any bonfire.

Contrary to: Town Police Clauses Act 1847 s.28

Max. sentence: Magistrates' Court: 14 days' imprisonment / £200 fine.

Power: Report / s.25 PACE

Offence: It is an offence for a person to:
(a) use a fire-hydrant otherwise than for fire-fighting purposes; or
(b) damage or obstruct any fire-hydrant.

Contrary to: Fire Services Act 1947 s.14(5)

Max. sentence: Magistrates' Court: £500 fine.

Power: Report / s.25 PACE

Offence: It is an offence for a person to wilfully obstruct or interfere with any member of a fire brigade who is engaged in operations for fire-fighting purposes.

Contrary to: Fire Services Act 1947 s.30(2)

Max. sentence: Magistrates' Court: £1,000 fine.

Power: Report / s.25 PACE

Offence: It is an offence for a person to knowingly give, or cause to be given, a false alarm of fire to any fire brigade or to any member of a fire brigade.

Contrary to: Fire Services Act 1947 s.31(1)

Max. sentence: Magistrates' Court: 3 months' imprisonment / £2,500 fine.

Power: Report / s.25 PACE

Offence: It is an offence for a person, without lawful authority or excuse, to light any fire within 50 ft of the centre of a highway which consists of or comprises a carriageway, and in consequence thereof the highway is damaged.

Contrary to: Highways Act 1980 s.131(1)

Max. sentence: Magistrates' Court: £1,000 fine.

Power: Report / s.25 PACE

Offence: It is an offence for a person, without lawful authority or excuse, to light any fire on or over a highway which consists of or comprises a carriageway, and in consequence thereof a user of the highway is injured, interrupted or endangered.

Contrary to: Highways Act 1980 s.161(2)

Max. sentence: Magistrates' Court: £1,000 fine.

Power: Report / s.25 PACE

Offence: It is an offence[1] for a person:

(a) to light a fire on any land not forming part of a highway which consists of or comprises a carriageway; or

(b) to direct or to permit a fire to be lit on any such land,

and in consequence a user of any highway which consists of or comprises a carriageway is injured, interrupted or endangered by, or by smoke from, that fire or any other fire caused by that fire.

Contrary to: Highways Act 1980 s.161A(1)

Max. sentence: Magistrates' Court: £5,000 fine.

Power: Report / s.25 PACE

General Powers

Any member of a maintained fire brigade who is on duty or any constable, may enter and if necessary break into any premises or place:

(a)   in which a fire has or is reasonably believed to have broken out; or

(b)   which it is necessary to enter for the purposes of extinguishing a fire or of protecting the premises or place from acts done for fire-fighting purposes;[2] and

may do all such things as he may deem necessary for extinguishing the fire or for protecting from fire any such premises or place or for rescuing any person or property therein.[3]

The senior officer of police present at any fire may close to traffic any street or may stop or regulate the traffic in any street whenever in the opinion of that officer it is necessary or desirable to do so for fire-fighting purposes.[4]

Notes

1   It shall be a defence for the accused to show that at the time the fire was lit he was satisfied on reasonable grounds that it was unlikely that users of any highway (carriageway) would be injured, interrupted or endangered by, or by smoke from, that fire or any other fire caused by that fire and that either that both before and after the fire was lit he did all he reasonably could to prevent users being so injured, interrupted or endangered or he had a reasonable excuse for not doing so.

2   Without the consent of the owner or occupier thereof.

3   Fire Services Act 1947 s.30(1).

4   Ibid., s.30(5).

FIREWORKS

See also Explosives, Fires and Smoke, Football, Highways and Roads, Metropolitan Police Act, Nuisance, PACE – Arrest, Town Police Clauses

Offence: It is an offence for a person to sell gunpowder[1] to any person apparently under the age of 16 years.

Contrary to: Explosives Act 1875 s.31

Max. sentence:	Magistrates' Court: £5,000 fine
Power:	Report / s.25 PACE

Offence: It is an offence for any person to throw, cast or fire any firework in or into any highway, street, thoroughfare, or public place.

Contrary to:	Explosives Act 1875 s.80
Max. sentence:	Magistrates' Court: £5,000 fine.
Power:	Report / s.25 PACE

Offence: It is an offence for a person, without lawful authority or excuse, to discharge any firework within 50 ft of the centre of a highway which consists of or comprises a carriageway, and in consequence thereof the highway is damaged.

Contrary to:	Highways Act 1980 s.131
Max. sentence:	Magistrates' Court: £1,000 fine.
Power:	Report / s.25 PACE

Offence: It is an offence for a person, without lawful authority or excuse, to discharge any firework within 50 ft of the centre of a highway which consists of or comprises a carriageway, and in consequence thereof a user of the highway is injured, interrupted or endangered.

Contrary to:	Highways Act 1980 s.161
Max. sentence:	Magistrates' Court: £1,000 fine.
Power:	Report / s.25 PACE

Offence: It is an offence for a person, without lawful authority, to have in his possession any firework:[2]

(a) at any time during the period of a designated sporting event when he is in any area of a designated sports ground from which the event may be directly viewed; or

(b)   while entering or trying to enter a designated
      sports ground at any time during the period of
      a designated sporting event at the ground.[3]

Contrary to: Sporting Events (Control of Alcohol etc.) Act 1985
                    s.2A(1)

Max. sentence: Magistrates' Court: 3 months' imprisonment /
                     £1,000 fine.

Power: Report / s.25 PACE

Notes

1   Including fireworks.

2   Applies also to any article or substance whose main purpose is the emission
    of a flare (other than for ignition or heating) or smoke or a visible gas and in
    particular to distress flares, fog-signals, and to pellets and capsules
    intended as fumigators or for testing pipes but not to matches, cigarette
    lighters or heaters, [Sporting Events (Control of Alcohol etc). Act 1985
    s.2A(3)].

3   For an explanation of these terms see page 181.

FOOTBALL

See also Breach of the Peace, Drunkenness, Fireworks, Highways and
Roads, Licensed Premises, Offensive Weapons, Public Order, Racial Hatred

Offence:

It is an offence for a person to knowingly cause or
permit intoxicating liquor to be carried on a
vehicle to which this section applies[1] if the vehicle is:

(a)   a public service vehicle and he is the operator
      of the vehicle or the servant or agent of the
      operator; or

(b)   a hired vehicle and he is the person to whom it
      is hired or the servant or agent of that person.

Contrary to: Sporting Events (Control of Alcohol etc.) Act 1985
                    s.1(2)

Max. sentence: Magistrates' Court: £2,500 fine.

Power: Report / s.25 PACE

Offence: It is an offence for a person to have intoxicating liquor in his possession while on a vehicle to which this section applies.[1]

Contrary to: Sporting Events (Control of Alcohol etc.) Act 1985 s.1(3)

Max. sentence: Magistrates' Court: 3 months' imprisonment / £1,000 fine.

Power: Report / s.25 PACE

Offence: It is an offence for a person to be drunk on a vehicle to which this section applies.[1]

Contrary to: Sporting Events (Control of Alcohol etc.) Act 1985 s.1(4)

Max. sentence: Magistrates' Court: £500 fine.

Power: Report / s.25 PACE

Offence: It is an offence for a person to knowingly cause or permit intoxicating liquor to be carried on a motor vehicle to which this section applies:[2]

(a) if he is its driver; or

(b) if he is not its driver but its keeper, the servant or agent of its keeper, a person to whom it is made available (by hire, loan or otherwise) by its keeper or the keeper's servant or agent, or the servant or agent of the person to whom it is made available.

Contrary to: Sporting Events (Control of Alcohol etc.) Act 1985 s.1A(2)

Max. sentence: Magistrates' Court: £2,500 fine.

Power: Report / s.25 PACE

Offence: It is an offence for a person to have intoxicating liquor in his possession while on a vehicle to which this section applies.[2]

Contrary to:	Sporting Events (Control of Alcohol etc.) Act 1985 s.1A(3)
Max. sentence:	Magistrates' Court: 3 months' imprisonment / £1,000 fine.
Power:	Report / s.25 PACE

Offence:

It is an offence for a person to be drunk on a vehicle to which this section applies.[2]

Contrary to:	Sporting Events (Control of Alcohol etc.) Act 1985 s.1A(4)
Max. sentence:	Magistrates' Court: £500 fine.
Power:	Report / s.25 PACE

Offence:

It is an offence for a person to have intoxicating liquor, or an article to which this section applies,[3] in his possession:

(a) at any time during the period[4] of a designated sporting event when he is in any area of a designated sports ground from which the event may be directly viewed; or

(b) while entering or trying to enter a designated sports ground at any time during the period[4] of a designated sporting event at that ground.

Contrary to:	Sporting Events (Control of Alcohol etc.) Act 1985 s.2(1)
Max. sentence:	Magistrates' Court: 3 months' imprisonment / £1,000 fine.
Power:	Report / s.25 PACE

Offence:

It is an offence for a person to be drunk in a designated sports ground at any time during the period[4] of the sporting event at that ground or to be drunk while entering or trying to enter such a ground at any time during the period of a designated sporting event at that ground.

Contrary to:	Sporting Events (Control of Alcohol etc.) Act 1985 s.2(2)
Max. sentence:	Magistrates' Court: £500 fine.
Power:	Report / s.25 PACE

Offence: It is an offence for a person to have an article or substance[5] to which this section applies:

(a) at any time during the period of a designated sporting event when he is in any area of a designated sports ground from which the event may be directly viewed; or

(b) while entering or trying to enter a designated sports ground at any time during the period of a designated sporting event at that ground.

Contrary to:	Sporting Events (Control of Alcohol etc.) Act 1985 s.2A(1)
Max. sentence:	Magistrates' Court: 3 months' imprisonment / £1,000 fine.
Power:	Report / s.25 PACE

Offence: It is an offence for a person subject of a banning order,[6] without reasonable excuse, to:

(a) fail to comply with any requirement imposed by that order; or

(b) fail to comply with any requirement imposed under s.19(2B)[7] or (2C).[8]

Contrary to:	Football Spectators Act 1989 s.14J[9]
Max. sentence:	Magistrates Court: 6 months' imprisonment / £5,000 fine.
Power:	Arrestable Offence[10]

Offence: It is an offence for a person, without lawful authority or excuse, at a designated football match[11] to throw anything at or towards:

(a)   the playing area, or any area adjacent to the playing area to which spectators are not generally admitted; or

(b)   any area in which spectators or other persons are or may be present.

Contrary to: Football (Offences) Act 1991, s.2
Max. sentence: Magistrates' Court: £1,000 fine.
Power: Arrestable Offence[12]

Offence:

It is an offence to engage or take part in chanting[13] of an indecent or racist nature[14] at a designated football match.

Contrary to: Football (Offences) Act 1991 s.3
Max. sentence: Magistrates' Court: £1,000 fine.
Power: Arrestable Offence[15]

Offence:

It is an offence for a person, without lawful authority or excuse, at a designated football match to go onto the playing area, or any area adjacent to the playing area to which spectators are not generally admitted.

Contrary to: Football (Offences) Act 1991 s.4
Max. sentence: Magistrates' Court: £1,000 fine.
Power: Arrestable Offence[16]

Offence:

It is an offence for an unauthorised person to sell, or offer or expose for sale, a ticket for a designated football match in any public place or place to which the public has access or, in the course of a trade or business, anywhere else.

Contrary to: Criminal Justice and Public Order Act 1994 s.166
Max. sentence: Magistrates' Court: £5,000.
Power: Arrestable Offence[17]

General Powers

Sporting Events (Control of Alcohol) Act 1985.

A constable may, at any time during the period of a designated sporting event at any designated sports ground, enter any part of the ground for the purposes of enforcing the provisions of the Act.[18]

A constable may search a person he has reasonable grounds to suspect is committing or has committed an offence under the 1985 Act, and may arrest such a person.[19]

A constable may stop a public service vehicle (within the meaning of s.1) or a motor vehicle to which s.1A applies and may search such a vehicle or a railway passenger vehicle if he has reasonable grounds to suspect that an offence is being or has been committed.[20]

If at any time during the period of a designated sporting event at any designated sporting ground it appears to a constable in uniform that the sale or supply of intoxicating liquor at any bar within the ground is detrimental to the orderly conduct or safety of spectators at that event, he may require any person having control of the bar to close it and keep it closed until the end of that period.[21]

Football Spectators Act 1989 [22]

During any control period in relation to a regulated football match outside England and Wales or an external tournament, if a constable in uniform:

(a) has reasonable grounds for suspecting that a person present before him has at any time caused or contributed to any violence or disorder in the United Kingdom or elsewhere, and

(b) has reasonable grounds to believe that making a banning order would help to prevent violence or disorder at or in connection with any regulated football matches,

he may detain that person in his custody (whether there or elsewhere) until he has decided whether or not to issue a notice,[23] and shall give the person his reasons for detaining him in writing.[24]

A constable may arrest a person to whom he is giving such a notice if he has reasonable grounds to believe that it is necessary to do so in order to secure that the person complies with the notice.[25]

Criminal Justice and Public Order Act 1994

There is a power of search in respect of vehicles where there are reasonable grounds to believe that they are being used for any purpose connected with the offence under s.166 of the 1994 Act (unauthorised sale of tickets).[26]

Definitions

Control period: in relation to a regulated football match outside England and Wales, means the period:

(a)   beginning 5 days before the day of the match; and

(b)   ending when the match is finished or cancelled.[27]

Designated sports ground: is a place used (wholly or partly) for sporting events where accommodation is provided for spectators, and for the time being designated, or of a class designated by the Secretary of State.

Designated football match: is an association football match in which one or both of the participating teams represents a club which is for the time being a member (full or associated) of the Football League or the Football Association Premier League, or which represents a club, country or territory outside England and Wales, and which is played at a sports ground which is designated by order under s.1(1) of the Safety of Sports Grounds Act 1975, or registered as the home ground of a club which is a member of the Football League or the Football Association Premier League at the time the match is played.[28]

Relevant period: Each of the following periods is 'relevant to' a designated football match, that is to say:

(a)   the period beginning

 (i)   2 hours before the start of the match;

 (ii)   2 hours before the time at which it is advertised to start; or

 (iii)   with the time at which spectators are first admitted to the premises, whichever is the earlier, and ending 1 hour after the end of the match;

(b) where a match advertised to start at a particular time, on a particular day, is postponed to a later day, or does not take place, the period in the advertised day beginning 2 hours before and ending 1 hour after that time.[29]

Regulated football match: means an association football match (whether in England and Wales or elsewhere) which is a prescribed match or a match of a prescribed description.

Notes

1   This section applies to a vehicle, which is a public service vehicle or railway passenger vehicle, and is being used for the principal purpose of carrying passengers for the whole or part of a journey to or from a designated sporting event. The only sporting events designated under this legislation are football matches. See *Definitions*. However the legislation does not apply to any sporting event or proposed sporting event where all competitors are to take part otherwise than for reward and to which all spectators are admitted free of charge.

2   Section 1A was added by the Public Order Act 1986. This section applies to a motor vehicle which is not a public service vehicle but is adapted to carry more than 8 passengers, and is being used for the principal purpose of carrying 2 or more passengers for the whole or part of a journey to or from a designated sporting event.

3   This is any article (or part of) capable of causing injury to a person struck by it, being a bottle, can or other portable container (including when crushed or broken) which is for holding drink, and is of a kind that when empty, is normally discarded or returned to, or left to be recovered by, the supplier. This does not include anything for holding a medicinal product.

4   The period of a designated sporting event is the period beginning 2 hours before the start of the event or (if earlier) 2 hours before the time at which it is advertised to start, and ending 1 hour after the end of the event. The period of a designated sporting event has been amended for the purposes of private viewing rooms to operate between 15 minutes before the start of the event until 15 minutes after the end of the event.

5   This section applies to any article or substance whose main purpose is the emission of a flare for the purpose of illuminating or signalling (as opposed to igniting or heating) or the emission of smoke or a visible gas; and in particular it applies to distress flares, fog-signals and pellets and capsules intended to be used as fumigators or for testing pipes, but not to matches, cigarette lighters or heaters. This section also applies to fireworks.

6   This is an order made by a court under the Football Spectators Act 1989 (as amended) which prohibits a person from attending regulated football matches and which requires that person to report to a police station.

7   To report to a police station at a specified time or to surrender a passport.

8   In the case of a regulated football match the person subject of a banning order may be required by notice in writing to comply with additional requirements.

9   As amended by the Football Disorder Act 2000.

10 This offence is an arrestable offence by virtue of s.24(2)(q) of the Police and Criminal Evidence Act 1984 (as amended).

11 An association football match designated, or of a description designated by the Home Secretary under the Football (Offences) (Designation of Football Matches) Order 1999.

12 Police and Criminal Evidence Act 1984 s.24(2)(e).

13 The repeated uttering of words or sounds.

14 Consisting of or including matter which is threatening, abusive or insulting to a person by reason of his colour, race nationality (inc. citizenship) or ethnic or national origins.

15 Police and Criminal Evidence Act 1984 s.24(2)(e).

16 Ibid., s.24(2)(e).

17 Ibid., s.24(2)(h).

18 Sporting Events (Control of Alcohol) Act 1985 s.7(1).

19 Ibid., s.7(2).

20 Ibid., s.7(3).

21 Ibid., s.6(1). Failure to comply is an offence.

22 As amended by the Football Disorder Act 2000.

23 This notice must be authorised by an officer of at least the rank of inspector and will require the person to appear before a magistrates' court within 24 hours while a banning order is applied for. The person may not leave England and Wales before that time and must surrender his passport if the match or tournament is outside the United Kingdom.

24 Football Spectators Act 1989 s.21A.

25 Ibid., s.21B(5). Failure to comply with a notice is an offence.

26 Police and Criminal Evidence Act 1984 s.32 as extended by the Criminal Justice and Public Order Act 1994.

27 In relation to a tournament the period is between 5 days before the first match of the tournament and ending with the finish of the last match.

28 Football Spectators (Designation of Football Matches in England and Wales) Order 1999.

29 Sporting Events (Control of Alcohol) Act 1985 s.8.

FOOTPATHS, FOOTWAYS AND BRIDLEWAYS

See also Drivers and Riders, Driving Off-Road, Highways and Roads, Metropolitan Police Act, Skips, Town Police Clauses

Offence: It is an offence for any person:

(a) to wilfully ride upon any footpath or causeway by the side of any road made or set apart for the use or accommodation of foot passengers;

(b) to wilfully lead or drive any horse, ass, sheep, mule, swine, cattle or carriage of any description, or any truck or sledge, upon any such footpath or causeway; or

(c) to tether any horse, ass, mule, swine or cattle on any highway so as to suffer or permit the tethered animal to be thereon.

Contrary to: Highways Act 1835 s.72
Max. sentence: Magistrates' Court: £500 fine.
Power: Report / s.25 PACE

Offence: It is an offence[i] for the occupier of a field or enclosure crossed by a right of way to permit a bull to be at large in the field or enclosure.

Contrary to: Wildlife and Countryside Act 1981 s.59
Max. sentence: Magistrates' Court: £1,000 fine.
Power: Report / s.25 PACE

Offence: It is an offence for a person to promote or take part in a trial of any description between motor vehicles on a footpath or bridleway unless the holding of the trial has been authorised by the local authority.

Contrary to: Road Traffic Act 1988 s.33(1)
Max. sentence: Magistrates' Court: £1,000 fine.

Power: Report / s.25 PACE

Offence: It is an offence for a person to place or maintain:

(a) on or near any access land;[2] or

(b) on or near a way leading to any access land,
a notice containing any false or misleading
information likely to deter the public from
exercising the right of access.

Contrary to: Countryside and Rights of Way Act 2000 s.14(1)[3]

Max. sentence: Magistrates' Court: £200 fine.

Power: Report / s.25 PACE

Definitions

Bridleway: means a highway over which the public have a right of way
on foot, on horseback or leading a horse or on a pedal cycle.[4]

Footpath: means a highway over which the public have a right of way on
foot only, not being a footway.[5]

Footway: means a way comprised in a highway which also comprises a
carriageway, being a way over which the public have a right of way on
foot only.[6]

Highway: means all roads, bridges, carriageways, cartways, horseways,
bridleways, footways, causeways, churchways and pavements.[7]

Restricted byway: means a highway over which the public have a right of
way on foot, on horseback or leading a horse as well as a right for
vehicles other than mechanically propelled vehicles.[8]

Notes

1   No offence is committed if the age of the bull does not exceed 10 months
or the bull is not a recognised dairy breed and is at large in any field or
enclosure in which cows or heifers are also at large. 'Recognised dairy
breed' includes Ayrshire, British Friesian, British Holstein, Dairy Shorthorn,
Guernsey, Jersey and Kerry.

2   Under this Act, access land is land detailed on public maps and is land to
which the general public have a right to wander over at will. The majority
of this Act will not come into force until 2004 at which time the maps will
have been prepared.

3   When in force.

4   Highways Act 1980 s.329. As amended by the Countryside Act 1964 s.30.

5   Highways Act 1980 s.329.

6   Ibid., s.329.

7   Highways Act 1835 s.5.

8   With or without a right to drive animals of any description along the highway, but no other rights of way. This description of highway was added by the Countryside and Rights of Way Act 2000.

FORGERY

See also Attempts, Bail, Conspiracy and Incitement, Criminal Justice, Deception, Driving Documents, Excise Licences, PACE – Arrest, Theft

Offence: It is an offence for a person, without lawful authority or excuse, to acknowledge in the name of any other any recognisance or bail, or any *cognovit actionem,* or judgment, or any deed or other instrument, before any court, judge or other person lawfully authorised in that behalf.

Contrary to: Forgery Act 1861 s.34

Max. sentence: Crown Court: 7 years' imprisonment / unlimited fine.

Power: Arrestable Offence

Offence: It is an offence for a person to make a false instrument, with the intention that he or another shall use it to induce somebody to accept it as genuine, and by reason of so accepting it to do or not to do some act to his own or any other person's prejudice.

Contrary to: Forgery and Counterfeiting Act 1981 s.1

Max. sentence: Magistrates' Court: 6 months' imprisonment / £5,000 fine.

Crown Court: 10 years' imprisonment / unlimited fine.

Power: Arrestable Offence

Offence: It is an offence for a person to make a copy of an instrument which is, and which he knows or believes to be, a false instrument, with the intention that he or another shall use it to induce somebody to accept it as a copy of a genuine instrument, and by reason of so accepting it to do or not to do some act to his own or any other person's prejudice.

Contrary to: Forgery and Counterfeiting Act 1981 s.2

Max. sentence: Magistrates' Court: 6 months' imprisonment / £5,000 fine.

Crown Court: 10 years' imprisonment / unlimited fine.

Power: Arrestable Offence

Offence: It is an offence for a person to use an instrument which is, and which he knows or believes to be, false, with the intention of inducing somebody to accept it as genuine, and by reason of so accepting it to do or not to do some act to his own or any other person's prejudice.

Contrary to: Forgery and Counterfeiting Act 1981 s.3

Max. sentence: Magistrates' Court: 6 months' imprisonment / £5,000 fine.

Crown Court: 10 years' imprisonment / unlimited fine.

Power: Arrestable Offence

Offence: It is an offence for a person to use a copy of an instrument which is, and which he knows or believes to be, a false instrument, with the intention of inducing somebody to accept it as a copy of a genuine instrument, and by reason of so accepting it to do or not to do some act to his own or any other person's prejudice.

Contrary to: Forgery and Counterfeiting Act 1981 s.4

Max. sentence: Magistrates' Court: 6 months' imprisonment / £5,000 fine.

Crown Court: 10 years' imprisonment / unlimited fine.

Power: Arrestable Offence

Offence:

It is an offence for a person to have in his custody or under his control an instrument to which this section applies[1] and which he knows or believes to be, false, with the intention that he or another shall use it to induce somebody to accept it as a copy of a genuine instrument, and by reason of so accepting it to do or not to do some act to his own or any other person's prejudice.

Contrary to: Forgery and Counterfeiting Act 1981 s.5(1)

Max. sentence: Magistrates' Court: 6 months' imprisonment / £5,000 fine.

Crown Court: 10 years' imprisonment / unlimited fine.

Power: Arrestable Offence

Offence:

It is an offence for a person to have in his custody or under his control, without lawful authority or excuse, an instrument to which this section applies which is and which he knows or believes to be, false.

Contrary to: Forgery and Counterfeiting Act 1981 s.5(2)

Max. sentence: Magistrates' Court: 6 months' imprisonment / £5,000 fine.

Crown Court: 2 years' imprisonment / unlimited fine.

Power: Report / s.25 PACE

Offence: It is an offence for a person to make or to have in his
custody or under his control, a machine or
implement, or paper or any other material, which
to his knowledge is or has been specially designed
or adapted for the making of an instrument to
which this section applies, with the intention that
he or another shall make such an instrument which
is false and that he or another shall use the
instrument to induce somebody to accept it as
genuine, and by reason of so accepting it to do or
not to do some act to his own or any other person's
prejudice.

Contrary to: Forgery and Counterfeiting Act 1981 s.5(3)

Max. sentence: Magistrates' Court: 6 months' imprisonment /
£5,000 fine.

Crown Court: 10 years' imprisonment / unlimited
fine.

Power: Arrestable Offence

Offence: It is an offence for a person to make or to have in his
custody or under his control, any such machine,
implement, paper or material, without lawful
authority or excuse.

Contrary to: Forgery and Counterfeiting Act 1981 s.5(4)

Max. sentence: Magistrates' Court: 6 months' imprisonment /
£5,000 fine.

Crown Court: 2 years' imprisonment / unlimited
fine.

Power: Report / s.25 PACE

Offence: It is an offence for a person to make a counterfeit of
a currency note or of a protected coin,[2] intending
that he or another shall pass or tender it as genuine.

Contrary to:	Forgery and Counterfeiting Act 1981 s.14(1)
Max. sentence:	Magistrates' Court: 6 months' imprisonment / £5,000 fine.
	Crown Court: 10 years' imprisonment / unlimited fine.
Power:	Arrestable Offence

Offence: It is an offence for a person to make a counterfeit of a currency note or of a protected coin without lawful authority or excuse.

Contrary to:	Forgery and Counterfeiting Act 1981 s.14(2)
Max. sentence:	Magistrates' Court: 6 months' imprisonment / £5,000 fine.
	Crown Court: 2 years' imprisonment / unlimited fine.
Power:	Report / s.25 PACE

Offence: It is an offence for a person:

(a) to pass or tender as genuine any thing which is, and which he knows or believes to be, a counterfeit of a currency note or of a protected coin; or

(b) to deliver to another any thing which is, and which he knows or believes to be, a counterfeit, intending that the person to whom it is delivered or another shall pass or tender it as genuine.

Contrary to:	Forgery and Counterfeiting Act 1981 s.15(1)
Max. sentence:	Magistrates' Court: 6 months' imprisonment / £5,000 fine.
	Crown Court: 10 years' imprisonment / unlimited fine.
Power:	Arrestable Offence

Offence: It is an offence for a person to deliver to another, without lawful authority or excuse, any thing which is, and which he knows or believes to be, a counterfeit of a currency note or of a protected coin.

Contrary to: Forgery and Counterfeiting Act 1981 s.15(2)

Max. sentence: Magistrates' Court: 6 months' imprisonment / £5,000 fine.

Crown Court: 2 years' imprisonment / unlimited fine.

Power: Report / s.25 PACE

Offence: It is an offence for a person to have in his custody or under his control any thing which is, and which he knows or believes to be, a counterfeit of a currency note or of a protected coin, intending either to pass or tender it as genuine or to deliver it to another with the intention that he or another shall pass or tender it as genuine.

Contrary to: Forgery and Counterfeiting Act 1981 s.16(1)

Max. sentence: Magistrates' Court: 6 months' imprisonment / £5,000 fine.

Crown Court: 10 years' imprisonment / unlimited fine.

Power: Arrestable Offence

Offence: It is an offence for a person to have in his custody or control, without lawful authority or excuse, any thing which is, and which he knows or believes to be, a counterfeit of a currency note or of a protected coin.

Contrary to: Forgery and Counterfeiting Act 1981 s.16(2)

Max. sentence: Magistrates' Court: 6 months' imprisonment / £5,000 fine.

Crown Court: 2 years' imprisonment / unlimited fine.

Power: Report / s.25 PACE

Offence:
It is an offence for a person to make, or to have in his custody or under his control, any thing which he intends to use, or to permit any other person to use, for the purpose of making a counterfeit of a currency note or of a protected coin with the intention that it be passed or tendered as genuine.

Contrary to: Forgery and Counterfeiting Act 1981 s.17(1)

Max. sentence: Magistrates' Court: 6 months' imprisonment / £5,000 fine.

Crown Court: 10 years' imprisonment / unlimited fine.

Power: Arrestable Offence

Offence:
It is an offence for a person, without lawful authority or excuse, to make, or to have in his custody or under his control, any thing which to his knowledge, is or has been specially designed or adapted for the making of a counterfeit of a currency note.

Contrary to: Forgery and Counterfeiting Act 1981 s.17(2)

Max. sentence: Magistrates' Court: 6 months' imprisonment / £5,000 fine.

Crown Court: 2 years' imprisonment / unlimited fine.

Power: Report / s.25 PACE

Offence:
It is an offence for a person, to make, or to have in his custody or under his control, any implement which, to his knowledge, is capable of imparting to any thing a resemblance to the whole or part of

either side of a protected coin, or to the whole or part of the reverse of the image on either side of a protected coin.

Contrary to: Forgery and Counterfeiting Act 1981 s.17(3)

Max. sentence: Magistrates' Court: 6 months' imprisonment / £5,000 fine.

Crown Court: 2 years' imprisonment / unlimited fine.

Power: Report / s.25 PACE

Offence:

It is an offence for a person, unless the relevant authority[3] has previously consented in writing, to reproduce on any substance whatsoever, and whether or not on the correct scale, any British currency note or any part of a British currency note.

Contrary to: Forgery and Counterfeiting Act 1981 s.18(1)

Max. sentence: Magistrates' Court: 6 months' imprisonment / £5,000 fine.

Crown Court: 2 years' imprisonment / unlimited fine.

Power: Report / s.25 PACE

Definitions

British currency note: means any note which has been lawfully issued in England and Wales, Scotland or Northern Ireland and is, or has been, customarily used as money in the country where it was issued and is payable on demand.

Counterfeit: a thing is counterfeit of a currency note or of a protected coin:

(a) if it is not a currency note or protected coin but resembles either (whether on one side or both) to such an extent that it is reasonably capable of passing for a currency note or protected coin of that description;

(b) if it is a currency note or protected coin which has been so altered that it is reasonably capable of passing for a currency note or protected coin of some other description.

False: an instrument is false for the purposes of this Act:-

(a)   if it purports to have been made in the form in which it is made by a person who did not in fact make it in that form; or

(b)   if it purports to have been made in the form in which it is made on the authority of a person who did in fact not authorise its making in that form; or

(c)   if it purports to have been made in the terms in which it is made by a person who did not in fact make it in those terms; or

(d)   if it purports to have been made in the terms in which it is made on the authority of a person who did in fact not authorise its making in those terms; or

(e)   if it purports to have been altered in any respect by a person who did not in fact alter it in that respect; or

(f)   if it purports to have been altered in any respect on the authority of a person who did not in fact authorise the alteration in that respect; or

(g)   if it purports to have been made or altered on a date on which, or at a place at which, or otherwise in circumstances in which, it was not in fact made or altered; or

(h)   if it purports to have been made or altered by an existing person but he did not in fact exist.[4]

Instrument: means any document (formal or informal), any stamp issued or sold by the Post Office, any Inland Revenue stamp and any disc, tape, sound track or other device on or in which information is recorded or stored by mechanical, electronic or other means. It may also include the original of a facsimile used to induce another to act to their or a third party's prejudice.[5] It does not mean a currency note.[6]

Protected coin: means any coin which is customarily used as money in any country, or is specified in an Order made by the Treasury for the purposes of the 1981 Act.

Notes

1   The instruments to which s.5 applies are money orders, postal orders, postage stamps, Inland Revenue stamps, share certificates, passports, cheques, travellers' cheques, cheque cards and credit cards.

2   A 'currency note' is any note issued or customarily used in any country and 'protected coin' means any coin which is used as money in any country or is specified in an Order made by the Treasury.

3   That is, the Bank of England.

4   Forgery and Counterfeiting Act 1981 s.9.

5   *R* v *Ondhia* (1998).

6   Forgery and Counterfeiting Act 1981 s.8.

GOING EQUIPPED

See also Attempts, Burglary, Deception, Knives and Bladed Articles, Offensive Weapons, PACE – Arrest, Taking a Conveyance, Theft

Offence: It is an offence for a person, when not at his place of abode, to have with him any article for use[1] in the course of or in connection with any burglary, theft[2] or cheat.[3]

Contrary to: Theft Act 1968 s.25(1)

Max. sentence: Magistrates' Court: 6 months' imprisonment / £5,000 fine.

Crown Court: 3 years' imprisonment / unlimited fine.

Power: Any person may arrest without warrant anyone who is, or whom he with reasonable cause suspects to be, committing an offence under this section.[4]

General Powers

A constable[5] may search any person or vehicle[6] or anything which is in or on a vehicle, for stolen or prohibited articles[7] or any article to which s.1(8A) of the Police and Criminal Evidence Act 1984 applies,[8] and may detain[9] a person or vehicle for the purpose of such a search.[10]

If in the course of such a search a constable discovers any article which he has reasonable grounds for suspecting to be stolen or prohibited articles or any article to which s.1(8A) applies, he may seize it.[11]

Definitions

Prohibited article: means an offensive weapon[12] or an article:

(a)   made or adapted for use in the course of or in connection with an offence of burglary, theft, taking a conveyance without authority or obtaining property by deception; or

(b)   intended by the person having it with him for such use by him or some other person.

Notes

1   That is, some future use.

2   For the purposes of this section 'theft' includes the taking of a conveyance under s.12(1) of the Theft Act 1968. See page 386.

3   That is, a deception under the Theft Act 1968 s.15.

4   Police and Criminal Evidence Act 1984 s.24(2)(d).

5   Section 1 of the 1984 Act does not give a constable power to search a person or vehicle or anything in or on a vehicle unless he has reasonable grounds for suspecting that he will find stolen or prohibited articles or any article to which s.1(8A) applies.

If a person is in a garden or yard occupied with and used for the purposes of a dwelling or on other land so occupied and used, a constable may not search him in the exercise of the power conferred by s.1 unless the constable has reasonable grounds for believing:

(a)   that he does not reside in the dwelling; and

(b)   that he is not in the place in question with the express or implied permission of a person who resides in the dwelling.

If a vehicle is in a garden or yard occupied with and used for the purposes of a dwelling or on other land so occupied and used, a constable may not search the vehicle or anything in or on it unless the constable has reasonable grounds for believing:

(a)   that the person in charge of the vehicle does not reside in the dwelling; and

(b)   that the vehicle is not in the place in question with the express or implied permission of a person who resides in the dwelling.

6   Includes vessels, aircraft and hovercraft.

7   See *Definitions*.

8   The articles identified by s.1(8A) are those with blades or points with the exception of certain folding pocket knives. See page 234.

9   The time for which a person or vehicle may be detained for the purposes of such a search is such time as is reasonably required to permit the search to be carried out either at the place where the person or vehicle was first detained or nearby. ibid., s.2(8). Reasonable force may be used. ibid., s.117.

10   Police and Criminal Evidence Act 1984 s.1. A constable may exercise any power conferred in this section:

   (a) in any place to which at the time when he proposes to exercise the power the public or any section of the public has access, on payment or otherwise, as of right or by virtue of express or implied permission; or

   (b) in any other place to which people have ready access at the time when he proposes to exercise the power but which is not a dwelling.

11   Ibid., s.1(6).

12   That is, any article made, adapted or intended by the person having it with him to cause injury. See page 279.

GOODS VEHICLES OPERATORS

See also Construction and Use, Drivers and Riders, Drivers' Records, Driving Documents, Trailers

Offence: It is an offence[1] for a person to use a goods vehicle on a road for the carriage of goods:

   (a)   for hire or reward; or

   (b)   for or in connection with any trade or business carried on by him

without a licence.[2]

Contrary to: Goods Vehicles (Licensing of Operators) Act 1995 s.2(1)

Max. sentence: Magistrates' Court: £5,000 fine.[3]

Power: Report / s.25 PACE

Offence: It is an offence for a person to use a place in the area of any traffic commissioner as an operating centre for vehicles authorised to be used under any operator's licence unless that place is specified as an operating centre of his in that licence.

Contrary to: Goods Vehicles (Licensing of Operators) Act 1995 s.7(1)

Max. sentence: Magistrates' Court: £2,500 fine.

Power: Report / s.25 PACE

Offence:

It is an offence for a person, with intent to deceive, to forge, alter, lend or allow to be used by any other person a document or other thing to which s.38 of the 1995 Act applies, or make or have in his possession any document or other thing so closely resembling a document to which se.38 applies as to be calculated to deceive.

Contrary to: Goods Vehicles (Licensing of Operators) Act 1995 s.38(1)

Max. sentence: Magistrates' Court: 6 months' imprisonment / £5,000 fine.

Crown Court: 2 years' imprisonment / unlimited fine.

Power: Report / s.25 PACE

Offence:

It is an offence for a person to knowingly make a false statement for the purpose of obtaining the issue of an operator's licence.

Contrary to: Goods Vehicles (Licensing of Operators) Act 1995 s.39(1)

Max. sentence: Magistrates' Court: £2,500 fine.

Power: Report / s.25 PACE

Offence:

It is an offence for the holder of an operator's licence to fail to cause a disc[4] appropriate to the vehicle to be fixed to,[5] and exhibited in a legible condition on, that vehicle in a waterproof container.

Contrary to:	Goods Vehicles (Licensing of Operators) Regulations 1995 r.32(1)
Max. sentence:	Magistrates' Court: £200 fine.
Power:	Report / s.25 PACE

General Powers

An officer[6] may, at any time which is reasonable having regard to the circumstances of the case, enter[7] any premises of a holder of an operator's licence and inspect any facilities on those premises for maintaining the vehicles used under the licence, in a fit and serviceable condition.[8]

The licence holder shall produce the licence for inspection by an officer or a police constable within 14 days of being required by such a person to do so, and the licence holder may do so at any operating centre covered by the licence or at his head or principal place of business or at a police station chosen by the licence holder.[9]

Definitions

Goods vehicle: a motor vehicle constructed or adapted for the carriage of goods, or a trailer so constructed or adapted, but does not include a tramcar or trolley vehicle.[10]

General Information

An operator's licence will specify the maximum number of motor vehicles and trailers that may be operated and will identify the operating centre from which those vehicles are to be used. Once issued such a licence will continue in force indefinitely unless revoked or terminated by the traffic commissioner for the area.

Notes

1 This subsection does not apply to the use of a small goods vehicle under 3.5 tonnes or with an unladen weight not exceeding 1,525 kg or to the use of a goods vehicle for international carriage by a haulier established outside the United Kingdom.

2 Issued by a traffic commissioner and referred to as an 'operator's licence', they may be standard or restricted. A standard operator's licence covers the carriage of goods for hire or reward or in connection with any trade or

business. A restricted licence covers the carriage of such goods for purposes other than any hire or reward.

3 As amended by the Transport Act 2000.

4 Issued by the traffic commissioner and indicating that the vehicle is used under an operator's licence.

5 If the vehicle has a windscreen, then the disc must be positioned in the lower near side of it and with the obverse side facing forwards.

6 This is an examiner or other authorised person appointed by the traffic commissioner and includes any police constable [Goods Vehicles (Licensing of Operators) Act 1995 s.42(2)].

7 Obstruction is a summary offence subject to a maximum fine of £1,000.

8 Goods Vehicles (Licensing of Operators) Act 1995 s.40(1).

9 Goods Vehicles (Licensing of Operators) Regulations 1995 r.26.

10 Goods Vehicles (Licensing of Operators) Act 1995 s.58.

HANDLING STOLEN GOODS

See also Blackmail, Burglary, Deception, PACE – Arrest, Taking a Conveyance, Theft

Offence: A person handles stolen[1] goods if (otherwise than in the course of the stealing) knowing or believing[2] them to be stolen goods he:

(a) dishonestly receives the goods; or

(b) dishonestly undertakes or assists in their

(i) retention,

(ii) removal,

(iii) disposal, or

(iv) realisation

by or for the benefit of another person,[3] or if he arranges to do so.

Contrary to: Theft Act 1968 s.22(1)

Max. sentence: Magistrates' Court: 6 months' imprisonment / £5,000 fine.

Crown Court: 14 years' imprisonment / unlimited fine.

Power: Arrestable Offence

Offence: It is an offence for any person[4] to make a public advertisement of a reward for the return of goods stolen or lost if such advertisement uses any words to the effect:

(a)   that no questions will be asked;

(b)   that the person producing the goods will be safe from apprehension or inquiry; or

(c)   that any money paid for the purchase of the goods, or advanced by way of loan on them, will be repaid.

Contrary to: Theft Act 1968 s.23

Max. sentence: Magistrates' Court: £1,000 fine.

Power: Report / s.25 PACE

Offence: A person is guilty of an offence if:

(a)   a wrongful credit[5] has been made to an account kept by him or in respect of which he has any right or interest;

(b)   he knows or believes that the credit is wrongful; and

(c)   he dishonestly fails to take such steps as are reasonable in the circumstances to secure that the credit is cancelled.

Contrary to: Theft Act 1968 s.24A

Max. sentence: Crown Court: 10 years' imprisonment / unlimited fine.

Power: Arrestable Offence

General Information

For the purposes of these provisions references to stolen goods shall include, in addition to the goods originally stolen and parts of them (whether in their original state or not):

(a) any other goods which directly or indirectly represent or have at any time represented the stolen goods in the hands of the thief as being the proceeds of any disposal or realisation of the whole or part of the goods stolen or of goods so representing the stolen goods; and

(b) any other goods which directly or indirectly represent or have at any time represented the stolen goods in the hands of a handler of the stolen goods, or any part of them, as being the proceeds of any disposal or realisation of the whole or part of the stolen goods handled by him or of goods so representing them.[6]

But no goods shall be regarded as having continued to be stolen goods after they have been restored to the person from whom they were stolen or to other lawful possession or custody, or after that person and any other person claiming through him, have otherwise ceased as regards those goods to have any right to restitution in respect of the theft.[7]

Once evidence has been laid before a court of a defendant having the stolen goods subject of the charge in his possession, or arranging to take them into his possession, or of his undertaking or assisting in the retention, removal, disposal or realisation of such goods, special rules allow for the admission of evidence that he had, within the 12 months preceding the offence charged, possessed or undertaken to assist in the retention, removal, disposal or realisation of any other stolen goods.[8]

Provided that 7 days' notice is given to the defendant, evidence of a previous conviction for theft or handling within the preceding 5 years may also be admitted by the court.[9]

The *doctrine of recent possession* is a rebuttable presumption that recently stolen property was either stolen by its possessor or received by him knowing that it was stolen.[10]

Notes

1   'Stolen' includes goods obtained by deception or blackmail. For a detailed examination of terms see page 402.

2 'Knowing' requires specific knowledge that the goods came from a theft. 'Belief' is something falling short of knowledge but is more than mere suspicion, [*R* v *Hall* (1985)].

3 The term 'by or for the benefit of another person' specifically covers the words 'retention', 'removal', 'disposal' and 'realisation' and needs to be associated in any charge where one of these is alleged, [*R* v *Sloggett* (1972)]. To 'realise' goods is to exchange them for money, [*R* v *Deakin* (1972)].

4 This includes both the person advertising the reward and any person who prints or publishes the advertisement. An offence of strict liability, [*Denham* v *Scott* (1983)].

5 That is, an amount of money. A credit is wrongful if it derives from a theft, any theft by deception, blackmail or from stolen goods.

6 Theft Act 1968 s.24(2).

7 Ibid., s.24(3).

8 Ibid., s.27(3)(a).

9 Ibid., s.27(3)(b).

10 *R* v *Seymour* (1954), *R* v *Cash* (1985).

HARASSMENT AND INTIMIDATION

See also Assaults, Criminal Justice, Drunkenness, Forgery, Industrial Relations, Offensive Weapons, PACE – Arrest, Post and Mail, Public Order, Racial Hatred, Telecommunications, Trespass

Offence: It is an offence for any person, with the object of coercing another person to pay money claimed from the other as a debt due under a contract to:

(a) harass the other with demands for payment which, in respect of their frequency or the manner or occasion of making any such demand, or of any threat or publicity by which any demand is accompanied, are calculated to subject him or members of his family or household to alarm, distress or humiliation;[1]

(b) falsely represent that criminal proceedings lie for failure to pay it;

(c) falsely represent himself to be authorised in

some official capacity to claim or enforce payment; or

(d) utter a document falsely represented by him to have some official character or purporting to have some official character which he knows it has not.

Contrary to: Administration of Justice Act 1970 s.40 (1)

Max. sentence: Magistrates' Court: 6 months' imprisonment / £5,000 fine.

Power: Report / s.25 PACE

Offence: It is an offence for any person to unlawfully deprive the residential occupier[2] of any premises of his occupation of those premises or any part thereof unless he proves that he believed, and had reasonable cause to believe, that the residential occupier had ceased to reside in the premises.

Contrary to: Protection from Eviction Act 1977 s.1(2)

Max. sentence: Magistrates' Court: 6 months' imprisonment / £5,000 fine.

Crown Court: 2 years' imprisonment / unlimited fine.

Power: Report / s.25 PACE

Offence: It is an offence for any person, with intent to cause the residential occupier of any premises:

(a) to give up the occupation of the premises or any part thereof; or

(b) to refrain from exercising any right or pursuing any remedy in respect of the premises or part thereof,

to do any acts likely to interfere with the peace or comfort of the residential occupier or members of his household, or to persistently withdraw or withhold services reasonably required for the occupation of the premises as a residence.

Contrary to: Protection from Eviction Act 1977 s.1(3)

Max. sentence: Magistrates' Court: 6 months' imprisonment / £5,000 fine.

Crown Court: 2 years' imprisonment / unlimited fine.

Power: Report / s.25 PACE

Offence:

It is an offence[3] for the landlord of a residential occupier, or an agent of the landlord:

(a) to do any act likely to interfere with the peace and comfort of the residential occupier or members of his household; or

(b) to persistently withdraw or withhold services reasonably required for the occupation of the premises in question as a residence,

and he knows, or has reasonable cause to believe, that that conduct is likely to cause the residential occupier to give up the occupation of the whole or part of the premises or to refrain from exercising any right or pursuing any remedy in respect of the whole or part of the premises.

Contrary to: Protection from Eviction Act 1977 s.1(3A)

Max. sentence: Magistrates' Court: 6 months' imprisonment / £5,000 fine.

Crown Court: 2 years' imprisonment / unlimited fine.

Power: Report / s.25 PACE

Offence:

It is an offence for a person to do to another person:

(a) an act which intimidates, and is intended to intimidate, that other person;[4]

(b) knowing or believing that the other person is

assisting in the investigation of an offence or is a witness or potential witness or a juror or potential juror in proceedings for an offence; and

(c)   intending thereby to cause the investigation or the course of justice to be obstructed, perverted or interfered with.

Contrary to: Criminal Justice and Public Order Act 1994 s.51(1)

Max. sentence: Magistrates' Court: 6 months' imprisonment / £5,000 fine.

Crown Court: 5 years' imprisonment / unlimited fine.

Power: Arrestable Offence

Offence:

It is an offence for a person to do, or threaten to do, to another person:

(a)   an act which harms[5] or would harm, and is intended to harm, that other person;

(b)   knowing or believing that the other person, or some other person, has assisted in an investigation into an offence or has given evidence or particular evidence in proceedings for an offence, or has acted as a juror or concurred in a particular verdict in proceedings for an offence; and

(c)   does or threatens to do the act because of what he knows or believes.

Contrary to: Criminal Justice and Public Order Act 1994 s.51(2)

Max. sentence: Magistrates' Court: 6 months' imprisonment / £5,000 fine.

Crown Court: 5 years' imprisonment / unlimited fine.

Power: Arrestable Offence

Offence: It is an offence for a person to pursue a course of conduct which amounts to harassment of another,[6] and which he knows or ought to know amounts to harassment of the other.[7]

Contrary to: Protection from Harassment Act 1997 s.2

Max. sentence: Magistrates' Court: 6 months' imprisonment / £5,000 fine.

Power: Arrestable Offence[8]

Offence: It is an offence for a person, without reasonable excuse, to do anything which he is prohibited from doing by an injunction granted by the High Court or a county court for the purpose of restraining that person from pursuing any conduct which amounts to harassment.

Contrary to: Protection from Harassment Act 1997 s.3(6)

Max. sentence: Magistrates' Court: 6 months' imprisonment / £5,000 fine.

Crown Court: 5 years' imprisonment / unlimited fine.

Power: Arrestable Offence

Offence: It is an offence[9] for a person to pursue a course of conduct which causes another to fear, on at least two occasions, that violence will be used against him if he knows or ought to know that his course of conduct will cause the other so to fear on each of those occasions.

Contrary to: Protection from Harassment Act 1997 s.4

Max. sentence: Magistrates' Court: 6 months' imprisonment / £5,000 fine.

Crown Court: 5 years' imprisonment / unlimited fine.

Power: Arrestable Offence

Offence:

It is an offence for a person subject to a restraining order, without reasonable excuse, to do anything which he is prohibited from doing by the order.

Contrary to: Protection from Harassment Act 1997 s.5(5)

Max. sentence: Magistrates' Court: 6 months' imprisonment / £5,000 fine.

Crown Court: 5 years' imprisonment / unlimited fine.

Power: Arrestable Offence

Offence:

It is an offence for a person to knowingly contravene a direction given by a constable under s.42 of this Act.[10]

Contrary to: Criminal Justice and Police Act 2001. s.42(7)

Max. sentence: Magistrates' Court: 3 months' imprisonment / £2,500 fine.

Power: A constable in uniform may arrest without warrant any person he reasonably suspects is committing this offence.[11]

General Powers

Under the provisions of the Criminal Justice and Police Act 2001, a constable[12] who is at the scene may give a direction to any person if:

(a) that person is present outside or in the vicinity of any premises that are used by an individual (the resident) as his dwelling;

(b) that constable believes, on reasonable grounds, that that person is present there for the purposes (by his presence or otherwise) of representing to the resident or another individual (whether or not one who uses the premises as his dwelling), or of persuading the resident or such other individual:

(i)   that he should not do something that he is entitled or required to do; or

(ii) that he should do something that he is not under any obligation to do; and

(c)   that constable also believes, on reasonable grounds, that the presence of that person (either alone or together with that of any other persons who are also present):

(i)   amounts to, or is likely to result in, the harassment of the resident; or

(ii)   is likely to cause alarm or distress to the resident.[13]

A direction[14] is a direction requiring the person to whom it is given to do all such things as the constable may specify as the things he considers necessary to prevent the harassment of the resident; or the causing of any alarm or distress to the resident.[15] A direction may include a requirement to leave the vicinity of the premises.[16]

General Information

A court sentencing or otherwise dealing with a person convicted of an offence under s.2 or s.4 of the Protection from Harassment Act 1997 may make a restraining order prohibiting the defendant from doing anything described in the order.

Notes

1   This does not apply to anything done by a person which is reasonable (and otherwise permissible in law) for the purpose of securing the discharge of an obligation due, to himself or to persons for whom he acts, or protecting himself or them from future loss, or of the enforcement of any liability by legal process.

2   The 'residential occupier' is any person occupying premises as a residence, whether under contract or by virtue of any enactment or rule of law giving him the right to remain in occupation or restricting the right of any other person to recover possession of the premises.

3   A person shall not be guilty of an offence under this subsection if he proves that he had reasonable grounds for doing the acts or withdrawing the services in question.

4   A person does an act 'to' another person with the intention of intimidating, or (as the case may be) harming, that other person not only where the act is done in the presence of that other and directed at him, but also where the act is done to a third person and is intended, in the circumstances, to intimidate or harm the person at whom the act is directed.

5   Includes financial harm.

6   'Another' is to be interpreted as 'others' and may be wide enough to allow

for a charge under s.2(1) where the conduct has affected a number of connected victims, [*DPP* v *Williams* (1998)].

7   For the purposes of this section, the person whose course of conduct is in question ought to know that it amounts to harassment of another if a reasonable person in possession of the same information would think the course of conduct amounted to harassment of the other. Conduct includes 'speech'. A 'course of conduct' must involve conduct on at least two occasions. Genuine attempts to commence a relationship may not amount to harassment if not intrusive or excessive, [*King* v *DPP* (2000)].

8   Police and Criminal Evidence Act 1984 s.24(2)(n).

9   Defences to a 'course of conduct' for both s.2 and s.4 include for the purpose of preventing or detecting crime, pursued under any enactment or rule of law or conduct that was reasonable in the circumstances.

10 See *General Powers*.

11 Criminal Justice and Police Act 2001 s.42(8).

12 That is, the most senior police officer present at the scene.

13 Criminal Justice and Police Act 2001 s.42(1).

14 May be oral.

15 Criminal Justice and Police Act 2001 s.42(2).

16 Will not apply to lawful and peaceful picketing.

HIGHWAYS AND ROADS

See also Abandoned Vehicles, Construction and Use, Drivers and Riders, Footpaths, Footways and Bridleways, Litter, Metropolitan Police Act, Parking, Skips, Straying Animals, Town Police Clauses, Traffic Signs and Directions

Offence: It is an offence for the driver of any carriage whatsoever on any part of the highway, by negligence or wilful[1] misbehaviour, to leave any cart or carriage on such highway, so as to obstruct the free passage there, or by negligence or misbehaviour prevent, hinder or interrupt the free passage of any person, wagon, cart or other carriage, or horses, mules or other beasts of burden on any highway.[2]

Contrary to:	Highways Act 1835 s.78
Max. sentence:	Magistrates' Court: £200 fine.
Power:	Report / s.25 PACE[3]

Offence:

It is an offence for a person, without lawful authority or excuse, to:

(a)   make a ditch or excavation in a highway which consists of or comprises a carriageway;

(b)   removes any soil or turf from any part of a highway, except for the purposes of improving the highway and with the consent of the highway authority;

(c)   deposit anything whatsoever on a highway so as to damage the highway; or

(d)   light any fire, or discharge any firearm or firework, within 50 feet from the centre of a highway which consists of or comprises a carriageway, and in consequence thereof the highway is damaged.

Contrary to:	Highways Act 1980 s.131(1)
Max. sentence:	Magistrates' Court: £1,000 fine.
Power:	Report / s.25 PACE

Offence:

It is an offence for a person, without either the consent of the highway authority or an authorisation by or under an enactment or a reasonable excuse, to paint, or otherwise inscribe, or affix any picture, letter, sign or other mark upon the surface of a highway or upon any tree, structure or works on or in a highway.

Contrary to:	Highways Act 1980 s.132(1)
Max. sentence:	Magistrates' Court: £2,500 fine.
Power:	Report / s.25 PACE

Offence: It is an offence for a person, without lawful authority or excuse, in any way to wilfully obstruct the free passage along a highway.

Contrary to: Highways Act 1980 s.137(1)

Max. sentence: Magistrates' Court: £1,000 fine.

Power: Report / s.25 PACE

Offence: It is an offence for a person, without lawful authority or excuse, to erect a building or fence, or to plant a hedge, in a highway which consists of or comprises a carriageway.

Contrary to: Highways Act 1980 s.138

Max. sentence: Magistrates' Court: £1,000 fine.

Power: Report / s.25 PACE

Offence: It is an offence[4] for the purpose of selling anything, or offering or exposing anything for sale, for a person to use any stall or similar structure or any container or vehicle, kept or placed on:

(a) the verge of a trunk road or a principal road;

(b) a lay-by on any such road; or

(c) unenclosed land within 15 metres of any part of any such road,

where its presence or its use for that purpose causes or is likely to cause danger on the road or interrupts or is likely to interrupt any user of the road.

Contrary to: Highways Act 1980 s.147A(1)

Max. sentence: Magistrates' Court: £1,000 fine.

Power: Report / s.25 PACE

Offence: It is an offence, without lawful authority or excuse:

(a) for a person to deposit any thing whatsoever on a highway to the interruption of any user of the highway; or

(b)   for a hawker or other itinerant trader to pitch a booth, stall or stand, or to encamp on a highway.

Contrary to: Highways Act 1980 s.148

Max. sentence: Magistrates' Court: £1,000 fine.

Power: Report / s.25 PACE

Offence:

It is an offence for a person, without lawful authority or excuse, to deposit any thing whatsoever on a highway in consequence of which a user of the highway is injured or endangered.

Contrary to: Highways Act 1980 s.161(1)

Max. sentence: Magistrates' Court: £1,000 fine.

Power: Report / s.25 PACE

Offence:

It is an offence for a person to play football or any other game on a highway to the annoyance of a user of the highway.

Contrary to: Highways Act 1980 s.161(3)

Max. sentence: Magistrates' Court: £200 fine.

Power: Report / s.25 PACE

Offence:

It is an offence[5] for any person to place a rope, wire or other apparatus across a highway in such a manner as to be likely to cause danger to persons using the highway.

Contrary to: Highways Act 1980 s.162

Max. sentence: Magistrates' Court: £1,000 fine.

Power: Report / s.25 PACE

Offence:

It is an offence[6] for a person to mix or deposit on a highway any mortar or cement or any other substance which is likely to stick to the surface of the highway or which, if it enters drains or sewers connected with the highway, is likely to solidify.

Contrary to:	Highways Act 1980 s.170
Max. sentence:	Magistrates' Court: £200 fine.
Power:	Report / s.25 PACE

Offence: It is an offence[7] for a person to carry out work[8] to a motor vehicle or trailer on any highway in Greater London.

Contrary to:	Greater London Council (General Powers) Act 1982 s.5(1)
Max. sentence:	Magistrates' Court: £1,000 fine.
Power:	Report / s.25 PACE

Offence: It is an offence for any person in charge of a motor vehicle or trailer to cause or permit the vehicle to stand on the road[9] so as to cause any unnecessary obstruction of the road.

Contrary to:	Road Vehicles (Construction and Use) Regulations 1986 r.103
Max. sentence:	Magistrates' Court: £1,000 fine.
Power:	Report / s.25 PACE

Offence: It is an offence for a person to intentionally and without lawful authority or reasonable cause to cause anything to be on or over a road,[10] in such circumstances that it would be obvious to a reasonable person that to do so would be dangerous.

Contrary to:	Road Traffic Act 1988 s.22A(1)
Max. sentence:	Magistrates' Court: 6 months' imprisonment / £5,000 fine.
	Crown Court: 7 years' imprisonment / unlimited fine.
Power:	Arrestable Offence

Definitions

Highway: means the whole or part of any highway other than a ferry or waterway and includes bridges and tunnels.

Carriageway: means a way constituting or comprised in a highway, being a way (other than a cycle track) over which the public have a right of way for the passage of vehicles.

Road: any highway and any other road to which the public has access. A 'highway' will be determined by the establishment of a public right of passage by foot, horseback or vehicle as a result of dedication or long usage. It need not look like a road or be called one in order to qualify as a road. The question of whether a place is a road is one of fact and a car park is not a road as it has a separate function other than enabling movement to a destination.[11]

Notes

1   That is, deliberately.

2   The obstruction need not be across the whole of the highway. Only a part need be obstructed for these offences.

3   Police and Criminal Evidence Act 1984 s.25(3)(d)(iv). See page 284.

4   This section does not apply:

   (a) to the sale of offer or exposure for sale of things from or on a vehicle which is used only for the purpose of itinerant trading with the occupiers of premises, or for purposes other than trading;

   (b) to the sale or exposure for sale of newspapers;

   (c) to anything done at a market; or

   (d) to the sale of anything authorised by a local authority.

5   Unless he shows that he had taken all necessary steps to give adequate warning.

6   This does not apply to any mixing or deposit in a receptacle or on a plate which prevents the substance from coming into contact with the highway or from entering the drains and sewers. Nor does it apply to work done by the highways authority or a person operating under a licence.

7   Does not apply to work carried out so not as to give reasonable cause for annoyance to persons in the vicinity and such work is done otherwise than in the course of a business or for gain or reward. It will be a defence to show that the work was necessary following an accident or breakdown and was carried out within 72 hours or with the permission of a police constable in uniform.

8   The work to which this section applies is works for the repair, maintenance, servicing, improvement or dismantling of, or of any part of or accessory to, a motor vehicle or trailer or work for the installation, replacement or renewal of any such part or accessory.

9   Includes a footpath.

10 'Road' does not include a footpath or bridleway.

11 *Cutter* v *Eagle Star Insurance* (1998).

HOMICIDE

See also Aggravated Vehicle-Taking, Aiding and Abetting, Conspiracy and Incitement, Dangerous and Careless Driving / Riding, Explosives, PACE – Arrest, Wounding and Grievous Bodily Harm

Offence: It is an offence for a person to unlawfully kill any person, under the peace, with malice aforethought, express or implied.

Contrary to: Common Law

Max. sentence: Crown Court: life imprisonment[1].

Power: Arrestable Offence

Offence: It is an offence to solicit, encourage, persuade or endeavour to persuade, or propose to any person, murder of any other person.

Contrary to: Offences Against the Person Act 1861 s.4

Max. sentence: Crown Court: life imprisonment / unlimited fine.

Power: Arrestable Offence

Offence: It is an offence for a person, without lawful excuse, to make to another a threat, intending that the other would fear it would be carried out, to kill that other or a third person.

Contrary to: Offences Against the Person Act 1861 s.16

Max. sentence: Magistrates' Court: 6 months' imprisonment / £5,000 fine.

Crown Court: 10 years' imprisonment / unlimited fine.

Power: Arrestable Offence

Offence:
It is an offence for a person to unlawfully and maliciously administer to, or cause to be administered to, or be taken by, any other person, any poison, or other destructive or noxious thing, so as thereby to endanger the life of such a person.

Contrary to: Offences Against the Person Act 1861 s.23

Max. sentence: Crown Court: 10 years' imprisonment / unlimited fine.

Power: Arrestable Offence

Offence:
It is an offence for a person to unlawfully abandon or expose any child, being under the age of 2 years, whereby the life of such child shall be endangered, or the health of such child shall have been or shall be likely to be permanently injured.

Contrary to: Offences Against the Person Act 1861 s.27

Max. sentence: Magistrates' Court: 6 months' imprisonment / £5,000 fine.

Crown Court: 5 years' imprisonment / unlimited fine.

Power: Arrestable Offence

Offence:
It is an offence:[2]

(a)   for a woman, being with child, with intent to procure her own miscarriage, to unlawfully administer to herself any poison or other noxious thing, or to unlawfully use any instrument or other means whatsoever with like intent; or

(b)   for whosoever with intent to procure the miscarriage of any woman, whether she be or be not with child, to unlawfully administer to her or cause to be taken by her any poison or other noxious thing, or to unlawfully use any instrument or other means whatsoever with the like intent.

Contrary to: Offences Against the Person Act 1861 s.58

Max. sentence: Crown Court: life imprisonment / unlimited fine.

Power: Arrestable Offence

Offence:

It is an offence for a person to unlawfully supply or procure any poison or other noxious thing, or any instrument or thing whatsoever, knowing that the same is intended to be unlawfully used or employed with intent to procure the miscarriage of any woman, whether she be or be not with child.

Contrary to: Offences Against the Person Act 1861 s.59

Max. sentence: Crown Court: 5 years' imprisonment / unlimited fine.

Power: Arrestable Offence

Offence:

It is an offence, if any woman shall be delivered of a child, for any person, by any secret disposition of the dead body of the child to endeavour to conceal the birth thereof.[3]

Contrary to: Offences Against the Person Act 1861 s.60

Max. sentence: Magistrates' Court: 6 months' imprisonment / £5,000 fine.

Crown Court: 2 years' imprisonment / unlimited fine.

Power: Report / s.25 PACE

Offence:

It is an offence[4] for a person, with intent to destroy the life of a child capable of being born alive, by any wilful act to cause a child to die before it has an existence independent of its mother.

Contrary to:	Infant Life (Preservation) Act 1929 s.1(1)
Max. sentence:	Crown Court: life imprisonment / unlimited fine
Power:	Arrestable Offence

Offence: It is an offence of infanticide for a woman, by any wilful act or omission, to cause the death of her child being a child under the age of 12 months whilst, at the time of the act or omission, the balance of her mind was disturbed by reason of her not having fully recovered from the effect of giving birth to the child or by reason of the effect of lactation consequent upon the birth of the child.[5]

Contrary to:	Infanticide Act 1938 s.1(1)
Max. sentence:	Crown Court: life imprisonment / unlimited fine.
Power:	Arrestable Offence

Offence: It is an offence of manslaughter for a person acting in pursuance of a suicide pact between him and another to kill the other or to be a party to the other being killed by a third person.

Contrary to:	Homicide Act 1957 s.4
Max. sentence:	Crown Court: life imprisonment / unlimited fine.
Power:	Arrestable Offence

Offence: It is an offence for a person to aid, abet, counsel or procure the suicide of another, or an attempt by another to commit suicide.

Contrary to:	Suicide Act 1961 s.2(1)
Max. sentence:	Crown Court: 14 years' imprisonment / unlimited fine.
Power:	Arrestable Offence

Definitions

Suicide pact: means a common agreement between two or more persons having for its object the death of all of them, whether or not each is to take his own life, but nothing done by a person who enters into a suicide pact shall be treated as done by him in pursuance of the pact unless it is done while he has the settled intention of dying in pursuance of the pact.

General Information

Where a death arises in the absence of any intention to kill, whilst still containing an unlawful element, the charge will normally be one of manslaughter which is punishable by a maximum term of life imprisonment.[6]

It shall be manslaughter, not murder, for a person acting in pursuance of a suicide pact between him and another to kill the other or be a party to the other being killed by a third person.[7]

Notes

1   This is the only sentence available for this offence.

2   But not if termination is by a registered medical practitioner in line with conditions made out by the Abortion Act 1967.

3   It is irrelevant whether the child died before, at or after its birth.

4   That is, 'child destruction'. For the purposes of this offence, evidence that a woman had at any material time been pregnant for a period of 28 weeks or more shall be *prima facie* proof that she was at the time pregnant of a child capable of being born alive.

5   The effect of this legislation is to reduce a charge from murder to manslaughter allowing a wider range of sentencing options.

6   Offences Against the Person Act 1861 s.5.

7   Homicide Act 1957 s.4(1).

HOSTAGES, KIDNAPPING AND FALSE IMPRISONMENT

See also Absconders and Escapees, Assaults, Children, PACE – Arrest, Sexual Offences

Offence: It is an offence of kidnapping[1] for any person without lawful excuse to take away another person without their consent, by force or by fraud.[2]

Contrary to:	Common Law
Max. sentence:	Crown Court: unlimited
Power:	Arrestable Offence

Offence: It is an offence of false imprisonment for any person without lawful excuse to detain,[3] compel or restrain the personal liberty of another.

Contrary to:	Common Law
Max. sentence:	Crown Court: unlimited
Power:	Arrestable Offence

Offence: It is an offence for any person,[4] to detain any other person and, in order to compel a State, international governmental organisation or person to do or abstain from doing any act, threaten to kill, injure or continue to detain the hostage.

Contrary to:	Taking of Hostages Act 1982 s.1(1)
Max. sentence:	Crown Court: life imprisonment / unlimited fine.[5]
Power:	Arrestable Offence

Offence: It is an offence[6] for any person, connected with a child[7] under 16, to take or send the child out of the United Kingdom without the appropriate consent.[8]

Contrary to:	Child Abduction Act 1984 s.1(1)
Max. sentence:	Magistrates' Court: 6 months' imprisonment / £5,000 fine.
	Crown Court: 7 years' imprisonment / unlimited fine.
Power:	Arrestable Offence

Offence: It is an offence[9] for a person,[10] without lawful authority or reasonable excuse, to take or detain a child under the age of 16:

(a) so as to remove him from the lawful control of any person having lawful control of the child; or

(b) so as to keep him out of the lawful control of any person entitled to lawful control of the child.

Contrary to: Child Abduction Act 1984 s.2(1)

Max. sentence: Magistrates, Court: 6 months' imprisonment / £5,000 fine.

Crown Court: 7 years' imprisonment / unlimited fine.

Power: Arrestable Offence

Offence:

It is an offence for a person, knowingly and without lawful authority or reasonable excuse, to:

(a) take a child to whom this section applies[11] away from the responsible person;[12]

(b) keep such a child away from the responsible person; or

(c) induce, assist or incite a child to run away or stay away from the responsible person.

Contrary to: Children Act 1989 s.49(1)

Max. sentence: Magistrates' Court: 6 months' imprisonment / £5,000 fine.

Power: Report / s.25 PACE[13]

Notes

1   In some circumstances a father may kidnap his own child [*R* v *D* (1984)] and a husband can kidnap his wife [*R* v *Reid* (1973)].

2   Except by or with the consent of the Director of Public Prosecutions no prosecution shall be instituted for an offence of kidnapping if it was committed against a child under the age of 16 and by a person connected with the child.

3   This does not require physical force provided the victim realises that he is under constraint [*Alderson* v *Booth* (1969)].

4   Whatever his nationality.

5   Proceedings require the consent of the Attorney General.

6   No offence is committed by a person in whose favour a residence order is in force if the period is for less than 1 month.

7   That is, parents, guardians and anyone with custody or in whose favour a residence order is in force.

8   The appropriate consent in relation to a child means the consent of:

   (a) the child's mother;

   (b) the child's father, if he has parental responsibility for him;

   (c) any guardian of the child;

   (d) any person in whose favour a residence order is in force with respect to the child;

   (e) any person who has custody of the child;

   (f) the court (under the provisions of Part II of the Children Act 1989);

   (g) if any person has custody of the child, the court which awarded custody.

9   It is a defence for an accused to prove that he was the child's father or believed, on reasonable grounds, that he was the child's father or that he believed that, at the time of the alleged offence, the child had attained the age of 16.

10 Other than the child's father and mother (if married at the time of birth), mother (if the parents were not married at the time of birth), guardian, person with a residence order or a person with custody.

11 This section applies to a child who is in care, the subject of an emergency protection order or in police protection.

12 That is, any person who for the time being has care of the child by virtue of the care order, the emergency protection order, or police officer.

13 See page 284.

INDECENT AND OBSCENE BEHAVIOUR

See also Assaults, Children and Young Persons, Football, Mental Health, Metropolitan Police Act, PACE – Arrest, Post and Mail, Sexual Offences, Public Order, Telecommunications, Town Police Clauses

Offence: It is an offence for a man to wilfully, openly, lewdly and obscenely expose his person,[1] with intent to insult any female.[2]

Contrary to: Vagrancy Act 1824 s.4

Max. sentence: Magistrates' Court: 3 months' imprisonment / £1,000 fine.

Power: Report / s.25 PACE

Offence:

It is an offence for any person in any thoroughfare or public place within the limits of the metropolitan police district, to sell or distribute or offer for sale or distribution, or exhibit to public view, any profane book, paper, print, drawing, painting or representation, or sing any profane, indecent or obscene song or ballad, or use any profane, indecent or obscene language to the annoyance of inhabitants or passengers.

Contrary to: Metropolitan Police Act 1839 s.54 (12)

Max. sentence: Magistrates' Court: £500 fine.

Power: Report / s.25 PACE[3]

Offence:

It is an offence for any person in any police station house to use any violent or indecent behaviour.

Contrary to: Metropolitan Police Act 1839 s.58

Max. sentence: Magistrates' Court: £200 fine.

Power: Report / s.25 PACE

Offence:

It is an offence for any person, in any street[4] to the obstruction, annoyance or danger of the residents or passengers:

(a)   to wilfully and indecently expose his person;

(b)   to publicly offer for sale or distribution or to exhibit to public view any profane book, paper, print, drawing or representation; or

(c)   to sing any profane or obscene song or ballad or use any profane or obscene language.

Contrary to: Town Police Clauses Act 1847 s.28

Max. sentence: Magistrates' Court: 14 days' imprisonment / £200 fine.

Power: Report / s.25 PACE

Offence: It is an offence for any person to be guilty of any violent or indecent behaviour in any police station.

Contrary to: Town Police Clauses Act 1847 s.29

Max. sentence: Magistrates' Court: 1 month's imprisonment / £200 fine.

Power: Report / s.25 PACE

Offence: It is an offence for a man:

(a) to commit an act of gross indecency with another man;[5]

(b) to be a party to the commission by a man of an act of gross indecency with another man; or

(c) to procure the commission by a man of an act of gross indecency.

Contrary to: Sexual Offences Act 1956 s.13(1)

Max. sentence: Magistrates' Court: 6 months' imprisonment / £5,000 fine.

Crown Court: 5 years' imprisonment[6] / unlimited fine.

Power: Arrestable Offence[7]

Offence: It is an offence[8] for a person[9] to make an indecent assault[10] on a woman.

Contrary to: Sexual Offences Act 1956 s.14(1)

Max. sentence: Magistrates' Court: 6 months' imprisonment / £5,000 fine.[11]

Crown Court: 10 years' imprisonment / unlimited fine.

Power: Arrestable Offence

Offence: It is an offence for a person to make an indecent assault on a man.[12]

Contrary to:	Sexual Offences Act 1956 s.15(1)
Max. sentence:	Magistrates' Court: 6 months' imprisonment / £5,000 fine.
	Crown Court: 10 years' imprisonment / unlimited fine.
Power:	Arrestable Offence

Offence:

It is an offence[13] for any person to commit an act of gross indecency with or towards[14] a child under the age of 16,[15] or to incite a child under that age to such an act with him or another.

Contrary to:	Indecency with Children Act 1960 s.1(1)
Max. sentence:	Magistrates' Court: 6 months' imprisonment / £5,000 fine.
	Crown Court: 10 years' imprisonment / unlimited fine.
Power:	Arrestable Offence

Offence:

It is an offence for a person:

(a) to take, or permit to be taken or to make,[16] any indecent photograph or pseudo-photograph of a child;[17]

(b) to distribute[18] or show such indecent photographs or pseudo-photographs;

(c) to have in his possession such indecent photographs or pseudo-photographs, with a view to their being distributed or shown[19] by himself or others; or

(d) to publish or cause to be published any advertisement likely to be understood as conveying that the advertiser distributes or shows such indecent photographs or pseudo-photographs, or intends to do so.

Contrary to:	Protection of Children Act 1978 s.1(1)
Max. sentence:	Magistrates' Court: 6 months' imprisonment / £5,000 fine.[20]
	Crown Court: 10 years' imprisonment / unlimited fine.[21]
Power:	Arrestable Offence

Offence:

It is an offence for any person to cause or permit any indecent matter to be publicly[22] displayed.

Contrary to:	Indecent Displays (Control) Act 1981 s.1(1)
Max. sentence:	Magistrates' Court: 6 months' imprisonment / £5,000 fine.
	Crown Court: 2 years' imprisonment / unlimited fine.
Power:	Report / s.25 PACE

Offence:

It is an offence for a person to have any indecent photograph or pseudo-photograph of a child in his possession.

Contrary to:	Criminal Justice Act 1988 s.160(1)
Max. sentence:	Magistrates' Court: 6 months' imprisonment / £5,000 fine.
	Crown Court: 5 years' imprisonment / unlimited fine.[23]
Power:	Arrestable Offence

General Powers

In respect of the offence under the Indecent Displays (Control) Act 1981 a constable may seize any article which he has reasonable grounds for believing to be or to contain indecent matter and to have been used in the commission of an offence. However, there is no accompanying power of entry other than one authorised by a warrant.

Where a constable has reasonable cause to believe that a child would otherwise be likely to suffer significant harm, he may:

(a)   remove the child to suitable accommodation and keep him there; or

(b)   take such steps as are reasonable to ensure that the child's removal from any hospital, or other place, in which he is then being accommodated is prevented.[24]

Definitions

Psuedo-photograph: means an image, whether made by computer-graphics or otherwise howsoever, which appears to be a photograph.[25]

General Information

A girl under 16 cannot in law, give any consent which would prevent an act being an indecent assault under section 14 of the Sexual Offences Act 1956. Similarly a woman who is a defective[26] cannot give consent to such an assault although an accused will only be found guilty in these circumstances if there is evidence that he knew, or had reason to suspect, that the woman was a defective.

The law relating to homosexual acts is currently governed by the Sexual Offences Act 1967 as amended by the Sexual Offences (Amendment) Act 2000. This permits acts of gross indecency, between men, in circumstances where the men are 16 years of age or older, the act takes place in private and there are no more than two men present. A public lavatory is specifically excluded as a private place.

Notes

1   That is, penis.

2   This offence can be committed in a private place.

3   Consider also Breach of the Peace.

4   The term 'street' is extended to mean any place of public resort or recreation ground belonging to, or under the control of, the local authority, and any unfenced land adjoining or abutting upon any street in an urban district by the Public Health Amendment Act 1906 s.81.

5   In public or private.

6   If the defendant is over 21 and the other person is under 16. Otherwise 2 years.

7   But see note 6.

8   There is a defence available to an accused in circumstances where he believes the woman to be his wife and has reasonable cause for that belief, even though the marriage is invalid due to the woman's age (under 16).

9   Male or female.

10 An assault in indecent circumstances. See page 28.

11 For sex offender orders. See page 375.

12 A boy under 16 cannot in law give any consent which would prevent an act being an assault for the purpose of this section.

13 No defence can be founded on the offender's mistaken belief as to their victim's age, [B v DPP (1998)].

14 No contact or assault is necessary and inactivity on the part of the accused may be sufficient in some cases, for example, where the child accepts an invitation to touch or to watch under indecent circumstances.

15 Raised from 14 to 16 years of age by the Criminal Justice and Court Services Act 2000.

16 The making must be a conscious act. The storage of images on the cache memory of a computer where the 'maker' was unaware of their presence is insufficient, [Atkins v DPP (2000)].

17 For the purposes of the 1978 Act a 'child' is a person under the age of 16 years.

18 For the purposes of the 1978 Act, a person is to be regarded as distributing an indecent photograph or pseudo-photograph if he parts with possession of it to, or exposes or offers it for acquisition by, another person.

19 That is, to others [R v ET (1999)].

20 Proceedings require the consent of the Director of Public Prosecutions.

21 As amended by the Criminal Justice and Court Services Act 2000.

22 That is, displayed in or visible from any public place. This does not include a place to which the public are permitted only on payment which is or includes payment for that display nor any shop, or part of a shop, to which the public can only gain access by passing beyond an adequate warning sign provided, in either case, persons under 18 are not permitted to enter. Other exceptions include museums and art galleries, Crown buildings and plays and films held under their respective governing legislation.

23 As amended by the Criminal Justice and Court Services Act 2000.

24 This is known as 'police protection'. See page 51.

25 But may not include a montage unless some further act takes place to turn the parts into a single piece, for example, making photocopies of the completed montage [Goodland v DPP (2000)].

26 'Defective' means a person suffering from a state of arrested or incomplete development of mind and includes severe impairment of intelligence and social functioning within the meaning of the Mental Health Acts.

See also Assaults, Breach of the Peace, Harassment and Intimidation, Public Order

Offence: It is an offence[1] for a person to wilfully and maliciously break a contract of service or hiring, knowing or having reasonable cause to believe that the probable consequences of doing so, either alone or in combination with others, will be:

(a) to endanger human life or cause serious bodily injury; or

(b) to expose valuable property, whether real or personal, to destruction or serious injury.

Contrary to: Trade Union and Labour Relations (Consolidation) Act 1992 s.240(1)

Max. sentence: Magistrates' Court: 3 months' imprisonment / £500 fine.

Power: Report / s.25 PACE

Offence: It is an offence for a person, with a view to compelling another person to abstain from doing or to do any act which that person has a legal right to do, or abstain from doing, wrongfully and without legal authority:

(a) to use violence to or intimidate that person or his wife or children, or to injure his property;

(b) to persistently follow that person about from place to place;

(c) to hide any tools, clothes or other property owned or used by that person, or to deprive him of or hinder him in the use thereof;

(d) to watch or beset the house or other place where that person resides, works, carries on business or happens to be, or the approach to any such house or place; or

(e)   to follow that person with two or more other persons in a disorderly manner in or through any street or road.

Contrary to: Trade Union and Labour Relations (Consolidation) Act 1992 s.241(1)

Max. sentence: Magistrates' Court: 6 months' imprisonment / £5,000 fine.

Power: A constable may arrest without warrant anyone he reasonably suspects is committing this offence.

General Information

It is lawful for a person in contemplation or furtherance of a trade dispute to picket at or near his own place of work, or if he is an official of a trade union, at or near the place of work of a member of the union whom he is accompanying and whom he represents.

Notes

1   This offence does not apply to seamen who are covered by separate legislation.

KNIVES AND BLADED ARTICLES

See also Burglary, Crossbows, Going Equipped, Offensive Weapons, PACE – Arrest, Schools

Offence: It is an offence for a person to manufacture, sell, hire or offer for sale or hire or expose or have in his possession for the purpose of sale or hire, or lend or give to any person:

(a)   any knife which has a blade which opens automatically by hand pressure applied to a button, spring or other device in or attached to the handle of the knife, sometimes known as a 'flick knife' or 'flick gun'; or

(b) any knife which has a blade which is released from the handle or sheath thereof by the force of gravity or the application of centrifugal force and which, when released, is locked in place by means of a button, spring, lever, or other device, sometimes known as a 'gravity knife'.

Contrary to: Restriction of Offensive Weapons Act 1959 s.1(1)

Max. sentence: Magistrates' Court: 6 months' imprisonment / £5,000 fine.

Power: Report / s.25 PACE

Offence:
It is an offence to import any knife as described in s.1(1).

Contrary to: Restriction of Offensive Weapons Act 1959 s.1(2)

Max. sentence: Magistrates' Court: 6 months' imprisonment / fine.[1]

Crown Court: 7 years' imprisonment / unlimited fine.

Power: Arrestable Offence

Offence:
It is an offence[2] for a person, without lawful authority or good reason, to have with him[3] in a public place, any article which has a blade or is sharply pointed except for a folding pocket-knife[4] which has a cutting edge to its blade not exceeding 3 inches.

Contrary to: Criminal Justice Act 1988 s.139(1)

Max. sentence: Magistrates' Court: 6 months' imprisonment / £5,000 fine.

Crown Court: 2 years' imprisonment / unlimited fine.

Power: Arrestable Offence[5]

Offence: It is an offence for a person, without lawful authority or good reason, to have with him on school premises any article to which s.139 applies.

Contrary to: Criminal Justice Act 1988 s.139A(1)

Max. sentence: Magistrates' Court: 6 months' imprisonment / £5,000 fine.

Crown Court: 2 years' imprisonment / unlimited fine.

Power: Arrestable Offence[6]

Offence: It is an offence[7] for a person to sell to a person under the age of 16 any knife,[8] knife blade, razor blade,[9] axe or any other article which has a blade or is sharply pointed and which is made or adapted for causing injury to the person.

Contrary to: Criminal Justice Act 1988 s.141A

Max. sentence: Magistrates' Court: 6 months' imprisonment / £5,000 fine.

Power: Report / s.25 PACE

Offence: It is an offence for a person to market[10] a knife in a way which:

(a)   indicates, or suggests, that it is suitable for combat;[11] or

(b)   is otherwise likely to stimulate or encourage violent behaviour involving the use of the knife as a weapon.

Contrary to: Knives Act 1997 s.1(1)

Max. sentence: Magistrates' Court: 6 months' imprisonment / £5,000 fine.

Crown Court: 2 years' imprisonment / unlimited fine.

Power: Report / s.25 PACE

Offence: It is an offence for a person to publish any written, pictorial or other material in connection with the marketing of any knife and that material indicates, or suggests, that the knife is suitable for combat; or is otherwise likely to stimulate or encourage violent behaviour involving the use of the knife as a weapon.

Contrary to: Knives Act 1997 s.2(1)

Max. sentence: Magistrates' Court: 6 months' imprisonment / £5,000 fine.

Crown Court: 2 years' imprisonment / unlimited fine.

Power: Report / s.25 PACE

General Powers

Under the provisions of the Police and Criminal Evidence Act 1984 s.1, a constable[12] may search any person or vehicle or anything which is in or on a vehicle, in a public place,[13] for prohibited articles[14] or any article to which s.139 of the Criminal Justice Act 1988 applies, and may detain the person or vehicle for the purpose of such a search.

A constable may enter school premises and search those premises and any person on those premises for any article to which s.139 of the Criminal Justice Act 1988 applies if he has reasonable grounds for believing that an offence under s.139A of the 1988 Act is being, or has been, committed. He may also seize and retain any such article if discovered and may use reasonable force, if necessary, in the exercise of these powers.

Notes

1   Punishment for this offence is controlled by the Customs and Excise Management Act 1979 s.170, which stipulates a fine on summary conviction of up to 3 times the duty payable on any goods.

2   It is a defence for an accused to prove that he had the article with him for use at work, or for religious reasons, or as part of a national costume. A knife which is made, adapted or intended for causing injury to the person is

an offensive weapon for the purposes of an offence under the Prevention of Crimes Act 1953 and is an Arrestable Offence under the Police and Criminal Evidence Act 1984 s.24(2)(k). See page 282.

3   For this offence it is necessary for the prosecution to show possession of the article and actual knowledge of the possession [*R* v *Daubney* (2000)].

4   A lock-knife is not a folding pocket-knife for the purposes of this section [*Harris* v *DPP* (1996), *Fuhmi* v *DPP* (1996), *R* v *Deegan* (1998)].

5   Police and Criminal Evidence Act 1984 s.24(2)(1).

6   Ibid., s.24(2)(m).

7   This offence does not apply to any article described in s.1 of the Restriction of Offensive Weapons Act 1959. It shall be a defence for a person charged with this offence to prove that he took all reasonable precautions and exercised all due diligence to avoid the commission of the offence.

8   But not a folding pocket-knife if the cutting edge of its blade does not exceed 7.62 centimetres (3 inches) [Criminal Justice Act 1988 (Offensive Weapons) (Exemption) Order 1996 s.2.art.2].

9   But not to any razor blade permanently enclosed in a cartridge or housing where less that 2 millimetres of any blade is exposed beyond the plane which intersects the highest point of the surfaces preceding and following such blades.

10 Includes selling, hiring, offering or exposing for sale or hire and having it in his possession for the purpose of sale or hire.

11 Includes being suitable for use as a weapon for inflicting injury on a person as well as causing a person to fear injury.

12 With reasonable grounds for suspecting that he will find stolen or prohibited articles or any article to which s.139 of the Criminal Justice Act 1988 applies.

13 Where the public have access, on payment or otherwise, as of right or by virtue of an express or implied permission. This will also include any other place to which the public have ready access at that time.

14 That is, offensive weapons.

LICENSED PREMISES

See also Children and Young Persons, Drink and Drive / Ride, Drunkenness, Metropolitan Police Act, Noise, Nuisance, Police, Prostitution, Public Order, Town Police Clauses

Offence: It is an offence for any person to supply or authorise the supply of intoxicating liquor on behalf of a club, unless the club is registered[1] in respect of those premises or the liquor is supplied under the authority of a justices' licence held by the club for those premises.

Contrary to: Licensing Act 1964 s.39(1)

Max. sentence: Magistrates' Court: 6 months' imprisonment / £2,500 fine.

Power: Report / s.25 PACE

Offence:

It is an offence for any person to supply or obtain intoxicating liquor by or on behalf of a club, for consumption off the premises except to a member in person.

Contrary to: Licensing Act 1964 s.39(2)

Max. sentence: Magistrates' Court: £1,000 fine.

Power: Report / s.25 PACE

Offence:

It is an offence for any person to supply or obtain intoxicating liquor by or on behalf of a registered club, to a member or guest except at premises in respect of which the club is registered or at any premises or place which the club is using on a special occasion for the accommodation of members and to which persons other than members and their guests are not permitted access.[2]

Contrary to: Licensing Act 1964 s.39(3)

Max. sentence: Magistrates' Court: £1,000 fine.

Power: Report / s.25 PACE

Offence:

It is an offence for the secretary of a registered club to fail, within 28 days, to notify the chief officer of police and the clerk to the local authority of any alteration made to the rules in respect of any premises.

Contrary to:	Licensing Act 1964 s.48
Max. sentence:	Magistrates' Court: £200 fine.
Power:	Report / s.25 PACE

Offence:

It is an offence[3] for any person, except during the permitted hours:

(a) himself, or his servant or agent,[4] to sell or supply to any person in licensed premises or registered club,[5] any intoxicating liquor, whether to be consumed on or off the premises; or

(b) to consume in[6] or take from such premises any intoxicating liquor.[7]

Contrary to:	Licensing Act 1964 s.59
Max. sentence:	Magistrates' Court: £1,000 fine.
Power:	Report / s.25 PACE

Offence:

It is an offence for any person:

(a) to sell or expose for sale by retail, any intoxicating liquor without holding a justices licence, canteen licence or occasional permission authorising the sale of that liquor; or

(b) holding a justices licence, occasional licence, canteen licence or occasional permission to sell or expose for sale by retail any intoxicating liquor except at the place for which that licence or permission authorises the sale of that liquor.

Contrary to:	Licensing Act 1964 s.160(1)
Max. sentence:	Magistrates' Court: 6 months' imprisonment / £2,500 fine.[8]
Power:	Report / s.25 PACE

Offence: It is an offence for the holder of a justices licence to knowingly[9] sell, or supply, intoxicating liquor to persons to whom he is not permitted by the conditions of the licence.

Contrary to: Licensing Act 1964 s.161(1)

Max. sentence: Magistrates' Court: 6 months' imprisonment / £2,500 fine.

Power: Report / s.25 PACE

Offence: It is an offence for the holder of a restaurant or residential licence to knowingly permit intoxicating liquor sold in pursuance of the licence to be consumed on the licensed premises by persons for whose consumption there he is not permitted by the conditions of the licence to sell it.

Contrary to: Licensing Act 1964 s.161(2)

Max. sentence: Magistrates' Court: 6 months' imprisonment / £2,500 fine.

Power: Report / s.25 PACE

Offence: It is an offence for a person, having purchased intoxicating liquor from the holder of a justices 'off' licence, and with the privity or consent of the licence holder, to drink the liquor:

(a) in the licensed premises; or

(b) in premises which adjoin or are near the licensed premises and which belong to the holder of the licence or are under his control or used by his permission, or on a highway adjoining or near those premises.

Contrary to: Licensing Act 1964 s.164(1)

Max. sentence: Magistrates' Court: £500 fine.

Power: Report / s.25 PACE

Offence: It is an offence for the holder of a justices 'off' licence to supply spirits or wine in open vessels.

Contrary to: Licensing Act 1964 s.164(4)

Max. sentence: Magistrates' Court: £200 fine.

Power: Report / s.25 PACE

Offence: It is an offence[10] for the holder of a justices licence to allow, or cause or procure, or attempt to cause or procure, a person under 14 years of age to be in the bar of licensed premises during the permitted hours.[11]

Contrary to: Licensing Act 1964 s.168

Max. sentence: Magistrates' Court: £200 fine.

Power: Report / s.25 PACE

Offence: It is an offence[12] for a person, in licensed premises:

(a) to sell intoxicating liquor to a person under 18;[13]

(b) to knowingly[14] allow any person to sell intoxicating liquor to a person under 18.

Contrary to: Licensing Act 1964 ss.169A and B[15]

Max. sentence: Magistrates' Court: £1,000 fine.

Power: Report / s.25 PACE

Offence: It is an offence[16] for a person, in licensed premises:

(a) to buy or attempt to buy intoxicating liquor under the age of 18; or

(b) to buy or attempt to buy intoxicating liquor on behalf of a person under 18.[17]

Contrary to: Licensing Act 1964 s.169C(1) and (2)

Max. sentence: Magistrates' Court: £1,000 fine.

Power: Report / s.25 PACE

Offence: It is an offence[18] for a person to buy or attempt to

buy intoxicating liquor for consumption in a bar in
licensed premises by a person under 18.

Contrary to: Licensing Act 1964 s.169C(3)

Max. sentence: Magistrates' Court: £1,000 fine.

Power: Report / s.25 PACE

Offence:
It is an offence for a person under 18, in a bar in
licensed premises, to consume intoxicating liquor.

Contrary to: Licensing Act 1964 s.169E(1)

Max. sentence: Magistrates' Court: £1,000 fine.

Power: Report / s.25 PACE

Offence:
It is an offence for a person who works in licensed
premises in a capacity[19] which gives him authority to
prevent consumption, to knowingly allow a person
under 18 to consume intoxicating liquor in a bar.[20]

Contrary to: Licensing Act 1964 s.169E(2)

Max. sentence: Magistrates' Court: £1,000 fine.

Power: Report / s.25 PACE

Offence:
It is an offence for a person who works in licensed
premises[21] to knowingly deliver to a person under
18 intoxicating liquor sold in those premises for
consumption off the premises.

Contrary to: Licensing Act 1964 s.169F(1)

Max. sentence: Magistrates' Court: £1,000 fine.

Power: Report / s.25 PACE

Offence:
It is an offence[22] for a person who works in licensed
premises in a capacity[23] which gives him authority to
prevent the delivery, to knowingly allow any person
to deliver to a person under 18 intoxicating liquor
sold in licensed premises for consumption off the
premises.

Contrary to:	Licensing Act 1964 s.169F(2)
Max. sentence:	Magistrates' Court: £1,000 fine.
Power:	Report / s.25 PACE

Offence:

It is an offence[24] for a person to knowingly send a person under 18[25] for the purpose of obtaining intoxicating liquor sold, or to be sold, in licensed premises for consumption off the premises.

Contrary to:	Licensing Act 1964 s.169G(1)
Max. sentence:	Magistrates' Court: £1,000 fine.
Power:	Report / s.25 PACE

Offence:

It is an offence for the holder of a justices licence to employ a person under 18 in a bar of licensed premises at a time when the bar is open for the sale or consumption of intoxicating liquor.

Contrary to:	Licensing Act 1964 s.170(1)
Max. sentence:	Magistrates' Court: £200 fine.
Power:	Report / s.25 PACE

Offence:

It is an offence to allow a person under 18 in off-licensed premises, or off-sales departments of on-licensed premises to make any sale of intoxicating liquor unless the sale has been specifically approved by the holder of the licence or by a person of or over the age of 18 acting on his behalf.

Contrary to:	Licensing Act 1964 s.171A(1)
Max. sentence:	Magistrates' Court: £200 fine.
Power:	Report / s.25 PACE

Offence:

It is an offence for the holder of a justices licence to permit drunkenness or any violent, quarrelsome or riotous conduct to take place in the licensed premises.

Contrary to:	Licensing Act 1964 s.172(1)
Max. sentence:	Magistrates' Court: £1,000 fine.[26]
Power:	Report / s.25 PACE

Offence:

It is an offence for the holder of a justices licence to sell intoxicating liquor to a drunken person.

Contrary to:	Licensing Act 1964 s.172(3)
Max. sentence:	Magistrates' Court: £500 fine.
Power:	Report / s.25 PACE

Offence:

It is an offence for a relevant person[27] to permit drunkenness or any violent, quarrelsome or riotous conduct to take place in the licensed premises.

Contrary to:	Licensing Act 1964 s.172A(1) [28]
Max. sentence:	Magistrates' Court: £1,000 fine.
Power:	Report / s.25 PACE

Offence:

It is an offence for a relevant person to sell intoxicating liquor to a drunken person.

Contrary to:	Licensing Act 1964 s.172A(3) [29]
Max. sentence:	Magistrates' Court: £1,000 fine.
Power:	Report / s.25 PACE

Offence:

It is an offence for any person in licensed premises to procure or attempt to procure any intoxicating liquor for consumption by a drunken person or who aids a drunken person in obtaining or consuming intoxicating liquor in licensed premises.

Contrary to:	Licensing Act 1964 s.173
Max. sentence:	Magistrates' Court: 1 month imprisonment / £200 fine.
Power:	Report / s.25 PACE

Offence: It is an offence for any person liable to be expelled from licensed premises, when requested by the holder of the justices licence, his agent or servant, the relevant person or any agent or servant of his, or any constable, to leave the premises, to fail to do so.

Contrary to: Licensing Act 1964 s.174(2)

Max. sentence: Magistrates' Court: £200 fine.

Power: Report / s.25 PACE

Offence: It is an offence for the holder of a justices licence:

(a)   to knowingly suffer to remain on the licensed premises any constable during any part of the time appointed for the constable's being on duty, except for the purposes of the execution of the constable's duty;

(b)   to supply any liquor or refreshment, whether by way of gift or sale, to any constable on duty except by authority of a superior officer of the constable; or

(c)   to bribe or attempt to bribe any constable.

Contrary to: Licensing Act 1964 s.178

Max. sentence: Magistrates' Court: £500 fine.

Power: Report / s.25 PACE

Offence: It is an offence for the licence holder, or any person in his employ or acting with his consent, to fail to admit a constable who demands entry to licensed premises.

Contrary to: Licensing Act 1964 s.186(2)

Max. sentence: Magistrates' Court: £200 fine.

Power: Report / s.25 PACE

General Powers

A constable may enter any licensed premises during permitted hours for the purpose of preventing or detecting any offence contrary to the Licensing Act 1964.[30]

A constable may enter any licensed premises at any time outside permitted hours when he reasonably suspects that an offence contrary to the Licensing Act 1964 is being committed or about to be committed.[31]

Any constable shall, on the demand of the holder of a justices licence or his agent or servant, help to expel from the licensed premises any person liable to be expelled from them, and may use such force as may be required for the purpose.[32]

Definitions

Intoxicating liquor: means any spirits, wine, beer, cider and any other fermented, distilled or spirituous liquor of an original gravity exceeding 1016 and a strength exceeding 1.2 per cent.

Bar: a place exclusively or mainly used for the sale and consumption of intoxicating liquor.

Permitted hours: currently 11.00 to 23.00 hours (weekdays), 12.00 to 22.30 hours (Sundays and Good Friday) and 12.00 to 15.00 hours and 19.00 to 22.30 hours (Christmas Day) for premises with an 'on' licence. 'Off' licences may open 08.00 to 23.00 hours (weekdays), 10.00 to 22.30 hours (Sundays), 08.00 to 22.30 hours (Good Friday) and 12.00 to 15.00 hours and 19.00 to 22.30 hours (Christmas Day).[33]

Registered club: means a club holding a registration certificate for which it qualifies by having rules which comply with s.41 of the Licensing Act 1964. These include the club being established in good faith, having not less than 25 members and intoxicating liquor is only supplied by or on behalf of the club. Members may not be admitted with less than an interval of 2 days between application and admission and the rules of the club must be notified to the police and to the magistrates.

Notes

1   See *Definitions*.

2   At any premises or place other than the premises in respect of which the club is registered, intoxicating liquor shall only be supplied for consumption in the premises or place.

3   This section does not apply to intoxicating liquor sold under an occasional licence. It also does not prohibit or restrict sale, supply or consumption by residents, to traders for the purposes of trade, to guests of a *bona fide* resident at his expense or employees at the expense of the employer.

4   The licensee will be liable vicariously for any act of his servant or agent which falls within the scope of their employment. This is the case regardless of any express order to the contrary which is disobeyed.

5   That is, in the premises for which the club is registered.

6   Regardless of where the liquor was obtained from.

7   No offence occurs where the consumption or taking away occurs during the first 20 minutes after the end of permitted hours or 30 minutes in the case of consumption by a person taking a meal there, provided that the liquor was supplied for consumption as an ancillary to the meal.

8   An offender's licence will be forfeit on a second conviction and he may be disqualified from holding a licence for 5 years. On a third conviction an offender may be disqualified for life.

9   This includes someone who deliberately looks away [*Ross* v *Moss* (1965)].

10 The holder of a justices licence may now apply for a children's certificate permitting children to be in any area of licensed premises which consists of or includes a bar. The existence of such a certificate, together with its conditions, must be displayed on a notice in some conspicuous place; see Licensing Act 1964 s.68A.

11 It is a defence for the licensee to show that he exercised all due diligence to prevent the commission of this offence or that the person under 14 had apparently attained that age. No offence is committed if the person under 14 is the licensee's child, resides in the premises or is merely passing through the bar in order to get to another part of the premises, there being no other convenient means of doing so. No offence is committed in premises that have another *bona fide* use other than that of supplying alcohol and where the supply is merely ancillary to the other use, for example, railway refreshment rooms.

12 No offence occurs in the case of a person who has attained the age of 16, the intoxicating liquor is beer, porter or cider and its sale is for consumption at a meal in a part of the licensed premises which is not a bar and is usually set aside for the service of meals.

13 It is a defence to prove that there was no reason to suspect that the person was under 18 or to prove that he had exercised all due diligence to avoid the commission of the offence by another's act or default.

14 Applies to a person who works in the premises in a capacity, whether paid or unpaid, which gives him authority to prevent the sale.

15 As amended by the Licensing (Young Persons) Act 2000.

16 In respect of (a) and (b) no offence occurs in the case of a person who has attained the age of 16, the intoxicating liquor is beer, porter or cider and its sale is for consumption at a meal in a part of the licensed premises which is not a bar and is usually set aside for the service of meals.

17 It is defence to prove that there was no reason to suspect that the person was under 18.

18 It is defence to prove that there was no reason to suspect that the person was under 18.

19 Whether paid or unpaid.

20 In licensed premises.

21 Whether paid or unpaid.

22 Section 169F(1) and (2) do not apply where:

    (a) the delivery is made at the residence or working place of the purchaser; or

    (b) the person under 18 works in the licensed premises in a capacity, whether paid or unpaid, which includes the delivery of intoxicating liquor.

23 Whether paid or unpaid.

24 This applies regardless of whether the liquor is to be obtained from licensed premises or from other premises from which it is delivered in pursuance of the sale.

25 This does not apply where the person under 18 works in the licensed premises where the sale has been or is to be made, in a capacity, whether paid or unpaid, which includes the delivery of intoxicating liquor.

26 As amended by the Criminal Justice and Police Act 2001 s.32(1), when in force.

27 That is, a person who works in licensed premises in any capacity, whether paid or unpaid, and has the authority to prevent drunkeness.

28 As inserted by the Criminal Justice and Police Act 2001 s.32(1), when in force.

29 As inserted by the Criminal Justice and Police Act 2001 s.32(1), when in force.

30 Licensing Act 1964 s.186(1). A power of entry exists for an occasional licence during the times specified within the licence.

31 Ibid., s.186(1).

32 Ibid., s.174(3). The licence holder may refuse to admit to, or may expel
    from, the licensed premises any person who is drunken, violent,
    quarrelsome or disorderly, or whose presence in the licensed premises
    would subject the licence holder to a penalty under the Licensing Act 1964.

33 These may however be varied by the Licensing Committee to suit the
    particular needs of an area.

LIGHTS ON VEHICLES

See also Construction and Use, Drivers and Riders

Offence: It is an offence for a vehicle to be fitted with a lamp
or retro reflective material, which is capable of
showing a red light to the front.[1]

Contrary to: Road Vehicles Lighting Regulations 1989 r.11(1)

Max. sentence: Magistrates' Court: £2,500 fine.

Power: Report / s.25 PACE

Offence: It is an offence for a vehicle to be fitted with a lamp
or retro reflective material which is capable of
showing any light to the rear, other than a red light.[2]

Contrary to: Road Vehicles Lighting Regulations 1989 r.11(2)

Max. sentence: Magistrates' Court: £2,500 fine.

Power: Report / s.25 PACE

Offence: It is an offence for a person to use, or cause or
permit to be used, on a road any vehicle to which, or
to any load or equipment to which, there is fitted a
lamp, reflector or marking which is capable of
being moved by swivelling, deflecting or otherwise
while the vehicle is in motion.[3]

Contrary to: Road Vehicles Lighting Regulations 1989 r.12(1)

Max. sentence: Magistrates' Court: £2,500 fine.

Power: Report / s.25 PACE

Offence: It is an offence for a vehicle to be fitted with a lamp which automatically emits a flashing light.[4]

Contrary to: Road Vehicles Lighting Regulations 1989 r.13(1)

Max. sentence: Magistrates' Court: £2,500 fine.

Power: Report / s.25 PACE

Offence: It is an offence for a vehicle, other than an emergency vehicle, to be fitted with:

(a)   a blue warning beacon or special warning lamp; or

(b)   a device which resembles a blue beacon or a special warning lamp, whether in working order or not.

Contrary to: Road Vehicles Lighting Regulations 1989 r.16(1)

Max. sentence: Magistrates' Court: £2,500 fine.

Power: Report / s.25 PACE

Offence: It is an offence for a vehicle of a class specified not to be fitted with lamps, reflectors, rear markings and devices which are specified by these regulations.[5]

Contrary to: Road Vehicles Lighting Regulations 1989 r.18(1)

Max. sentence: Magistrates' Court: £2,500 fine.

Power: Report / s.25 PACE

Offence: It is an offence for a person to use, or cause or permit to be used, on a road a vehicle unless every lamp, reflector, rear marking and device is in good working order and, in the case of a lamp, clean.[6]

Contrary to: Road Vehicles Lighting Regulations 1989 r.23(1)

Max. sentence: Magistrates' Court: £2,500 fine.

Power: Report / s.25 PACE

Offence: It is an offence for a person:

(a)   to use, or cause or permit to be used, on a road any vehicle which is in motion between sunset and sunrise, or in seriously reduced visibility between sunrise and sunset; or

(b)   to allow to remain at rest, or cause or permit to be allowed to remain at rest, on a road any vehicle between sunset and sunrise,

unless every front position lamp, rear position lamp, rear registration plate lamp, side marker lamp and end-outline marker lamp with which the vehicle is required to be fitted is kept lit and unobscured.

Contrary to: Road Vehicles Lighting Regulations 1989 r.24(1)

Max. sentence: Magistrates' Court: £2,500 fine.

Power: Report / s.25 PACE

Offence:

It is an offence for a person to use, or cause or permit to be used, on a road a vehicle which is fitted with obligatory dipped-beam headlamps unless every such lamp is kept lit:

(a)   during the hours of darkness, except on a restricted road,[7] and

(b)   in seriously reduced visibility.

Contrary to: Road Vehicles Lighting Regulations 1989 r.25(1)

Max. sentence: Magistrates' Court: £2,500 fine.

Power: Report / s.25 PACE

Offence:

It is an offence for a person to use, or cause or permit to be used, on a road any vehicle on which any lamp or hazard warning signal device is being used in a prohibited manner; that is:

Headlamp

Used so as to cause undue dazzle or discomfort to other persons using the road or lit when the vehicle is parked.

Front fog lamp

> Used so as to cause undue dazzle or discomfort to other persons using the road, lit at any time other than in conditions of seriously reduced visibility, or lit when the vehicle is parked.

Rear fog lamp

> Used so as to cause undue dazzle or discomfort to other persons using the road, lit at any time other than in conditions of seriously reduced visibility, or lit when the vehicle is parked.[8]

Reversing lamp

> Used so as to be lit except for the purpose of reversing the vehicle.

Hazard warning device

> Used other than:
>
> (a) to warn persons using the road of a temporary obstruction when the vehicle is at rest;
>
> (b) on a motorway or unrestricted dual-carriageway, to warn following drivers of a need to slow down due to a temporary obstruction ahead; or
>
> (c) in the case of a bus, to summon assistance or when children under 16 are entering or leaving.

Contrary to: Road Vehicles Lighting Regulations 1989 r.27

Max. sentence: Magistrates' Court: £2,500 fine.

Power: Report / s.25 PACE

General Powers

The provisions of r.74 of the Road Vehicles (Construction and Use) Regulations 1986 apply in respect of lighting equipment and reflectors in the same way as it applies to brakes, silencers, steering gear and tyres.[9]

General Information

The regulations are intricate and contain lists of exceptions. Generally any motor vehicle having 3 or more wheels is required to have front side lights, a dipped-beam headlamp and a main beam headlamp, direction indicators, a hazard warning device, side marker lamps, rear side lights, a rear fog lamp, stop lamps, and a rear registration plate lamp.

While these regulations stipulate that obligatory front lamps must be white or selective yellow the newer blue laser bulbs also fall within the colour range acceptable to the regulations.

The lamps detailed in r.24 do not need to be lit between the hours of sunset and sunrise when parked on a road on which a speed limit of 30 mph or less is in force provided the vehicle:[10]

(a) is parked in a designated parking place or a parking place which is set apart; or

(b) in a lay-by; or

(c) is parked with its near side as close as may be, and parallel, to the edge of the carriageway[11] and no part of the vehicle is less than 10 metres from a junction.

Notes

1   The exceptions include a red and white chequered domed lamp or a red and white segmented mast mounted warning beacon fitted to a fire service control vehicle, a side marker and a traffic sign.

2   The long list of exceptions include the amber light from a direction indicator or side marker lamp, the white light from a reversing lamp, the light to illuminate the interior of the vehicle, the rear registration plate light and the lights used by police, fire and ambulance units in an emergency.

3   Exceptions include a headlamp which can be dipped only by movement of the headlamp or its reflector, a headlamp or fog lamp which can be totally or partially retracted or concealed, a work lamp and a warning beacon.

4   Exceptions include a direction indicator, a warning beacon and a lamp fitted to a vehicle used for police purposes.

5　The specifications for lights and the vehicles to which they must be fitted are contained in Sch.1 to the Road Vehicles Lighting Regulations 1989.

6　This subsection applies to every front and rear position lamp (side lights), headlamp, rear registration plate lamp, side marker lamp, end-outline marker lamp, rear fog lamp, retro reflector, stop lamp, direction indicator, running lamp, dim-dip device and hazard warning signal device. It does not apply to a defective lamp on a vehicle in use on a road between sunrise and sunset if such became defective during the journey in progress or if arrangements have been made to remedy the defect with all reasonable expedition.

7　Identifiable by a system of street lighting no more than 200 yards apart.

8　Save in the case of an emergency vehicle.

9　Regulation 74 provides for testing and inspection by authorised police officers. See page 61.

10　Being a goods vehicle with an unladen weight which does not exceed 1,525 kg, a passenger vehicle other than a bus, an invalid carriage, a motor cycle or a pedal cycle and not being a vehicle to which a trailer is attached.

11　Or on either side in a one-way street.

LITTER

See also Abandoned Vehicles, Highways and Roads, Parks, Gardens and Open Spaces

Offence:　It is an offence[1] for any person to throw any rubbish into any town garden.

Contrary to:　Town Gardens Protection Act 1863 s.5

Max. sentence:　Magistrates' Court: 14 days' imprisonment / £200 fine.

Power:　Report / s.25 PACE

Offence:　It is an offence for any person, without lawful authority, to abandon on any land in the open air, or on any other land forming part of a highway, any thing other than a motor vehicle, being a thing which he has brought to the land for the purpose of abandoning it there.[2]

Contrary to:	Refuse Disposal (Amenity) Act 1978 s.2(1)(b)
Max. sentence:	Magistrates' Court: 3 months' imprisonment / £2,500 fine.[3]
Power:	Report / s.25 PACE

Offence: It is an offence for a person, without lawful authority or excuse, to allow any filth, dirt, lime or other offensive matter or thing to run or flow on to a highway from any adjoining premises.

Contrary to:	Highways Act 1980 s.161(4)
Max. sentence:	Magistrates' Court: £200 fine.
Power:	Report / s.25 PACE

Offence: It is an offence for any person to wilfully remove or otherwise interfere with any litter bin or notice board provided or erected under this Act.[4]

Contrary to:	Litter Act 1983 s.5(9)
Max. sentence:	Magistrates' Court: £200 fine.
Power:	Report / s.25 PACE

Offence: It is an offence[5] for a person to throw down, drop or otherwise deposit in, into or from any place to which this section applies, and leave, any thing whatsoever in such circumstances as to cause, or contribute to, or tend to lead to, the defacement by litter of any such a place.

Contrary to:	Environmental Protection Act 1990 s.87(1)
Max. sentence:	Magistrates' Court: £2,500 fine.
Power:	Report / s.25 PACE

General Information

The Environmental Protection Act 1990 applies to any public open place[6] and, in so far as the place is not a public open place, also includes any relevant highway or relevant road and any trunk road which is a special road;[7] any place on relevant land of a principal litter authority; any place on relevant Crown land; any place on relevant land of a designated educational institution; any place on relevant land within a litter control area.

Notes

1   This section applies to any enclosed garden or ornamental garden set aside in any public square, crescent, circus, street or other public place for the use or enjoyment of the inhabitants in any city or borough but does not apply to Crown property.

2   For the purposes of this offence, a person who leaves any thing on any land in such circumstances or for such period that he may reasonably be assumed to have abandoned it or to have brought it to the land for the purpose of abandoning it there shall be deemed to have done so unless the contrary is shown.

3   On an application by the local authority, a person convicted of this offence may be required to repay any removal costs.

4   The Litter Act 1983, together with s.185 of the Highways Act 1980, places a duty on local authorities to provide litter bins. Any removal or interference will be an offence regardless of which of the two Acts a bin was sited and maintained under.

5   No offence is committed if the depositing and leaving was authorised by law or done with the consent of the owner or occupier.

6   A 'public open place' is a place in the open air to which the public are entitled or permitted to have access without payment; and any covered place open to the air on at least one side. This will not include a four-sided telephone kiosk, [*Felix* v *DPP* (1998)].

7   Every highway which is maintainable at public expense, other than a trunk road which is a special road, is a 'relevant highway'.

MENTAL HEALTH

See also Absconders and Escapees, Sexual Offences

Offence: It is an offence:[1]

(a)   for a man who is an officer on the staff of or is otherwise employed in, or is one of the managers of, a hospital or mental nursing home to have unlawful sexual intercourse with a woman, buggery with another man or an act of gross indecency with another man, who is for the time being receiving treatment for mental disorder in that hospital or home, or to do such on the premises of which the hospital or home forms part with a person receiving treatment as an out-patient; and

(b)   for a man to commit such an act with a person who is a mentally disordered patient and who is subject to his guardianship or is otherwise in his custody or care under the Mental Health Act 1983.

Contrary to: Mental Health Act 1959 s.128(1)

Max. sentence: Crown Court: 2 years' imprisonment / unlimited fine.

Power: Report / s.25 PACE

Offence:

It is an offence for any person who is an officer on the staff of, or otherwise employed in, or who is one of the managers of, a hospital or mental nursing home to ill-treat[2] or wilfully to neglect any patient receiving treatment as an in-patient or to ill-treat or wilfully to neglect, on the premises of which the hospital or home forms part, a patient receiving such treatment as an out-patient.

Contrary to: Mental Health Act 1983 s.127(1)

Max. sentence: Magistrates' Court: 6 months' imprisonment / £5,000 fine.

Crown Court: 2 years' imprisonment / unlimited fine.

Power: Report / s.25 PACE

Offence:

It is an offence for a person to ill-treat or wilfully to neglect a mentally disordered patient who is for the time being subject to his guardianship or otherwise in his custody or care.

Contrary to: Mental Health Act 1983 s.127(2)

Max. sentence: Magistrates' Court: 6 months' imprisonment / £5,000 fine.

Crown Court: 2 years' imprisonment / unlimited fine.

Power: Report / s.25 PACE

Offence:

It is an offence for a person to ill-treat or wilfully to neglect a mentally disordered patient who is for the time being subject to after-care under supervision.

Contrary to: Mental Health Act 1983 s.127(2A)

Max. sentence: Magistrates' Court: 6 months' imprisonment / £5,000 fine.

Crown Court: 2 years' imprisonment / unlimited fine.

Power: Report / s.25 PACE

Offence:

It is an offence for any person to induce or knowingly assist another person who is liable to be detained in a hospital, or is subject to guardianship, within the meaning of this Act to absent himself without leave or to knowingly harbour a patient who is absent without leave or is otherwise at large, or to give him any assistance with intent to prevent, hinder or interfere with his being taken into custody or returned to the hospital or other place where he ought to be.

Contrary to: Mental Health Act 1983 s.128

Max. sentence: Magistrates' Court: 6 months' imprisonment / £5,000 fine.

Crown Court: 2 years' imprisonment / unlimited fine.

Power: Report / s.25 PACE

General Powers

If a constable finds in a place to which the public have access a person who appears to him to be suffering from mental disorder and to be in immediate need of care or control, the constable may, if he thinks it necessary to do so in the interests of that person or for the protection of other persons, remove that person to a place of safety where he may be detained for a maximum of 72 hours for the purpose of enabling him to be examined by a registered medical practitioner and interviewed by an approved social worker.[3]

If a person absconds from a place to which he has been remanded under s.35,[4] s.38,[5] or s.137[6] of the Mental Health Act 1983 or while being conveyed to or from that place, he may be arrested without warrant by any constable.[7]

Definitions

Mental disorder: means mental illness, arrested or incomplete development of mind, psychopathic disorder and any other disorder or disability of mind.

Severe mental impairment: means a state of arrested or incomplete development of mind which includes severe impairment of intelligence and social functioning and is associated with abnormally aggressive or seriously irresponsible conduct on the part of the person concerned.

Mental impairment: means a state of arrested or incomplete development of mind (not amounting to severe mental impairment) which includes significant impairment of intelligence and social functioning and is associated with abnormally aggressive or seriously irresponsible conduct on the part of the person concerned.

Psychopathic disorder: means a persistent disorder or disability of mind (whether or not including significant impairment of intelligence) which results in abnormally aggressive or seriously irresponsible conduct on the part of the person concerned.

Place of safety: means residential accommodation provided by a local social services authority, a hospital, a police station, a mental nursing home, a residential home for mentally disordered persons or any other suitable place.

Section 2 order: compulsory admission for assessment. Application is by nearest relative or approved social worker and requires the approval of two doctors. Admission is for 28 days only.

Section 3 order: compulsory admission for treatment. Initially for six months but renewable.

Section 4 order: emergency admission for assessment requiring the approval of only one doctor. Admission is for a maximum of 72 hours.

Section 5 order: compulsory admission for voluntary in-patients. Lasts for a maximum of 72 hours.

Notes

1   It shall not be an offence if he did not know and had no reason to believe that the other person was a mentally disordered patient. The consent of the Director of Public Prosecutions is required before any proceedings may be initiated for this offence.

2   Requires some deliberate conduct. [*R* v *Newington* (1990)].

3   Mental Health Act 1983 s.136.

4   This section is concerned with remands to a hospital in cases where a criminal offence has been committed and the accused is suffering from mental illness, psychopathic disorder, severe mental impairment or mental impairment.

5   That is, under an interim hospital order.

6   Any person required or authorised by or by virtue of this Act to be conveyed to any place or to be kept in custody or detained in a place of safety shall be deemed to be in lawful custody.

7   Mental Health Act 1983 s.138.

METROPOLITAN POLICE ACT

See also Animals, Begging, Damage, Dogs, Drivers and Riders, Firearms – Criminal Use, Fireworks, Highways and Roads, Indecent and Obscene Behaviour, Litter, Loudspeakers, Noise, Nuisance, Straying Animals, Town Police Clauses

Offence: It is an offence for a person, within the limits of the metropolitan police district, in any thoroughfare or public place,[1] to:

(1) expose[2] for show or sale,[3] or feed or fodder, any horse or other animal, or show any caravan containing any animal or any other show or public entertainment, or shoe, bleed or farry any horse or animal,[4] or clean, dress, exercise, train, or break any horse or animal, or clean, make or repair any part of any cart or carriage;[5]

(2) turn loose any horse or cattle, or suffer to be at large any unmuzzled ferocious dog, or set on or urge any dog or other animal to attack, worry, or put in fear any person, horse or other animal;

(3) cause any mischief to be done by negligence or ill-usage in driving cattle, or in anywise misbehave in the driving, care or management of such cattle, or to wantonly and unlawfully pelt, drive or hunt any such cattle;

(4) ride[6] on any part of any cart or carriage, or on the shafts, or on any horse or other animal drawing the same, without having and holding the reins, or to be at such a distance from such cart or carriage as not to have the complete control over every horse or other animal drawing the same;

(5) ride or drive furiously so as to endanger the life or limb of any person, or to the common danger of the passengers in any thoroughfare;

(6) cause any cart, public carriage, sledge, truck or barrow, with or without horses, to stand

longer than may be necessary for loading or unloading or for taking up or setting down passengers,[7] or, by means of any cart, carriage, sledge, truck or barrow or any horse or other animal, wilfully interrupt any public crossing, or wilfully cause any obstruction in any thoroughfare;

(7) lead or ride any horse or other animal, or draw or drive any cart or carriage, sledge, truck or barrow, upon any footway or curbstone, or fasten any horse or other animal so that it can stand upon or across any footway;

(8) roll or carry any cask, tub, hoop, or wheel, or any ladder, plank, pole, showboard or placard, upon any footway except for the purpose of loading or unloading any cart or carriage, or of crossing the footway;

(9) wilfully disregard or not conform to the regulations[8] or directions which the commissioners of police shall have made for regulating the route of horses, carts or carriages or for preventing obstructions during public processions;

(10) affix, without the consent of the owner or occupier, any posting bill or other paper against or upon any building, wall, fence or pale, or write upon, soil, deface or mark any such building, wall, fence or pale with chalk or paint, or in any other way whatsoever, or wilfully break, destroy, or damage any part of any such building, wall, fence or pale, or any fixture or appendage thereunto, or any tree, shrub or seat in any public walk, park or garden;

(12) sell or distribute, or offer for sale or distribution, or exhibit to public view, any profane book, paper, print, drawing, painting or representation, or sing any profane, indecent or obscene song or ballad, or use any profane, indecent or obscene language to the annoyance of the inhabitants or passengers;

(14) blow any horn or use any other noisy instrument for the purpose of calling persons together, or of announcing any show or entertainment, or for the purpose of hawking, selling, distributing or collecting any article whatsoever, or of obtaining money or alms;

(15) wantonly discharge any firearm or throw or discharge any stone or other missile to the damage or danger of any person, or make any bonfire or throw or set fire to any firework;

(16) wilfully and wantonly disturb any inhabitants by pulling or ringing any door-bell or knocking at any door without lawful excuse, or to wilfully and unlawfully extinguish the light of any lamp;

(17) fly any kite or play any game to the annoyance of the inhabitants or passengers, or make or use any slide upon ice or snow in any street or other thoroughfare, to the common danger of passengers.

Contrary to: Metropolitan Police Act 1839 s.54

Max. sentence: Magistrates' Court: £500 fine.

Power: Report / s.25 PACE

Notes

1   Undefined.

2   To the annoyance of the inhabitants or passengers.

3   Except in an authorised market.

4   Except in cases of accident or emergency.

5   Except in cases of accident where repair on the spot is necessary.

6   Being the person having the care of such cart or carriage.

7   Except hackney carriages standing for hire in any place not forbidden by law.

8   Having first been acquainted with them.

MIRRORS

See also Construction and Use, Drivers and Riders

Offence: It is an offence for a motor vehicle of any class not to be fitted with such mirror or mirrors as specified.

Contrary to: Road Vehicles (Construction and Use) Regulations 1986 r.33(1)

Max. sentence: Magistrates' Court: £2,500 fine.[1]

Power: Report / s.25 PACE

Offence: It is an offence, in the case of a motor vehicle first used on or after 1 April 1969, for the edges of any mirror fitted internally not to be surrounded by some material such as will render it unlikely that severe cuts would be caused if the mirror were struck by the occupant of the vehicle.

Contrary to: Road Vehicles (Construction and Use) Regulations 1986 r.33(3)

Max. sentence: Magistrates' Court: £1,000 fine.

Power: Report / s.25 PACE

Offence: It is an offence[2] to fail to comply with any of the following requirements:

(a)   each mirror shall be fixed to the vehicle in such a way that it remains steady under normal driving conditions;

    (b)   each exterior mirror shall be visible to the driver;

    (c)   each interior mirror shall be capable of being adjusted by the driver when in his driving position;

    (d)   except in the case of a mirror which, if knocked out of its alignment, can be returned to its former position without needing to be adjusted, each exterior mirror on the driver's side of the vehicle shall be capable of being adjusted from the driver's position.[3]

Contrary to: Road Vehicles (Construction and Use) Regulations 1986 r.33(4)

Max. sentence: Magistrates' Court: £1,000 fine.

Power: Report / s.25 PACE

General Information

Generally a wheeled motor vehicle is required to have fitted the following:

(a)   at least one mirror fitted externally on the off side of the vehicle; and

(b)   at least one mirror fitted internally, unless a mirror so fitted would give the driver no view to the rear of the vehicle; and

(c)   at least one mirror fitted externally on the near side of the vehicle unless a mirror which gives the driver an adequate view to the rear is fitted internally.

There is no requirement for mirrors to be fitted to a two-wheeled motor cycle with, or without, a side-car attached.

Notes

1   In the case of a goods vehicle or one designed for the carrying of more than 8 passengers. In any other case the maximum fine is £1,000.

2   This offence can be committed by a wheeled motor vehicle first used on or after 1 June 1978 but which is not a locomotive, motor tractor, a bus, a goods vehicle or a two-wheeled motor cycle. These are, however, subject to similar regulations under a variety of EC Directives.

3   This provision does not prevent the mirror from being locked into position
     from outside the vehicle.

MOTOR CYCLES

See also Construction and Use, Drivers and Riders, Driving Documents,
Driving Off-Road, Excise Licences, Lights on Vehicles, Pedal Cycles,
Registration and Licensing, Trailers

Offence: It is an offence for a motor cycle first used on or
after 1 April 1986 to be fitted with any sidestand[1]
which is capable of:

(a)   disturbing the stability or direction of the
      motor cycle when it is in motion under its own
      power; or

(b)   closing automatically if the angle of the
      inclination of the motor cycle is inadvertently
      altered when it is stationary.

Contrary to: Road Vehicles (Construction and Use) Regulations
1986 r.38

Max. sentence: Magistrates' Court: £1,000 fine.

Power: Report / s.25 PACE

Offence: It is an offence for any person to use, cause or
permit to be used on a road a motor cycle which
does not meet the noise limit requirements set by
regulations.[2]

Contrary to: Road Vehicles (Construction and Use) Regulations
1986 r.57B

Max. sentence: Magistrates' Court: £1,000 fine.

Power: Report / s.25 PACE

Offence: It is an offence for any person to use, cause or
permit to be used on a road any two-wheeled motor
cycle registered on or after 1 August 1981, not
being a motor cycle brought temporarily into Great

Britain by a person resident abroad, if there is a side-car attached to the right (or off) side of the motor cycle.

Contrary to: Road Vehicles (Construction and Use) Regulations 1986 r.93

Max. sentence: Magistrates' Court: £1,000 fine.

Power: Report / s.25 PACE

Offence:

It is an offence for any person to be carried astride a two-wheeled motor cycle, on a road, in addition to the driver without suitable supports or rests for the feet being available on the motor cycle for that person.

Contrary to: Road Vehicles (Construction and Use) Regulations 1986 r.102

Max. sentence: Magistrates' Court: £1,000 fine.

Power: Report / s.25 PACE

Offence:

It is an offence:

(a) for more than one person in addition to the driver to be carried on a motor bicycle;

(b) for a person carried in addition to the driver to be carried otherwise than sitting astride the motor cycle and on a proper seat securely fixed to the motor cycle behind the driver's seat.

Contrary to: Road Traffic Act 1988 s.23

Max. sentence: Magistrates' Court: £1,000 fine.

Power: Report / s.25 PACE

Offence:

It is an offence for a person:

(a) to contravene or fail to comply with any construction and use requirement as to brakes, steering gear or tyres; or

(b) to use on a road a motor vehicle or trailer which does not comply with such a requirement, or causes or permits a motor vehicle or trailer to be so used.

Contrary to: Road Traffic Act 1988 s.41A
Max. sentence: Magistrates' Court: £5,000 fine.
Power: Report / s.25 PACE

Offence:
It is an offence for a person to drive a motor cycle on a road otherwise than in accordance with a licence authorising him to drive that class of motor vehicle.[3]

Contrary to: Road Traffic Act 1988 s.87(1)
Max. sentence: Magistrates' Court: £1,000 fine.[4]
Power: Report / s.25 PACE

Offence:
It is an offence[5] for a person to use, cause or permit to be used, a solo motor bicycle not fitted with a front position lamp, on a road between sunset and sunrise or in seriously reduced visibility between sunrise and sunset, unless a headlamp is kept lit and unobscured.

Contrary to: Road Vehicles Lighting Regulations 1989 r.24(2)
Max. sentence: Magistrates' Court: £2,500 fine.
Power: Report / s.25 PACE

Offence:
It is an offence[6] for a person to allow to remain parked, or cause or permit to be allowed to remain parked between sunset and sunrise a solo motor bicycle which is not required to be fitted with a front position lamp, unless a front position lamp is fitted and kept lit and unobscured.

Contrary to: Road Vehicles Lighting Regulations 1989 r.24(4)
Max. sentence: Magistrates' Court: £2,500 fine.
Power: Report / s.25 PACE

Offence:

It is an offence[7] for a person to drive or ride (otherwise than in a side-car) on a motor bicycle when on a road without wearing protective headgear.[8]

Contrary to: Motor Cycles (Protective Helmets) Regulations 1998 r.4(1)

Max. sentence: Magistrates' Court: £500 fine.

Power: Report / s.25 PACE

Definitions

Motor cycle: means a mechanically propelled vehicle, not being an invalid carriage, with less than four wheels, and the weight of which unladen does not exceed 410 kg.[9]

Motor bicycle: means a two-wheeled motor cycle.

Learner motor bicycle: is a motor bicycle which is either propelled by electric power or has the following characteristics:

(a)   the cylinder capacity of its engine does not exceed 125 cubic centimetres,

(b)   the maximum net power output of the engine does not exceed 11 kilowatts.[10]

General Information

A provisional licence shall not authorise a person under the age of 21 years, before he has passed a test of competence to drive a motor bicycle :

(a)   to drive a motor bicycle without a side-car unless it is a learner motor bicycle or its first use occurred before 1 January 1982 and the cylinder capacity of its engine does not exceed 125 cubic centimetres, or

(b)   to drive a motor bicycle with a side-car unless its power to weight ratio is less than or equal to 0.16 kilowatts per kilogram.[11]

   A provisional licence shall not authorise a person, before he has passed a test of competence to drive, to drive on a road a motor bicycle except where he has successfully completed an approved training course for motor cyclists or is undergoing training on such a course and is driving the motor bicycle on the road as part of the training.[12]

Notes

1   'Sidestand' means a device fitted to a motor cycle which, when fully extended or pivoted to its open position, supports the vehicle from one side only and so that both wheels of the motor cycle are on the ground.

2   These are set by the Road Vehicles (Construction and Use) Regulations 1986, as amended.

3   No person submitting himself for a test of competence to drive a motor cycle shall be permitted to take the test unless he furnishes the prescribed certificate of completion by him of an approved training course for motor cyclists.

4   Plus discretionary disqualification or obligatory endorsement.

5   No offence is committed if the motor bicycle is parked or being pushed along the left-hand edge of a carriageway.

6   Exceptions include parking on a road with a 30 mph speed limit where the motor bicycle is parked within a parking place, lay-by or parked close to the kerb.

7   This does not apply to any person driving or riding on a motor bicycle if it is a mowing machine, or it is for the time being propelled by a person on foot. By virtue of the Road Traffic Act 1988 s.16(2) no offence will be committed by a follower of the Sikh religion while he is wearing a turban.

8   This is headgear which complies to British Standards.

9   Road Traffic Act 1988 s.185. The motorised scooters known as Gopeds are mechanically propelled vehicles intended or adapted for use on a road and as such require a driving licence and compulsory insurance, [*DPP* v *Saddington* (2000)].

10 Road Traffic Act 1988 s.97(5).

11 Ibid., s.97(3)(d).

12 Ibid., s.97(3)(e).

MOTORWAYS

See also Drivers and Riders, Highways and Roads, Speeding, Traffic Signs and Directions

Offence: It is an offence for a person to drive a vehicle on any part of a motorway, which is not a carriageway.

Contrary to:	Motorways Traffic (England and Wales) Regulations 1982 r.5
Max. sentence:	Magistrates' Court: £2,500 fine.
Power:	Report/ s.25 PACE

Offence: It is an offence, where there is a traffic sign indicating that there is no entry to a carriageway at a particular place, to drive or move a vehicle onto that carriageway at that particular place.

Contrary to:	Motorways Traffic (England and Wales) Regulations 1982 r.6(1)
Max. sentence:	Magistrates' Court: £2,500 fine.
Power:	Report/ s.25 PACE

Offence: It is an offence, where there is a traffic sign indicating that there is no left or right turn into a carriageway at a particular place, to drive or move a vehicle as to cause it to turn to the left or to the right into that carriageway at that particular place.

Contrary to:	Motorways Traffic (England and Wales) Regulations 1982 r.6(2)
Max. sentence:	Magistrates' Court: £2,500 fine.
Power:	Report/ s.25 PACE

Offence: It is an offence to fail to drive a vehicle in such a direction on a length of carriageway that the central reservation is at all times on the right hand or off side of the vehicle.

Contrary to:	Motorways Traffic (England and Wales) Regulations 1982 r.6(3)
Max. sentence:	Magistrates' Court: £2,500 fine.
Power:	Report/ s.25 PACE

Offence: It is an offence for a vehicle to stop or remain at rest on a motorway carriageway.[1]

Contrary to:	Motorways Traffic (England and Wales) Regulations 1982 r.7(1)
Max. sentence:	Magistrates' Court: £2,500 fine.
Power:	Report/ s.25 PACE

Offence:

It is an offence for a vehicle to be driven or remain at rest[2] on a hard shoulder for longer than is necessary in the circumstances or the purposes for which it was placed there.

Contrary to:	Motorways Traffic (England and Wales) Regulations 1982 r.7(3)(b) and r.9
Max. sentence:	Magistrates' Court: £2,500 fine.
Power:	Report/ s.25 PACE

Offence:

It is an offence for a vehicle on a motorway to be driven or moved backwards.[3]

Contrary to:	Motorways Traffic (England and Wales) Regulations 1982 r.8
Max. sentence:	Magistrates' Court: £2,500 fine.
Powers:	Report/ s.25 PACE

Offence:

It is an offence for a vehicle to be driven or moved or to stop or remain at rest on a central reservation or verge.

Contrary to:	Motorways Traffic (England and Wales) Regulations 1982 r.10
Max. sentence:	Magistrates' Court: £2,500 fine.
Power:	Report/ s.25 PACE

Offence:

It is an offence for a person to drive on a motorway a motor vehicle which he is authorised to drive only by virtue of his being the holder of a provisional licence.[4]

Contrary to:	Motorways Traffic (England and Wales) Regulations 1982 r.11(1)

| **Max. sentence:** | Magistrates' Court: £2,500 fine. |
| **Power:** | Report/ s.25 PACE |

Offence:

It is an offence for a vehicle to which this regulation applies[5] to be driven, moved or stopped, or allowed to remain at rest, on the right hand or off side lane of a length of carriageway which has three or more traffic lanes at any place where all the lanes are open for use by traffic proceeding in the same direction.

Contrary to:	Motorways Traffic (England and Wales) Regulations 1982 r.12(2)
Max. sentence:	Magistrates' Court: £2,500 fine.
Power:	Report/ s.25 PACE

Offence:

It is an offence for a person in charge of any animal which is carried by a vehicle using a motorway, to fail, so far as is practicable, to secure that:

(a) the animal shall not be removed from or permitted to leave the vehicle while the vehicle is on a motorway; and

(b) if it escapes from, or it is necessary for it to be removed from, or permitted to leave the vehicle:

　(i) it shall not go or remain on any part of the motorway other than a hard shoulder; and

　(ii) it shall whilst it is not on or in the vehicle be held on a lead or otherwise be kept under proper control.

Contrary to:	Motorways Traffic (England and Wales) Regulations 1982 r.14
Max. sentence:	Magistrates' Court: £2,500 fine.
Power:	Report/ s.25 PACE

General Information

Nothing in these regulations shall preclude anyone from using a motorway otherwise than in accordance with the provisions in any of the following circumstances:

(a) in accordance with any direction or permission given by a constable in uniform or with the indication given by a traffic sign;

(b) where, in accordance with any permission given by a constable, he does so for the purpose of investigating any accident which has occurred on or near a motorway;

(c) where it is necessary for him to do so to avoid or prevent an accident or to obtain or give help required as a result of accident or emergency, and he does so in such manner as to cause as little danger or inconvenience as possible to other traffic on a motorway;

(d) where he does so in exercise of his duty as a constable or as a member of a fire brigade or ambulance service;

(e) where it is necessary for the efficient maintenance, repair, cleaning, clearance, alteration, or improvement of a motorway; or the removal of a vehicle;

(f) where it is necessary for him to do so in connection with any inspection, survey, investigation or census which is carried out with the authority of the Secretary of State.

Notes

1   This will not apply where a vehicle is forced to stop because of other vehicles, people or objects on the carriageway. Where it is necessary for a vehicle to be stopped by reason of breakdown, accident, illness, other emergency, to recover or move any object on the carriageway or to allow assistance to be given, then the vehicle should be removed to the hard shoulder.

2   A vehicle which is at rest on a hard shoulder shall so far as is reasonably practicable be allowed to remain there in such a position only that no part of it or of any load shall obstruct or be a cause of danger to vehicles using the carriageway.

3   Except in so far as it is necessary to back the vehicle to enable it to proceed forwards or to be connected to any other vehicle.

4   This regulation applies to:

(a)   a motor vehicle in category A or B or sub-category C1+E (8.5 tonnes), D1 (not for hire or reward), D1+E (not for hire or reward) or P; and

(b)   a motor vehicle in category B+E or sub-category C1 if the provisional licence authorising the driving of such a motor vehicle was in force at any time before 1 January 1997.

This will not apply once a certificate of competence has been gained.

5   This regulation applies to:

(a)   a goods vehicle having a maximum laden weight exceeding 7.5 tonnes;

(b)   a passenger vehicle which is constructed or adapted to carry more than 8 seated passengers in addition to the driver, the maximum weight of which exceeds 7.5 tonnes;

(c)   a motor vehicle drawing a trailer; and

(d)   a vehicle which is a motor tractor, a light locomotive or a heavy locomotive.

NOISE

See also Audible Warning Instruments, Breach of the Peace, Construction and Use, Drunkenness, Indecent and Obscene Behaviour, Motor Cycles, Nuisance, Public Order, Trespass

Offence: It is an offence[1] to operate or permit the operation of a loudspeaker in a street:

(a)   between 21.00 hours and 08.00 hours the following morning, for any purpose;

(b)   at any other time, for the purpose of advertising any entertainment, trade or business.

Contrary to: Control of Pollution Act 1974 s.62(1)

Max. sentence: Magistrates' Court: £5,000 fine.

Power: Report / s.25 PACE

Offence: It is an offence not to have fitted and maintained in good and efficient working order, on every vehicle propelled by an internal combustion engine, an exhaust system including a silencer through which the exhaust gases from the engine must pass before escaping into the atmosphere.

Contrary to: Road Vehicles (Construction and Use) Regulations 1986 r.54

Max. sentence: Magistrates' Court: £1,000 fine.

Power: Report / s.25 PACE

Offence:

It is an offence for a person to use a motor vehicle on a road in such manner as to cause any excessive noise which could have been avoided by the exercise of reasonable care on the part of the driver.

Contrary to: Road Vehicles (Construction and Use) Regulations 1986 r.97

Max. sentence: Magistrates' Court: £1,000 fine.

Power: Report / s.25 PACE

Offence:

It is an offence[2] for the driver of a vehicle, when the vehicle is stationary, to fail to stop the action of any machinery attached to or forming part of the vehicle so far as may be necessary for the prevention of noise or exhaust emissions.

Contrary to: Road Vehicles (Construction and Use) Regulations 1986 r.98(1)

Max. sentence: Magistrates' Court: £1,000 fine.

Power: Report / s.25 PACE

General Information

Car alarms fitted for the purpose of preventing theft are subject to a requirement that they be designed to stop sounding after a maximum continuous period of 5 minutes. Any failure to comply with this requirement is an offence under the Road Vehicles (Construction and Use) Regulations 1986.[3]

Notes

1   Exceptions include the use of a loudspeaker by the police, fire or
    ambulance services and where the loudspeaker is fixed to the vehicle and is
    operated solely for the entertainment of or communicating with the driver
    provided it does not give annoyance to persons in the vicinity. Section
    62(1)(b) shall not apply to the use of a loudspeaker between 12.00 hours
    and 19.00 hours if it is fixed to a vehicle which is conveying perishable
    commodities, it is operated to inform members of the public that such
    commodity is for sale from the vehicle otherwise than by the use of words
    and it does not cause annoyance.

2   This does not apply:

    (a) when the vehicle is stationary owing to the necessities of traffic;

    (b) so as to prevent the examination or working of the machinery where
         the examination is necessitated by any failure or derangement of the
         machinery or where the machinery is required to be worked for a
         purpose other than driving the vehicle; or

    (c) in respect of a gas propelled vehicle where the gas is produced on the
         vehicle.

3   See r.37(7) and (8). See page 58.

NUISANCE

See also Anti-Social Behaviour, Breach of the Peace, Harassment and
Intimidation, Highways and Roads, Indecent and Obscene Behaviour, Litter,
Noise, Skips, Telecommunications, Trespass

Offence: It is an offence of public nuisance at Common Law
for any person by any unwarranted act[1] or omission[2]
to endanger the life or health of another, or
damage their property, morals or comfort.

Contrary to: Common Law

Max. sentence: Magistrates' Court: 6 months' imprisonment /
£5,000 fine.

Crown Court: unlimited.

Power: Arrestable Offence

General Information

While many examples of public nuisance are now subject to statutory prohibition or control, the Common Law liability remains. Although no clear definition exists, a public nuisance is one that inflicts damage, injury or inconvenience to a group[3] of the population although it may be only one person who complains. Its effects must be widespread and indiscriminate.[4] Whether the act is sufficiently wide is a matter of fact for the court to decide. Cases held to be a public nuisance have included the keeping of highly inflammatory matter in a manner calculated to terrify the neighbourhood;[5] indecent exposure on a roof visible to other houses;[6] allowing land to be used as a gypsy encampment;[7] the making of a hoax bomb call that affected the public by excluding them from part of the highway or other public place[8] and the making of nuisance telephone calls to at least 13 different people.[9]

Notes

1   That is, without lawful authority.

2   For example, a failure to carry out some legal duty.

3   That is, a considerable number of people or a section of the public [*R* v *Madden* (1975)].

4   *Attorney General* v *PYA Quarries Ltd* (1957).

5   *R* v *Lister and Biggs* (1857).

6   *R* v *Thallman* (1863).

7   *Attorney General* v *Stone* (1895).

8   *R* v *Madden* (1975). In this particular case the hoax bomb call only affected the 8 security officers inside the target factory and was held to be a private nuisance rather than a public nuisance. However the ruling indicated that if a public highway had been affected, then the circumstances would have been sufficient for this offence.

9   *R* v *Norbury* (1978), *R* v *Johnson* (1996).

OFFENSIVE WEAPONS

See also Air Weapons, Crossbows, Firearms – Criminal Use, Knives and Bladed Articles, Public Order, PACE – Arrest, Schools, Trespass

Offence: It is an offence for a person without lawful authority

or reasonable excuse,[1] to have with him in any public place[2] any offensive weapon.[3]

Contrary to: Prevention of Crime Act 1953 s.1(1)

Max. sentence: Magistrates' Court: 6 months' imprisonment / £5,000 fine.

Crown Court: 4 years' imprisonment / unlimited fine.

Power: Arrestable Offence.[4]

Offence:

It is an offence for a person who is on any premises as a trespasser, after having entered as such, and without lawful authority or reasonable excuse, to have with him on the premises any weapon of offence.

Contrary to: Criminal Law Act 1977 s.8(1)

Max. sentence: Magistrates' Court: 3 months' imprisonment / £5,000 fine.

Power: A constable in uniform may arrest anyone whom he reasonably suspects to be committing this offence.[5]

Offence:

It is an offence for any person without lawful authority or reasonable excuse[6] to have with him:

(a) in any aircraft registered in the United Kingdom, whether at a time when the aircraft is in the United Kingdom or not;

(b) in any other aircraft at a time when it is in, or in a flight over, the United Kingdom;

(c) in any part of an aerodrome in the United Kingdom; or

(d) in any air navigation installation in the United Kingdom, which does not form part of an aerodrome,

any article made or adapted for use for causing injury to or incapacitating a person or for destroying or damaging property, or intended by the person having it with him for such use, whether by him or any other person.

Contrary to: Aviation Security Act 1982 s.4(1)

Max. sentence: Magistrates' Court: 3 months' imprisonment / £5,000 fine.

Crown Court: 5 years' imprisonment / unlimited fine.

Power: Arrestable Offence.

Offence: It is an offence[7] for a person, without lawful authority or good reason, to have an offensive weapon with him on school premises.

Contrary to: Criminal Justice Act 1988 s.139A(2)

Max. sentence: Magistrates' Court: 6 months' imprisonment / £5,000 fine.

Crown Court: 4 years' imprisonment / unlimited fine.

Power: Arrestable offence.[8]

Offence: It is an offence for any person:

(a)   to manufacture,

(b)   to sell,

(c)   to hire or

(d)   to offer for sale or hire, or expose or have in his possession for the purpose of sale or hire, or

(e)   to lend or

(f)   to give to any person, a weapon to which this section applies.[9]

Contrary to: Criminal Justice Act 1988 s.141(1)

Max. sentence: Magistrates' Court: 6 months' imprisonment / £5,000 fine.

Power: Report / s.25 PACE

General Powers

Under the Police and Criminal Evidence Act 1984 s.1, a constable who has reasonable grounds for suspecting that he will find prohibited articles,[10] may search any person or vehicle, or anything which is in or on a vehicle, and may detain[11] the person or vehicle for the purpose of such a search.[12]

A constable may also enter any school premises and search those premises and any person on those premises for an offensive weapon if he has reasonable grounds for believing that an offence under s.139A of the Criminal Justice Act 1988 is being, or has been, committed.[13] If the constable discovers an article or weapon which he has reasonable grounds for suspecting is an offensive weapon, he may seize and retain it. The constable may use reasonable force, if necessary, in the exercise of these powers.[14]

Definitions

Offensive weapon: means any article made or adapted for use for causing injury to the person, or intended by the person having it with him for such use by him or by some other person.[15]

General Information

The prohibition under s.141(1) of the Criminal Justice Act 1988 applies to the following:[16]

(a) a knuckle-duster, that is, a band of metal or other hard material worn on one or more fingers, and designed to cause injury;

(b) a swordstick, that is, a hollow walking stick or cane containing a blade that may be used as a sword;

(c) a 'handclaw', that is, a band of metal or other hard material from which a number of sharp spikes protrude, and worn around the hand;

(d) a 'belt buckle knife', that is, a buckle which incorporates a knife;

(e) a 'push dagger', that is, a knife the handle of which fits within a clenched fist and the blade of which protrudes from between two fingers;

(f) a 'hollow kubatan', that is, a cylindrical container containing a number of sharp spikes;

(g) a 'footclaw', that is, a bar of metal or other hard material from which a number of sharp spikes protrude, and worn strapped to the foot;

(h) a 'shuriken', 'shaken' or 'death star', that is, a hard non-flexible plate having three or more sharp radiating points and designed to be thrown;

(i) a 'balisong' or 'butterfly knife', that is, a blade enclosed by its handle, which is designed to split down the middle, without the operation of a spring or other mechanical means, to reveal the blade;

(j) a 'telescopic truncheon', that is, a truncheon which extends automatically by hand pressure applied to a button, spring or other device in or attached to its handle;

(k) a blow pipe or blow gun, that is, a hollow tube out of which hard pellets or darts are shot by the use of breath;

(l) a 'kusari gama', that is, a length of rope, cord, wire or chain fastened at one end to a sickle;

(m) a 'kyoketsu shoge', that is, a length of rope, cord, wire or chain fastened at one end to a hooked knife;

(n) a 'manrikgusari' or 'kusari', that is, a length of rope, cord, wire or chain fastened at each end to a hard weight or hand grip.

Notes

1 The onus of proof lies on the defence. Lack of knowledge that an article is an offensive weapon is not a 'reasonable excuse', [*R* v *Densu* (1991)].

2 May include the communal landing within a block of flats, *Knox* v *Anderton* (1983)].

3 Defined by s.1(4) of the Prevention of Crime Act 1953. A flick knife is an offensive weapon per se, [*Gibson* v *Wales* (1983), *R* v *Veasey* (1999)].

4 Police and Criminal Evidence Act 1984 s.24(2)(k).

5 Criminal Law Act 1977 s.8(1).

6   The proof of which lies with the defence.

7   It will be a defence for a person to show that he had the article or weapon with him for use at work, educational purposes, religious reasons or as part of any national costume. See also page 234.

8   Police and Criminal Evidence Act 1984 s.24(2)(m).

9   See *General Information*.

10 That is, offensive weapons. See also page 195.

11 The time for which a person or vehicle may be detained for the purposes of such a search is such time as is reasonably required to permit the search to be carried out either at the place where the person or vehicle was first detained or nearby [Police and Criminal Evidence Act 1984 s.2(8)] Reasonable force may be used. [ibid., s.117].

12 Police and Criminal Evidence Act 1984 s.1. A constable may exercise any power conferred in this section:

   (a) in any place to which at the time when he proposes to exercise the power the public or any section of the public has access, on payment or otherwise, as of right or by virtue of express or implied permission; or

   (b) in any other place to which people have ready access at the time when he proposes to exercise the power but which is not a dwelling

13 Criminal Justice Act 1988 s.139B(1). As amended by the Offensive Weapons Act 1996.

14 Criminal Justice Act 1988 s.139B(3).

15 Prevention of Crimes Act 1953 s.1(4).

16 Criminal Justice Act 1988 (Offensive Weapons) Order 1988. This list does not include antiques, which are defined as being more than 100 years old.

PACE – ARREST

See also Bail, Football, Going Equipped, Harassment and Intimidation, Indecent and Obscene Behaviour, Knives and Bladed Articles, Offensive Weapons, Public Order, Schools, Sexual Offences, Taking a Conveyance, Theft

General Powers

Any person may arrest without warrant:

(a) anyone who is in the act of committing an arrestable offence;

(b) anyone whom he has reasonable grounds for suspecting to be committing such an offence.[1]

Where an arrestable offence has been committed, any person may arrest without warrant:

(a) anyone who is guilty of the offence;

(b) anyone whom he has reasonable grounds for suspecting to be guilty of it.[2]

Where a constable[3] has reasonable grounds for suspecting that an arrestable offence has been committed, he may arrest without warrant anyone whom he has reasonable grounds for suspecting to be guilty of the offence.[4]

A constable may arrest without warrant:

(a) anyone who is about to commit an arrestable offence;

(b) anyone whom he has reasonable grounds for suspecting to be about to commit an arrestable offence.[5]

Where a constable has reasonable grounds for suspecting that any offence, which is not an arrestable offence, has been committed or attempted, or is being committed or attempted, he may arrest the relevant person if it appears to him that service of a summons is impracticable or inappropriate because any of the general arrest conditions is satisfied.[6]

Definitions

Arrest: the taking of a person's liberty in order that he may answer to an alleged or suspected charge or offence.

Arrestable offence: defined by s.24 of the Police and Criminal Evidence Act 1984 these are:

* offences for which the sentence is fixed by law;

* offences for which a person of 18[7] years of age or over[8] may be sentenced to imprisonment for a term of 5 years;[9] and

* offences to which subsection (2) applies. These are:

(a) offences for which the person may be arrested under the Customs and Excise Acts, as defined in s.1(1) of the Customs and Excise Management Act 1979;

(b) offences under the Official Secrets Act 1920 that are not arrestable offences by virtue of the term of imprisonment for which a person may be sentenced in respect of them;

(bb) offences under any provision of the Official Secrets Act 1989 except s.8(1), (4) or (5);

(c) offences under s.22[10] or section 23[11] of the Sexual Offences Act 1956;

(ca) an offence under s.46(6) of the Criminal Justice and Police Act 2001;[12]

(d) offences under s.12(1)[13] or s.25(1)[14] of the Theft Act 1968;

(e) any offence under the Football (Offences) Act 1991;

(f) an offence under s.2 of the Obscene Publications Act 1959;[15]

(g) an offence under s.1 of the Protection of Children Act 1978;[16]

(ga) an offence under s.1 of the Sexual Offences Act 1985;[17]

(gb) an offence under s.170(4) of the Road Traffic Act 1988;[18]

(h) an offence under s.166 of the Criminal Justice and Public Order Act 1994;[19]

(i) an offence under s.19 of the Public Order Act 1986;[20]

(j) an offence under s.167 of the Criminal Justice and Public Order Act 1994;[21]

(k) an offence under s.1(1) of the Prevention of Crime Act 1953;[22]

(l) an offence under s.139(1) of the Criminal Justice Act 1988;[23]

(m) an offence under s.139A(1) or (2) of the Criminal Justice Act 1988;[24]

(n) an offence under s.2 of the Protection from Harassment Act 1997;[25]

(o) an offence under s.60(8)(b) of the Criminal Justice and Public Order Act 1994;[26]

(p) an offence falling within s.32(1)(a) of the Crime and Disorder Act 1998;[27]

(q) an offence under ss.14J or 21C of the Football Spectators Act 1989;[28]

(qa) an offence under s.12(4) of the Criminal Justice and Police Act 2001;[29]

(r) [30]

(s) an offence under s.1(1) or (2) of the Wildlife and Countryside Act 1981[31] in respect of a bird included in Sch.1 to that Act or any part of, or anything derived from, such a bird;[32]

(t) an offence under s.1(5),[33] s.9, s.13(1)(a) or (2)[34] or s.14[35] of the Wildlife and Countryside Act 1981.[36]

[s.25] *General arrest conditions:* these are:

(a) the name of the relevant person is unknown to, and cannot be readily ascertained by, the constable;

(b) that the constable has reasonable grounds for doubting whether a name furnished by the relevant person as his name, is his real name;

(c) that

    (i) the relevant person has failed to furnish a satisfactory address for service; or

    (ii) the constable has reasonable grounds for doubting whether the address furnished by the relevant person is a satisfactory address for service;

(d) that the constable has reasonable grounds for believing that arrest is necessary to prevent the relevant person:

    (i) causing physical injury to himself or any other person;

    (ii) suffering personal injury;

    (iii) causing loss of or damage to property;

    (iv) committing an offence against public decency; or

    (v) causing an unlawful obstruction of the highway;

(e) that the constable has reasonable grounds for believing that an arrest is necessary to protect a child or other vulnerable person from the relevant person.

Following arrest, a constable may search the prisoner if he believes the person may be a danger, may use something to escape or may have evidence [s.32].

General Information

Without prejudice to s.2 of the Criminal Attempts Act 1981, the powers of summary arrest shall also apply to the offences of:

(a) conspiring to commit any of the offences mentioned in s.24(2) of the Police and Criminal Evidence Act 1984;

(b) attempting to commit any such offence other than an offence under s.12(1) of the Theft Act 1968;

(c) inciting, aiding, abetting, counselling or procuring the commission of any such offence; and such offences are also arrestable for the purposes of the 1984 Act.[37]

It is an indictable offence to refuse to assist a constable in the execution of his duty when called upon to do so. Such a refusal renders the offender liable to a fine or imprisonment at Common Law.[38]

The powers of arrest contained within the Police and Criminal Evidence Act 1984 are not the only powers available to the police and many other enactments include their own powers of arrest. Generally these powers of arrest are distinguishable from arrestable offences by requiring some specific circumstance or warning before arrest is permissible; for example, 'found committing'.

A special constable has all the powers of a constable in the police area where they were appointed as well as adjoining police areas. Special constables appointed in the City of London have powers throughout the Metropolitan Police area and also in the police areas contiguous to that.

Notes

1 Police and Criminal Evidence Act 1984 s.24(4).

2 Ibid., s.24(5)

3 A constable may enter and search any premises for the purpose of executing a warrant of arrest or of arresting a person for an arrestable offence.

4 Police and Criminal Evidence Act 1984 s.24(6)

5 Ibid., s.24(7)

6 Ibid., s.25(1)

7 As amended by the Criminal Justice and Court Service Act 2000.

8 Not previously convicted.

9 Or might be so sentenced but for the restrictions imposed by s.33 of the

Magistrates' Courts Act 1980, which limits penalties in cases where the value involved is small. There is an irrebuttable presumption in law that persons under 10 years of age cannot form the necessary *mens rea* for the completion of an offence.

10 Causing prostitution of women.

11 Procuration of a girl under 21. See page 315.

12 Placing of advertisements relating to prostitution. See page 321.

13 Taking motor vehicle or other conveyance without authority, etc. See page 386.

14 Going equipped for stealing etc. See page 195.

15 Publication of obscene matter.

16 Indecent photographs and pseudo-photographs of children. As a result of the Criminal Justice and Court Services Act 2000, this offence is now subject to a maximum penalty on indictment of 10 years. See page 227.

17 Kerb crawling, as amended by the Criminal Justice and Police Act 2001, in force 1 October 2001. See page 320.

18 Failing to stop and report a road traffice accident involving personal injury as inserted by the Criminal Justice and Police Act 2001, in force 1 October 2001. See page 354.

19 Sale of tickets for designated football matches by unauthorised persons. See page 179.

20 Publishing, etc. material intended or likely to stir up racial hatred. See page 333.

21 Touting for car hire services. See page 386.

22 Prohibition on the carrying of offensive weapons. See page 277.

23 Offence of having an article with blade or point in a public place. See page 232.

24 Offence of having an article with blade or point (or offensive weapon) on school premises. See page 233.

25 Offence of a person pursuing a course of conduct which amounts to harassment of another. See page 207.

26 Failing when required to remove mask, etc. See page 327.

27 Racially aggravated harassment. See page 337.

28 Failure to comply with the requirements of a banning order. See page 178.

29 Failing to comply with a requirement in relation to the consumption of alcohol in public places. When in force. See page 138.

30 Repealed by the Football (Disorder) Act 2000.

31 Taking, possessing, selling etc., of wild birds. See page 436.

32 For full details of the Schedules to this Act, see *A-Z of Countryside Law second edition*.

33 Disturbance of wild birds.

34 Taking, possessing, selling, etc., of wild animals or plants.

35 Introduction of new species, etc.

36 As amended by the Countryside and Rights of Way Act 2000.

37 Police and Criminal Evidence Act 1984 s.24(3).

38 See page 307.

PARKING

See also Drivers and Riders, Driving Off-Road, Highways and Roads, Lights on Vehicles, Traffic Signs and Directions, Trailers; Vehicle Interference

Offence: It is an offence[1] for a person:

(a) being the driver of a vehicle, to leave the vehicle in a designated parking place otherwise than as authorised by or under an order relating to the parking place, or to leave the vehicle in a designated parking place for longer after the excess charge has been incurred than the time so authorised, or to fail to pay any charge payable, or to contravene or fail to comply with any provision of an order relating to the parking place as to the manner in which vehicles shall stand in, or be driven into or out of, the parking place; or

(b) whether being the driver of a vehicle or not, to otherwise contravene or fail to comply with any order relating to designated parking places.

Contrary to: Road Traffic Regulation Act 1984 s.47

Max. sentence: Magistrates' Court: £500 fine.[2]

Power: Report / s.25 PACE

Offence: It is an offence for a person, with intent to defraud:

(a)   to interfere with a parking device, or operate or attempt to operate any parking device otherwise than in the manner prescribed; or

(b)   to display a parking device otherwise than in the manner prescribed.

Contrary to: Road Traffic Regulation Act 1984 s.52(1)

Max. sentence: Magistrates' Court: £500 fine.

Power: Report / s.25 PACE

Offence: It is an offence[3] for a person to park a heavy commercial vehicle wholly or partly on the verge of a road, or on any land situated between two carriageways and which is not a footway, or on a footway.

Contrary to: Road Traffic Act 1988 s.19(1)

Max. sentence: Magistrates' Court: £1,000 fine.

Power: Report / s.25 PACE

Offence: It is an offence[4] for a person, without lawful authority, to drive or park a motor vehicle wholly or partly on a cycle track.

Contrary to: Road Traffic Act 1988 s.21(1)

Max. sentence: Magistrates' Court: £1,000 fine.

Power: Report / s.25 PACE

Offence: It is an offence for a person in charge of a motor vehicle to cause or permit the vehicle or a trailer drawn by it to remain at rest on a road in such a position or in such condition or in such circumstances as to involve a danger of injury to other persons using the road.

Contrary to: Road Traffic Act 1988 s.22

Max. sentence: Magistrates' Court: £1,000 fine.

Power: Report / s.25 PACE

Offence:

It is an offence in London for a person, other than the owner of the vehicle or a person acting on the authority of the London authority for the place in which the vehicle was found, to remove or interfere with a fixed penalty notice fixed to the vehicle by a parking attendant.

Contrary to: Road Traffic Act 1991 s.66(5)

Max. sentence: Magistrates' Court: £500 fine.

Power: Report / s.25 PACE

Offence:

It is an offence in London for a person, without being authorised to do so, to remove or attempt to remove an immobilisation device fixed to the vehicle in a designated parking space by a parking attendant.

Contrary to: Road Traffic Act 1991 s.69(7)

Max. sentence: Magistrates' Court: £1,000 fine.

Power: Report / s.25 PACE

Definitions

Footway: means a way comprised in a highway which also comprises a carriageway, being a way over which the public have a right of way on foot only.

Heavy commercial vehicle: means any goods vehicle which has an operating weight exceeding 7.5 tonnes.[5]

General Information

Further parking offences occur where traffic signs indicate a prohibition. In such cases the offence is one of failing to conform to the direction given by the traffic sign.[6]

Notes

1   This offence does not apply to the Greater London area which is controlled

by ss.43, 50 and 53 of the Road Traffic Regulation Act 1984, the Greater London Council (General Powers) Act 1982 and the Road Traffic Act 1991.

2 £1,000 if the parking place is designated for a disabled person's use only.

3 It is not an offence where the accused can prove that:

(a) it was parked in accordance with permission given by a constable in uniform;

(b) it was parked for the purpose of saving life or extinguishing fire, in an emergency; or

(c) it was parked for the purpose of loading or unloading which could not satisfactorily have been performed if it had not been parked on the footway or verge and the vehicle was not left unattended.

4 No offence will be committed where the vehicle was driven or parked in an emergency involving life or fire; or where the driving or parking was concerned with the cleansing, maintenance or improvement of the cycle track or its verges or any apparatus.

5 That is, in the case of a motor vehicle *or* trailer its maximum laden weight; in the case of an articulated vehicle its maximum laden weight or the aggregate weight of its parts and in the case of a motor vehicle and trailer, its aggregate maximum laden weight.

6 For example, double white lines and clearways. See also page 412.

PARKS, GARDENS AND OPEN SPACES

See also Damage, Litter, Metropolitan Police Act, Nuisance, Theft, Town Police Clauses, Trespass

Offence: It is an offence for any person in respect of a town garden[1] to:

(a) throw any rubbish into such a garden;

(b) trespass therein or to get over the railings or fence;

(c) steal or damage any flowers or plants; or

(d) commit any nuisance therein.

Contrary to: Town Gardens Protection Act 1863 s.5

Max. sentence: Magistrates' Court: 14 days' imprisonment / £200 fine.

Power: Report / s.25 PACE

Offence: It is an offence for any person who, within the view of a park constable,[2] acts in contravention of any park regulations[3] and when required by any park or police constable[4] to give his name and address, gives a false name or false address.

Contrary to: Parks Regulation Act 1872 s.5[5]

Max. sentence: Magistrates' Court: £200 fine.

Power: Report / s.25 PACE

Offence: It is an offence for any person to assault a park constable in the execution of his duty.

Contrary to: Parks Regulation Act 1872, s.6

Max. sentence: Magistrates' Court: 6 months' imprisonment / £500 fine.

Power: Report / s.25 PACE

Offence: It is an offence for any person in respect of a park[6] to fail to comply with any regulations made to secure the proper management of the park, the preservation of order and the prevent of abuses within it.

Contrary to: Parks Regulation (Amendment) Act 1926 s.2(1)

Max. sentence: Magistrates' Court: £200 fine.

Power: Report / s.25 PACE

Offence: It is an offence for any person to fail to comply with, or act in contravention of, a park trading regulation.

Contrary to: Royal Parks (Trading) Act 2000 s.1(2)

Max. sentence: Magistrates' Court: £1,000 fine.

Power: Report / s.25 PACE

Offence: It is an offence for any person to place or maintain;

(a) on or near any access land; or

(b)   on or near a way leading to access land,

a notice containing any false or misleading information likely to deter the public exercising their right to enter on access land.

Contrary to: Countryside and Rights of Way Act 2000 s.14[7]

Max. sentence: Magistrates' Court: £200 fine.[8]

Power: Report / s.25 PACE

General Powers

A park constable who reasonably suspects that a person has committed a park trading offence may[9] seize anything of a non-perishable nature which the person has in his possession or control, and the constable reasonably believes it to have been used in the commission of an offence.

Notes

1   This applies to enclosed or ornamental gardens in streets and public places for the enjoyment of the inhabitants, but not to Crown land or gardens under the control of the Department for Environment, Food and Rural Affairs or to any gardens protected by other legislation.

2   Within a park, a park constable has all the powers, privileges, immunities and duties of a police constable.

3   In the park where the constable has jurisdiction.

4   A police constable has within the park, all the powers, privileges and immunities of a park constable. Parks Regulation Act 1872 s.8.

5   As amended by the Police and Criminal Evidence Act 1984.

6   Includes all parks, gardens, recreation grounds, open spaces and other land vested in or under the control or management of the Secretary of State or the Minister for Environmental, Food and Rural Affairs.

7   When in force.

8   £1,000 for a second conviction.

9   In the park where he has jurisdiction.

PEDAL CYCLES

See also Dangerous and Careless Driving / Riding, Drink and Drive / Ride, Drivers and Riders, Footpaths, Footways and Bridleways, Highways and Roads, Motor Cycles, Parking, Taking a Conveyance, Traffic Signs and Directions

Offence: It is an offence for any person to wilfully ride upon any footpath or causeway by the side of any road made or set apart for the use of foot passengers.

Contrary to: Highways Act 1835 s.72

Max. sentence: Magistrates' Court: £500 fine.

Power: Report / s.25 PACE

Offence: It is an offence for any person driving any sort of carriage[1] to ride or drive the same furiously so as to endanger the life or limb of any passenger.

Contrary to: Highways Act 1835 s.78

Max. sentence: Magistrates' Court: £200 fine.

Power: Report / s.25 PACE

Offence: It is an offence for a person to be drunk while in charge on any highway or other public place of any carriage.

Contrary to: Licensing Act 1872 s.12

Max. sentence: Magistrates' Court: 1 month imprisonment / £200 fine.

Power: Report / s.25 PACE

Offence: It is an offence for a person to ride, or cause or permit to be ridden, on a road a pedal cycle[2] to which the Electrically Assisted Pedal Cycle Regulations 1983 apply unless it is fitted with:

(a) a securely fixed plate in a conspicuous position showing the name of the manufacturer, the nominal voltage of the battery and the continuous rated output of the vehicle;

(b) braking systems which are so designed and constructed that they comply with s.6 of the 1981 British Standard;

(c) a battery which does not leak so as to be a source of danger; and

(d) a device biased to the off position which allows power to come from the motor only when the device is operated so as to achieve that result.

Contrary to: Pedal Cycles (Construction and Use) Regulations 1983 r.4

Max. sentence: Magistrates' Court: £1,000 fine.

Power: Report / s.25 PACE

Offence:

It is an offence[3] for a person to ride, or cause or permit to be ridden, on a road a pedal cycle to which the Electrically Assisted Pedal Cycle Regulations 1983 do not apply unless:

(a) it is equipped with at least one braking system;

(b) in the case of a bicycle or tricycle the height of the saddle of which is 635 millimetres or more above the ground and every cycle with four or more wheels:

    (i) it is equipped with a braking system operating on the front wheel or, if it has more than one front wheel, on at least two front wheels;[4]

    (ii) it is equipped with two independent braking systems one of which operates on the front wheel or, if it has more than one front wheel, on at least two front wheels, and the other of which operates on the rear wheel, or if it has more than one rear wheel at least two rear wheels.[5]

Contrary to: Pedal Cycles (Construction and Use) Regulations 1983 r.6

Max. sentence: Magistrates' Court: £1,000 fine.

Power: Report / s.25 PACE

Offence:

It is an offence for a person to ride, or cause or permit to be ridden, on a road a pedal cycle to which r.6 applies unless the braking system or systems with which it is required to be fitted are in efficient working order.

Contrary to: Pedal Cycles (Construction and Use) Regulations 1983 r.10

Max. sentence: Magistrates' Court: £1,000 fine.

Power: Report / s.25 PACE

Offence:

It is an offence[6] for more than one person to be carried[7] on a road[8] on a bicycle not propelled by mechanical power unless it is constructed or adapted for the carriage of more than one person.

Contrary to: Road Traffic Act 1988 s.24(1)

Max. sentence: Magistrates' Court: £200 fine.

Power: Report / s.25 PACE

Offence:

It is an offence for a person to promote or to take part in a race or trial of speed on a public way between cycles unless the race is authorised and conducted within the conditions of such an authorisation.

Contrary to: Road Traffic Act 1988 s.31(1)

Max. sentence: Magistrates' Court: £200 fine.

Power: Report / s.25 PACE

Offence:

It is an offence for a person:

(a) under the age of 14 to drive an electrically assisted pedal cycle;

(b) knowing or suspecting that another person is under the age of 14, to cause or permit him to drive such a pedal cycle.

Contrary to: Road Traffic Act 1988 s.32

Max. sentence: Magistrates' Court: £500 fine.

Power: Report / s.25 PACE

Offence:

It is an offence for a person riding a cycle on a road to fail to stop when required to do so by a constable in uniform.

Contrary to: Road Traffic Act 1988 s.163(3)

Max. sentence: Magistrates' Court: £1,000 fine.

Power: Report / s.25 PACE

General Powers

A person riding a cycle on a road must stop the cycle on being required to do so by a constable in uniform.[9]

Any constable in uniform may test and inspect a pedal cycle for the purpose of ascertaining whether any of the requirements with regard to braking systems are being complied with, provided he does so either:

(a) on any premises where the cycle is if the cycle has been involved in an accident, and the test and inspection are carried out within 48 hours of the accident and the owner of the cycle consents; or

(b) on a road.[10]

Definitions

Cycle track: means a way constituting or comprised in a highway, being a way over which the public have a right of way on pedal cycles with or without a right of way on foot.[11]

Notes

1   Pedal cycles are carriages, whether ridden or pushed [*Corkery* v *Carpenter* (1951)]. See also *Drink and Drive/Ride.*

2   Defined for the purposes of these regulations as a pedal cycle which is either not propelled by mechanical power or is an electrically assisted pedal cycle. For the purposes of the Traffic Signs Regulations and General Directions 1994, the definition is a unicycle, bicycle, tricycle or cycle having four or more wheels, not being in any case mechanically propelled unless it is electrically assisted.

3   This offence does not apply to a pedal cycle so constructed that the pedals act on any wheel or on the axle of any wheel or to any pedal cycle brought temporarily into Great Britain.

4   This applies in cases where the cycle is so constructed that one or more of the wheels is incapable of rotating independently of the pedals, sometimes known as a 'fixed wheel'.

5   This applies in cases where the cycle is not so constructed that one or more of the wheels is incapable of rotating independently of the pedals; that is, if the rider stops rotating the pedals, the cycle's wheels continue to operate.

6   If this section is contravened each of the persons carried is liable.

7   Includes 'riding'.

8   Includes 'bridleway'.

9   Road Traffic Act 1988 s.163(2).

10 Pedal Cycles (Construction and Use) Regulations 1983 r.11.

11 Highways Act 1980 s.329.

POACHING[1]

See also Animals, Attempts, Damage, Firearms – Criminal Use, PACE – Arrest, Theft, Trespass, Wildlife

Offence: It is an offence for a person, by night,[2] to unlawfully take or destroy any game[3] or rabbits in any land,[4] whether open or enclosed, or to unlawfully enter or be in any such land, with any gun, net, engine, or other instrument for the purpose of taking or destroying game.

Contrary to: Night Poaching Act 1828 s.1

Max. sentence: Magistrates' Court: £1,000 fine.

Power:	Report / s.25 PACE

Offence:

It is an offence for a person lawfully seized and apprehended[5] by the owner or occupier of any land, or their gamekeeper or servant, to assault any such person or to offer violence with any gun, crossbow, firearms, bludgeon, stick, club, or any other offensive weapon whatsoever towards any person authorised to seize and apprehend him.

Contrary to:	Night Poaching Act 1828 s.2
Max. sentence:	Magistrates' Court: 6 months' imprisonment / £2,500 fine.
Power:	Report / s.25 PACE

Offence:

It is an offence for any persons, to the number of three or more together, by night, to unlawfully enter or be in any land whether open or enclosed, for the purpose of taking or destroying any game or rabbits, and any of such persons are armed with any gun, crossbow, firearms, bludgeon, or any other offensive weapon.

Contrary to:	Night Poaching Act 1828 s.9
Max. sentence:	Magistrates' Court: 6 months' imprisonment / £2,500 fine.
Power:	Report / s.25 PACE

Offence:

It is an offence for any person whatsoever to kill or take:

(a) any game,[6] or use any dog, gun, net or other engine[7] or instrument for the purpose of taking or killing any game, on a Sunday or Christmas Day;

(b) any partridge between 1 February and 1 September in any year;

(c)   any pheasant between 1 February and 1 October in any year;

(d)   any black game between 10 December in any year and 20 August in the succeeding year;

(e)   any grouse between 10 December in any year and 12 August in the succeeding year;

(f)   any bustard between 1 March and 1 September in any year.

Contrary to: Game Act 1831 s.3

Max. sentence: Magistrates' Court: £200 fine.[8]

Power: Report / s.25 PACE

Offence:

It is an offence for any person to buy or sell any dead bird of game after the expiration of 10 days from the respective days in each year on which it shall become unlawful to kill or take such birds.

Contrary to: Game Act 1831 s.4[9]

Max. sentence: Magistrates' Court: £200 fine.

Power: Report / s.25 PACE

Offence:

It is an offence[10] for any person, not having obtained a game certificate:

(a)   to kill or take any game, or use any dog, gun, net, or other instrument for the purpose of searching for or killing or taking game;[11]

(b)   to sell or offer for sale any game to any person whatsoever except such person licensed to deal in game;

(c)   to buy any game from any person whatsoever except from a person licensed to deal in game, or *bona fide* from a person displaying a board purporting to be the board of a person licensed to deal in game.

Contrary to:	Game Act 1831 s.23, s.25 and s.27
Max. sentence:	Magistrates' Court: £500 fine.
Power:	Report / s.25 PACE

Offence:

It is an offence for any person, not having the right of killing game upon any land, nor having permission from the person having such right, to wilfully take out of the nest or to destroy in the nest the eggs of any bird of game, or of any swan, wild duck, teal or widgeon, or to knowingly have in his house, shop, possession or control, any such eggs so taken.

Contrary to:	Game Act 1831 s.24
Max. sentence:	Magistrates' Court: £200 fine.
Power:	Report / s.25 PACE

Offence:

It is an offence for any person to commit any trespass[12] by entering or being in the daytime upon any land in search or pursuit of game, woodcocks, snipe or conies.

Contrary to:	Game Act 1831 s.30
Max. sentence:	Magistrates' Court: £1,000 fine.[13]
Power:	Report / s.25 PACE

Offence:

It is an offence[14] for a person to take or destroy, or attempt to take or destroy, any fish in water which is private property or in which there is any private right of fishery.

Contrary to:	Theft Act 1968 Sch.1(2)(1)
Max. sentence:	Magistrates' Court: 3 months' imprisonment / £1,000 fine.
Power:	A constable may arrest without warrant anyone who is, or who he, with reasonable cause suspects to be, committing this offence.

Offence: It is an offence[15] for any person to use, or intend to use, or have in his possession, for the purpose of taking or killing any salmon, trout or freshwater fish:

(a) a firearm;

(b) an otter lath or jack, wire or snare;

(c) a crossline or setline;

(d) a spear, gaff, stroke-haul, snatch or other like instrument;[16] or

(e) a light; or

(f) to throw or discharge any stone or other missile for such purposes or to facilitate the taking or killing of such a fish.

Contrary to: Salmon and Freshwater Fisheries Act 1975 s.1(1)

Max. sentence: Magistrates' Court: 3 months' imprisonment / £5,000 fine.

Crown Court: 2 years' imprisonment / unlimited fine.

Power: Report / s.25 PACE

Offence: It is an offence for any person to take, kill, or attempt to take or kill any fish during the close season or close times applicable to that species of fish.[17]

Contrary to: Salmon and Freshwater Fisheries Act 1975 s.19

Max. sentence: Magistrates' Court: £2,500 fine.

Power: Report / s.25 PACE

Offence: It is an offence for any person, in any place in which fishing for fish of any description is regulated by a system of licensing, to fish for or take fish otherwise than by the means authorised by virtue of a fishing licence or otherwise than in accordance with the conditions of the licence or to have in his possession with intent to use it for such purpose any

instrument other than one which he is authorised
to use by virtue of such a licence.

Contrary to: Salmon and Freshwater Fisheries Act 1975 s.27

Max. sentence: Magistrates' Court: 3 months' imprisonment /
£5,000 fine.

Crown Court: 2 years' imprisonment / unlimited
fine.

Power: Report / s.25 PACE

Offence:
It is an offence[18] for any person, without the consent
of the owner or occupier or other lawful authority:

(a)   to enter any land in search or pursuit of any
deer with the intention of taking, killing or
injuring it;

(b)   while on any land to intentionally take, kill or
injure, or to attempt to take, kill or injure any
deer or to search for or pursue any deer with
the intention of taking, killing or injuring it,
or to remove the carcass of any deer.

Contrary to: Deer Act 1991 s.1(1)

Max. sentence: Magistrates' Court: 3 months' imprisonment /
£2,500 fine.

Power: Report / s.25 PACE

Offence:
It is an offence[19] for any person to take or
intentionally kill any deer during the prescribed
close season.[20]

Contrary to: Deer Act 1991 s.2(1)

Max. sentence: Magistrates' Court: 3 months' imprisonment /
£2,500 fine.

Power: Report / s.25 PACE

Offence:
It is an offence[21] for a person to take or intentionally
kill any deer between the expiry of the first hour

after sunset and the beginning of the last hour before sunrise.

Contrary to: Deer Act 1991 s.3

Max. sentence: Magistrates' Court: 3 months' imprisonment / £2,500 fine.

Power: Report / s.25 PACE

Offence:

It is an offence for any person:

(a) to set in position any article which is a trap, snare, or poisoned or stupefying bait and is of such a nature and so placed as to be calculated to cause bodily injury to any deer coming in contact with it;

(b) to use for the purpose of taking or killing any deer any trap, snare, poisoned or stupefying bait, or net;

(c) to use for the purpose of taking or killing or injuring any deer:

    (i) any smooth-bore gun;

    (ii) any rifle having a calibre of less than .240 inches or a muzzle energy of less than 2,305 joules (1,700 ft.lbs);

    (iii) any air gun, air rifle or air pistol;

    (iv) any cartridge for use in a smooth-bore gun;

    (v) any bullet for use in a rifle other than a soft-nosed or hollow-nosed bullet;

    (vi) any arrow, spear or similar missile, or

    (vii) any missile, whether discharged from a firearm or otherwise, carrying or containing any poison, stupefying drug or muscle-relaxing agent;

(d) to discharge any firearm, or to project any missile, from any mechanically propelled vehicle at a deer or to use any mechanically propelled vehicle for the purpose of driving deer.

Contrary to: Deer Act 1991 s.4

Max. sentence: Magistrates' Court: 3 months' imprisonment / £2,500 fine.

Power: Report / s.25 PACE

General Powers

A constable may require any person found committing an offence under the Game Act 1831 s.30 to give his name and address and to quit the land.[22]

A constable may, in any place in Great Britain and Ireland, in any highway, street, or public place search any person, cart or other conveyance, which he may have good cause to suspect of coming from any land where such person shall have been unlawfully in pursuit of game,[23] or any person aiding or abetting such person, and having in his possession any game unlawfully obtained, or any gun or part of a gun, cartridges or other ammunition, nets, traps, snares or other devices used for killing game.[24]

A police constable who has reasonable cause for suspecting that a person is committing an offence on any land[25] under s.1 or s.9 of the Night Poaching Act 1828, or under section 30 of the Game Act 1831, may enter on the land for the purpose of exercising the power to demand that person's name and address and to require him to quit the land or to arrest him.[26]

A constable may require any person who is fishing, or whom he reasonably suspects of being about to fish or to have within the preceding half hour fished in any area, to produce his licence or other authority to fish and to state his name and address.[27]

Notes

1   See also *A-Z of Countryside Law*, Second Edition.

2   'Night' commences at the end of the first hour after sunset and concludes at the beginning of the last hour before sunrise.

3   The word 'game' includes hares, pheasants, partridges, grouse, heath or moor game, black game and bustards.

4   Includes any public road or path. [Night Poaching Act 1844].

5   Whilst the Night Poaching Act 1828 retains a power of seizure and apprehension for specified persons, a constable's powers are now dictated by the Police and Criminal Evidence Act 1984.

6   Rabbits are not included under this section.

7   For example, a snare.

8   For each head of game taken.

9   There is a similar offence concerning deer under s.10 of the Deer Act 1991.

10 The occupiers or owners of land with the right to take game, and persons authorised by them, do not require a game certificate in order to take or kill hares, [Hares Act 1848]. See also the Game Licences Act 1860 s.4.

11 Exceptions include the taking of woodcock and snipe with nets, the taking of rabbits by a warrener or occupier of land or a person authorised by them, hare coursing with hounds, deer hunting with hounds and members of the Royal Family.

12 This does not extend to any person hunting or coursing with hounds or greyhounds who are in fresh pursuit of any deer, hare or fox already started upon any other land.

13 Where 5 or more persons together commit this offence the penalty rises to £5,000 for each offender.

14 This shall not apply to the taking or destroying of fish by angling in the daytime, but a person who by angling in the daytime unlawfully takes or destroys, or attempts to take or destroy, any fish in water which is private property or in which there is any private right of fishery shall on summary conviction be liable to a fine of £200 [Theft Act 1968 Sch.1].

15 No offence is committed if an accused can show that the act was done for the preservation or development of a private fishery and the previous written permission of the National Rivers Authority had been obtained.

16 This does not apply to the use of a gaff or trailer as an auxiliary to angling with a rod and line.

17 Different close seasons apply to the methods by which fish are to be taken or killed. Generally the close season for salmon is between 31 August and the following 1 February and for trout between 31 August and the following 1 March. In the case of other freshwater fish, unless specified by local byelaws the close season will operate between 14 March and 16 June.

18　It is a defence for the accused person to show that he believed that he would have had the consent of the owner or occupier of the land if they had known of the circumstances.

19　No offence is committed in the case of farmed deer, or where the killing is done to prevent the suffering of an injured or diseased deer or other act of mercy or where the occupier of land is protecting crops where the action taken was necessary to protect land.

20　For Red Deer, Fallow Deer and Sika Deer stags this is 1 May until 31 July while for the hinds the close season commences on 1 March and continues to 31 October. In the case of Roe Deer stags the close season is from 1 November until 31 March whilst the hinds may not be taken between 1 March until 31 October.

21　See note 18.

22　Any failure is punishable by a £200 fine. If there are 5 or more together and any of them is armed and violence, intimidation or menace is used to prevent or discourage an exercise of these powers then the punishment rises to £5,000 for each offender, [Game Act 1831 s.31A].

23　For the purposes of this power the term 'game' includes hares, pheasants, partridges, eggs of pheasants or partridges, woodcocks, snipes, rabbits, grouse, black or moor game, and the eggs of black or moor game.

24　Poaching Prevention Act 1862 s.2.

25　Not including land occupied or managed by the armed forces or the Atomic Energy Authority.

26　Game Laws (Amendment) Act 1960 s.2 alternatively, the Police and Criminal Evidence Act 1984 s.25. See page 284.

27　Salmon and Freshwater Fisheries Act 1975 s.35.

POLICE

See also Assaults, Breach of the Peace, Criminal Justice, Metropolitan Police Act, PACE – Arrest, Public Order, Town Police Clauses

Offence:	It is an offence for a person to assault a constable in the execution of his duty, or a person assisting a constable in the execution of his duty.
Contrary to:	Police Act 1996 s.89(1)
Max. sentence:	Magistrates' Court: 6 months' imprisonment / £5,000 fine.
Power:	Report / s.25 PACE / Breach of the Peace

Offence: It is an offence for a person to resist or wilfully obstruct[1] a constable in the execution of his duty,[2] or a person assisting a constable in the execution of his duty.

Contrary to: Police Act 1996 s.89(2)

Max. sentence: Magistrates' Court: 1 months' imprisonment / £1,000 fine.

Power: Report / s.25 PACE / Breach of the Peace

Offence: It is an offence for a person, with intent to deceive, to impersonate a member of a police force or special constable, or to make any statement or to do any act calculated to falsely suggest that he is such a member or constable.

Contrary to: Police Act 1996 s.90(1)

Max. sentence: Magistrates' Court: 6 months' imprisonment / £5,000 fine.

Power: Report / s.25 PACE

Offence: It is an offence for a person, not being a constable, to wear any article of police uniform in circumstances where it gives him an appearance so nearly resembling that of a member of a police force as to be calculated to deceive.

Contrary to: Police Act 1996 s.90(2)

Max. sentence: Magistrates' Court: £1,000 fine.

Power: Report / s.25 PACE

Offence: It is an offence for a person, not being a member of a police force or special constable, to have in his possession any article of police clothing unless he proves that he obtained possession lawfully and has possession of it for a lawful purpose.

Contrary to: Police Act 1996 s.90(3)

Max. sentence: Magistrates' Court: £200 fine.

Power: Report / s.25 PACE

Offence: It is an offence for a person to cause, or attempt to cause, or to do any act calculated to cause disaffection amongst members of any police force,[3] or to induce or attempt to induce, or to do any act calculated to induce, any member of a police force to withhold his services.

Contrary to: Police Act 1996 s.91(1)

Max. sentence: Magistrates' Court: 6 months' imprisonment / £5,000 fine.

Crown Court: 2 years' imprisonment / unlimited fine.

Power: Report / s.25 PACE

Notes

1   This does not include a refusal to answer questions which the person is not legally obliged to respond to.

2   Generally a constable must be acting lawfully and with due authority to satisfy this requirement.

3   This includes special constables.

POST AND MAIL

See also Damage, Explosives, Harassment and Intimidation, Indecent and Obscene Behaviour, Telecommunications, Theft

Offence: It is an offence for a person to send to another person:

(a)   a letter, electronic communication or article of any description which conveys:

     (i)   a message which is indecent or grossly offensive;

    (ii)   a threat; or

      (iii) information which is false and known or believed to be false by the sender; or

  (b) any article or electronic communication which is, in whole or part, of an indecent or grossly offensive nature,

if his purpose, or one of his purposes, in sending it is that it should cause distress or anxiety to the recipient or to any other person to whom he intends that it or its contents or nature should be communicated.

Contrary to:	Malicious Communications Act 1988 s.1(1)[1]
Max. sentence:	Magistrates' Court: 6 months' imprisonment / £5,000 fine.
Power:	Report / s.25 PACE

Offence:

It is an offence[2] for a person who is engaged in the business of a postal operator, contrary to his duty and without reasonable excuse, to:

  (a) intentionally delay or open a postal packet in the course of its transmission by post, or

  (b) intentionally open a mail bag.

Contrary to:	Postal Services Act 2000 s.83(1)
Max. sentence:	Magistrates' Court: 6 months' imprisonment / £5,000 fine.
	Crown Court: 2 years' imprisonment / unlimited fine.
Power:	Report / s.25 PACE

Offence:

It is an offence for a person, without reasonable excuse, to:

  (a) intentionally delay or open a postal packet in the course of its transmission by post, or

  (b) intentionally open a mail bag.

Contrary to:	Postal Services Act 2000 s.84(1)

Max. sentence:	Magistrates' Court: 6 months' imprisonment / £5,000 fine.
Power:	Report / s.25 PACE

Offence: It is an offence for a person, intending to act to a person's detriment and without reasonable excuse, to open a postal packet which he knows or reasonably suspects has been incorrectly delivered to him.

Contrary to:	Postal Services Act 2000 s.84(3)
Max. sentence:	Magistrates' Court: 6 months' imprisonment / £5,000 fine.
Power:	Report / s.25 PACE

Offence: It is an offence for a person to send by post a postal packet which encloses any creature, article or thing of any kind which is likely to injure other postal packets in the course of their transmission by post or any person engaged in the business of a postal operator.

Contrary to:	Postal Services Act 2000 s.85(1)
Max. sentence:	Magistrates' Court: 6 months' imprisonment / £5,000 fine.
	Crown Court: 1 year imprisonment / unlimited fine.
Power:	Report / s.25 PACE

Offence: It is an offence for a person to send by post a postal packet which encloses:

(a) any indecent or obscene print, painting, photograph, lithograph, engraving, cinematograph film or other record of a picture or pictures, book, card or written communication; or

(b) any other indecent or obscene article.[3]

Contrary to:	Postal Services Act 2000 s.85(3)

Max. sentence:	Magistrates' Court: 6 months' imprisonment / £5,000 fine.
	Crown Court: 1 year imprisonment / unlimited fine.
Power:	Report / s.25 PACE

Offence:

It is an offence for a person to send by post a postal packet which has on the packet, or on the cover of the packet, any words, marks or designs which are of an indecent or obscene character.

Contrary to:	Postal Services Act 2000 s.85(4)
Max. sentence:	Magistrates' Court: 6 months' imprisonment / £5,000 fine.
	Crown Court: 1 year imprisonment/ unlimited fine.
Power:	Report / s.25 PACE

Offence:

It is an offence for a person, without due authority, to affix any advertisement, document, board or thing in or on any universal postal service post office, universal postal service letter box or to other property belonging to, or used by, a universal service provider in connection with the provision of a universal postal service.

Contrary to:	Postal Services Act 2000 s.86(1)
Max. sentence:	Magistrates' Court: £1,000 fine.
Power:	Report / s.25 PACE

Offence:

It is an offence for a person, without due authority, to paint or in any way disfigure any universal postal service post office, universal postal service letter box or other property belonging to, or used by, a universal service provider in connection with the provision of a universal postal service.

Contrary to:	Postal Services Act 2000 s.86(2)
Max. sentence:	Magistrates' Court: £1,000 fine.
Power:	Report / s.25 PACE

Offence:

It is an offence for a person, without authority,[4] to place or maintain in or on any house, wall, door, window, box, post, pillar or other place belonging to him or under his control:

(a) the words 'letter box' accompanied with words, letters or marks which signify or imply, or may reasonably lead the public to believe, that it is a universal postal service letter box, or

(b) any words, letters or marks which signify or imply, or may reasonably lead the public to believe, that any house, building, room, vehicle or place is a universal postal service post office, or that any box or receptacle is a universal postal service letter box.

Contrary to:	Postal Services Act 2000 s.87(1)
Max. sentence:	Magistrates' Court: £1,000 fine.
Power:	Report / s.25 PACE

Offence:

It is an offence for a person, without authority,[5] to:

(a) place or maintain in or on any ship, vehicle, aircraft or premises belonging to him or under his control, or

(b) use in any document in relation to himself or any other person or in relation to any ship, vehicle, aircraft or premises,

any words, letters or marks which signify or imply, or may reasonably lead the public to believe, that he or that other person is authorised to collect, receive, sort, deliver or convey postal packages or that the ship, vehicle, aircraft or premises is so authorised.

Contrary to: Postal Services Act 2000 s.87(2)

Max. sentence: Magistrates' Court: £1,000 fine.

Power: Report / s.25 PACE

Offence:

It is an offence for a person, without reasonable excuse, to:

(a) obstruct a person engaged in the business of a universal service provider in the execution of his duty in connection with the provision of a universal postal service; or

(b) obstruct, while in any universal postal service post office or related premises, the course of business of a universal service provider.

Contrary to: Postal Services Act 2000 s.88(1)

Max. sentence: Magistrates' Court: £500 fine.

Power: Report / s.25 PACE

Offence:

It is an offence for a person, without reasonable excuse, to fail to leave a universal postal service post office or related premises when required to do so.[6]

Contrary to: Postal Services Act 2000 s.88(3)

Max. sentence: Magistrates Court: £500 fine.

Power: Report / s.25 PACE

Definitions

Universal postal service letter box: means any box or receptacle provided by a universal service provider for the purpose of receiving postal packets, or any class of postal packets, for onwards transmission in connection with the provision of a universal postal service.

Universal postal service post office: includes any house, building, room, vehicle or place used for the provision of any postal services in connection with the provision of a universal postal service or a part of such a service.

Related premises: means any premises belonging to a universal postal service post office or used together with any such post office.

General Information

Section 88(5) of the Postal Services Act 2000 places a duty on any constable to remove or assist in removing any person committing an offence under s.88(3).

Notes

1   As amended by the Criminal Justice and Police Act 2001 s.43.

2   This will not apply to the delaying or opening of a postal packet in accordance with any terms or conditions applicable to its transmission by post or in accordance with any legislation. Nor does it apply to delays caused by a trade dispute.

3   Whether or not of a similar kind to those mentioned in (a).

4   Of the universal postal service provider concerned.

5   Of the universal postal service provider concerned.

6   By a person who is engaged in the business of a universal service provider and who reasonably suspects him of committing an offence of obstruction under s.88(1) of the Postal Services Act 2000.

PROSTITUTION

See also Breach of the Peace, Children and Young Persons, Harassment and Intimidation, Indecent and Obscene Behaviour, Mental Health, Nuisance, PACE – Arrest, Sexual Offences, Town Police Clauses

Offence: It is an offence for the keeper of any house, shop, room, or other place of public resort for the sale or consumption of refreshments of any kind, to knowingly suffer common prostitutes[1] or reputed thieves to assemble and continue in his premises.

Contrary to: Town Police Clauses Act 1847 s.35

Max. sentence: Magistrates' Court: 14 days' imprisonment / £1,000 fine.

Power: Report / s.25 PACE

Offence: It is an offence for a person:

(a)   to procure a woman to become, in any part of the world, a common prostitute; or

(b)   to procure a woman to leave the United Kingdom, intending her to become an inmate of or frequent a brothel elsewhere; or

(c)   to procure a woman to leave her usual place of abode in the United Kingdom intending her to become an inmate of or frequent a brothel in any part of the world for the purposes of prostitution.

Contrary to: Sexual Offences Act 1956 s.22(1)

Max. sentence: Crown Court: 2 years' imprisonment / unlimited fine.

Power: Arrestable Offence[2]

Offence: Its is an offence for a person to procure a girl under the age of 21 to have unlawful sexual intercourse in any part of the world with a third person.

Contrary to: Sexual Offences Act 1956 s.23(1)

Max. sentence: Crown Court: 2 years' imprisonment / unlimited fine.

Power: Arrestable Offence[3]

Offence: It is an offence for a person to detain a woman against her will on any premises with the intention that she shall have unlawful sexual intercourse[4] with men or with a particular man, or to detain a woman against her will in a brothel.

Contrary to: Sexual Offences Act 1956 s.24(1)

Max. sentence: Crown Court: 2 years' imprisonment / unlimited fine.

Power:	Report / s.25 PACE

Offence: It is an offence for a person who is the owner or occupier of any premises, or who has, or acts or assists in, the management or control of any premises, to induce or knowingly suffer a girl under the age of 13 to resort to or be on those premises for the purpose of having unlawful sexual intercourse with men or with a particular man.

Contrary to:	Sexual Offences Act 1956 s.25
Max. sentence:	Crown Court: life imprisonment / unlimited fine.
Power:	Arrestable Offence

Offence: It is an offence for a person who is the owner or occupier of any premises, or who has, or acts or assists in, the management or control of any premises, to induce or knowingly suffer a girl under the age of 16 to resort to or be on those premises for the purpose of having unlawful sexual intercourse with men or with a particular man.

Contrary to:	Sexual Offences Act 1956 s.26
Max. sentence:	Magistrates' Court: 6 months' imprisonment / £5,000 fine.
	Crown Court: 2 years' imprisonment / unlimited fine.
Power:	Report / s.25 PACE

Offence: It is an offence[5] for a person who is the owner or occupier of any premises, or who has, or acts or assists in, the management or control of any premises, to induce or knowingly suffer a woman who is a defective[6] to resort to or be on those premises for the purpose of having unlawful sexual intercourse with men or with a particular man.

Contrary to:	Sexual Offences Act 1956 s.27
Max. sentence:	Crown Court: 2 years' imprisonment / unlimited fine.
Power:	Report / s.25 PACE

Offence: It is an offence for a person to cause or encourage the prostitution of, or the commission of unlawful sexual intercourse with, or of an indecent assault on, a girl under the age of 16 for whom he is responsible.[7]

Contrary to:	Sexual Offences Act 1956 s.28
Max. sentence:	Crown Court: 2 years' imprisonment / unlimited fine.
Power:	Report / s.25 PACE

Offence: It is an offence[8] for a person to cause or encourage the prostitution in any part of the world of a woman who is a defective.

Contrary to:	Sexual Offences Act 1956 s.29
Max. sentence:	Crown Court: 2 years' imprisonment / unlimited fine.
Power:	Report / s.25 PACE

Offence: It is an offence for a man knowingly to live[9] wholly or partly on the earnings of prostitution.

Contrary to:	Sexual Offences Act 1956 s.30
Max. sentence:	Magistrates' Court: 6 months' imprisonment / £5,000 fine.
	Crown Court: 7 years' imprisonment / unlimited fine.
Power:	Arrestable Offence

Offence: It is an offence, for a woman for purposes of gain to exercise control, direction or influence over a prostitute's movements in a way which shows she is aiding, abetting or compelling her prostitution.

Contrary to: Sexual Offences Act 1956 s.31

Max. sentence: Magistrates' Court: 6 months' imprisonment / £5,000 fine.

Crown Court: 7 years' imprisonment / unlimited fine.

Power: Arrestable Offence

Offence:
It is an offence for a man persistently[10] to solicit or importune in a public place for immoral purposes.[11]

Contrary to: Sexual Offences Act 1956 s.32

Max. sentence: Magistrates' Court: 6 months' imprisonment / £5,000 fine.

Crown Court: 2 years' imprisonment / unlimited fine.

Power: Report / s.25 PACE[12]

Offence:
It is an offence for a person to keep a brothel,[13] or to manage or act in the management of, a brothel.

Contrary to: Sexual Offences Act 1956 s.33

Max. sentence: Magistrates' Court: 3 months' imprisonment / £1,000 fine.[14]

Power: Report / s.25 PACE

Offence:
It is an offence for the lessor or landlord of any premises or his agent to let the whole or part of the premises with the knowledge that it is to be used, in whole or in part, as a brothel, or, where the whole or part of the premises is used as a brothel, to be wilfully a party to that use continuing.

Contrary to: Sexual Offences Act 1956 s.34

Max. sentence:	Magistrates' Court: 3 months' imprisonment / £1,000 fine.
Power:	Report / s.25 PACE

Offence: It is an offence for the tenant or occupier, or person in charge, of any premises knowingly to permit the whole or part of the premises to be used as a brothel.

Contrary to:	Sexual Offences Act 1956 s.35(1)
Max. sentence:	Magistrates' Court: 3 months' imprisonment / £1,000 fine.
Power:	Report / s.25 PACE

Offence: It is an offence for the tenant or occupier, or person in charge, of any premises knowingly to permit the whole or part of the premises to be used for the purposes of habitual prostitution.

Contrary to:	Sexual Offences Act 1956 s.36
Max. sentence:	Magistrates' Court: 3 months' imprisonment / £1,000 fine.
Power:	Report / s.25 PACE

Offence: It is an offence for a common prostitute to loiter or solicit in a street[15] or public place for the purposes of prostitution.

Contrary to:	Street Offences Act 1959 s.1(1)
Max. sentence:	Magistrates' Court: £500 fine.[16]
Power:	A constable may arrest without warrant anyone he finds in a street or public place and suspects, with reasonable cause, to be committing this offence.

Offence: It is an offence[17] for the holder of a justices licence to knowingly allow the licensed premises to be the habitual resort or place of meeting of reputed prostitutes, whether the object of their so resorting or meeting is or is not prostitution.

Contrary to: Licensing Act 1964 s.175

Max. sentence: Magistrates' Court: £500 fine.

Power: Report / s.25 PACE

Offence:

It is an offence for a man or a woman to knowingly live wholly or partly on the earnings of prostitution of another man.

Contrary to: Sexual Offences Act 1967 s.5

Max. sentence: Magistrates' Court: 6 months' imprisonment / £5,000 fine.

Crown Court: 7 years' imprisonment / unlimited fine.

Power: Arrestable Offence

Offence:

It is an offence for a man to solicit a woman (or different women) for the purposes of prostitution:

(a) from a motor vehicle while in a street or public place; or

(b) in a street or public place while in the immediate vicinity of a motor vehicle that he has just got out of or off,

persistently or in such manner or in such circumstances as to be likely to cause annoyance to the woman (or any of the women) solicited, or nuisance to other persons in the neighbourhood.

Contrary to: Sexual Offences Act 1985 s.1(1)

Max. sentence: Magistrates' Court: £1,000 fine.

Power: Report / s.25 PACE / Arrestable Offence[18]

Offence:

It is an offence for a man in a street or public place to persistently solicit a woman (or different women) for the purposes of prostitution.

Contrary to:	Sexual Offences Act 1985 s.2(1)
Max. sentence:	Magistrates' Court: £1,000 fine.
Power:	Report / s.25 PACE

Offence:

It is an offence for a person to:

(a) place on, or in the immediate vicinity of, a public telephone an advertisement relating to prostitution,[19] and

(b) to do so with the intention that the advertisement should come to the attention of any person or persons.

Contrary to:	Criminal Justice and Police Act 2001 s.46(1)[20]
Max. sentence:	Magistrates' Court: 6 months' imprisonment / £5,000 fine.
Power:	Arrestable Offence[21]

General Information

For the offence under s.1(1) of the Street Offences Act 1959 a system of cautioning was introduced by the police whereby a woman found soliciting, who had no previous convictions for such offences, would be cautioned on two occasions before being charged with the offence. While this method of dealing with acts of loitering and soliciting facilitated the acquisition of proof that a woman was a 'common prostitute', no powers exist for it and a constable may only proceed with the co-operation of the woman involved. Any woman so cautioned has a right to appeal against that caution to a magistrates' court.

Notes

1 Undefined by any statute.

2 Police and Criminal Evidence Act 1984 s.24(2)(c).

3 As note 2.

4 That is, outside the bounds of marriage.

5 No offence is committed if the accused can prove that he did not know and had no reason to suspect her to be a defective.

6   In this Act 'defective' means a person suffering from a state of arrested or incomplete development of mind which includes severe impairment of intelligence and social functioning.

7   That is, parents, any other person with parental responsibility and any person who has care of her.

8   See note 6.

9   For the purposes of this section a man who lives with or is habitually in the company of a prostitute, or who exercises control, direction or influence over a prostitute's movements in a way which shows he is aiding, abetting or compelling her prostitution with others, shall be presumed to be knowingly living on the earnings of prostitution unless he proves otherwise.

10 Requires a degree of repetition.

11 Such purpose need not be in itself a criminal offence [*R* v *Ford* (1978)] but must involve some kind of sexual activity [*R* v *Kirkup* (1993)].

12 Anyone may arrest without warrant a person found committing an offence under s.32 of the 1956 Act except a constable who may only do so in accordance with s.25 of the Police and Criminal Evidence Act 1984. [Sexual Offences Act 1956 s.41 as amended].

13 That is, a place where people of opposite sexes gather for illicit intercourse.

14 Rising to 6 months' imprisonment and a fine of £2,500 for a second offence. This also applies to ss.34, 35 and 36 of the Sexual Offences Act 1956.

15 'Street' includes any bridge, road, lane, footway, subway, square, court, alley or passage, whether a thoroughfare or not, which is for the time being open to the public. The doorways and entrances of premises abutting on a street, and any ground adjoining and open to a street, shall also be treated as forming part of the street.

16 Or £1,000 for a second offence. Home Office advice is that court proceedings should not be initiated until an offender has 2 police cautions.

17 This section does not prohibit the allowing of such persons to remain in the premises for the purpose of obtaining reasonable refreshment for such time as is necessary for that purpose.

18 The Criminal Justice and Police Act 2001 s.71, in force 1 October 2001, amends the Police and Criminal Evidence Act 1984 s.24(2) by the addition of (ga). See page 283.

19 An advertisement is an advertisement relating to prostitution if it is for the services of a prostitute, whether male or female, or indicates that premises are premises at which such services are offered.

20 In force from 1 September 2001.

21 Police and Criminal Evidence Act 1984 s.24(2)(ca).

PUBLIC ORDER

See also Assaults, Breach of the Peace, Conspiracy and Incitement, Drunkenness, Football, Harassment and Intimidation, Industrial Relations, Noise, Nuisance, PACE – Arrest, Racial Hatred, Town Police Clauses, Trespass

Offence: It is an offence for any person at a lawful public meeting:

(a) to act in a disorderly manner for the purpose of preventing the transaction of the business for which the meeting was called together;

(b) to incite others to commit an act under this section.

Contrary to: Public Meeting Act 1908 s.1

Max. sentence: Magistrates' Court: 6 months' imprisonment / £5,000 fine.

Power: Report / s.25 PACE

Offence: It is an offence[1] for any person in any public place, or at any public meeting, to wear uniform signifying his association with any political organisation or with the promotion of any political object.

Contrary to: Public Order Act 1936 s.1(1)

Max. sentence: Magistrates' Court: 3 months' imprisonment / £2,500 fine.

Power: A constable may arrest without warrant any person reasonably suspected by him to be committing this offence.

Offence: It is an offence[2] where 12 or more persons who are present together[3] use or threaten unlawful violence for a common purpose[4] and the conduct of them (taken together) is such as would cause a person of reasonable firmness present[5] at the scene to fear for his personal safety.

Contrary to: Public Order Act 1986 s.1(1)

Max. sentence: Crown Court: 10 years' imprisonment / unlimited fine.

Power: Arrestable Offence

Offence:

It is an offence[6] where 3 or more persons who are present together[7] use or threaten unlawful[8] violence and the conduct of them (taken together) is such as would cause a person of reasonable firmness present[9] at the scene to fear for his personal safety.

Contrary to: Public Order Act 1986 s.2(1)

Max. sentence: Magistrates' Court: 6 months' imprisonment / £5,000 fine.

Crown Court: 5 years' imprisonment / unlimited fine.

Power: Arrestable Offence

Offence:

It is an offence[10] to use or threaten[11] unlawful violence[12] towards another where the conduct is such as would cause a person of reasonable firmness, present at the scene,[13] to fear for their personal safety.

Contrary to: Public Order Act 1986 s.3(1)

Max. sentence: Magistrates' Court: 6 months' imprisonment / £5,000 fine.

Crown Court: 3 years' imprisonment / unlimited fine.

Power: A constable may arrest without warrant any person he suspects is committing this offence.

Offence:

It is an offence[14] for a person:[15]

(a) to use towards another person threatening, abusive or insulting words or behaviour, or

(b) to distribute or display to another person any writing, sign or other visible representation which is threatening, abusive or insulting,

with intent to cause that person to believe that immediate unlawful violence will be used against him or another by any person, or to provoke the immediate use of unlawful violence by that person or another, or whereby that person is likely to believe that such violence will be used or it is likely that such violence will be provoked.

Contrary to: Public Order Act 1986 s.4(1)

Max. sentence: Magistrates' Court: 6 months' imprisonment / £5,000 fine.

Power: A constable may arrest without warrant any person he suspects is committing this offence.

Offence: It is an offence[16] for any person, with intent to cause a person harassment, alarm or distress:

(a) to use threatening, abusive or insulting words or behaviour, or disorderly behaviour; or

(b) to display any writing, sign or other visible representation which is threatening, abusive or insulting,

thereby causing that or another person harassment, alarm or distress.

Contrary to: Public Order Act 1986 s.4A(1)

Max. sentence: Magistrates' Court: 6 months' imprisonment / £5,000 fine.

Power: A constable may arrest without warrant any person he suspects is committing this offence.

Offence: It is an offence[17] for a person:

(a) to use threatening, abusive or insulting words or behaviour, or disorderly behaviour; or

(b) to display any writing, sign or other visible representation which is threatening, abusive or insulting,

within the hearing or sight of a person[18] likely to be caused harassment, alarm or distress.

Contrary to: Public Order Act 1986 s.5(1)

Max. sentence: Magistrates' Court: £1,000 fine.

Power: A constable may arrest without warrant a person for this offence if that person engages in offensive conduct[19] which a constable warns him to stop, and he engages in further offensive conduct immediately or shortly after the warning.

Offence:

It is an offence[20] for a person, with a view to compelling another person to abstain from doing or to do any act which that person has a legal right to do, or abstain from doing, wrongfully and without legal authority:

(a) to use violence to or intimidate that person or his wife or children, or to injure his property;

(b) to persistently follow that person about from place to place;

(c) to hide any tools, clothes or other property owned or used by that person, or to deprive him of or hinder him in the use thereof;

(d) to watch or beset the house or other place where that person resides, works, carries on business or happens to be, or the approach to any such house or place;

(e) to follow that person with two or more other persons in a disorderly manner in or through any street or road.

Contrary to: Trade Union and Labour Relations (Consolidation) Act 1992 s.241(1)

Max. sentence:	Magistrates' Court: 6 months' imprisonment / £5,000 fine.
Power:	A constable may arrest without warrant anyone he reasonably suspects is committing this offence.

Offence: It is an offence for a person to fail to stop, or to stop a vehicle when required by a constable in the exercise of his powers under s.60 of the Criminal Justice and Public Order Act 1994.

Contrary to:	Criminal Justice and Public Order Act 1994 s.60(8)(a)
Max. sentence:	Magistrates' Court: 1 month's imprisonment / £1,000 fine.
Power:	Report / s.25 PACE

Offence: It is an offence for a person to fail to remove an item worn by him when required by a constable in the exercise of his powers under s.60 of the Criminal Justice and Public Order Act 1994.

Contrary to:	Criminal Justice and Public Order Act 1994 s.60(8)(b)
Max. sentence:	Magistrates' Court: 1 month's imprisonment / £1,000 fine.
Power:	Arrestable Offence[21]

General Powers

If any constable reasonably suspects any person of committing an offence under s.1 of the Public Meeting Act 1908 he may, if requested to do so by the chairman of the meeting, require that person to declare to him immediately his name and address.[22]

A constable may enter and search any premises for the purpose of arresting a person for an offence under s.1 of the Public order Act 1936 or s.4 of the Public Order Act 1986.[23]

Where an authorisation under s.60 of the Criminal Justice and Public Order Act 1994[24] has been given, a constable in uniform may:

(a) stop any pedestrian and search him or anything carried by him for offensive weapons or dangerous instruments;

(b) stop any vehicle and search the vehicle, its driver and any passenger for offensive weapons or dangerous instruments; or

(c) require any person to remove any item which the constable reasonably believes that the person is wearing wholly or mainly for the purpose of concealing his identity.

If in the course of a search under s.60 a constable discovers an offensive weapon, dangerous instrument or item worn for the purpose of concealing the person's identity, he may seize it.

Definitions

Violence: means any violent conduct, so that:

(a) except in the context of affray, it includes violent conduct towards property as well as violent conduct towards persons; and

(b) it is not restricted to conduct causing or intended to cause injury or damage but includes any other violent conduct (for example, throwing at or towards a person a missile of a kind capable of causing injury which does not hit or falls short).[25]

General Information

In relation to the offences under the Public Order Act 1986 a person is guilty

(a) of riot only if he intends to use violence or is aware[26] that his conduct may be violent;

(b) of violent disorder only if he intends to use or threaten violence or is aware that his conduct may be violent or threaten violence;

(c) of an offence under s.4 only if he intends his words or behaviour, or the writing, sign or other visible representation, to be threatening, abusive or insulting, or is aware that it may be threatening, abusive or insulting;

(d) of an offence under s.5 only if he intends his words or behaviour, or the writing, sign or other visible representation, to be threatening, abusive or insulting, or is aware that it may be threatening, abusive or insulting or (as the case may be) he intends his behaviour to be or is aware that it may be disorderly.

Processions are controlled and a written notice is required to be given of any public procession intended to demonstrate support or opposition to the views or action of any person or body of persons, or to publicise a cause or campaign, or to mark or commemorate an event. This allows the police to consider the imposition of any conditions considered necessary to avoid public disorder, serious damage or serious disruption to the life of the community and facilitates the prohibition of such a procession if the imposition of conditions is considered insufficient to avoid serious public disorder. Offences are committed by any person organising a prohibited assembly, taking part in one or inciting others to take part.[27]

Notes

1   A chief constable may give permission for the wearing of uniforms for ceremonial or special occasions provided he is satisfied that such is not likely to provoke any public disorder.

2   This offence is commonly referred to as 'Riot' and may be committed in private as well as in public places.

3   It is immaterial whether or not the 12 or more use or threaten violence simultaneously.

4   The common purpose may be inferred from conduct.

5   No person of reasonable firmness need actually be, or be likely to be, present at the scene.

6   Referred to as 'Violent Disorder', this offence may also be committed in both public and private places.

7   As note 3.

8   Lawful will include self-defence and the reasonable defence of another, [*R* v *Rothwell and Barton* (1993)].

9   As note 5.

10   This is an 'Affray' and can be committed in both public and private places.

11   This cannot be by words alone. However, the public and open carrying of weapons (for example, petrol bombs) is capable of constituting a threat of unlawful violence and it is a reasonable inference that a person there at the time would be in fear. Affray does require the presence of a person threatened although it does not need to be proved that they perceived the threat [*R* v *West London Youth Court, ex parte M* (1990)].

12   Where 2 or more persons use or threaten the unlawful violence, it is the conduct of them taken together which must be considered.

13 No person of reasonable firmness need actually be, or be likely to be, present at the scene. [Public Order Act 1986 s.3(4)].

14 This offence may be committed in public or private, except that no offence is committed where the words or behaviour used, or the writing, sign or other visible representation is distributed or displayed, by a person inside a dwelling and the other person is also inside that or another dwelling. The common parts of a block of flats are not a 'dwelling' for this purpose [*Rukwira* v *DPP* (1993)].

15 Intentionally or with an awareness that the words or behaviour are, or may be, threatening, abusive or insulting [*Winn* v *DPP* (1992)].

16 See note 14. It is a defence for the accused to prove that he was inside a dwelling and had no reason to believe that the words or behaviour used, or the writing, sign or other visible representation displayed, would be heard or seen by a person outside that or any other dwelling, or that his conduct was reasonable.

17 See notes 14 and 16. In addition to that outlined in note 14, there is a defence where the accused can prove that he had no reason to believe that there was any person within hearing or sight who was likely to be caused harassment, alarm or distress.

18 This may include a police officer [*DPP* v *Orum* (1988)].

19 'Offensive conduct' means conduct the constable reasonably suspects to constitute an offence under s.5(1), and the conduct mentioned in (a) and the further conduct need not be of the same nature. The warning may be given by a different constable to the one who affects an arrest.

20 This offence is not restricted to trade disputes and may be applied to the actions of an anti-road protestor [*Todd* v *DPP* (1996)].

21 Police and Criminal Evidence Act 1984 s.24(2)(o), as amended by the Crime and Disorder Act 1998.

22 Failure is an offence, subject to a £200 fine.

23 Police and Criminal Evidence Act 1984, s.17.

24 This may be given by an inspector or above where he believes that incidents of serious violence may occur within a locality and it is expedient to give a s.60 authorisation in order to prevent such occurrence or that persons are carrying dangerous instruments or offensive weapons without good reason. This authorisation only lasts for 24 hours but may be extended for a further 24 hours by a superintendent or above.

25 Public Order Act 1986 s.8.

26 Such awareness is not affected by intoxication either through drink or drugs, unless the accused can show that his intoxication was not self-induced or that it was caused solely by the taking or administration of a substance in the course of medical treatment.

27 Public Order Act 1986 ss.11–14.

PUBLIC SERVICE VEHICLES

See also Drivers and Riders, Drivers' Records, Driving Documents, Goods
Vehicles Operators, Taxis and Private Hire

Offence: It is an offence for a public service vehicle to be used on a road for carrying passengers for hire or reward except under a PSV operator's licence.

Contrary to: Public Passenger Vehicles Act 1981 s.12(1)

Max. sentence: Magistrates' Court: £2,500 fine.

Power: Report / s.25 PACE

Offence: It is an offence for a vehicle being used in circumstances such that a PSV operator's licence is required, to do so without there being fixed and exhibited on the vehicle an operator's disc.

Contrary to: Public Passenger Vehicles Act 1981 s.18(1)

Max. sentence: Magistrates' Court: £1,000 fine.

Power: Report / s.25 PACE

Offence: It is an offence for a driver, inspector or conductor on any public service vehicle or tramcar to contravene, or fail to comply with, a provision of regulations concerned with their conduct.

Contrary to: Public Passenger Vehicles Act 1981 s.24(2)

Max. sentence: Magistrates' Court: £500 fine.

Power: Report / s.25 PACE

Offence: It is an offence for a passenger on any public service vehicle or tramcar to contravene, or fail to comply with, a provision of regulations concerned with their conduct.

Contrary to: Public Passenger Vehicles Act 1981 s. 25(3)

Max. sentence: Magistrates' Court: £500 fine.

Power: Report / s.25 PACE

General Powers

Any passenger on a vehicle who is reasonably suspected by the driver, inspector or conductor of the vehicle of contravening any provision of the regulations shall give his name and address to the driver, inspector or conductor on demand. Any passenger on a vehicle who contravenes any provision of the regulations may be removed from the vehicle by the driver, inspector or conductor of the vehicle or, on the request of the driver, inspector or conductor, by a police constable.[1]

Definitions

Public service vehicle: means a motor vehicle (other than a tramcar) which:

(a)   being a vehicle adapted to carry more than 8 passengers, is used for carrying passengers for hire or reward; or

(b)   being a vehicle not so adapted, is used for carrying passengers for hire or reward at separate fares in the course of a business of carrying passengers.

General Information

The Public Service Vehicles (Conduct of Drivers, Inspectors, Conductors and Passengers) Regulations 1990 control conduct on PSVs and prohibit on any person:

(a)   putting at risk or unreasonably impeding or causing discomfort to any person travelling on or entering or leaving the vehicle, or a driver, inspector, conductor or employee of the operator when doing his work on the vehicle;

(b)   throwing or trailing any article from the vehicle;

(c)   smoking where it is prohibited;

(d)   selling or offering for sale any article without the permission of the operator;

(e)   distracting the driver's attention;

(f)   remaining on the vehicle when directed to leave;

(g)   failing to declare, on request, the journey he intends to take, or is taking, or has taken;

(h) failing to pay the fare for the journey.

Notes

1   Public Service Vehicles (Conduct of Drivers, Inspectors, Conductors and Passengers) Regulations 1990.

RACIAL HATRED

See also Assaults, Breach of the Peace, Damage, Football, Harassment and Intimidation, Indecent and Obscene Behaviour, Public Order

Offence: It is an offence[1] for a person to use threatening, abusive or insulting words or behaviour, or to display any written material which is threatening, abusive or insulting if:

(a)   he intends thereby to stir up racial hatred; or

(b)   having regard to all the circumstances racial hatred is likely to be stirred up thereby.

Contrary to: Public Order Act 1986 s.18(1)

Max. sentence: Magistrates' Court: 6 months' imprisonment / £5,000 fine.

Crown Court: 2 years' imprisonment / unlimited fine.

Power: A constable may arrest without warrant any person he suspects is committing this offence.

Offence: It is an offence[2] for a person to publish or distribute[3] written material which is threatening, abusive or insulting words or behaviour, if:

(a)   he intends thereby to stir up racial hatred; or

(b)   having regard to all the circumstances racial hatred is likely to be stirred up thereby.

Contrary to: Public Order Act 1986 s.19(1)

Max. sentence: Magistrates' Court: 6 months' imprisonment / £5,000 fine.

Crown Court: 2 years' imprisonment / unlimited fine.

Power: Report / s.25 PACE / Breach of the Peace

Offence:

It is an offence for a person to distribute,[1] or show or play, a recording of visual images or sounds which are threatening, abusive or insulting if:

(a)   he intends thereby to stir up racial hatred; or

(b)   having regard to all the circumstances racial hatred is likely to be stirred up thereby.

Contrary to: Public Order Act 1986 s.21(1)

Max. sentence: Magistrates' Court: 6 months' imprisonment / £5,000 fine.

Crown Court: 2 years' imprisonment / unlimited fine.

Power: Report / s.25 PACE / Breach of the Peace

Offence:

It is an offence for a person to have in his possession written material which is threatening, abusive or insulting, or a recording of visual images or sounds which are threatening, abusive or insulting, with a view to:

(a)   in the case of written material, it being displayed, published, distributed, or included in a programme service whether by himself or another; or

(b)   in the case of a recording, its being distributed, shown, played, or included in a programme service whether by himself or another,

intending that racial hatred be stirred up thereby, or, having regard to all the circumstances, racial hatred is likely to be stirred up thereby.

Contrary to: Public Order Act 1986 s.23 (1)

Max. sentence:	Magistrates' Court: 6 months' imprisonment / £5,000 fine.
	Crown Court: 2 years' imprisonment / unlimited fine.
Power:	Report / s.25 PACE / Breach of the Peace

Offence:

It is an offence for a person to take part at a designated football match in chanting of a racialist nature.[5]

Contrary to:	Football (Offences) Act 1991 s.3
Max. sentence:	Magistrates' Court: £1,000 fine.
Power:	Report / s.25 PACE / Breach of the Peace

Offence:

It is an offence for a person to commit an offence under s.20 of the Offences Against the Person Act 1861 which is racially aggravated.

Contrary to:	Crime and Disorder Act 1998 s.29(1)(a)
Max. sentence:	Magistrates' Court: 6 months' imprisonment / £5,000 fine.
	Crown Court: 7 years' imprisonment / unlimited fine
Power:	Arrestable Offence

Offence:

It is an offence for a person to commit a racially aggravated assault falling within s.47 of the Offences Against the Person Act 1861.

Contrary to:	Crime and Disorder Act 1998, s.29(1)(b)
Max. Penalty:	Magistrates' Court: 6 months' imprisonment/ £5,000 fine.
	Crown Court: 7 years' imprisonment/ unlimited fine.
Power:	Arrestable Offence

Offence:

It is an offence for a person to commit a racially aggravated common assault.

Contrary to:	Crime and Disorder Act 1998 s.29(1)(c)
Max. Penalty:	Magistrates' Court: 6 months' imprisonment / £5,000 fine.
	Crown Court: 2 years' imprisonment/ unlimited fine.
Power:	Report / s.25 PACE / Breach of the Peace

Offence:

It is an offence for a person to commit an offence under s.1(1) of the Criminal Damage Act 1971[6] which is racially aggravated.

Contrary to:	Crime and Disorder Act 1998 s.30(1)
Max. sentence:	Magistrates' Court: 6 months' imprisonment / £5,000 fine.
	Crown Court: 14 years' imprisonment / unlimited fine.
Power:	Arrestable Offence

Offence:

It is an offence for a person to commit an offence under s.4[7] or 4A[8] of the Public Order Act 1986, which is racially aggravated.

Contrary to:	Crime and Disorder Act 1998 s.31(1)(a) and (b).
Max. sentence:	Magistrates' Court: 6 months' imprisonment / £5,000 fine.
	Crown Court: 2 years' imprisonment / unlimited fine.
Power:	A constable may arrest without warrant anyone whom he reasonably suspects is committing this offence.[9]

Offence:

It is an offence for a person to commit an offence under s.5[10] of the Public Order Act 1986, which is racially aggravated.

Contrary to:	Crime and Disorder Act 1998 s.31(1)(c)
Max. sentence:	Magistrates' Court: £2,500 fine.

Power:	A constable may arrest without warrant where a person engages in conduct which a constable reasonably suspects to constitute an offence under s.31(1)(c), he is warned by that constable to stop, and he engages in further such conduct immediately or shortly after the warning.

Offence:

It is an offence for a person, to commit an offence under s.2 of the Protection from Harassment Act 1997 which is racially aggravated.

Contrary to:	Crime and Disorder Act 1998 Act 1998 s.32(1) (a)
Max. sentence:	Magistrates' Court: 6 months' imprisonment / £5,000 fine.
	Crown Court: 2 years' imprisonment / unlimited fine.
Power:	Arrestable Offence[11]

Offence:

It is an offence for a person, to commit an offence under s.4 of the Protection from Harassment Act 1997 which is racially aggravated.

Contrary to:	Crime and Disorder Act 1998 Act 1998 s.32(1)(b)
Max. sentence:	Magistrates' Court: 6 months' imprisonment / £5,000 fine.
	Crown Court: 7 years' imprisonment / unlimited fine.
Power:	Arrestable Offence.

Definitions

Chanting: means the repeated uttering of any words or sounds in concert with one or more others.

Racial group: means a group of persons defined by reference to race, colour, nationality (including citizenship) or ethnic or national origins.

Racial hatred: means hatred against a group of persons in Great Britain defined by reference to colour, race, nationality (including citizenship) or ethnic or national origins.[12]

Racially aggravated: An offence is racially aggravated for the purposes of the Crime and Disorder Act 1998 s.32 if:

(a) at the time of committing the offence, or immediately before or after doing so, the offender demonstrates towards the victim of the offence hostility based on the victim's membership[13] (or presumed[14] membership) of a racial group; or

(b) the offence is motivated (wholly or partly) by hostility towards members of a racial group based on their membership of that group.

It is immaterial for the purposes of either (a) or (b) whether or not the offender's hostility is also based to any extent on the fact or presumption that any person or group of persons belongs to any religious group, or any other factor.

Notes

1   This offence may be committed in public or private, except that no offence is committed where the words or behaviour used, or the written material is displayed, by a person inside a dwelling and are not heard or seen except by other persons in that or another dwelling.

2   It is a defence for an accused who is not shown to have intended to stir up racial hatred to prove that he was not aware of the content of the material and did not suspect, and had no reason to suspect, that it was threatening, abusive or insulting.

3   That is, to the public or to a section of the public.

4   That is, to the public or a section of the public.

5   This includes chanting which is threatening, abusive or insulting by reason of reference to colour, race, nationality (including citizenship) or ethnic or national origins [Football (Offences) Act 1991 s.3(2)].

6   See page 74.

7   Fear or provocation of violence. See page 325.

8   Intentional harassment, alarm or distress. See pages 207 and 325.

9   Crime and Disorder Act 1998 s.31(2).

10   Harassment, alarm or distress. See page 326.

11   Police and Criminal Evidence Act 1984 s.24(2)(p).

12 Public Order Act 1986 s.17.

13 Includes association with members of that group.

14 That is, by the offender.

RAILWAYS

See also Damage, Drink and Drive / Ride, Trespass

Offence: It is an offence[1] for a person to:

(a) wilfully obstruct or impede any officer or agent of any railway company in the execution of his duty upon any railway;[2]

(b) wilfully trespass upon any railway and refuse to quit when requested to do so by any officer or agent of the company.

Contrary to: Railway Regulation Act 1840 s.16

Max. sentence: Magistrates' Court: 1 month imprisonment / £1,000 fine.

Power: Report / s.25 PACE

Offence: It is an offence for an employee of the railway company[3] to:

(a) commit any offence against any of the byelaws, rules or regulations of the company;

(b) wilfully, maliciously or negligently do or omit to do any act whereby the life or limb of any person passing along or being upon the railway might be injured or endangered;

(c) obstruct or impede the passage of any engines, carriages or trains.

Contrary to: Railway Regulation Act 1842 s.17

Max. sentence: Magistrates' Court: 3 months' imprisonment / £1,000 fine.

Power: Any officer or agent, or persons called to assist, may seize and detain the person.[4]

Offence: It is an offence for any person to omit to shut and fasten any gate, or to lower any barrier set up at either side of a railway for the accommodation of the owners or occupiers of the adjoining lands as soon as he and the carriage, cattle or other animals under his care, have passed through.

Contrary to: Railway Clauses Consolidation Act 1845 s.75

Max. sentence: Magistrates' Court: £1,000 fine.

Power: Report / s.25 PACE

Offence: It is an offence for any person, knowingly and wilfully and on arriving at the point to which he has paid his fare, to refuse or neglect to quit the carriage.

Contrary to: Railway Clauses Consolidation Act 1845 s.103

Max. sentence: Magistrates' Court: £500 fine.

Power: A constable may arrest anyone committing or attempting to commit this offence.[5]

Offence: It is an offence for any person to:

(a) carry, or require the railway company to carry, upon the railway any goods which may be of a dangerous nature;[6] or

(b) send by the railway, any such goods without clearly marking their nature on the outside of the package, or otherwise giving notice to the company.

Contrary to: Railway Clauses Consolidation Act 1845 s.105

Max. sentence: Magistrates' Court: £500 fine.

Power: Report / s.25 PACE.

Offence: It is an offence for any person to pull down or injure any board put up or affixed for the purpose of publishing any byelaw of the railway company or any penalty imposed, or shall obliterate any of the letters or figures thereon.

Contrary to: Railway Clauses Consolidation Act 1845 s.144

Max. sentence: Magistrates' Court: £200 fine.

Power: Report / s.25 PACE.

Offence:

It is an offence for any person, unlawfully and maliciously, to:

  (a) put or throw upon or across any railway, any wood, stone or other matter or thing;

  (b) take up, remove, or displace any rail, sleeper, or other matter or thing belonging to any railway;

  (c) turn, move or divert any points or other machinery belonging to any railway;

  (d) make or show, hide or remove, any signal or light upon or near to any railway; or

  (e) do or cause to be done any other matter or thing,

with intent to endanger the safety of any person travelling or being upon any such railway.

Contrary to: Malicious Damage Act 1861 s.32

Max. sentence: Crown Court: life imprisonment / unlimited fine.

Power: Arrestable Offence

Offence:

It is an offence for any person, unlawfully and maliciously, to throw, or cause to fall or strike, at, into or upon any engine, tender, carriage, or truck used upon any railway, any wood, stone, or other matter or thing, with intent to injure or endanger the safety of any person being in or upon such engine, tender, carriage, or truck, or in or upon any other engine, tender, carriage, or truck of any train of which the first-mentioned engine, tender, carriage, or truck shall form part.

Contrary to: Malicious Damage Act 1861 s.33

Max. sentence: Crown Court: life imprisonment / unlimited fine.

Power: Arrestable Offence

Offence:

It is an offence for any person,[7] by any unlawful act or wilful omission or neglect, to endanger or cause to be endangered the safety of any person conveyed or being in or upon a railway.

Contrary to: Malicious Damage Act 1861 s.34

Max. sentence: Magistrates' Court: 6 months' imprisonment / £5,000 fine.

Crown Court: 2 years' imprisonment / unlimited fine.

Power: Report / s.25 PACE

Offence:

It is an offence for any person to unlawfully and maliciously:

(a) put, place, cast, or throw upon or across any railway, any wood, stone or other matter or thing;

(b) take up, remove, or displace any rail, sleeper, or other matter or thing belonging to any railway;

(c) turn, move or divert any points or other machinery belonging to any railway;

(d) make or show, hide or remove, any signal or light upon or near to any railway; or

(e) do or cause to be done any other matter or thing,

with intent to obstruct, upset, overthrow, injure, or destroy any engine, tender, carriage or truck using the railway.

Contrary to:	Malicious Damage Act 1861 s.35
Max. sentence:	Crown Court: life imprisonment / unlimited fine.
Power:	Arrestable Offence

Offence: It is an offence for any person,[8] by any unlawful act or wilful omission or neglect, to obstruct or cause to be obstructed any engine or carriage using the railway.

Contrary to:	Malicious Damage Act 1861 s.36
Max. sentence:	Magistrates' Court: 6 months' imprisonment / £5,000 fine.
	Crown Court: 2 years' imprisonment / unlimited fine.
Power:	Report / s.25 PACE[9]

Offence: It is an offence for a person to:

(a) unlawfully and maliciously put or throw upon or across any railway any wood, stone or other matter or thing;

(b) unlawfully and maliciously take up, remove or displace any rail, sleeper, or other matter or thing belonging to any railway;

(c) unlawfully and maliciously turn, move or divert any points or other machinery belonging to any railway;

(d) unlawfully and maliciously make or show, hide or remove, any signal or light upon or near any railway; or

(e) unlawfully and maliciously do or cause to be done any other matter or thing,

with intent to endanger the safety of any person travelling or being upon such railway.

Contrary to:	Offences Against the Person Act 1861 s.32
Max. sentence:	Crown Court: life imprisonment / unlimited fine.

| **Power:** | Arrestable Offence |

Offence:

It is an offence for any person, having received a warning[10] not to go or pass thereon to be or pass upon any railway[11] except for the purpose of crossing at an authorised crossing.

Contrary to:	Regulation of Railways Act 1868 s.23
Max. sentence:	Magistrates' Court: £200 fine.
Power:	Report / s.25 PACE

Offence:

It is an offence for any passenger on a railway, on the request of an officer or servant of a railway company, to fail to:

(a) produce or deliver up a ticket showing that his fare is paid;

(b) pay his fare from the place whence he started; or

(c) give his name and address.

Contrary to:	Regulation of Railways Act 1889 s.5(1)
Max. sentence:	Magistrates' Court: £200 fine.
Power:	Any officer or servant of the railway company may detain the person.[12]

Offence:

It is an offence for any person:

(a) to travel or attempt to travel on a railway without having previously paid his fare and with intent to avoid payment thereof;

(b) having paid for a certain distance, knowingly and wilfully, proceeds beyond that distance without paying the additional fare and with intent to avoid payment thereof; or

(c) having failed to pay his fare, gives in reply to a request by an officer of a railway company a false name and address.

Contrary to:	Regulation of Railways Act 1889, s.5(3)
Max. sentence:	Magistrates' Court: 3 months' imprisonment / £1,000 fine.
Power:	Report / s.25 PACE

Offence: It is an offence for any person to trespass upon any of the lines of railway or sidings or in any tunnel, or upon any railway embankment, cutting or similar work belonging or leased to any of the railway boards,[13] or in dangerous proximity to any such lines of railway or other works, or to any electrical apparatus used for or in connection with the railway.[14]

Contrary to:	British Transport Commission Act 1949 s.55
Max. sentence:	Magistrates' Court: £1,000 fine.
Power:	Report / s.25 PACE

Offence: It is an offence for any person to unlawfully throw or cause to fall or strike at or against, into or upon any engine, tender, motor, carriage, truck works or apparatus used upon any railway or siding belonging to or leased by any of the railway boards, any stone, matter or thing likely to cause damage or injury to persons or property.

Contrary to:	British Transport Commission Act 1949 s.56
Max. sentence:	Magistrates' Court: £1,000 fine.
Power:	Report / s.25 PACE

Offence: It is an offence[15] for a person who works on a transport system to which this Act applies:[16]

(a) as a driver, guard, conductor or signalman or in any other capacity in which he can control or affect the movement of a vehicle; or

(b) in a maintenance capacity or as a supervisor of, or look-out for, persons working in a maintenance capacity,

to be unfit to carry out that work[17] through drink or drugs.

Contrary to: Transport and Works Act 1992 s.27(1)

Max. sentence: Magistrates' Court: 6 months' imprisonment / £5,000 fine.

Power: A constable may arrest a person without warrant if he has reasonable cause to suspect that that person is or has been committing this offence.

Offence:

It is an offence[18] for a person who works on a transport system:

(a) as a driver, guard, conductor or signalman or in any other capacity in which he can control or affect the movement of a vehicle; or

(b) in a maintenance capacity or as a supervisor of, or look-out for, persons working in a maintenance capacity,

after consuming so much alcohol that the proportion of it in his breath, blood or urine exceeds the prescribed limit.[19]

Contrary to: Transport and Works Act 1992 s.27(2)

Max. sentence: Magistrates' Court: 6 months' imprisonment / £5,000 fine.

Power: See General Powers

Offence:

It is an offence for a person, without reasonable excuse, to fail to provide a specimen of breath when required to do so in pursuance of s.29.

Contrary to: Transport and Works Act 1992 s.29(5)

Max. sentence: Magistrates' Court: £1,000 fine.

Power: See General Powers

Offence: It is an offence for a person, without reasonable excuse, to fail or refuse to provide a specimen[20] when required to do so in pursuance of s.31.

Contrary to: Transport and Works Act 1992 s.31(8)

Max. sentence: Magistrates' Court: £1,000 fine.

Power: See General Powers

General Powers

For the purpose of arresting a person under s.27(1) of the Transport and Works Act 1992, a constable may enter (if need be by force) any place where that person is or where the constable, with reasonable cause, suspects him to be.

Where a constable in uniform has reasonable cause to suspect:

(a) that a person working on a transport system in any capacity[21] has alcohol in his body; or

(b) that a person has been working on a transport system with alcohol in his body and still has alcohol in his body,

he may require that person to provide a specimen of breath for a breath test.[22]

Where an accident or dangerous incident occurs on a transport system,[23] a constable in uniform may require a person to provide a specimen of breath for a breath test if he has reasonable cause to suspect that:

(a) at the time of the accident or incident that person was working on the transport system in a capacity as mentioned in s.27(1) or (2); and

(b) an act or omission of that person while he had been so working may have been a cause of the accident or incident.[24]

A person may be required to provide a specimen either at or near the place where the requirement is made or, if the requirement is made under s.29(2) and the constable making the requirement thinks fit, at a police station specified by the constable.[25]

A constable may arrest[26] a person without warrant if:

(a)   as a result of a breath test he has reasonable cause to suspect that the proportion of alcohol in that person's breath or blood exceeds the prescribed limit; or

(b)   that person has failed or refused to provide a specimen of breath for a breath test when required to do so and the constable has reasonable cause to suspect that he has alcohol in his body.[27]

A constable may, for the purpose of:

(a)   requiring a person to provide a specimen of breath under s.29(2) in the case of an accident which the constable has reasonable cause to suspect involved the death of, or injury to, another person; or

(b)   arresting a person in such a case under s.30(2), enter[28] any place where that person is or where the constable, with reasonable cause, suspects him to be.[29]

In the course of an investigation into whether a person has committed an offence under s.27, a constable may require him:

(a)   to provide two specimens of breath[30] for analysis by means of an approved device; or

(b)   to provide a specimen of blood or urine,[31] for a laboratory test.[32]

A person may be required to provide a specimen of blood or urine notwithstanding that he has already provided or been required to provide two specimens of breath.[33]

General Information

The Railway Byelaws 2001[34] provide extensive provisions for the protection of railway property and the control of passengers. Prohibitions under these byelaws include the carriage of potentially dangerous articles, smoking in certain areas, intoxication, unacceptable behaviour, gambling and carrying on a trade on railway property.

Notes

1   It is also an offence to aid or assist.

2   Including stations, premises or other works connected with a railway.

3   Includes engine drivers, guards, porters, servants or other employees as

well as the employees of other companies involved with conducting railway traffic or repairing or maintaining the railway.

4   Police officers may be called upon to assist, in which case s.30 the Police and Criminal Evidence Act 1984 applies.

5   Railway Clauses Consolidation Act 1845 s.104.

6   In the opinion of the company.

7   Or to aid or assist.

8   Or to aid or assist.

9   But see the powers for criminal damage offences on page 73.

10 From the company or any of its agents or servants.

11 Does not include platforms.

12 Police officers may be called upon to assist.

13 And their successors.

14 It is a defence to show that clearly exhibited notices warning people against trespass had not been affixed and maintained at the nearest station.

15 Unless the responsible operator has exercised due diligence to prevent the commission of this offence, they will also be liable.

16 This applies to railways, tramways and any other system specified in an Order by the Secretary of State, used wholly or party for the carriage of members of the public.

17 That is, if his ability is for the time being impaired.

18 Unless the responsible operator has exercised due diligence to prevent the commission of this offence, they will also be liable.

19 See page 100.

20 A constable shall, on requiring a person to provide a specimen, warn him that a failure to provide may render him liable to prosecution.

21 Mentioned in s.27(1) or (2) of the Transport and Works Act 1992.

22 Ibid., s.29(1).

23 That is, that involves, in the constable's opinion, a danger of death or personal injury.

24 Transport and Works Act 1992 s.29(2).

25 Ibid., s.29(4).

26 But not while the person is at a hospital as a patient.

27 Transport and Works Act 1992 s.30(2).

28 If need be by force.

29 Transport and Works Act 1992 s.30(4).

30 This requirement can only be made at a police station.

31 The choice is the constable's unless advised against blood by a medical practitioner. A specimen of urine must be provided within 1 hour of the requirement and after the provision of a previous specimen of urine. This requirement can only be made at a police station or a hospital and cannot be made at a police station unless:

(a)   the constable making the requirement has reasonable cause to believe that for medical reasons a specimen of breath cannot be provided or should not be required;

(b)   at the time that the requirement is made, either a reliable device of the approved type is not available or it is not practicable to use such a device;

(bb) an approved device has been used but the constable has reasonable cause to believe that the device has not produced a reliable indication of the proportion of alcohol in the breath of the person concerned; or

(c)   the suspected offence is one under s.27(1) and the constable has been advised by a medical practitioner that the condition of the person required to provide the specimen might be due to a drug.

32 Transport and Works Act 1992 s.31(1), (2) and (3).

33 Ibid., s.31(5).

34 Where adopted by the rail operators.

REGISTRATION AND LICENSING

See also Driving Documents, Excise Licences, Goods Vehicles Operators, Public Service Vehicles, Taxis and Private Hire

Offence: It is an offence[1] for a registration mark not to be fixed on a vehicle so as to comply with the regulations.[2]

Contrary to: Vehicle Excise and Registration Act 1994 s.42(1)

Max. sentence: Magistrates' Court: £1,000 fine.

Power: Report / s.25 PACE

Offence: It is an offence[3] for a registration mark to be in any way obscured, or rendered, or allowed to become, not easily distinguishable.

Contrary to: Vehicle Excise and Registration Act 1994 s.43

Max. sentence: Magistrates' Court: £1,000 fine.

Power:	Report / s.25 PACE

Offence: It is an offence for a person to use or keep on a road an exempt vehicle for which regulations require a nil licence to be in force and a nil licence is not, for the time being, in force in respect of the vehicle.

Contrary to:	Vehicle Excise and Registration Act 1994 s.43A
Max. sentence:	Magistrates' Court: £1,000 fine.
Power:	Report / s.25 PACE

Offence: It is an offence for a person to forge, fraudulently alter, fraudulently use, fraudulently lend or fraudulently allow to be used by another person a registration mark, registration document or trade plate.[4]

Contrary to:	Vehicle Excise and Registration Act 1994 s.44(1)
Max. sentence:	Magistrates' Court: 6 months' imprisonment / £5,000 fine. Crown Court: 2 years' imprisonment / unlimited fine.
Power:	Report / s.25 PACE

Offence: It is an offence for a person to carry on a business as a registration plate supplier without being registered by the Secretary of State.

Contrary to:	Vehicles (Crime) Act 2001 s.17(1)[5]
Max. sentence:	Magistrates' Court: £5,000 fine.
Power:	Report / s.25 PACE

Offence: It is an offence for a person required to keep records under the provisions of the regulations made under this Act, to fail to do so.

Contrary to:	Vehicles (Crime) Act 2001 s.24(4)
Max. sentence:	Magistrates' Court: £1,000 fine.
Power:	Report / s.25 PACE

Offence: It is an offence for a person to obstruct a constable exercising his powers under this Act.

Contrary to: Vehicles (Crime) Act 2001 s.26(7)

Max. sentence: Magistrates' Court: £500 fine.

Power: Report / s.25 PACE

Offence: It is an offence for a person to knowingly, or recklessly, sell a plate or other device which is not a registration plate as a registration plate.

Contrary to: Vehicles (Crime) Act 2001 s.28(1)

Max. sentence: Magistrates' Court: £2,500 fine.

Power: Report / s.25 PACE

General Powers

The owner of a mechanically propelled vehicle in respect of which a registration book has been issued shall produce it for inspection if he is at any time reasonably required to do so by a police officer.[6]

A constable may at any reasonable time enter[7] and inspect premises for the time being entered in the register as premises which are occupied by a person carrying on business as a registration plate supplier.[8]

A constable may at any reasonable time :

(a)   require production of, and inspect, any registration plates kept at the premises of a registration plate supplier; and

(b)   require production of, inspect and take copies of or extracts from any records which the person carrying on business as a registration plate supplier is required to keep.[9]

General Information

British Standard specification BS AU 145 details the requirements for registration mark layouts which affect vehicles falling into three categories, those registered before 1 January 1973, those registered between 1 January 1973 and 1 September 2001 and those registered after 1 September 2001. Specifications included in the regulations include:

(a)   a registration plate must be fixed to the rear of the vehicle;[10]

(b)   a registration plate must be fixed to the front of the vehicle;[11]

(c)   where the vehicle is being used on a road between sunset and sunrise the rear registration plate must be lit;[12]

(d)   no reflex-reflecting material may be applied to any part of a registration plate and the plate must not be treated in such a way that the characters of the registration mark become, or are caused to act as, retroreflective characters;

(e)   a registration mark must not be treated in any other way which renders the characters of the registration mark less easily distinguishable to the eye or which would prevent or impair the making of a true photographic image of the plate through the medium of a camera and film or any other device;

(f)   a registration plate must not be fixed to the vehicle by means of a screw, bolt or other fixing device of any type or colour, by the placing of a screw, bolt or other fixing device in any position or in any other manner, which has the effect of changing the appearance or legibility of any of the characters of the registration mark, which renders the characters of the registration mark less easily distinguishable to the eye or which prevents or impairs the making of a true photographic image of the plate through the medium of a camera and film or any other device.

The size, spacing and style of characters used in a registration mark are also detailed within the regulations. Non-vertical and italic scripts are not permitted. Nor is forming characters in such a way as to make them appear like a different character.

Notes

1   This offence is committed by the person driving the vehicle or, where it is not being driven, the person keeping it.

2   Road Vehicles (Display of Registration Marks) Regulations 2001. These regulations came into force on 1 September 2001.

3   As note 1.

4   'Fraudulently' includes for the purpose of deceiving a police officer. 'Use' is use on a public road.

5   When in force.

6   Road Vehicles (Registration and Licensing) Regulations 1971 r.8(2).

7   But not by force unless with a warrant.

8   Vehicles (Crime) Act 2001 s.26(1) when in force.

9   Ibid., s.26(2).

10 Or where the vehicle is towing a trailer, the rear of the trailer, or where the vehicle is towing more than one trailer, the rearmost trailer.

11 In the case of a motor cycle or motor tricycle which does not have a body of a type which is characteristic of the body of a 4-wheeled vehicle, a registration plate must not be fixed to the front if the vehicle was registered after 1 September 2001 and need not be if registered before that date.

12 Does not apply to works trucks, road rollers, agricultural machines and vehicles first registered before 1 October 1938. Where required the plate must be lit so as to be easily distinguishable from 18 metres or 15 metres in the case of plates having characters with a width of 44 millimetres.

ROAD TRAFFIC COLLISIONS

See also Dangerous and Careless Driving / Riding, Drink and Drive / Ride, Drivers and Riders, Driving Documents

Offence: It is an offence where an accident occurs, for the driver of the mechanically propelled vehicle to fail to stop;[1] or to fail to give his name and address[2] and also the name and address of the owner and the registration marks of the vehicle if required to do so by any person having reasonable grounds for so requiring.

Contrary to: Road Traffic Act 1988 s.170(2) and (4)

Max. sentence: Magistrates' Court: 6 months' imprisonment / £5,000 fine.

Power: Report / s.25 PACE / Arrestable Offence[3]

Offence: It is an offence, in circumstances where an accident occurs, for the driver of the mechanically propelled vehicle who for any reason,[4] has not given his name and address to any person having reasonable grounds for so requiring, to fail to report[5] the accident.

Contrary to: Road Traffic Act 1988 s.170(3) and (4)

Max. sentence: Magistrates' Court: 6 months' imprisonment / £5,000 fine.

Power: Report / s.25 PACE / Arrestable Offence[6]

Offence:

It is an offence in circumstances where an accident occurs by which personal injury is caused to a person other than the driver of the mechanically propelled vehicle, for the driver to fail to produce a certificate of insurance or security to a constable or some other person who has reasonable grounds for requiring him to produce it.[7]

Contrary to: Road Traffic Act 1988 s.170(5) and (7)

Max. sentence: Magistrates' Court: £1,000 fine.

Power: Report / s.25 PACE

Definitions

Road traffic accident: owing to the presence of a mechanically propelled vehicle on a road or other public place,[8] an accident occurs by which:

(a) personal injury is caused to a person other than the driver of that mechanically propelled vehicle;

(b) damage is caused:

  (i) to a vehicle[9] other than that mechanically propelled vehicle or a trailer drawn by that mechanically propelled vehicle; or

  (ii) to an animal other than an animal in or on that mechanically propelled vehicle or a trailer drawn by that mechanically propelled vehicle; or

  (iii) to any other property constructed on, fixed to, growing in or otherwise forming part of the land on which the road or place in question is situated or land adjacent to such land.[10]

Animal: means any horse, cattle, ass, mule, sheep, pig, goat or dog.

General Information

Section 170 of the Road Traffic Act 1988 places obligations on the drivers of mechanically propelled vehicles to stop following a collision on a road or other public place[11] and then to provide their details, those of the owner of the vehicle (if different) and the registration number to anyone who has a good reason for needing them. If this does not or cannot happen, then the obligation is on the driver to report the matter either to a constable or at a police station. This must occur as soon as practicable or in any case within 24 hours. There is a further obligation in the case of accidents involving personal injury.

This requires that the driver either produce a certificate of insurance at the time or when reporting the accident.[12]

Notes

1   The obligation to stop is immediate [*Hallinan* v *DPP* (1998)]. The stopping must be for a reasonable amount of time to allow for any requirement to be made [*Lee* v *Knapp* (1966)]. However there is no obligation on a driver to search for any person who would have reasonable grounds for requesting such information [*Mutton* v *Bates* (1983)].

2   This is not restricted to the person's home address [*DPP* v *McCarthy* (1998)].

3   The Criminal Justice and Police Act 2001 s.71, in force 1 October 2001, amends the Police and Criminal Evidence Act 1984 s.24(2) by the addition of (gb). This makes a failure to stop and report an accident an arrestable offence in the case of accidents involving injury. See page 283.

4   For example, no one else was present. If the driver was unaware of the accident then he will commit no offence. However, if he subsequently becomes aware he still has an obligation to report within 24 hours of the accident occurring [*DPP* v *Drury* (1988)].

5   This must be at a police station or to a constable and the driver must do so as soon as is reasonably practicable and, in any case, within 24 hours of the occurrence of the accident.

6   See note 3.

7   However, no offence is committed if, within 7 days of the occurrence of the accident, the certificate or other evidence is produced at a police station specified at the time when the accident was reported.

8   As amended by the Motor Vehicles (Compulsory Insurance) Regulations 2000.

9 Includes cycles.

10 Road Traffic Act 1988 s.170(1).

11 As amended by the Motor Vehicles (Compulsory Insurance) Regulations 2000.

12 This does not apply to drivers of invalid carriages.

ROBBERY

See also Assaults, Blackmail, Firearms – Criminal Use, Knives and Bladed Articles, Offensive Weapons, PACE – Arrest, Theft, Wounding and Grievous Bodily Harm

Offence: It is an offence[1] for a person to steal, and immediately before or at the time of doing so, and in order to do so, he uses force on any person or puts or seeks to put any person in fear of being then and there subjected to force.

Contrary to: Theft Act 1968 s.8(1)

Max. sentence: Crown Court: life imprisonment / unlimited fine.

Power: Arrestable Offence

Offence: It is an offence for a person to assault another with intent to rob.

Contrary to: Theft Act 1968 s.8(2)

Max. sentence: Crown Court: life imprisonment / unlimited fine.

Power: Arrestable Offence

Definitions

Steal: a person is guilty of theft when he dishonestly appropriates property belonging to another with the intention of permanently depriving the other person of it. 'Thief' and 'steal' shall be construed accordingly.[2]

General Information

The offence of robbery contains the elements of theft coupled with those of an assault, provided that the use of force takes place before or at the time of the offence or, where the force is merely threatened, that the threat is of the use of force at that time and not at any later time.[3]

Force applied after the theft has taken place is not sufficient for a charge with robbery unless the theft is continuing and force is used during the course of that continuing appropriation.

The force does not have to be applied to the person from whom the theft takes place.

Notes

1   See *Theft* for a discussion regarding the defences available to an accused.

2   Theft Act 1968 s.1. See page 400.

3   As an alternative see *Blackmail*.

SCHOOLS

See also Assaults, Breach of the Peace, Children and Young Persons, Indecent and Obscene Behaviour, Knives and Bladed Articles, Noise, Nuisance, Offensive Weapons, Traffic Signs and Directions, Trespass

Offence: It is an offence for any person, without lawful authority on premises to which this applies,[1] to cause or permit any nuisance or disturbance to the annoyance of persons who lawfully use those premises.[2]

Contrary to: Local Government (Misc. Provisions) Act 1982 s.40(1)

Max. sentence: Magistrates' Court: £500 fine.

Power: Report / s.25 PACE

Offence: It is an offence for a person required by a school crossing patrol[3] to stop a vehicle:

(a)   to fail to cause the vehicle to stop before reaching the place where a person[4] is crossing (or seeking to cross) and so as not to stop or impede their crossing; and

(b) to put the vehicle in motion again so as to reach the place so long as the sign continues to be exhibited.

Contrary to: Road Traffic Regulation Act 1984 s.28(3)

Max. sentence: Magistrates' Court: £1,000 fine.

Power: Report / s.25 PACE

Offence:

It is an offence for a person, without lawful authority or good reason, to have with him on school premises any article to which s.139 applies.

Contrary to: Criminal Justice Act 1988 s.139A(1)

Max. sentence: Magistrates' Court: 6 months' imprisonment / £5,000 fine.

Crown Court: 2 years' imprisonment / unlimited fine.

Power: Arrestable Offence[5]

Offence:

It is an offence[6] for a person, without lawful authority or good reason, to have an offensive weapon with him on school premises.

Contrary to: Criminal Justice Act 1988 s.139A(2)

Max. sentence: Magistrates' Court: 6 months' imprisonment / £5,000 fine.

Crown Court: 4 years' imprisonment / unlimited fine.

Power: Arrestable Offence[7]

Offence:

It is an offence for any person, without lawful authority, to be on premises[8] and cause or permit nuisance or disturbance to the annoyance of persons who lawfully use those premises.

Contrary to: Education Act 1996 s.547(1)

| **Max. sentence:** | Magistrates' Court: £500 fine. |
| **Power:** | Report / s.25 PACE / Breach of the Peace |

General Powers

A constable may remove from the premises any person who he has reasonable cause to suspect is committing, or has committed, an offence under s.40 of the Local Government (Misc. Provisions) Act 1982 or s.547 of the Education Act 1996.

A constable may enter school premises and search those premises and any person on those premises[9] for an article which has a blade or is sharply pointed if he has reasonable grounds for believing that an offence under s.139 of the Criminal Justice Act 1988 is being committed.

If the constable finds an article or weapon in the course of a search he may seize and retain it.

Where a local authority has notified the chief officer of police that it has designated premises to which children and young persons of compulsory school age may be removed and a police superintendent[10] has directed that the power shall be exercised,[11] if a constable has reasonable cause to believe that a child or young person found by him in a public place[12] is of compulsory school age and is absent from a school without lawful authority,[13] then he may remove the child or young person to:

(a)   the designated premises; or

(b)   to the school from which he is absent.[14]

Definitions

School premises: means land used for the purposes of a school excluding land occupied solely as a dwelling by a person employed at the school.

Notes

1   Playgrounds, playing fields and other premises for outdoor recreation of schools or institutions providing higher or further education which are either maintained by a local education authority or grant maintained.

2   Whether or not present.

3   School crossing patrols must wear an approved uniform and the uniform
    worn will be deemed to have been approved. The only indication of what is
    a 'uniform' for these purposes can be found in HO Circular 3/89, which
    indicates a peaked cap, beret or yellow turban and a white raincoat, dust
    coat or other white coat. The headgear may not be essential. This may
    include traffic wardens as a result of the Functions of Traffic Wardens Order
    1970.

4   Amended from 'children' by the Transport Act 2000.

5   Police and Criminal Evidence Act 1984 s.24(2)(m).

6   It will be a defence for a person to show that he had the article or weapon
    with him for use at work, educational purposes, religious reasons or as part
    of any national costume. See also page 234.

7   Police and Criminal Evidence Act 1984 s.24(2)(m).

8   This section applies to premises, including playgrounds, playing fields and
    other premises for outdoor recreation, of any school maintained by a local
    education authority or any grant-maintained school.

9   By reasonable force if need be.

10 Or above.

11 Within a specified area and within a specified period.

12 Within the specified area and within the specified period.

13 Lawful authority includes sickness and religious observance.

14 Crime and Disorder Act 1998 s.16.

SCRAP METAL DEALERS

See also Deception, Handling Stolen Goods, PACE – Arrest, Theft

Offence: It is an offence for any person to carry on business
                   as a scrap metal dealer unless the appropriate
                   particulars relating to him are for the time being
                   entered in the register maintained by the local
                   authority.

Contrary to: Scrap Metal Dealers Act 1964 s.1(7)

Max. sentence: Magistrates' Court: £1,000 fine.

Power: Report / s.25 PACE

Offence: It is an offence for a scrap metal dealer, at each
                   place occupied by him as a scrap metal store, to fail

to keep a book[1] or to fail to enter in the book particulars[2] with respect to:

(a) all scrap metal received at that place; and

(b) all scrap metal either processed at, or despatched from, that place.

Contrary to: Scrap Metal Dealers Act 1964 s.2(6)

Max. sentence: Magistrates' Court: £1,000 fine.

Power: Report / s.25 PACE

Offence:

It is an offence for a person required to provide notification of the destruction of motor vehicles under the provisions of the regulations made under this Act, to fail to do so.

Contrary to: Scrap Metal Dealers Act 1964 s.4A(4)[3]

Max. sentence: Magistrates' Court: £1,000 fine.

Power: Report / s.25 PACE

Offence:

It is an offence for a scrap metal dealer to acquire any scrap metal from a person apparently under the age of 16 years.[4]

Contrary to: Scrap Metal Dealers Act 1964 s.5(1)

Max. sentence: Magistrates' Court: £200 fine.

Power: Report / s.25 PACE

Offence:

It is an offence for any person to give a false name or false address on selling scrap metal to a scrap metal dealer.

Contrary to: Scrap Metal Dealers Act 1964 s.5(2)

Max. sentence: Magistrates' Court: £200 fine.

Power: Report / s.25 PACE

Offence:

It is an offence for any person to obstruct the exercise of any right of entry or inspection, or to fail to produce any book or any other document which a person has a right to inspect.

Contrary to:	Scrap Metal Dealers Act 1964 s.6(5)
Max. sentence:	Magistrates' Court: £200 fine.
Power:	Report / s.25 PACE

Offence: It is an offence for any person to carry on business as a motor salvage operator[5] in the area of a local authority without being registered for that area by the authority.

Contrary to:	Vehicles (Crime) Act 2001 s.1(1)[6]
Max. sentence:	Magistrates' Court: £5,000 fine.
Power:	Report / s.25 PACE

Offence: It is an offence for a person required to keep records under the provisions of the regulations made under this Act, to fail to do so.

Contrary to:	Vehicles (Crime) Act 2001 s.7(4)[7]
Max. sentence:	Magistrates' Court: £2,500 fine
Power:	Report / s.25 PACE

Offence: It is an offence for a person required to provide notification of the destruction of motor vehicles under the provisions of the regulations made under this Act, to fail to do so.

Contrary to:	Vehicles (Crime) Act 2001 s.8(3)[8]
Max. sentence:	Magistrates' Court: £1,000 fine.
Power:	Report / s.25 PACE

Offence: It is an offence for a person, in making an application to be registered in the local authority register, to make a statement which he knows to be false in any material particular or to recklessly make a statement which is false in a material particular.

Contrary to:	Vehicles (Crime) Act 2001 s.10(1)[9]
Max. sentence:	Magistrates' Court: £5,000 fine.

Power:	Report / s.25 PACE

Offence:
It is an offence for a person, on selling a motor vehicle to a motor salvage operator, to give that person a false name or address.

Contrary to:	Vehicles (Crime) Act 2001 s.12[10]
Max. sentence:	Magistrates' Court: £1,000 fine.
Power:	Report / s.25 PACE

General Powers

Any constable shall have the right at all reasonable times:

(a) to enter and inspect any place for the time being registered with the local authority as a place which is occupied by a scrap metal dealer as a scrap metal store, or occupied wholly or partly for the purposes of his business; or

(b) to require production of, and to inspect, any scrap metal kept at that place and any book or record which the dealer is required by the Scrap Metal Dealers Act 1964 to keep at that place, and to take copies of or extracts from any such book.[11]

A constable may at any reasonable time enter[12] and inspect premises for the time being entered in the register of a local authority as premises which are:

(a) occupied as a motor salvage yard by persons carrying on business as a motor salvage operator; or

(b) occupied by a person carrying on business as a motor salvage operator wholly or partly for the purposes of his business so far as it consists of any of the relevant activities.[13]

A constable may at any reasonable time:

(a) require production of, and inspect, any motor vehicles or salvageable parts kept at such premises; and

(b) require production of, inspect and take copies of or extracts from any records which the person carrying on the business as a motor salvage operator is required to keep.

General Information

The particulars required to be recorded in respect of the receipt of scrap metal at a store are:

(a)   the description and weight of the scrap metal;

(b)   the date and time of the receipt of the scrap metal;

(c)   the full name and address of the person the scrap metal is received from;

(d)   the price, if any, paid;

(e)   the estimated value of the scrap metal if no payment is made;

(f)   the registration mark of the mechanically propelled vehicle delivering the scrap metal, if delivered by such a vehicle.

Where the scrap metal is processed or sold the book must record:

(a)   the description and weight of the scrap metal;

(b)   the date of processing or despatch of the scrap metal and, if appropriate, details of the process applied;

(c)   the full name and address of the person to whom the scrap metal is sold or with whom it is exchanged;

(d)   the estimated value of the scrap metal immediately before its processing or despatch if dealt with other than by way of sale or exchange.

Notes

1   Or two books dealing with (a) and (b) separately. The book or books must be kept for 2 years from the date of the last entry. These requirements do not apply to itinerant collectors.

2   See *General Information*.

3   As amended by the Vehicles (Crime) Act 2001, when in force.

4   It is irrelevant whether the scrap metal is offered by that person on his own behalf or on behalf of another person.

5   A person carries on business as a motor salvage operator if he carries on a business which consists:

(a)   wholly or partly in the recovery for re-use or sale of salvageable parts from motor vehicles and the subsequent sale or other disposal for scrap of the remainder of the vehicle concerned;

(b)   wholly or mainly in the purchase of written-off vehicles and their subsequent repair and re-sale;

(c) wholly or mainly in the sale or purchase of motor vehicles which are to be the subject (whether immediately or on a subsequent re-sale) of any of the activities in (a) or (b); or

(d) wholly or mainly in activities falling within (b) or (c).

6   When in force.

7   When in force.

8   When in force.

9   When in force.

10 When in force.

11 Scrap Metal Dealers Act 1964 s.6(1).

12 Force may only be used where there is a warrant.

13 Vehicles (Crime) Act 2001 s.9(1). The relevant activities are those detailed in note 5.

SEAT BELTS

See also Construction and Use, Drivers and Riders

Offence: It is an offence for a wheeled motor car, three-wheeled motor cycle or heavy motor car to which the regulations apply,[1] not to be fitted with seat belt anchorage points.

Contrary to: Road Vehicles (Construction and Use) Regulations 1986 r.46[2]

Max. sentence: Magistrates' Court: £2,500 fine.[3]

Power: Report / s.25 PACE

Offence: It is an offence for a vehicle[4] to which the regulations apply[5] not to be provided with

(a) a three-point body restraining belt, designed for use by an adult, for the driver's seat;

(b) a three-point body restraining belt for the specified passenger's seat;[6]

(c) a seat belt for other forward-facing seats.

Contrary to: Road Vehicles (Construction and Use) Regulations 1986 r.47

Max. sentence:	Magistrates' Court: £2,500 fine.[7]
Power:	Report / s.25 PACE

Offence: It is an offence for a person without reasonable excuse to drive a motor vehicle on a road where a child under the age of 14 years is in the front[8] unless the child is wearing a seat belt.

Contrary to:	Road Traffic Act 1988 s.15(2)
Max. sentence:	Magistrates' Court: £500 fine.
Power:	Report / s.25 PACE

Offence: It is an offence[9] for a person without reasonable excuse to drive a motor vehicle on a road where a child under the age of 14 years is in the rear, and any seat belt is fitted in the rear of that vehicle, unless the child is wearing a seat belt.

Contrary to:	Road Traffic Act 1988 s.15(3) and (4)
Max. sentence:	Magistrates' Court: £500 fine.
Power:	Report / s.25 PACE

Offence: It is an offence for a person without reasonable excuse to drive a passenger car[10] on a road where:

(a) a child who is under the age of 12 years and less than 150 centimetres in height is in the rear;

(b) no seat belt is fitted in the rear; and

(c) a seat in the front of the passenger car is provided with a seat belt but is not occupied by any person.

Contrary to:	Road Traffic Act 1988 s.15(3A)
Max. sentence:	Magistrates' Court: £500 fine.
Power:	Report / s.25 PACE

Offence: It is an offence for any person[11] of 14 years or more, unless otherwise exempted:

(a) to drive a motor vehicle (other than a two-wheeled motor cycle with or without a side-car);

(b) to ride in a front seat of a motor vehicle (other than a two-wheeled motor cycle with or without a side-car); or

(c) to ride in a rear seat of a motor car or a passenger car which is not a motor car;

whilst not wearing an adult seat belt.

Contrary to: Motor Vehicles (Wearing of Seat Belts) Regulations 1993 r.5

Max. sentence: Magistrates' Court: £500 fine.

Power: Report / s.25 PACE

General Information

The requirements of r.5 of the 1993 Regulations do not apply to:

(a) a person holding a medical certificate;[12]

(b) a person using a vehicle constructed or adapted for the delivery of goods or mail to consumers or addresses, as the case may be, while engaged in making local rounds of deliveries or collections;

(c) a person driving a vehicle while performing a manoeuvre which includes reversing;

(d) a qualified driver who is supervising the holder of a provisional licence while that holder is performing a manoeuvre which includes reversing;

(e) a person by whom a test of competence to drive is being conducted and his wearing of a seat belt would endanger himself or any other person;

(f) a person driving or riding in a vehicle while it is being used for fire brigade or police purposes or for carrying a person in lawful custody;

(g) the driver of

(i) a licensed taxi while it is being used as a taxi, or

      (ii)   a private hire vehicle while it is being used to carry a passenger for hire;

(h)   a person riding in a vehicle being used under a trade licence, for the purpose of investigating or remedying a mechanical fault in the vehicle;

(i)   a disabled person who is wearing a disabled person's belt;

(j)   a person riding in a vehicle while it is taking part in a procession organised by or on behalf of the Crown; or

(k)   a person driving or riding in a vehicle where no belt is provided for him.

Notes

1   New regulations from 1 October 2001 apply to all vehicles although the exact nature of the requirement will vary depending upon the type of vehicle and the date when it was first used. Most importantly they apply to any vehicle first used before 1 April 1982 (on the driver's seat and specified passenger seat), passenger or dual-purpose vehicles (other than a bus) first used on or after 1 April 1982 (every forward-facing seat constructed or adapted to accommodate no more than one adult) and any other vehicle (not a bus) first used on or after 1 April 1982 (every forward-facing front seat and every non-protected seat). The requirement for minibuses, goods vehicles and coaches is dependent upon their age. See further the Road Vehicles (Construction and Use)(Amendment) (No. 2) Regulations 2001.

2   Road Traffic Act 1988 s.14(3)

3   In the case of any goods vehicle or any vehicle adapted to carry more than 8 passengers; £1,000 in any other case.

4   This term includes 'passenger vehicles' and 'dual purpose vehicles'. Also minibuses first used on or after 1 October 1988, motor ambulances, motor caravans and coaches.

5   As note 1.

6   This is the front passenger seat, alongside and furthest from, the driver's seat.

7   As note 3.

8   That is, everything forward of the rearmost part of the driver's seat.

9   Exemptions include a child for whom there is a medical certificate, a child under 1 year in a carry-cot provided the cot is restrained by straps and disabled children wearing suitable restraints. Licensed taxis and hire cars are also excluded where the rear seats are separated from the driver by a partition.

10 'Passenger car' means a motor vehicle which:

    (a) is constructed or adapted for use for the carriage of passengers and is not a goods vehicle;

    (b) has no more than 8 seats in addition to the driver's seat;

    (c) has four or more wheels;

    (d) has a maximum design speed exceeding 25 kph; and

    (e) has a maximum laden weight not exceeding 3.5 tonnes.

11 Only the person committing the contravention is guilty of an offence [Road Traffic Act 1988 s.14(3)].

12 This may be produced at a police station within 7 days or as soon as is reasonably practicable.

SEXUAL OFFENCES

See also Children and Young Persons, Indecent and Obscene Behaviour, Mental Health, PACE – Arrest, Prostitution

Offence: It is an offence[1] for a man to rape a woman or another man.

Contrary to: Sexual Offences Act 1956 s.1

Max. sentence: Crown Court: life imprisonment / unlimited fine.

Power: Arrestable Offence

Offence: It is an offence for a person to procure a woman by threats or intimidation, to have sexual intercourse[2] in any part of the world.

Contrary to: Sexual Offences Act 1956 s.2

Max. sentence: Crown Court: 2 years' imprisonment / unlimited fine.

Power: Report / s.25 PACE

Offence: It is an offence for a person to procure a woman, by false pretences or false representations, to have sexual intercourse in any part of the world.

Contrary to: Sexual Offences Act 1956 s.3

Max. sentence:	Crown Court: 2 years' imprisonment / unlimited fine.
Power:	Report / s.25 PACE

Offence: It is an offence for a person to apply or administer to, or cause to be taken by, a woman any drug, matter or thing with intent to stupefy or overpower her so as thereby to enable any man to have un-lawful[3] sexual intercourse with her.

Contrary to:	Sexual Offences Act 1956 s.4
Max. sentence:	Crown Court: 2 years' imprisonment / unlimited fine.
Power:	Report / s.25 PACE

Offence: It is an offence for a man to have unlawful sexual intercourse with a girl under the age of 13.

Contrary to:	Sexual Offences Act 1956 s.5
Max. sentence:	Crown Court: life imprisonment / unlimited fine.
Power:	Arrestable Offence

Offence: It is an offence[4] for a man to have unlawful sexual intercourse with a girl under the age of 16.

Contrary to:	Sexual Offences Act 1956 s.6
Max. sentence:	Magistrates' Court: 6 months' imprisonment / £5,000 fine.
	Crown Court: 2 years' imprisonment / unlimited fine.
Power:	Report / s.25 PACE

Offence: It is an offence[5] for a man to have unlawful sexual intercourse with a woman who is a defective.

Contrary to:	Sexual Offences Act 1956 s.7
Max. sentence:	Crown Court: 2 years' imprisonment / unlimited fine.

Power:	Report / s.25 PACE

Offence: It is an offence for a person to procure a woman who is a defective to have unlawful sexual intercourse in any part of the world.

Contrary to:	Sexual Offences Act 1956 s.9
Max. sentence:	Crown Court: 2 years' imprisonment / unlimited fine.
Power:	Report / s.25 PACE

Offence: It is an offence for a man to have sexual intercourse with a woman he knows to be his granddaughter, daughter, sister or mother.[6]

Contrary to:	Sexual Offences Act 1956 s.10
Max. sentence:	Crown Court: 7 years' imprisonment[7] / unlimited fine.
Power:	Arrestable Offence

Offence: It is an offence for a woman of the age of 16 or over to permit a man whom she knows to be her grandfather, father, brother or son to have sexual intercourse with her.

Contrary to:	Sexual Offences Act 1956 s.11
Max. sentence:	Crown Court: 7 years' imprisonment / unlimited fine.
Power:	Arrestable Offence

Offence: It is an offence[8] for a person to commit buggery with another person or with an animal.

Contrary to:	Sexual Offences Act 1956 s.12
Max. sentence:	Crown Court: life imprisonment / unlimited fine.[9]
Power:	Arrestable Offence[10]

Offence: It is an offence for a person to assault another person with intent to commit buggery.

Contrary to:	Sexual Offences Act 1956 s.16
Max. sentence:	Crown Court: 10 years' imprisonment / unlimited fine.
Power:	Arrestable Offence

Offence:

It is an offence for a person to take away or detain a woman against her will with the intention that she shall marry or have unlawful sexual intercourse with that or any other person, if she is so taken away or detained either by force or for the sake of her property or expectations of property.

Contrary to:	Sexual Offences Act 1956 s.17
Max. sentence:	Crown Court: 14 years' imprisonment / unlimited fine.
Power:	Arrestable Offence

Offence:

It is an offence[11] for a person to take an unmarried girl under the age of 18 out of the possession of her parent or guardian against his will, if she is so taken with the intention that she shall have unlawful sexual intercourse with men or with a particular man.

Contrary to:	Sexual Offences Act 1956 s.19
Max. sentence:	Crown Court: 2 years' imprisonment / unlimited fine.
Power:	Report / s.25 PACE

Offence:

It is an offence for a person acting without lawful authority or excuse to take an unmarried girl under the age of 16 out of the possession of her parent or guardian against his will.

Contrary to:	Sexual Offences Act 1956 s.20
Max. sentence:	Crown Court: 2 years' imprisonment / unlimited fine.

Power: Report / s.25 PACE

Offence:
It is an offence for a person to take a woman who is a defective out of the possession of her parent or guardian against his will, if she is so taken with the intention that she shall have unlawful sexual intercourse with men or with a particular man.

Contrary to: Sexual Offences Act 1956 s.21

Max. sentence: Crown Court: 2 years' imprisonment / unlimited fine.

Power: Report / s.25 PACE

Offence:
It is an offence for a man to incite to have sexual intercourse with him a girl under the age of 16 whom he knows to be his granddaughter, daughter or sister.

Contrary to: Criminal Law Act 1977 s.54(1)

Max. sentence: Magistrates' Court: 6 months' imprisonment / £5,000 fine.

Crown Court: 2 years' imprisonment / unlimited fine.

Power: Report / s.25 PACE

Offence:
It is an offence for a person subject of the notification requirements in relation to sex offenders to:

(a)   fail to notify, without reasonable excuse and within 72 hours, the police of his name and his home address;[12]

(b)   fail to notify, without reasonable excuse and within 14 days, the police of any change of home address;[13]

(c)   notify to the police in purported compliance of his obligations, any information which he knows to be false.

Contrary to:	Sex Offenders Act 1997 s.3(1)
Max. sentence:	Crown Court: 5 years' imprisonment / unlimited fine.
Power:	Arrestable Offence

Offence: It is an offence for a person subject of a sex offender order, without reasonable excuse, to do anything prohibited by that order.

Contrary to:	Crime and Disorder Act 1998 s.2(8)
Max. sentence:	Magistrates' Court: 6 months' imprisonment / £5,000 fine.
Power:	Arrestable Offence

Offence: It is an offence[14] for a person aged 18 or over:

(a) to have sexual intercourse (whether vaginal or anal) with a person under that age; or

(b) to engage in any other sexual activity with or directed towards such a person,

if (in either case) he is in a position of trust in relation to that person.

Contrary to:	Sexual Offences (Amendment) Act 2000 s.3(1)
Max. sentence:	Magistrates' Court: 6 months' imprisonment / £5,000 fine.
	Crown Court: 5 years' imprisonment / unlimited fine.
Power:	Arrestable Offence

Definitions

Rape: sexual intercourse with a person (whether vaginal or anal) who at the time of the intercourse does not consent to it and, at the time, the offender knows that the person does not consent or is reckless as to whether the person consents or not.

Position of trust: a person over 18 is in a position of trust if any of the following is fulfilled:

(a) he looks after persons who are detained in an institution by virtue of a court order or under any enactment;

(b) he looks after persons under 18 who are resident in a home or other place where accommodation is provided;[15]

(c) he looks after persons who are accommodated and cared for in an institution which is a hospital; residential care home; nursing home; mental nursing home; private hospital; community home; voluntary home; children's home or residential establishment;

(d) he looks after persons under 18 who are receiving full-time education at an educational institution.

General Information

A man also commits rape if he induces a married woman to have sexual intercourse with him by impersonating her husband.

Notes

1 Any relationship between offender and victim is irrelevant [*R* v *R (Rape: Marital Exemption)*(1992)]. While a person under 16 cannot give lawful consent to other offences, rape relies on an absence of consent and can only be committed against the person's actual will [*R* v *Howard* (1965)]. Consent fraudulently obtained may be rape [*R* v *Linekar* (1995)].

2 Where, on the trial of any offence under the Sexual Offences Act 1956, it is necessary to prove sexual intercourse (whether natural or unnatural), it shall not be necessary to prove the completion of intercourse by the emission of seed, but the intercourse shall be deemed complete upon proof of penetration only; see Sexual Offences Act (s.44, 1956).

3 That is, outside marriage [*R* v *Chapman* (1959)].

4 Exceptions include a marriage which is invalid due to the girl's age although the man believes her to be his wife and has reasonable cause for that belief. A man also has a defence if he is under the age of 24, has not previously been charged with a like offence and he believed the girl to be of the age of 16 or over and had reasonable cause for that belief. Consent is no defence.

5 See *Mental Health*. It is a defence to show that he did not know and had no reason to suspect the woman to be a defective.

6 For the purposes of this legislation, 'sister' includes half-sister and 'brother' includes half-brother.

7 If the offence charged concerns a girl under 13 years of age the punishment rises to life imprisonment.

8   A homosexual act in private shall not be an offence provided that the parties consent and have attained the age of 16. However 'private' does not include circumstances where more than 2 people take part or are present or lavatories to which the public have access, whether on payment or otherwise.

9   When committed with a person under 16 years or with an animal. Where the accused is over 21 and the other is under 18 the sentence is 5 years. In any other case 2 years.

10 But see note 9.

11 A person is not guilty of an offence under s.19 if he believes the girl to be of the age of 18 or over and has reasonable cause for the belief.

12 That is, his sole or main residence.

13 If a registered sex offender stays for 14 days or more at another premises he must notify the police. This includes two periods in any 12 months which taken together amount to 14 days.

14 It will be a defence to show that at the time he did not know and could not reasonably been expected to know, that the victim was under 18 or was a person in relation to whom he was in a position of trust. Lawful marriage is also a defence.

15 That is, by a local authority or voluntary organisation under the Children Act 1989.

SKIPS

See also Highways and Roads, Litter

Offence:

It is an offence for a person to deposit a builder's skip on a highway without the permission of the highway authority.

Contrary to: Highways Act 1980 s.139(1)

Max. sentence: Magistrates' Court: £1,000 fine.

Power: Report / s.25 PACE

Offence:

It is an offence, where a builder's skip has been deposited on a highway in accordance with a permission, for the owner of the skip to fail:

(a)   to secure that the skip is properly lit during the hours of darkness;

(b) to secure that the skip is clearly and indelibly marked with the owner's name and telephone number or address;

(c) to remove the skip as soon as practicable after it has been filled;

(d) to comply with any condition subject to which that permission was granted.

Contrary to: Highways Act 1980 s.139(4)

Max. sentence: Magistrates' Court: £1,000 fine.

Power: Report / s.25 PACE

General Powers

A constable in uniform may require the owner of a skip to remove or reposition it or cause it to be removed or repositioned notwithstanding that it was deposited in accordance with a permission of the highway authority.[1]

General Information

Highway authority conditions may relate to:

(a) the siting of the skip;

(b) its dimensions;

(c) the manner in which it is to be coated with paint and other material for the purpose of making it immediately visible to oncoming traffic;

(d) the care and disposal of its contents;

(e) the manner in which it is to be lighted or guarded; and

(f) its removal at the end of the period of permission.

Notes

1   Any failure to comply with such a requirement is an offence subject to a maximum fine of £1,000. In such circumstances, or where the owner cannot be traced, a constable may arrange for the skip's removal or repositioning.

SPEEDING

See also Construction and Use, Dangerous and Careless Driving / Riding, Drink and Drive / Ride, Drivers and Riders, Motorways, Pedal Cycles, Traffic Signs and Directions

Offence: It is an offence for a person to drive a motor vehicle on a restricted road at a speed exceeding 30 mph.[1]

Contrary to: Road Traffic Regulation Act 1984 s.81

Max. sentence: Magistrates' Court: £1,000 fine.

Power: Report / s.25 PACE

Offence: It is an offence for a person to drive a motor vehicle of any class on a road at a speed greater than that specified as the maximum speed for a vehicle of that class.[2]

Contrary to: Road Traffic Regulation Act 1984 s.86

Max. sentence: Magistrates' Court: £1,000 fine.

Power: Report / s.25 PACE

Offence: It is an offence for any person to drive a motor vehicle on a road at a speed exceeding a limit imposed by any enactment to which this section applies.[3]

Contrary to: Road Traffic Regulation Act 1984 s.89

Max. sentence: Magistrates' Court: £1,000 fine.

Power: Report / s.25 PACE

Offence: It is an offence for a person to promote or take part in a race or trial of speed between motor vehicles on a public way.

Contrary to: Road Traffic Act 1988 s.12

Max. sentence: Magistrates' Court: £2,500 fine.

Power: Report / s.25 PACE

Definitions

Restricted road: a road is a restricted road for the purposes of s.81 if there is provided on it a system of street lighting furnished by means of lamps placed not more than 200 yards apart.

General Information

No person prosecuted for an offence of exceeding a speed limit shall be convicted solely on the evidence of one witness to the effect that, in the opinion of the witness, the person prosecuted was driving the vehicle at a speed exceeding a specified limit.[4]

These offences require the driver of the offending motor vehicle to be provided with a Notice of Intended Prosecution either at the time of the offence or within 14 days.[5]

The Road Vehicles (Construction and Use) Regulations 1986 require that every motor vehicle be fitted with a speedometer which, if the vehicle was first used on or after 1 April 1984, shall be capable of indicating speed in both miles per hour and kilometres per hour, either simultaneously or, by the operation of a switch, separately.[6] Once fitted, speedometers are required to be maintained and kept free from obstruction.[7]

Notes

1   No statutory provision imposing a speed limit on motor vehicles shall apply to a vehicle when it is being used for fire brigade, ambulance or police purposes, if compliance would be likely to hinder the use of the vehicle [Road Traffic Regulation Act 1984 s.87].

2   A variety of restrictions apply to motor vehicles of different types and the road on which they are being driven, for example, a passenger vehicle, motor caravan or dual purpose vehicle not drawing a trailer and with an unladen weight exceeding 3.05 tonnes and not exceeding 12 metres in length may travel at 70 mph on a motorway, 60 mph on a dual carriageway and 50 mph elsewhere.

3   Including the Road Traffic Regulation Act 1984, the Parks Regulation (Amendment) Act 1926 and enactment passed after 1 September 1960.

4   The evidence of one witness may be sufficient in circumstances where corroboration is gained from a speedometer, stop watch, radar meter or other such measuring device.

5   See page 82.

6   Road Vehicles (Construction and Use) Regulations 1986 r.35. Exceptions
     include vehicles having a maximum speed not exceeding 25 mph;
     agricultural motor vehicles not driven at more than 20 mph; motor cycles
     first used before 1 April 1984 with a cc not exceeding 100cc; invalid
     carriages used before 1 April 1984; works trucks and vehicles first used
     before 1 October 1937.

7   Road Vehicles (Construction and Use) Regulations 1986 r.36. Failure is an
     offence. See page 58.

STEERING

See also Brakes, Construction and Use, Drivers and Riders

Offence: It is an offence:

(a)   to contravene or fail to conform with a
      construction and use requirement as to
      steering gear;

(b)   to use on a road a motor vehicle or trailer
      which does not comply with such a
      requirement; or

(c)   to cause or permit a motor vehicle or trailer to
      be so used.

Contrary to: Road Traffic Act 1988 s.41A

Max. sentence: Magistrates' Court: £5,000 fine.[1]

Power: Report / s.25 PACE

Offence: It is an offence for a person to fail to maintain all
               steering gear fitted to a motor vehicle, in good and
               efficient working order and properly adjusted.

Contrary to: Road Vehicles (Construction and Use) Regulations
                    1986 r.29

Max. sentence: Magistrates' Court: £2,500 fine.

Power: Report / s.25 PACE

General Powers

A constable in uniform has the power to stop a mechanically propelled vehicle, or cycle, being driven on a road.[2]

Notes

1   In the case of a goods vehicle or a vehicle adapted to carry 8 or more passengers; £2,500 in any other case.

2   Road Traffic Act 1988 s.163.

STRAYING ANIMALS

See also Animals, Dogs, Highways and Roads, Metropolitan Police Act, Town Police Clauses, Wildlife

Offence: It is an offence for any horses, cattle, sheep, goat or swine to be at any time found straying on or lying at the side of a highway.[1]

Contrary to: Highways Act 1980 s.155(1)

Max. sentence: Magistrates' Court: £1,000 fine.

Power: Report / s.25 PACE

Offence: It is an offence for the owner of a dog or the person in charge of a dog, without lawful authority or excuse, proof of which shall lie on him, to cause or permit the dog to be in a highway or in a place of public resort not wearing a collar with the name and address of the owner thereon.[2]

Contrary to: Animal Health Act 1981 s.13(2)(a)[3]

Max. sentence: Magistrates' Court: 6 months' imprisonment / £5,000 fine.

Power: Report / s.25 PACE

Offence: It is an offence for a person to cause or permit a dog to be on a designated road[4] without the dog being held on a lead.

Contrary to:	Road Traffic Act 1988 s.27
Max. sentence:	Magistrates' Court: £200 fine.
Power:	Report / s.25 PACE

General Powers

If any cattle be at any time found at large in any street without any person having charge thereof any constable may seize and impound such cattle.[5]

Where a police officer has reason to believe that any dog found in a highway or place of public resort is a stray dog, he may seize the dog and may detain it until the owner has claimed it and paid all expenses incurred by reason of its detention.[6]

Notes

1   This does not apply in relation to a part of a highway passing over any common, waste or unenclosed land.

2   Exceptions include packs of hounds, dogs being used for sporting purposes, dogs driving cattle or sheep, police dogs and guide dogs. Any dog contravening this section may be treated as a stray.

3   As amended by the Control of Dogs Order 1992.

4   This is a length of road specified by an order of a local authority. The exceptions to this section are dogs proved to be kept for driving or tending sheep or cattle in the course of trade or business and dogs being used for sporting purposes which are under proper control.

5   Town Police Clauses Act 1847 s.24. See page 406.

6   Dogs Act 1906 s.3. See also page 89.

STREET TRADING

See also Begging, Children and Young Persons, Highways and Roads, Vagrancy

Offence: It is an offence for a person, without reasonable excuse:

    (a)   to contravene any of the conditions of a street trading licence or a temporary licence; or

(b) in connection with an application for a street trading licence or a temporary licence, to make a statement which he knows to be false in a material particular; or

(c) resists or obstructs any authorised officer of a Borough council in the execution of his duties; or

(d) fails on demand and without reasonable excuse, to produce his licence to an authorised officer of the Borough council or to a constable.

Contrary to: London Local Authorities Act 1990 s.34

Max. sentence: Magistrates' Court: £1,000 fine.

Power: Report / s.25 PACE

Offence:

It is an offence[1] for a person:

(a) who is not the holder of a street trading licence or a temporary licence to engage in street trading in a Borough; or

(b) who is the holder of a temporary licence to engage in street trading in a Borough on a day or in a place not specified in that temporary licence.

Contrary to: London Local Authorities Act 1990 s.38

Max. sentence: Magistrates' Court: £1,000 fine.

Powers: Report / s.25 PACE

Notes

1   Does not apply to an itinerant ice cream trader in any street except where that street is a licence street or has been designated as a prohibited street.

SUBSTANCE ABUSE

See also Children and Young Persons, Drugs, Drunkenness, PACE – Arrest

Offence: It is an offence for a person to supply or offer to supply a substance other than a controlled drug:

(a) to a person under the age of 18 whom he knows or has reasonable cause to believe to be under that age; or

(b) to a person:

(i) who is acting on behalf of a person under that age; and

(ii) whom he knows, or has reasonable cause to believe, to be so acting,

if he knows or has reasonable cause to believe that the substance is, or its fumes are, likely to be inhaled by the person under the age of 18 for the purpose of causing intoxication.

Contrary to: Intoxicating Substances (Supply) Act 1985 s.1(1)

Max. sentence: Magistrates' Court: 6 months' imprisonment / £5,000 fine.

Power: Report / s.25 PACE

Offence: It is an offence[1] for a person to supply any cigarette lighter refill canister containing butane or a substance with butane as a constituent part to any person under the age of 18.

Contrary to: Cigarette Lighter Refill (Safety) Regulations 1999 r.2

Max. sentence: Magistrates' Court: 6 months' imprisonment / £1,000 fine.

Power: Report / s.25 PACE

General Information

In proceedings against any person for the offence under the Intoxicating Substances (Supply) Act 1985, it is a defence for him to show that at the time he made the supply or offer he was under the age of 18 and was acting otherwise than in the course or furtherance of a business.

There is no offence of possession of an intoxicating substance. In the case of any child or young person, action may be taken if they are in need of care.[2]

Notes

1   It is a defence to show that all reasonable steps were taken, and all due diligence exercised to avoid the commission of the offence.

2   See page 51.

TAKING A CONVEYANCE

See also Aggravated Vehicle-Taking, Drivers and Riders, Driving Documents, Theft

Offence: It is an offence[1] for a person without the consent[2] of the owner or other lawful authority:

   (a)   to take[3] any conveyance[4] for his own or another's use; or

   (b)   knowing that any conveyance has been taken without such authority, to drive[5] it or allow himself to be carried in or on it.

Contrary to: Theft Act 1968 s.12(1)

Max. sentence: Magistrates' Court: 6 months' imprisonment / £5,000 fine.

Power: Arrestable Offence[6]

Offence: It is an offence for a person, without the consent of the owner or other lawful authority:

(a) to take a pedal cycle for his own or another's use; or

(b) to ride a pedal cycle knowing it to have been taken without such authority.

Contrary to: Theft Act 1968 s.12(5)

Max. sentence: Magistrates' Court: £1,000 fine.

Power: Report / s.25 PACE

Definitions

Conveyance: means any conveyance constructed or adapted for the carriage of a person or persons whether by land, water or air, except that it does not include a conveyance constructed or adapted for use only under the control of a person not carried in or on it, and 'drive' shall be construed accordingly.

General Information

For the purposes of this section 'owner', in relation to a conveyance which is the subject of a hiring agreement or hire-purchase agreement, means the person in possession of the conveyance under that agreement.

Notes

1   A person does not commit an offence under this section by anything done in the belief that he has lawful authority to do it or that he would have had the owner's consent if the owner knew of his doing it and the circumstances of it.

2   This must be true consent and not obtained through any fraud or misrepresentation.

3   This term is not limited to 'driven' but must involve some movement [*R* v *Bogacki* (1973)].

4   This does not include pedal cycles [Theft Act 1968 s.12(5)].

5   Includes ride, row, fly and so on.

6   Police and Criminal Evidence Act 1984 s.24(2)(d).

See also Deception, Drivers and Riders, Driving Documents, Public Service Vehicles

Offence: It is an offence for the driver of a London hackney carriage, standing in a street or place and not already hired, to refuse hire.

Contrary to: London Hackney Carriage Act 1831 s.35

Max. sentence: Magistrates' Court: £500 fine.

Power: Report / s.25 PACE

Offence: It is an offence for the proprietor or driver of any London hackney carriage, or any other person having the care thereof, to, by intoxication, or by wanton and furious driving, or by any other wilful misconduct, injure or endanger any person in his life, limbs or property, or make use of any abusive or insulting language, or use other rude behaviour to or towards any person, or assault or obstruct any constable in the execution of his duty.

Contrary to: London Hackney Carriage Act 1831 s.56[1]

Max. sentence: Magistrates' Court: £200 fine.

Power: Report / s.25 PACE

Offence: It is an offence for the licensed driver of a London hackney carriage to fail to wear his badge conspicuously upon his breast during his employment or when attending before any justice of the peace.

Contrary to: London Hackney Carriage Act 1843 s.17

Max. sentence: Magistrates' Court: £200 fine.

Power: Report / s.25 PACE

Offence: It is an offence for the driver of a London hackney carriage, to ply for hire elsewhere than at some standing or place appointed for that purpose, or by loitering or any wilful behaviour, to cause any obstruction in or upon any public street, road or place.

Contrary to: London Hackney Carriage Act 1843 s.33

Max. sentence: Magistrates' Court: £200 fine.

Power: Report / s.25 PACE

Offence: It is an offence, in respect of hackney carriages, for a person to permit the use of, or to drive, or to stand or to ply for hire without a licence.

Contrary to: Town Police Clauses Act 1847 s.45

Max. sentence: Magistrates' Court: £2,500 fine.

Power: Report / s.25 PACE

Offence: It is an offence, in respect of hackney carriages, for a driver to act without a driver's licence or a proprietor to employ an unlicensed driver.

Contrary to: Town Police Clauses Act 1847 s.47

Max. sentence: Magistrates' Court: £1,000 fine.

Power: Report / s.25 PACE

Offence: It is an offence, in respect of hackney carriages, for a driver on a hackney carriage stand to refuse, without reasonable excuse, to drive to any place within the prescribed limit.

Contrary to: Town Police Clauses Act 1847 s.53

Max. sentence: Magistrates' Court: £500 fine.

Power: Report / s.25 PACE

Offence: It is an offence, in respect of hackney carriages, for a driver to demand more than the sum agreed.

Contrary to:	Town Police Clauses Act 1847 s.54
Max. sentence:	Magistrates' Court: £2000 fine.
Power:	Report / s.25 PACE

Offence:

It is an offence for the driver of a London hackney carriage to:

(a) demand or take more than the proper fare;

(b) refuse to admit and carry the number of persons marked or specified;

(c) refuse to carry a reasonable quantity of luggage for any person hiring or intending to hire the carriage;

(d) refuse to drive to the limits of the Act, not exceeding 20 miles to which he shall be required to drive any person hiring or intending to hire the carriage;

(e) refuse to drive for any time not exceeding one hour, if so required by the person hiring or intending to hire the carriage;

(f) drive at an improper and unreasonable speed or less than 6 miles per hour except in cases of unavoidable delay or when required to do so by the hirer;

(g) ply for hire with a carriage that is at that time unfit for public use.

Contrary to:	London Hackney Carriage Act 1853 s.17
Max. sentence:	Magistrates' Court: £1,000 fine.
Power:	Report / s.25 PACE

Offence:

It is an offence for a London hackney carriage to ply for hire unless the driver is licensed.

Contrary to:	Metropolitan Public Carriage Act 1869 s.8[2]
Max. sentence:	Magistrates' Court: £1,000 fine.
Power:	Report / s.25 PACE

Offence: It is an offence for any person, with respect to a London cab, to:

    (a)   hire a cab knowing or having reason to believe that he cannot pay the lawful fare, or with intent to avoid payment;

    (b)   fraudulently endeavour to avoid payment of a fare lawfully due; or

    (c)   (having failed or refused to pay a fare lawfully due) refuse to give to the driver an address at which he can be found or, with intent to deceive, gives a false address.

Contrary to: London Cab Act 1896 s.1

Max. sentence: Magistrates' Court: £200 fine.

Power: Report / s.25 PACE

Offence: It is an offence for a person:

    (a)   being the proprietor of any vehicle, not being a hackney carriage or a London cab in respect of which a vehicle licence is in force, to knowingly use or permit the vehicle to be used in a controlled district as a private hire vehicle without having for such a vehicle a current private hire vehicle licence issued by a district council;

    (b)   in a controlled district, to knowingly act as driver of any private hire vehicle without having a current licence to drive such a vehicle granted by a district council;

    (c)   being the proprietor of a licensed private hire vehicle to knowingly employ any unlicensed driver;

    (d)   in a controlled district, to knowingly operate any vehicle as a private hire vehicle without

having a current operator's licence issued by a
district council;

(e) licensed as an operator of private hire vehicles
to operate any vehicle as a private hire vehicle
if the driver and vehicle are not themselves
licensed.

Contrary to: Local Government (Misc. Provisions) Act 1976 s.46

Max. sentence: Magistrates' Court: £1,000 fine.

Power: Report / s.25 PACE

Offence:
It is an offence for a person, without reasonable
excuse, to use or permit to be used in a controlled
district as a private hire vehicle, a vehicle in respect
of which a licence has been granted unless the
plate or disc issued is exhibited on the vehicle in
such a manner as prescribed by the district
authority.

Contrary to: Local Government (Misc. Provisions) Act 1976
s.48(6)

Max. sentence: Magistrates' Court: £1,000 fine.

Power: Report / s.25 PACE

Offence:
It is an offence for the licensed driver of a private
hire vehicle, without reasonable excuse, when
acting in accordance with the licence granted to
him, to fail to wear such a badge as issued by the
district council in such a position and manner as to
be plainly and distinctly visible.

Contrary to: Local Government (Misc. Provisions) Act 1976
s.54(2)

Max. sentence: Magistrates' Court: £1,000 fine.

Power: Report / s.25 PACE

Offence:
It is an offence for a person, being the driver of a
hackney carriage or private hire vehicle licensed by

a district council, to, without reasonable cause, unnecessarily prolong, in distance or in time, the journey for which the hackney carriage or private hire vehicle has been hired.

Contrary to: Local Government (Misc. Provisions) Act 1976 s.69
Max. sentence: Magistrates' Court: £1,000 fine.
Power: Report / s.25 PACE

Offence:

It is an offence for any person:

(a) to wilfully obstruct a constable acting in pursuance of this Act or the Act of 1847;[3]

(b) without reasonable excuse, to fail to comply with any requirement properly made to him by a constable; or

(c) without reasonable cause, to fail to give a constable so acting any other assistance or information which he may reasonably require of such person for the purpose of the performance of his functions under this Act or the Act of 1847.

Contrary to: Local Government (Misc. Provisions) Act 1976 s.73
Max. sentence: Magistrates' Court: £1,000 fine.
Power: Report / s.25 PACE

Offence:

It is an offence,[4] in any part of England and Wales outside the metropolitan police district and the City of London, to display on or above the roof of any vehicle which is used for carrying passengers for hire or reward but which is not a taxi:

(a) any sign which consists of or includes the word 'taxi' or 'cab', whether in the singular or plural, or 'hire', or any word of similar meaning or appearance to any of those words whether alone or as part of another word; or

(b) any sign, notice, mark, illumination or other feature which may suggest that the vehicle is a taxi.

Contrary to:	Transport Act 1980 s.64
Max. sentence:	Magistrates' Court: £1,000 fine.
Power:	Report / s.25 PACE

Offence: It is an offence[5] for a person, in a public place, to solicit persons to hire vehicles to carry them as passengers.

Contrary to:	Criminal Justice and Public Order Act 1994 s.167
Max. sentence:	Magistrates' Court: £2,500 fine.
Power:	Arrestable Offence[6]

Offence: It is an offence for a person in London to make provision for the invitation or acceptance of, or to accept, private hire bookings unless he is the holder of a private hire vehicle operator's licence for London.

Contrary to:	Private Hire Vehicles (London) Act 1998 s.2(2)
Max. sentence:	Magistrates' Court: £2,500 fine.
Power:	Report / s.25 PACE

Offence: It is an offence for a person[7] to use a vehicle as a private hire vehicle on a road in London unless a private hire licence is in force for that vehicle.

Contrary to:	Private Hire Vehicles (London) Act 1998 s.6(5)
Max. sentence:	Magistrates' Court: £2,500 fine.
Power:	Report / s.25 PACE

Offence: It is an offence for a vehicle to which a London private hire vehicle licence relates to be fitted with a taximeter.

Contrary to:	Private Hire Vehicles (London) Act 1998 s.11(1)

| **Max. sentence:** | Magistrates' Court: £1,000 fine. |
| **Power:** | Report / s.25 PACE |

Offence: It is an offence for a vehicle to be used as a private hire vehicle on a road in London unless the driver[8] holds a private hire vehicle driver's licence.

Contrary to:	Private Hire Vehicles (London) Act 1998 s.12(1)
Max. sentence:	Magistrates' Court: £2,500 fine.
Power:	Report / s.25 PACE

Offence: It is an offence for a person granted a London private hire vehicle driver's licence not to wear the badge when he is the driver of a vehicle being used as a private hire vehicle, in such position and manner as to be plainly and distinctly visible.

Contrary to:	Private Hire Vehicles (London) Act 1998 s.14(5)
Max. sentence:	Magistrates' Court: £1,000 fine.
Power:	Report / s.25 PACE

General Powers

Any constable shall have the power at all reasonable times to inspect and test, for the purposes of ascertaining its fitness, any hackney carriage or private hire vehicle licensed by a district council, or any taximeter affixed to such a vehicle, and if he is not satisfied as to the fitness of the hackney carriage or private hire vehicle or as to the accuracy of its taximeter he may by notice in writing require the proprietor of the hackney carriage or private hire vehicle to make it or its taximeter available for further inspection and testing at such reasonable time and place as may be specified in the notice and suspend the vehicle licence until such time as the constable is satisfied.[9]

A constable has the power at all reasonable times to inspect and test, for the purpose of ascertaining its fitness, any vehicle to which a London private hire vehicle licence relates.[10]

If a constable is not satisfied as to the fitness of such a vehicle he may, by notice to the owner of the vehicle:

(a) require the owner to make the vehicle available for further inspection and testing at such reasonable time and place as may be specified; and

(b) if he thinks fit, suspend the London private hire vehicle licence relating to that vehicle until such time as a constable is satisfied as to the fitness of the vehicle.[11]

Definitions

Hackney carriage: defined as 'every wheeled carriage, whatever may be its form or construction, used in standing or plying for hire in any street...'.[12] Any carriage for the conveyance of passengers, which plies for hire within the metropolitan police district or the City of London and is not a stage carriage.[13] Includes motor vehicles.[14]

Controlled district: means any area for which Part II of the Local Government (Misc. Provisions) Act 1976 is in force by virtue of a resolution passed by a district council.

Private hire vehicle: means a motor vehicle constructed or adapted to seat fewer than 9 passengers, other than a hackney carriage or public service vehicle or a London cab or tramcar, which is provided for hire with the services of a driver for the purposes of carrying passengers.

Taxi: means a vehicle licensed under the Town Police Clauses Act 1847 s.37, the Metropolitan Public Carriage Act 1869 s.6, or any similar local enactment.

Taximeter: means a device for calculating the fare to be charged in respect of any journey by reference to the distance travelled or time elapsed since the start of the journey (or a combination of both).[15]

Notes

1 A similar offence is made out by the London Hackney Carriage Act 1843 s.28.

2 In such circumstances the owner of the carriage will also be liable to a fine of £2,500 [Metropolitan Public Carriage Act 1869 s.7].

3 This applies to Part II of the Local Government (Misc. Provisions) Act 1976 which is concerned with the licensing of hackney carriages and private hire vehicles and to the relevant parts of the Town Police Clauses Act 1847.

4   This offence is committed by any person who knowingly drives the vehicle
     or causes or permits its use.

5   This does not imply that the soliciting must refer to any particular vehicle
     nor is the mere display of a sign on a vehicle that the vehicle is for hire
     soliciting within this section. No offence is committed under this section
     where soliciting persons to hire licensed taxis is permitted or where a
     person is soliciting passengers for public service vehicles.

6   Police and Criminal Evidence Act 1984 s.24(2)(j).

7   The driver and operator of a vehicle used in contravention of this section
     are each guilty of an offence. The owner of a vehicle used in contravention
     of this section will also be liable.

8   As note 7.

9   Local Government (Misc. Provisions) Act 1976 s.68.

10   Private Hire Vehicles (London) Act 1998 s.9(1).

11   Ibid., s.9(2).

12   Town and Police Clauses Act 1847.

13   Metropolitan Public Carriage Act 1869 s.4.

14   Road Traffic Act 1988 s.191.

15   Private Hire Vehicles (London) Act 1998 s.11(3).

TELECOMMUNICATIONS

See also Computers and the Internet, Harassment and Intimidation,
Indecent and Obscene Behaviour, Post and Mail, Theft

Offence: It is an offence for a person to dishonestly obtain a
                service which is provided by means of a licensed
                telecommunication system, with intent to avoid
                payment of any charge applicable to the provision
                of that service.

Contrary to: Telecommunications Act 1984 s.42

Max. sentence: Magistrates' Court: 6 months' imprisonment /
                      £5,000 fine.

                      Crown Court: 5 years' imprisonment[1] / unlimited
                      fine.

Power: Arrestable Offence

Offence: It is an offence for a person:

(a) to send by means of a public telecommunication system, a message or other matter that is grossly offensive or of an indecent, obscene or menacing character; or

(b) to send by those means, for the purpose of causing annoyance, inconvenience or needless anxiety to another, a message that he knows to be false or persistently makes use for that purpose of a public telecommunication system.

Contrary to: Telecommunications Act 1984 s.43

Max. sentence: Magistrates' Court: 6 months' imprisonment / £5,000 fine.

Power: Report / s.25 PACE

Offence: It is an offence for a person to send to another person:

(a) an electronic communication which conveys:

(i) a message which is indecent or grossly offensive;

(ii) a threat; or

(iii) information which is false and known or believed to be false by the sender; or

(b) any electronic communication which is, in whole or part, of an indecent or grossly offensive nature,

if his purpose, or one of his purposes, in sending it is that it should cause distress or anxiety to the recipient or to any other person to whom he intends that it or its contents or nature should be communicated.

Contrary to: Malicious Communications Act 1988 s.1(1)[2]

Max. sentence:	Magistrates' Court: 6 months' imprisonment / £5,000 fine.
Power:	Report / s.25 PACE

Offence: It is an offence for a person, intentionally and without lawful authority, to intercept at any place in the United Kingdom, any communication in the course of its transmission by means of:

(a) a public postal service, or

(b) a public telecommunications system, or

(c) a private telecommunication system.[3]

Contrary to:	Regulation of Investigatory Powers Act 2000 s.1(1) and (2)
Max. sentence:	Magistrates' Court: £5,000 fine.
	Crown Court: 2 years' imprisonment / unlimited fine.
Power:	Report / s.25 PACE

Notes

1 A person's conduct is excluded from criminal liability if he has the right to control the operation or use of the system or has such a person's express or implied permission.

2 As amended by the Criminal Justice and Police Act 2001 s.43.

3 Exceptions include any interception under a warrant issued by the Home Secretary; where there is a belief that consent has been given by the receiver of the communication or the enforcement of postal or telecommunication Acts.

THEFT

See also Abstracting Electricity, Aggravated Vehicle-Taking, Blackmail, Burglary, Deception, Going Equipped, Handling Stolen Goods, PACE – Arrest, Poaching, Robbery, Taking a Conveyance

Offence: It is an offence[1] for a person to dishonestly appro-

	priate property belonging to another with the intention of permanently depriving the other of it.
Contrary to:	Theft Act 1968 s.1
Max. sentence:	Magistrates' Court: 6 months' imprisonment / £5,000 fine.
	Crown Court: 7 years' imprisonment / unlimited fine.
Power:	Arrestable Offence

Offence: It is an offence,[2] where the public have access to a building in order to view the building or part of it, or a collection or part of a collection[3] housed in it, for a person, without lawful authority, to remove from the building or its grounds the whole or part of any article displayed or kept for display to the public in the building or that part of it or in its grounds.

Contrary to:	Theft Act 1968 s.11
Max. sentence:	Magistrates' Court: 6 months' imprisonment / £5,000 fine.
	Crown Court: 5 years' imprisonment / unlimited fine.
Power:	Arrestable Offence

Offence: It is an offence for a person, dishonestly with a view to gain for himself or another or with intent to cause loss[4] to another:

(a) to destroy, deface, conceal or falsify any account or any record or document made or required for any accounting purpose; or

(b) in furnishing information for any purpose to produce or make use of any account, or any such record or document as aforesaid, which to his knowledge is or may be misleading, false or deceptive in a material particular.

Contrary to: Theft Act 1968 s.17

Max. sentence: Magistrates' Court: 6 months' imprisonment / £5,000 fine.

Crown Court: 7 years' imprisonment / unlimited fine.

Power: Arrestable Offence

Offence:

It is an offence for a person[5] in any advertisement of a reward for the return of any goods which have been stolen or lost to use any words to the effect that no questions will be asked, or that the person producing the goods will be safe from apprehension or inquiry, or that any money paid for the purchase of the goods or advanced by way of loan on them will be repaid.

Contrary to: Theft Act 1968 s.23

Max. sentence: Magistrates' Court: £1,000 fine.

Power: Report / s.25 PACE

Offence:

It is an offence for a person, where a wrongful[6] credit[7] has been made to an account kept by him or in respect of which he has a right or interest, and knowing or believing that the credit is wrongful, to dishonestly fail to take such steps as are reasonable in all the circumstances to secure that the credit is cancelled.

Contrary to: Theft Act 1968 s.24A

Max. sentence: Crown Court: 10 years' imprisonment / unlimited fine.

Power: Arrestable Offence

Offence:

It is an offence[8] for a person, knowing that payment on the spot for any goods supplied or service done is required or expected from him, to dishonestly make off[9] without having paid as required or expected and with intent to avoid payment of the amount due.

Contrary to: Theft Act 1978 s.3(1)

Max. sentence: Magistrates' Court: 6 months' imprisonment / £5,000 fine.

Crown Court: 2 years' imprisonment / unlimited fine.

Power: Any person may arrest without warrant any person who is or whom he, with reasonable cause, suspects to be, committing or attempting to commit this offence.[10]

General Powers

A constable may search any person or vehicle, or anything which is in or on a vehicle, for stolen articles and may detain a person or vehicle for the purpose of such a search.[11]

Definitions

Dishonesty: a person's appropriation of property belonging to another is not to be regarded as dishonesty:

(a) if he appropriates the property in the belief that he has in law the right to deprive the other of it, on behalf of himself or another person;

(b) if he appropriates the property in the belief that he would have the other's consent if he knew of the appropriation and the circumstances of it; or

(c) (except where the property came to him as trustee or personal representative) if he appropriates the property in the belief that the person to whom the property belongs cannot be discovered by taking reasonable steps.

A person's appropriation of property belonging to another may be dishonest notwithstanding that he is willing to pay for the property.

Appropriate: any assumption by a person of the rights of an owner amounts to an appropriation, and this includes, where he has come by the property (innocently or not) without stealing it, any later assumption of a right to be keeping or dealing with it as owner. Where property or a right or interest in property is or purports to be transferre for value (not a gift) to a person acting in good faith, no later assumption by him of rights which he believed himself to be acquiring shall, by reason of any defect in the transferor's title, amount to theft of the property. An appropriation can be complete through the use of innocent agents.

Property: includes money and all other property, real or personal, including things in action[12] and other intangible property. A person cannot steal land, or things forming part of land and severed from it by him or by his directions, except:

(a) when he is the trustee or personal representative, or is authorised by power of attorney, or as liquidator of a company, or otherwise, to sell or dispose of land belonging to another, and he appropriates the land or anything forming part of it by dealing with it in breach of the confidence reposed in him;

(b) when he is not in possession of the land and appropriates anything forming part of the land by severing it or causing it to be severed, or after it has been severed; or

(c) when, being in possession of the land under a tenancy, he appropriates the whole or part of any fixture or structure let to be used with the land.

'Land' does not include incorporeal hereditaments; 'tenancy' means a tenancy for years or any less period and includes an agreement for such a tenancy, but a person who after the end of a tenancy remains in possession as statutory tenant or otherwise is to be treated as having possession under the tenancy, and 'let' shall be construed accordingly.

A person who picks mushrooms[13] growing wild on any land, or who picks flowers, fruit or foliage from a plant growing wild on any land, does not (although not in possession of the land) steal what he picks, unless he does it for reward or for sale or other commercial purpose.[14]

Wild creatures, tamed or untamed, shall be regarded as property, but a person cannot steal a wild creature not tamed nor ordinarily kept in captivity, or the carcass of any such creature, unless either it has been reduced into possession by or on behalf of another person and possession of it has not since been lost or abandoned, or another person is in course of reducing it into possession.

Belonging to another: property shall be regarded as belonging to any person having possession or control of it, or having in it any proprietary right or interest (not being an equitable interest arising only from an agreement to transfer or grant an interest).

Where property is subject to a trust, the persons to whom it belongs shall be regarded as including any person having a right to enforce the trust, and an intention to defeat the trust shall be regarded accordingly as an intention to deprive of the property any person having that right.

Where a person receives property from or on account of another, and is under an obligation to the other to retain and deal with that property or its proceeds in a particular way, the property or proceeds shall be regarded (as against him) as belonging to the other.[15]

Where a person gets property by another's mistake, and is under an obligation to make restoration (in whole or in part) of the property or its proceeds or of the value thereof, then to the extent of that obligation the property or proceeds shall be regarded (as against him) as belonging to the person entitled to restoration, and an intention not to make restoration shall be regarded accordingly as an intention to deprive that person of the property or proceeds.

Property of a corporation sole shall be regarded as belonging to the corporation notwithstanding a vacancy in the corporation.

Intention of permanently depriving the other of it: a person appropriating property belonging to another without meaning the other permanently to lose the thing itself is nevertheless to be regarded as having the intention of permanently depriving the other of it if his intention is to treat the thing as his own to dispose of regardless of the other's rights;[16] and a borrowing or lending of it may amount to so treating it if, but only if, the borrowing or lending is for a period and in circumstances making it equivalent to an outright taking or disposal.

Without prejudice to the generality of the above, where a person, having possession or control (lawfully or not) of property belonging to another, parts with the property under a condition as to its return which he may not be able to perform, this (if done for purposes of his own and without the other's authority) amounts to treating the property as his own to dispose of regardless of the other's rights.

Notes

1   It is immaterial whether the appropriation is made with a view to gain, or is made for the thief's own benefit.

2   A person does not commit an offence under this section if he believes that he has lawful authority for the removal of the thing in question or that he would have it if the person entitled to give it knew of the removal and the circumstances of it.

3   For this purpose 'collection' includes a collection got together for a temporary purpose, but references in this section to a collection do not apply to a collection made or exhibited for the purpose of effecting sales or other commercial dealings.

4   'Gain' and 'loss' are to be construed as extending only to gain or loss in money or other property, but as extending to such gain or loss whether temporary or permanent; and

   (a)   'gain' includes a gain by keeping what one has, as well as a gain by getting what one has not; and

   (b)   'loss' includes a loss by not getting what one might get, as well as a loss by parting with what one has.

5   This offence may be committed by the person advertising the reward and any person who prints or publishes the advertisement. This offence is one of strict liability.

6   A credit to an account is wrongful if it is the credit side of a money transfer obtained contrary to s.15A of the Theft Act 1968 (see page 84) or where it derives from theft, deception (s.15A), blackmail or stolen goods.

7   That is, money.

8   This will not apply where the supply of goods or the doing of a service is contrary to law, or where the service done is such that payment is not legally enforceable.

9   Must be an intention to avoid payment, not merely to defer it [*R* v *Allan* (1985)].

10 Theft Act 1968 s.3(4).

11 Police and Criminal Evidence Act 1984 s.1.

12 For example, a cheque.

13 'Mushroom' includes any fungus and 'plant' includes any shrub or tree.

14 Other offences may, however, be committed.

15 For example, the treasurer of a holiday fund or a fund used to provide tea and coffee for a group of employees.

16 Using up the value or virtue in a ticket is sufficient [*R* v *Marshall* (1998)].

TOWN POLICE CLAUSES

See also Animals, Assaults, Breach of the Peace, Dogs, Fires and Smoke, Fireworks, Highways and Roads, Indecent and Obscene Behaviour, Litter, Metropolitan Police Act, Noise, Nuisance, Public Order, Straying Animals, Taxis and Private Hire

Offence: It is an offence in any street to the obstruction, annoyance or danger of residents or passengers,[1] for a person:

(a) to expose for show, hire or sale[2] any horse or other animal, or to exhibit in a caravan or otherwise any show or public entertainment, or to shoe, bleed or farry any horse or animal,[3] or clean, dress, exercise, train, break or turn loose any horse or animal, or make or repair any part of any cart or carriage;[4]

(b) to suffer to be at large any unmuzzled ferocious dog, or to set on or urge any dog or other animal to attack, worry or put in fear any person or animal;

(c) to slaughter or dress any cattle[5] or part thereof,[6]

(d) having the care of any wagon, cart or carriage,[7] to ride on the shafts thereof, or without having reins and holding the same to ride upon such wagon, cart or carriage, or on any animal drawing the same, or to be at such a distance from such wagon, cart or carriage as not to have due control over every animal drawing the same, or to fail in meeting another carriage, to keep his wagon, cart or carriage to the left or near side, or, when passing any other carriage, to keep his wagon, cart or carriage on the right or off side, or, by obstructing the street, to wilfully prevent any person or carriage from passing him, or any wagon, cart or carriage in his care;

(e) to ride or drive furiously any horse or carriage, or to drive furiously any cattle;

(f) to cause any public carriage, sledge, truck or barrow, with or without horses, or any beast of burden, to stand longer than necessary for loading or unloading goods, or for taking up or setting down passengers,[8] or, by means of any public carriage, sledge, truck or barrow, or any animal, or other means, to wilfully interrupt any public crossing or wilfully cause any obstruction in any public footpath, or other public thoroughfare;

(g) to cause any tree, timber or iron beam to be drawn in or upon any carriage without there being sufficient means of safely guiding the same;

(h) to lead or ride any horse or other animal, or draw or drive any cart or carriage, sledge, truck or barrow, upon any footway of any street, or to fasten any horse or other animal so that it stands across or upon any footway;

(i)   to place or leave any furniture, goods, wares, or merchandise, or any cask, tub, basket, pail or bucket, or to place or use any standing place, stool, bench, stall or showboard on any footway, or to place any blind, shade, covering, awning, or other projection over or along any such footway unless it is at least 8 feet from the ground in every part;

(j)   to place, hang up or otherwise expose for sale any goods, wares, merchandise, matter or thing whatsoever, that projects into or over any footway so as to obstruct or incommode the passage of any person over or along such a footway;

(k)   to roll or carry any cask, tub, hoop or wheel, or any ladder, plank, pole, timber or log of wood upon any footway;[9]

(l)   to place any line, cord or pole across any street, or to hang or place any clothes thereon;

(m) to wilfully and indecently expose the person;[10]

(n)   to publicly offer for sale or distribution, or to exhibit to public view, any profane book, paper, print, drawing, painting, or representation, or to sing any profane song or ballad, or use any profane or obscene language;

(o)   to wantonly discharge any firearm, or throw or discharge any stone or other missile, or to make any bonfire, or throw or set fire to any firework;

(p)   to wilfully and wantonly disturb any inhabitant by pulling or ringing any door-bell, or knocking at any door,[11] or to wilfully and wantonly extinguish the light of any lamp;

(q) to fly any kite or to make or use any slide upon snow or ice;

(r) to cleanse, hoop, fire, wash, or scald any cask or tub, or to hew, saw, bore, or cut any timber or stone, or to slack, sift or screen any lime;

(s) to throw down or lay down stones, coal, slate, shells, lime, bricks, timber, iron or other materials;[12]

(t) to beat or shake any carpet, rug, or mat;[13]

(u) to fix or place any flower-pot or box or other heavy article in any upper window without sufficiently guarding it from being blown down;

(v) to throw from the roof or any part of any house or other building any slate, brick, wood, rubbish, or other thing;[14]

(w) to order or permit[15] any person to stand on the sill of any window in order to clean, paint or perform any other operation unless the window be in the basement storey;

(x) to leave open any vault or cellar, or the entrance from any street to any cellar or underground room, without a sufficient fence or handrail, or leave defective the door, window or other covering of any vault or cellar, or not sufficiently to fence any area, pit or sewer left open, or to leave such open area, sewer or pit without sufficient light after sunset to warn and prevent persons from falling thereinto;

(y) to throw or lay any dirt, litter or ashes, or night

soil or any carrion, fish, offal, or rubbish on any street,[16] or to cause any offensive matter to run from any factory, brewery, slaughterhouse, butcher's shop or dung-hill onto any street;

(z) to keep any pigsty to the front of any street not being shut out from the street by a wall or fence, or to keep any swine in or near any street so as to be a common nuisance.

Contrary to: Town Police Clauses Act 1847 s.28

Max. sentence: Magistrates' Court: 14 days' imprisonment / £1,000 fine.

Power: Report / s.25 PACE

Offence:

It is an offence for a person to use any violent or indecent behaviour in any police office or police station.

Contrary to: Town Police Clauses Act 1847 s.29

Max. sentence: Magistrates' Court: 1 month imprisonment / £200 fine.

Power: Report / s.25 PACE

Offence:

It is an offence for a person keeping any house, shop, room, or other place of public resort for the sale or consumption of refreshments of any kind, to knowingly suffer common prostitutes or reputed thieves to assemble and continue in his premises.

Contrary to: Town Police Clauses Act 184 s.35

Max. sentence: Magistrates' Court: £200 fine.

Power: Report / s.25 PACE

Notes

1   That is, people passing through.

2   This does not apply to a lawful market, market-place or fair.

3   Except in cases of accident.

4   Except in an emergency.

5   This term includes any horses, asses, mules, sheep, goats and swine.

6   Except in the interests of public safety.

7   A bicycle is a 'carriage' for these purposes.

8   This does not apply to hackney carriages standing for hire at any place set aside for them. See page 389.

9   Except for loading and unloading or for crossing the footway.

10   As the term 'person' means penis, this offence can obviously only be committed by males. See page 224.

11   In a similar vein, under the Town Improvements Clauses Act 1847 it is also an offence for any person to destroy, pull down or deface any number of a house, or name of a street put up by a local authority or to put up a different number or name.

12   Except building materials that are enclosed so as to prevent mischief to passengers.

13   Except door-mats before 08.00 hours.

14   Except snow thrown so not as to fall on any passenger.

15   This only applies to occupiers ordering or permitting some person in their service.

16   It is not an offence to lay sand or other materials in time of frost to prevent accidents or the freezing of water in pipes if the party laying them causes them to be removed after the frost.

TRAFFIC SIGNS AND DIRECTIONS

See also Drivers and Riders, Highways and Roads, Motorways, Parking, Road Traffic Collisions, Speeding, Zebra, Pelican and Puffin Crossings

Offence: It is an offence for a person without lawful authority or excuse to pull down or obliterate a traffic sign placed on or over a highway, or a milestone or direction post (not being a traffic sign) so placed.

Contrary to: Highways Act 1980 s.131(2)

Max. sentence: Magistrates' Court: £1,000 fine.

Power: Report / s.25 PACE

Offence: It is an offence for a person intentionally and without lawful authority or reasonable cause to interfere (directly or indirectly) with traffic equipment in such circumstances that it would be obvious to a reasonable person that to do so would be dangerous.[1]

Contrary to: Road Traffic Act 1988 s.22A(1)(c)

Max. sentence: Magistrates' Court: 6' months imprisonment / £5,000 fine.

Crown Court: 7 years' imprisonment / unlimited fine.

Power: Arrestable Offence

Offence: It is an offence for any person driving or propelling a vehicle,[2] to neglect or refuse to stop the vehicle, or make it proceed in, or keep to, a particular line of traffic when directed to do so by a constable in the execution of his duty for the time being engaged in the regulation of traffic in a road.

Contrary to: Road Traffic Act 1988 s.35(1)

Max. sentence: Magistrates' Court: £1,000 fine.

Power: Report / s.25 PACE

Offence: It is an offence where:

(a) a traffic survey of any description is being carried out on or in the vicinity of a road; and

(b) a constable gives to a person driving or propelling a vehicle a direction:[3]

(i) to stop the vehicle,

(ii) to make it proceed in, or keep to, a particular line of traffic, or

(iii) to proceed to a particular point on or near the road on which the vehicle is being driven or propelled,being a direction given for the purposes of the survey,[4]

for a person to neglect or refuse to comply with the direction.

Contrary to: Road Traffic Act 1988 s.35(2)
Max. sentence: Magistrates' Court: £1,000 fine.
Power: Report / s.25 PACE

Offence: It is an offence for any person driving or propelling a vehicle, to fail to comply with the indication[5] given by a traffic sign[6] that has been lawfully placed[7] on or near a road.

Contrary to: Road Traffic Act 1988 s.36
Max. sentence: Magistrates' Court: £1,000 fine.
Power: Report / s.25 PACE

Offence: It is an offence for a person on foot to proceed across or along the carriageway in contravention of a direction to stop given by a constable in the execution of his duty for the time being engaged in the regulation of vehicular traffic in a road.

Contrary to: Road Traffic Act 1988 s.37
Max. sentence: Magistrates' Court: £1,000 fine.
Power: Report / s.25 PACE

Offence: It is an offence for a person committing an offence under s.37 of the Road Traffic Act 1988 to fail to give his name and address to a constable so requiring.

Contrary to: Road Traffic Act 1988 s.169
Max. sentence: Magistrates' Court: £200 fine.
Power: Report / s.25 PACE

General Powers

A constable may require a person committing an offence under s.37 of the Road Traffic Act 1988 to give his name and address.

Definitions

Traffic equipment: means:

(a)   anything lawfully placed on or near a road by a highway authority;

(b)   a traffic sign lawfully placed on or near a road by a person other than a highway authority;

(c)   any fence, barrier or light lawfully placed on or near a road in pursuance of the Highways Act 1980, the Public Utilities Street Works Act 1950 or the New Roads and Street Works Act 19918 or by a constable or a person acting under the instructions (whether general or specific) of a chief officer of police.9

For these purposes anything placed on or near a road shall unless the contrary is proved be deemed to have been lawfully placed there.[10]

General Information

A Notice of Intended Prosecution is required to be given for the offences under s.35 and s.36. The form and meaning of traffic signs are laid down in the Traffic Sign Regulations and General Directions 1994.

A failure on the part of a person to observe a provision of the Highway Code shall not of itself render that person liable to criminal proceedings of any kind but any such failure may in any proceedings be relied upon as tending to establish or negative any liability which is in question.[11]

Notes

1   This refers to danger either of injury to any person while on or near a road, or of serious damage to property on or near a road.

2   This is not limited to mechanically propelled vehicles.

3   The power to give such a direction shall be exercised so as not to cause any unreasonable delay to a person who indicates that he is unwilling to provide any information for the purposes of the survey.

4   But not a direction requiring any person to provide any information for the purposes of a traffic survey.

5   This section also applies to traffic surveys. See note 4 above.

6   Being a sign of the prescribed size, colour and type, or of another character authorised by the Secretary of State under the Road Traffic Regulation Act 1984. A traffic sign placed on or near a road shall be deemed to be of the prescribed size, colour and type and to have been lawfully placed unless the contrary is proved. An absolute offence (no *mens rea* required).

7   A traffic sign shall not be treated as having been lawfully placed unless either the indication given by the sign is an indication of a statutory prohibition, restriction or requirement, or it is expressly provided by or under any provision of the Road Traffic Acts that this section shall apply to the sign or to signs of a type of which the sign is one.

8   These provide for guarding, lighting and signing in streets where works are undertaken.

9   Road Traffic Act 1988 s.22A(3).

10 Ibid, s.22A(4).

11 Ibid., s.38(7).

TRAILERS

See also Construction and Use, Drivers and Riders, Driving Documents, Goods Vehicles Operators, Highways and Roads, Motor Cycles

Offence: It is an offence[1] for a person to use, or cause or permit to be used, on a road, while drawing a trailer any:

(a)   straddle carrier;

(b)   invalid carriage;

(c)   articulated bus;

(d)   bus not being an articulated bus or a minibus;[2]

(e)   locomotive;[3]

(f)   motor tractor;[4]

(g)   heavy motor car or a motor car not described in (a), (c) or (d) above;[5]

(h)   agricultural motor vehicle.[6]

Contrary to:	Road Vehicles (Construction and Use) Regulations 1986 r.83
Max. sentence:	Magistrates' Court: £2,500 fine.[7]
Power:	Report / s.25 PACE

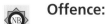

Offence: It is an offence[8] for a person to use, or cause or permit to be used, on a road a motor cycle:

(a) drawing behind it more than one trailer;

(b) drawing behind it any trailer carrying a passenger;

(c) drawing behind it a trailer with an unladen weight exceeding 254 kg;

(d) with not more than 2 wheels, without a side-car, and with an engine capacity which does not exceed 125 cc, drawing behind it any trailer; or

(e) with not more than 2 wheels, without a side-car, and with an engine capacity exceeding 125 cc, drawing behind it any trailer unless:

(i) the trailer has an overall width not exceeding 1 metre;

(ii) the distance between the rear axle of the motor cycle and the rearmost part of the trailer does not exceed 2.5 metres;

(iii) the motor cycle is clearly and indelibly marked in a conspicuous and readily accessible position with its kerbside weight;

(iv) the motor cycle is clearly and indelibly marked in a conspicuous and readily accessible position with its unladen weight; and

(v) the laden weight of the trailer does not exceed 150 kg or two-thirds of the kerbside weight of the motor cycle, whichever is the less.

Contrary to: Road Vehicles (Construction and Use) Regulations 1986 r.84

Max. sentence: Magistrates' Court: £2,500 fine.

Power: Report / s.25 PACE

Offence:

It is an offence, where a trailer is attached to the vehicle immediately in front of it solely by means of a rope or chain, for the distance between the trailer and that vehicle:

(a)   in any case to exceed 4.5 metres;

(b)   to exceed 1.5 metres unless the rope or chain is made clearly visible to any other person using the road within a reasonable distance from either side.

Contrary to: Road Vehicles (Construction and Use) Regulations 1986 r.86

Max. sentence: Magistrates' Court: £2,500 fine.

Power: Report / s.25 PACE

Offence:

It is an offence for a person in charge of a motor vehicle, or trailer drawn thereby, to cause or permit such trailer to stand on a road when detached from the drawing vehicle unless one at least of the wheels of the trailer is prevented from revolving by the setting of a parking brake or the use of a chain, chock or other efficient device.

Contrary to: Road Vehicles (Construction and Use) Regulations 1986 r.89

Max. sentence: Magistrates' Court: £2,500 fine.

Power: Report / s.25 PACE

Offence:

It is an offence[9] for any person to use, or cause or

permit to be used, on a road any trailer for the carriage of passengers for hire or reward.

Contrary to: Road Vehicles (Construction and Use) Regulations 1986 r.90

Max. sentence: Magistrates' Court: £2,500 fine.

Power: Report / s.25 PACE

Offence:

It is an offence[10] for any person to use, or cause or permit to be used, on a road any wheeled trailer in which any person is carried and which is a living van having either less than 4 wheels or 4 wheels consisting of two close-coupled wheels on each side.

Contrary to: Road Vehicles (Construction and Use) Regulations 1986 r.90(3)

Max. sentence: Magistrates' Court: £2,500 fine.

Power: Report / s.25 PACE

Definitions

Trailer: means a vehicle drawn by a motor vehicle but does not include any part of an articulated bus and for the purposes of r.83 only a composite trailer shall be treated as 1 trailer (not being a semi-trailer or converter dolly). Not included is any vehicle drawn by a steam-powered vehicle and which is used solely for carrying water.

Living van: a vehicle used primarily as living accommodation by one or more persons, and which is not also used for the carriage of goods or burden which are not needed by such one or more persons for the purpose of their residence in the vehicle.

Notes

1   Does not apply to articulated buses.

2   Except (a) 1 broken down bus where no person other than the driver is carried in either vehicle, or (b) 1 trailer.

3   Except 3 trailers.

4   Except 1 trailer or 2 trailers if neither is laden.

5   Except 2 trailers if one of them is a towing implement and part of the other is secured to and either rests on or is suspended from that implement or, in any other case, 1 trailer.

6   Except

   (1) in respect of trailers other than agricultural trailers and agricultural trailed appliances, such trailers as are permitted in (e), (f) and (g) above, as the case may be; or

   (2) in respect of agricultural trailers and agricultural trailed appliances:

      (i)   2 unladen agricultural trailers, or

      (ii) 1 agricultural trailer and 1 agricultural trailed appliance, or

      (iii) 2 agricultural trailed appliances.

7   In the case of goods vehicles and vehicles adapted to carry more than 8 passengers. £1,000 in any other case.

8   The restrictions in (b), (d) and (e) do not apply if the trailer is a broken down motor cycle and 1 passenger is riding it.

9   This does not apply in respect of a wheeled trailer which is, or is carrying, a broken down motor vehicle if the trailer is drawn at a speed not exceeding 30 mph and where the trailer is, or is carrying, a broken down bus, it is attached to the drawing vehicle by a rigid draw bar.

10   This does not apply in respect of a trailer which is being tested by its manufacturer, a person by whom it has been, or is being, repaired, or a distributor of, or dealer in, trailers.

TRESPASS

See also Begging, Burglary, Firearms – Criminal Use, Harassment and Intimidation, PACE – Arrest, Offensive Weapons, Poaching, Public Order, Vagrancy

Offence: It is an offence[1] for any person to trespass in, or get over the railings or fence of, any town garden or to commit any nuisance therein.

Contrary to: Town Gardens Protection Act 1863 s.5

Max. sentence: Magistrates' Court: 14 days' imprisonment / £200 fine.

Power: Report / s.25 PACE

Offence: It is an offence[2] for any person, without lawful authority, to use or threaten violence for the purpose of securing entry into any premises for himself or any other person[3] provided that:

(a) there is someone present on those premises at the time who is opposed to the entry which the violence is intended to secure; and

(b) the person using or threatening the violence knows that that is the case.

Contrary to: Criminal Law Act 1977 s.6(1)

Max. sentence: Magistrates' Court: 6 months' imprisonment / £5,000 fine.

Power: A constable in uniform may arrest without warrant anyone who is, or whom he suspects to be, guilty of this offence.

Offence: It is an offence[4] for any person who is on any premises as a trespasser, after having entered as such, to fail to leave those premises on being required to do so by or on behalf, of:

(a) a displaced residential occupier of the premises; or

(b) an individual who is a protected intending occupier of the premises.

Contrary to: Criminal Law Act 1977 s.7(1)

Max. sentence: Magistrates' Court: 6 months' imprisonment / £5,000 fine.

Power: A constable in uniform may arrest without warrant anyone who is, or whom he suspects to be, guilty of this offence.

Offence: It is an offence for a person who is on any premises as a trespasser, after having entered as such, without lawful authority or reasonable excuse, to have with him on the premises any weapon of offence.[5]

Contrary to: Criminal Law Act 1977 s.8(1)

Max. sentence: Magistrates' Court: 3 months' imprisonment / £5,000 fine.

Power: A constable in uniform may arrest without warrant anyone who is, or whom he suspects to be, guilty of this offence.

Offence:

It is an offence for a person to enter or be on, as a trespasser:

(a) the premises of a diplomatic mission;[6]

(b) consular premises;[7]

(c) any other premises in respect of which any organisation or body is entitled to inviolability by or under any enactment;

(d) any premises which are the private residence of a diplomatic agent or any other person who is entitled to inviolability of residence by or under any enactment.

Contrary to: Criminal Law Act 1977 s.9(1)

Max. sentence: Magistrates' Court: 6 months' imprisonment / £5,000 fine.

Power: A constable in uniform may arrest without warrant anyone who is, or whom he suspects to be, guilty of this offence.

Offence:

It is an offence for a person to resist or intentionally obstruct any officer of a court engaged in executing any process issued by the High Court or by any county court for the purpose of enforcing a judgment or order for the recovery of any premises or for the delivery of possession of any premises.

Contrary to: Criminal Law Act 1977 s.10(1)

Max. sentence:	Magistrates' Court: 6 months' imprisonment / £5,000 fine.
Power:	A constable in uniform may arrest without warrant anyone who is, or whom he with reasonable cause suspects to be, guilty of this offence.

Offence: It is an offence for a person, in relation to a trespassory assembly prohibited under s.14A of the Public Order Act 1986[8] to:

(a) knowingly organise such an assembly;

(b) knowingly take part in such an assembly; or

(c) incite another to take part in such an assembly.

Contrary to:	Public Order Act 1986 s.14B
Max. sentence:	Magistrates' Court: 3 months' imprisonment / £2,500 fine.[9]
Power:	A constable in uniform may arrest without warrant anyone he reasonably suspects to be committing any of these offences.

Offence: It is an offence for a person, in relation to a trespassory assembly prohibited under s.14A of the Public Order Act 1986 to fail to comply with a direction given by a constable directing him to stop and/or not to proceed in the direction of the assembly.

Contrary to:	Public Order Act 1986 s.14C(3)
Max. sentence:	Magistrates' Court: £1,000 fine.
Power:	A constable in uniform may arrest without warrant anyone he reasonably suspects to be committing this offence.

Offence: It is an offence for a person, knowing that a direction[10] to leave land[11] has been given which applies to him:

> (a) to fail to leave the land as soon as reasonably practicable; or
>
> (b) having left again to enter the land as a trespasser within the period of 3 months beginning with the day on which the direction was given.

Contrary to: Criminal Justice and Public Order Act 1994 s.61(4) and s.69(3)

Max. sentence: Magistrates' Court: 3 months' imprisonment / £2,500 fine.

Power: A constable in uniform may arrest without warrant anyone whom he reasonably suspects to be committing this offence.

Offence:

It is an offence[12] for a person, knowing that a direction to leave land, at which amplified music is to be played during the night, has been given which applies to him:

> (a) to fail to leave the land as soon as reasonably practicable; or
>
> (b) having left again to enter the land as a trespasser within the period of 7 days beginning with the day on which the direction was given.

Contrary to: Criminal Justice and Public Order Act 1994 s.63(6)

Max. sentence: Magistrates' Court: 3 months' imprisonment / £2,500 fine.

Power: A constable in uniform may arrest without warrant anyone whom he reasonably suspects to be committing this offence.

Offence:

It is an offence for a person, knowing that a direction under s.61(1)[13] of the Criminal Justice and Public Order Act 1994 has been given to him, to fail to comply with that direction.

Contrary to: Criminal Justice and Public Order Act 1994 s.65(4)

Max. sentence: Magistrates' Court: £1,000 fine.

Power: A constable in uniform who reasonably suspects that a person is committing this offence may arrest him without warrant.

Offence:

It is an offence of aggravated trespass for a person to trespass on land in the open air and, in relation to any lawful activity which persons are engaging in or are about to engage in or on that or adjoining land in the open air, to do anything which is intended by him to have the effect:

(a)   of intimidating those persons or any of them so as to deter them or any of them from engaging in that activity;

(b)   of obstructing that activity; or

(c)   of disrupting that activity.

Contrary to: Criminal Justice and Public Order Act 1994 s.68(1)

Max. sentence: Magistrates' Court: 3 months' imprisonment / £2,500 fine.

Power: A constable in uniform may arrest without warrant anyone whom he reasonably suspects to be committing this offence.

Offence:

It is an offence for a person, knowing that a direction under s.69 has been given which applies to him, to fail to leave the land as soon as practicable or having left, again enters as a trespasser within 3 months of the direction being given.

Contrary to: Criminal Justice and Public Order Act 1994 s.69(3)

Max. sentence: Magistrates' Court: 3 months' imprisonment / £2,500 fine.

Power: A constable in uniform may arrest without warrant anyone whom he reasonably suspects to be committing this offence.

General Powers

If a constable in uniform reasonably believes that a person is on his way to an assembly within an area to which an order under s.14A of the Public Order Act 1984 applies which the constable reasonably believes is likely to be an assembly which is prohibited by that order, he may stop that person and direct him not to proceed in the direction of the assembly.[14]

In respect of the Criminal Justice and Public Order Act 1994, if the senior police officer present at the scene reasonably believes that 2 or more persons are trespassing on land[15] and are present there with the common purpose of residing for any period, that reasonable steps have been taken by or on behalf of the occupier to ask them to leave and:

(a)　that any of those persons has caused damage to the land or to property on the land or used threatening, abusive or insulting words or behaviour towards the occupier, a member of his family or an employee or agent of his; or

(b)　that those persons have between them 6 or more vehicles on the land,

he may direct[16] those persons, or any of them, to leave the land and to remove any vehicles or other property they have with them on the land.[17]

If, as respects any land in the open air, a police officer of at least the rank of superintendent reasonably believes that:

(a)　2 or more persons are making preparations for the holding there of a gathering to which s.63 of the Criminal Justice and Public Order Act 1994 applies;[18]

(b)　10 or more persons are waiting for such a gathering to begin there; or

(c)　10 or more persons are attending such a gathering which is in progress,

he may give a direction that those persons or any other persons who come to prepare or wait for or to attend the gathering are to leave the land and remove any vehicles or other property which they have with them on the land.[19]

If a police officer of at least the rank of superintendent reasonably believes that circumstances exist in relation to any land which would justify the giving of a direction under s.63 of the Criminal Justice and Public Order Act 1994 he may authorise any constable to enter the land:

(a)   to ascertain whether such circumstances exist; and

(b)   to exercise any power conferred by the Act.[20]

If a constable in uniform reasonably believes that a person is on his way to a gathering to which s.63 of the Criminal Justice and Public Order Act 1994 applies and in relation to which a direction is in force he may stop that person, and direct him not to proceed in the direction of the gathering.[21]

If the senior police officer at the scene believes that:

(a)   a person is committing, has committed or intends to commit the offence of aggravated trespass on land in the open air; or

(b)   2 or more persons are trespassing on land in the open air and are present there with the common purpose of intimidating persons so as to deter them from engaging in a lawful activity or of obstructing or disrupting a lawful activity, he may direct that person or persons to leave the land.[22]

Notes

1   This applies to any enclosed garden or ornamental garden set aside in any public square, crescent, circus, street or other public place for the use or enjoyment of the inhabitants in any city or borough but does not apply to Crown property.

2   This legislation was originally designed to deal with squatters and therefore does not apply to a person who is a displaced residential occupier or a protected intending occupier. A 'displaced residential occupier' is any person who was occupying the premises as a residence immediately before being excluded by anyone who entered those premises as a trespasser. A person is a 'protected intending occupier' if he has a freehold interest or a lease with 2 years yet to run, or a tenancy, and he requires the premises for his own occupation but is excluded by a trespasser.

3   The fact that a person has any interest in or right to possession or occupation of any premises shall not for the purposes of this offence constitute lawful authority for the use or threat of violence by him or anyone else for the purpose of securing his entry into those premises, [Criminal Law Act 1977 s.6(2)]. It is immaterial whether the violence in question is directed against the person or against property or whether the entry is for the purpose of acquiring possession or for any other purpose [Ibid., s.6(4)].

4   It is a defence for the accused to prove that he believed that the person requiring him to leave was not a displaced residential occupier nor a protected intending occupier or that the premises, or part of them, were used mainly for non-residential purposes.

5   'Weapon of offence' means any article made or adapted for use for causing injury to or incapacitating a person, or intended by the person having it with him for such use.

6   Open or closed. As defined by Article 1 of the Vienna Convention on Diplomatic Relations and the Diplomatic Privileges Act 1964.

7   Open or closed. Consular Relations Act 1968 sch.1

8   These are assemblies prohibited by a council for a district under s.14A of the Public Order Act 1986.

9   In the case of (a) and (c). A £1,000 fine is the maximum penalty for (b).

10 Such a direction may be given by the senior police officer at the scene.

11 'Land' does not include buildings other than agricultural buildings or scheduled monuments or land forming part of a highway (or a road) unless it is a footpath, bridleway, byway or cycle track.

12 This is an offence in relation to the gathering on land of 100 persons or more at which such music is played.

13 See *General Powers*.

14 Public Order Act 1986 s.14C(1). See also note 8 above.

15 Where the persons in question are reasonably believed to be persons who were not originally trespassers but have become trespassers on the land, the officer must reasonably believe that the conditions in s.61(1) of the 1994 Act are satisfied after those persons became trespassers before he can exercise this power.

16 This may be communicated to such persons by any constable at the scene.

17 Criminal Justice and Public Order Act 1994 s.61(1).

18 This section applies to a gathering on land in the open air of 100 or more persons (whether or not trespassers) at which amplified music is played during the night and is such as, by reason of its loudness and duration and the time at which it is played, is likely to cause serious distress to the inhabitants of the locality.

19 Criminal Justice and Public Order Act 1994 s.63(2).

20 Ibid., s.64(1).

21 Ibid., s.65(1). This power may only be exercised within 5 miles of the boundary of the site of the gathering. Failure to comply is an offence subject to a £1,000 fine on summary conviction.

22 Ibid., s.69(1).

TYRES

See also Brakes, Construction and Use, Drivers and Riders, Steering

Offence: It is an offence[1] for pneumatic tyres of different types of structure to be fitted to the same axle of a wheeled vehicle.

Contrary to: Road Vehicles (Construction and Use) Regulations 1986 r.26(1)

Max. sentence: Magistrates' Court: £5,000 fine.[2]

Power: Report / s.25 PACE

Offence: It is an offence[3] for a wheeled motor vehicle having only 2 axles each of which is equipped with 1 or 2 single wheels, to be fitted with:

(a)   a diagonal-ply tyre or a bias-belted tyre on its rear axle if a radial-ply tyre is fitted on its front axle; or

(b)   a diagonal-ply tyre on its rear axle if a bias-belted tyre is fitted on the front axle.

Contrary to: Road Vehicles (Construction and Use) Regulations 1986 r.26(2)

Max. sentence: Magistrates' Court: £2,500 fine.

Power: Report / s.25 PACE

Offence: It is an offence[4] for pneumatic tyres fitted to:

(a)   the steerable axles of a wheeled vehicle; or

(b)   the driven axles of a wheeled vehicle, not being steerable axles,

not to be of the same type of structure.

Contrary to:	Road Vehicles (Construction and Use) Regulations 1986 r.26(4)
Max. sentence:	Magistrates' Court: £2,500 fine.
Power:	Report / s.25 PACE

Offence:

It is an offence[5] for a wheeled motor vehicle or trailer a wheel of which is fitted with a pneumatic tyre to be used on a road, if:

(a) the tyre is unsuitable having regard to the use to which the motor vehicle or trailer is being put or to the types of tyre fitted to its other wheels;

(b) the tyre is not so inflated as to make it fit for the use to which the motor vehicle or trailer is being put;

(c) the tyre has a cut in excess of 24 millimetres or 10 per cent of the section width of the tyre, whichever is the greater, measured in any direction on the outside of the tyre and deep enough to reach the ply or cord;

(d) the tyre has any lump, bulge or tear caused by the separation or partial failure of its structure;

(e) the tyre has any of the ply or cord exposed;

(f) the base of any groove which showed in the original tread pattern of the tyre is not clearly visible;

(g) either

    (i) the grooves of the tread pattern of the tyre do not have a depth of at least 1 millimetre[6] throughout a continuous band measuring at least three quarters of the breadth of the tyre and round the entire outer circumference of the tyre; or

(ii) if the grooves of the original tread pattern on the tyre did not extend beyond three quarters of the breadth of the tread, any groove which showed in the original tread pattern does not have a depth of at least 1 millimetre; or

(h) the tyre is not maintained in such condition as to be fit for the use to which the vehicle or trailer is being put or has a defect which might in any way cause damage to the surface of the road or damage to persons on or in the vehicle or to other persons using the road.

Contrary to: Road Vehicles (Construction and Use) Regulations 1986 r.27

Max. sentence: Magistrates' Court: £2,500 fine.

Power: Report / s.25 PACE

Notes

1 No offence is committed under r.26(1), (2) or (4) in relation to the fitting of a temporary use tyre to the wheel of a passenger vehicle (not being a bus) unless it is driven at a speed exceeding 50 mph.

2 In the case of goods vehicles or vehicles adapted to carry more than 8 passengers. £2,500 in any other case.

3 This does not apply to a vehicle to the axle of which there are fitted wide tyres not specially constructed for use on engineering plant or to a vehicle which has a maximum speed not exceeding 30 mph.

4 As note 3.

5 This does not prohibit the use on a road of a motor vehicle or trailer by reason only of the fact that a wheel of the vehicle or trailer is fitted with a tyre which is deflated or not fully inflated and which has any of the defects in (c), (d) or (e) if the tyre and the wheel to which it is fitted are so constructed as to make the tyre in that condition fit for use. Nothing in (a) to (g) applies to an agricultural motor vehicle that is not driven at more than 20 mph or an agricultural trailer or drawn appliance or to a broken down vehicle or a vehicle proceeding to a place where it is to be broken up, being drawn, in either case, by a motor vehicle at a speed not exceeding 20 mph. Nothing in (g) applies to a motor cycle with an engine capacity which does not exceed 50 cc.

6   That is, 1.6 millimetres in the central three quarters of the breadth of the tyre and around its entire circumference in the case of passenger vehicles capable of carrying 8 passengers plus the driver or less, light goods vehicles under 3.5 tonnes and light trailers.

VAGRANCY

See also Begging, Children and Young Persons, Indecent and Obscene Behaviour, Trespass

Offence: It is an offence for any person:

(a)   to wander abroad and lodge in any barn or outhouse, or in any deserted or unoccupied building, or in the open air, or under a tent, or in any cart or wagon[1] and fail to give a good account of himself or herself;

(b)   to be found in or upon any dwelling-house, warehouse, coach-house, stable, or outhouse, or in any enclosed yard, garden or area, for any unlawful purpose.

Contrary to: Vagrancy Act 1824 s.4[2]

Max. sentence: Magistrates' Court: 3 months' imprisonment / £1,000 fine.

Power: Any person may arrest an offender found committing.[3]

Notes

1   But not a tent, cart or wagon with or in which he travels.

2   As amended by the Vagrancy Act 1935. No conviction is possible unless the offender has been redirected to a 'reasonably accessible' place of shelter and has refused or he causes damage, an infestation of vermin or there is some other offensive consequence.

3   Vagrancy Act 1824 s.6. This includes police officers [*Gapper* v *CC Avon & Somerset Constabulary* (1998)]. If not found committing, then proceedings are by way of summons unless any of the conditions of s.25 of the Police and Criminal Evidence Act 1984 apply. See page 284.

VEHICLE INTERFERENCE

See also Aggravated Vehicle-Taking, Damage, Highways and Roads, Parking, Taking a Conveyance, Theft, Traffic Signs and Directions

Offence: It is an offence for a person to interfere with a motor vehicle or trailer or with anything carried in or on a motor vehicle or trailer with the intention[1] that a specified offence shall be committed by himself or some other persons.

Contrary to: Criminal Attempts Act 1981 s.9

Max. sentence: Magistrates' Court: 3 months' imprisonment / £2,500 fine.

Power: Report / s.25 PACE

Offence: It is an offence for a person, intentionally and without lawful authority or reasonable cause to interfere with a motor vehicle, trailer or cycle, in such circumstances that it would be obvious to a reasonable person that to do so would be dangerous.

Contrary to: Road Traffic Act 1988 s.22A(1)

Max. sentence: Magistrates' Court: 6 months' imprisonment / £5,000 fine.

Crown Court: 7 years' imprisonment / unlimited fine.

Power: Arrestable Offence

Offence: It is an offence for a person without lawful authority or reasonable cause, while a motor vehicle is on a road or on a parking place, to get on to the vehicle, or tamper with the brake or other parts of its mechanism.

Contrary to: Road Traffic Act 1988 s.25

Max. sentence:	Magistrates' Court: £1,000 fine.
Power:	Report / s.25 PACE

Offence:

It is an offence for a person without lawful authority or reasonable cause, for the purpose of being carried or drawn, to take or retain hold of, or get on to, a motor vehicle or trailer while it is in motion on a road.

Contrary to:	Road Traffic Act 1988 s.26
Max. sentence:	Magistrates' Court: £200 fine.
Power:	Report / s.25 PACE

Offence:

It is an offence for a person to remove or interfere with any notice fixed to a vehicle under s.62 of this Act, unless with the authority of the driver or person in charge of the vehicle or the person liable for the fixed penalty offence in question.

Contrary to:	Road Traffic Offenders Act 1988 s.62(2)
Max. sentence:	Magistrates' Court: £200 fine.
Power:	Report / s.25 PACE

General Information

The specified offences under s.9 of the Criminal Attempts Act 1981 are:

(a) theft of the motor vehicle or part of it;

(b) theft of anything carried in or on the motor vehicle or trailer; and

(c) an offence under s.12(1) of the Theft Act 1968.[2]

Notes

1   If it is shown that a person accused of an offence under this section intended that one of the specified offences should be committed, it is immaterial that it cannot be shown which it was.

2   That is, taking a conveyance.

See also Construction and Use, Drivers and Riders

Offence: It is an offence to fail to maintain all glass or other transparent material fitted to a motor vehicle in such condition that it does not obscure the vision of the driver while the vehicle is being driven on a road.

Contrary to: Road Vehicles (Construction and Use) Regulations 1986 r.30(3)

Max. sentence: Magistrates' Court: £2,500 fine.[1]

Power: Report / s.25 PACE

Offence: It is an offence for a vehicle fitted with a windscreen, unless the driver can obtain an adequate view to the front of the vehicle without looking through the windscreen, not to be fitted with one or more automatic windscreen wipers capable of clearing the windscreen so that the driver has an adequate view of the road in front of both sides of the vehicle and to the front of the vehicle.

Contrary to: Road Vehicles (Construction and Use) Regulations 1986 r.34(1)

Max. sentence: Magistrates' Court: £1,000 fine.

Power: Report / s.25 PACE

Offence: It is an offence[2] for every wheeled vehicle required to be fitted with a wiper or wipers not to be fitted with a windscreen washer capable of cleaning, in conjunction with the windscreen wiper, the area of the windscreen swept by the wiper of mud or similar deposit.

Contrary to: Road Vehicles (Construction and Use) Regulations 1986 r.34(2)

Max. sentence:	Magistrates' Court: £1,000 fine.
Power:	Report / s.25 PACE

Offence: It is an offence for every wiper and washer, fitted in accordance with regulations, while a vehicle is being used on a road not to be maintained at all times in efficient working order and properly adjusted.

Contrary to:	Road Vehicles (Construction and Use) Regulations 1986 r.34(6)
Max. sentence:	Magistrates' Court: £1,000 fine.
Power:	Report / s.25 PACE

Notes

1   In the case of goods vehicles and vehicles adapted for the carriage of more than 8 passengers. £1,000 in any other case.

2   This does not apply to an agricultural motor vehicle (other than a vehicle used on or after 1 June 1986 which is driven at more than 20 mph); a track-laying vehicle, a vehicle having a maximum speed of 20 mph and a vehicle used to provide a local service, as defined by the Transport Act 1985.

WILDLIFE

See also Animals, Dogs, PACE – Arrest, Poaching, Straying Animals, Theft

Offence: It is an offence for any person:

(a)   to keep any dangerous wild animal[1] except under the authority of a licence granted by a local authority; or

(b)   being the person to whom the licence was granted, and any other person who is entitled to keep any animal under the authority of the licence, to contravene or fail to comply with any condition of the licence.

Contrary to:	Dangerous Wild Animals Act 1976 s.2(5) and (6)

Max. sentence:	Magistrates' Court: £5,000 fine.
Power:	Report / s.25 PACE

Offence: It is an offence for any person to intentionally or recklessly:

(a) kill, injure or take any wild bird;[2]

(b) take, damage or destroy the nest of any wild bird while that nest is in use or being built; or

(c) take or destroy an egg of any wild bird.

Contrary to:	Wildlife and Countryside Act 1981 s.1(1)
Max. sentence:	Magistrates' Court: £1,000 fine.[3]
Power:	Arrestable Offence[4]

Offence: It is an offence[5] for a person to have in his possession or control:

(a) any live or dead wild bird or any part of, or anything derived from, such a bird; or

(b) an egg of a wild bird or any such part of a egg.

Contrary to:	Wildlife and Countryside Act 1981 s.1(2)
Max. sentence:	Magistrates' Court: £1,000 fine.
Power:	Arrestable Offence[6]

Offence: It is an offence for a person intentionally or recklessly to:

(a) disturb any wild bird included in Sch.1 while it is building a nest or is in, on or near a nest containing eggs or young; or

(b) disturbs dependent young of such a bird.

Contrary to:	Wildlife and Countryside Act 1981 s.1(5)
Max. sentence:	Magistrates' Court: £1,000 fine.
Power:	Arrestable Offence[7]

Offence: It is an offence for a person:

(a) to set in position any of the following articles, being an article which is of such a nature and is so placed as to be calculated to cause bodily injury to any wild bird coming into contact therewith; that is to say, any springe, trap, gin, snare, hook and line, any electrical device for killing, stunning or frightening or any poisonous, poisoned or stupefying substance;

(b) to use for the purpose of killing or taking any wild bird any such article as aforesaid, whether or not of such a nature and so placed as aforesaid, or any net, baited board, bird-lime or substance of a like nature to bird-lime;

(c) to use for the purpose of killing or taking any wild bird:

   (i) any bow or crossbow;

   (ii) any explosive other than ammunition for a firearm;

   (iii) any automatic or semi-automatic weapon;

   (iv) any shotgun of which the barrel has a internal diameter at the muzzle of more than 1¼ inches;

   (v) any device for illuminating a target or any sighting device for night shooting;

   (vi) any form of artificial lighting or any mirror or other dazzling device;

   (vii) any gas or smoke;

   (viii) any chemical wetting agent;

(d) to use as a decoy, for the purpose of killing or taking any wild bird, any sound recording or any live bird or other animal whatever which is tethered, or which is secured by means of braces or other similar appliances, or which is blind, maimed or injured;

(e)   to use any mechanically propelled vehicle in immediate pursuit of a wild bird for the purpose of killing or taking that bird; or

(f)   to knowingly cause or permit to be done any act as aforesaid.

Contrary to: Wildlife and Countryside Act 1981 s.5(1)

Max. sentence: Magistrates' Court: £5,000 fine.

Power: Report / s.25 PACE

Offence:

It is an offence for any person:[8]

(a)   to sell, offer or expose for sale, or have in his possession or to transport for the purposes of sale, any

(i)   live wild bird[9] or an egg of a wild bird or any part of such an egg;

(ii)   dead wild bird[10] or any part of, or anything derived from, such a wild bird; or

(b)   to publish or cause to be published any advertisement likely to be understood as conveying that he buys or sells, or intends to buy or sell, any of those things.

Contrary to: Wildlife and Countryside Act 1981 s.6(1) and (2)

Max. sentence: Magistrates' Court: £1,000 fine.

Power: Arrestable Offence[11]

Offence:

It is an offence[12] for a person to keep or confine any bird whatever in a cage or other receptacle which is not sufficient in height, length or breadth to permit the bird to stretch its wings freely.

Contrary to: Wildlife and Countryside Act 1981 s.8(1)

Max. sentence: Magistrates' Court: £2,500 fine.

Power: Report / s.25 PACE

Offence: It is an offence for any person to promote, arrange, conduct, assist in, receive money for, or take part in any event whatever at or in the course of which captive birds are liberated by hand or by any other means whatever for the purpose of being shot immediately after their liberation, or being the owner or occupier of any land, permit that land to be used for the purposes of such an event.

Contrary to: Wildlife and Countryside Act 1981 s.8(3)

Max. sentence: Magistrates' Court: £2,500 fine.

Power: Report / s.25 PACE

Offence: It is an offence[13] for any person to intentionally or recklessly kill, injure or take any wild animal included in Sch.5.[14]

Contrary to: Wildlife and Countryside Act 1981 s.9(1)

Max. sentence: Magistrates' Court: £1,000 fine.

Power: Arrestable Offence[15]

Offence: It is an offence[16] for any person to have in his possession or control any live or dead wild animal included in Sch.5 or any part of, or anything derived from, such an animal.

Contrary to: Wildlife and Countryside Act 1981 s.9(2)

Max. sentence: Magistrates' Court: £1,000 fine.

Power: Arrestable Offence[17]

Offence: It is an offence[18] for a person to intentionally:

(a) damage or destroy, or obstruct access to, any structure or place which any wild animal included in Sch.5 uses for shelter or protection; or

(b) disturb any such animal while it is occupying a structure or place which it uses for that purpose.

Contrary to:	Wildlife and Countryside Act 1981 s.9(4)
Max. sentence:	Magistrates' Court: £1,000 fine.
Power:	Arrestable Offence[19]

Offence:

It is an offence for any person:

(a) to sell, offer or expose for sale, or have in his possession or to transport for the purposes of sale, any live or dead wild[20] animal included in Sch.5 or any part of, or anything derived from, such an animal; or

(b) to publish or cause to be published any advertisement likely to be understood as conveying that he buys or sells, or intends to buy or sell, any of those things.

Contrary to:	Wildlife and Countryside Act 1981 s.9(5)
Max. sentence:	Magistrates' Court: £1,000 fine.
Power:	Arrestable Offence[21]

Offence:

It is an offence for any person:

(a) to set in position any self-locking snare which is of such a nature and so placed as to be calculated to cause bodily injury to any wild animal coming into contact therewith;

(b) to use for the purpose of killing or taking any wild animal any self-locking snare, whether or not of such a nature or so placed as aforesaid, any bow or crossbow or any explosive other than for a firearm;

(c) to use as a decoy, for the purpose of killing or taking any wild animal, any live mammal or bird whatever; or

(d) to knowingly cause or permit to be done an act which is mentioned above.

| **Contrary to:** | Wildlife and Countryside Act 1981 s.11(1) |

Max. sentence: Magistrates' Court: £1,000 fine.

Power: Report / s.25 PACE

Offence:

It is an offence for any person:

(a) to set in position any of the following articles, being an article which is of such a nature and so placed as to be calculated to cause bodily injury to any wild animal included in Sch.6[22] which comes into contact therewith; that is to say, any trap or snare, any electrical device for killing or stunning or any poisonous, poisoned or stupefying substance;[23]

(b) to use for the purpose of killing or taking any such wild animal any such article as aforesaid, whether or not of such a nature and so placed as aforesaid, or any net;

(c) to use for the purpose of killing or taking any such wild animal:

(i) any automatic or semi-automatic weapon;

(ii) any device for illuminating a target or any sighting device for night shooting;

(iii) any form of artificial lighting or any mirror or other dazzling device;

(iv) any gas or smoke;

(d) to use as a decoy, for the purpose of killing or taking any such wild animal, any sound recording;

(e) to use any mechanically propelled vehicle in immediate pursuit of any such wild animal for the purpose of killing or taking that animal; or

(f) to knowingly cause or permit to be done any act as aforesaid.

Contrary to:	Wildlife and Countryside Act 1981 s.11(2)
Max. sentence:	Magistrates' Court: £1,000 fine.
Power:	Report / s.25 PACE

Offence:

It is an offence for a person:

(a) to set in position or knowingly cause or permit to be set in position any snare which is of such a nature and so placed as to be calculated to cause bodily injury to any wild animal coming into contact therewith; and

(b) while the snare remains in position, to fail, without reasonable excuse, to inspect it, or cause it to be inspected, at least once every day.

Contrary to:	Wildlife and Countryside Act 1981 s.11(3)
Max. sentence:	Magistrates' Court: £1,000 fine.
Power:	Report / s.25 PACE

Offence:

It is an offence[24] for a person:

(a) to intentionally pick, uproot or destroy any wild plant included in Sch.8;[25] or

(b) not being an authorised person, to intentionally uproot any wild plant not included in that Schedule.

Contrary to:	Wildlife and Countryside Act 1981 s.13(1)
Max. sentence:	Magistrates' Court: £1,000 fine.
Power:	(a) Arrestable Offence;[26] (b) Report / s.25 PACE

Offence:

It is an offence for any person:

(a) to sell, offer or expose for sale, or have in his possession or to transport for the purposes of sale, any live or dead wild plant included in Sch.8 or any part of, or anything derived from, such a plant; or

(b) to publish or cause to be published any advertisement likely to be understood as conveying that he buys or sells, or intends to buy or sell, any of those things.

Contrary to: Wildlife and Countryside Act 1981 s.13(2)

Max. sentence: Magistrates' Court: £1,000 fine.

Power: Arrestable Offence[27]

Offence:

It is an offence for a person to release or allow to escape into the wild any animal which is of a kind which is not ordinarily resident in and is not a regular visitor to Great Britain in a wild state.

Contrary to: Wildlife and Countryside Act 1981 s.14(1)(a)

Max. sentence: Magistrates' Court: £1,000 fine.

Power: Arrestable Offence[28]

Offence:

It is an offence for a person, except as permitted under this Act,[29] to wilfully kill, injure or take, or attempt to kill, injure or take, a badger or to have in his possession or under his control any dead badger or any part of, or anything derived from, a dead badger.

Contrary to: Protection of Badgers Act 1992 s.1

Max. sentence: Magistrates' Court: 6 months' imprisonment / £5,000 fine.

Power: Report / s.25 PACE

Offence:

It is an offence for a person to:

(a) cruelly ill-treat a badger;

(b) use any badger tongs in the course of killing, taking, or attempting to kill or take, a badger;

(c) except as permitted, dig for a badger;

(d) use for any purpose of killing or taking a badger any firearm other than a smooth bore weapon of not less than 20 bore or a rifle using ammunition having a muzzle energy not less than 160 ft.lbs and a bullet weighing not less than 38 grains.

Contrary to: Protection of Badgers Act 1992 s.2

Max. sentence: Magistrates' Court: 6 months' imprisonment / £5,000 fine.

Power: Report / s.25 PACE

Offence:

It is an offence for a person, except as permitted under this Act,[30] to interfere with a badger sett by damaging it or any part of it, destroying it, obstructing access to, or to any entrance of, a badger sett, or to cause a dog to enter or disturb a badger when it is occupying a sett, intending to do any of those things or being reckless as to whether his actions would have any of those consequences.

Contrary to: Protection of Badgers Act 1992 s.3

Max. sentence: Magistrates' Court: 6 months' imprisonment / £5,000 fine.

Power: Report / s.25 PACE

Offence:

It is an offence for a person, except as permitted under this Act, to sell a live badger or offer one for sale or to have a live badger in his possession or under his control.

Contrary to: Protection of Badgers Act 1992 s.4

Max. sentence: Magistrates' Court: £5,000 fine.

Power: Report / s.25 PACE

Offence:

It is an offence[31] for any person to mutilate, kick, beat, nail or otherwise impale, stab, burn, stone, crush, drown, drag or asphyxiate any wild animal[32] with intent to inflict unnecessary suffering.

Contrary to: Wild Mammals (Protection) Act 1996

Max. sentence:	Magistrates' Court: 6 months' imprisonment / £5,000 fine.
Power:	Report / s.25 PACE

Offence:

It is an offence for any person to use, cause or permit another to use, lead shot for the purpose of shooting with a shotgun:

(a) on or over any area below the high-water mark of ordinary spring tides;

(b) on or over any site of special scientific interest included in Sch.1;[33] or

(c) any wild bird mentioned in Sch.2.[34]

Contrary to:	Environmental Protection (Restriction of Lead Shot) (England) Regulations 1999 r.3
Max. sentence:	Magistrates' Court: £1,000 fine.
Power:	Report / s.25 PACE

General powers

If a constable suspects with reasonable cause that any person is committing or has committed any of these offences under the Wildlife and Countryside Act 1981, the constable may without warrant:

(a) stop and search that person if the constable suspects with reasonable cause that evidence of the commission of the offence is to be found on that person;

(b) search or examine any thing which that person may be using or have in his possession if the constable suspects with reasonable cause that evidence of the commission of the offence is to be found on that thing;

(c) seize and detain for the purposes of proceedings any thing which may be evidence of the commission of an offence;

(d) enter any land other than a dwelling-house.[35]

Where a constable has reasonable grounds for suspecting that a person has committed an offence under the provisions of the

Protection of Badgers Act 1992 and that evidence of the commission of the offence may be found on that person or in or on any vehicle he may have with him, the constable may stop and search that person and any vehicle or article he may have with him and seize and detain anything which may be evidence of the commission of an offence or which may be liable to be forfeited.

Where a constable has reasonable grounds for suspecting that a person has committed the offence under the Wild Mammals (Protection) Act 1996 and that evidence of the commission of the offence may be found on that person or in or on any vehicle he may have with him, the constable may:

(a) without warrant, stop and search that person and any vehicle or article he may have with him; and

(b) seize and detain for the purposes of proceedings anything which may be evidence of the commission of an offence.

Notes

1 These are detailed in the Schedule to the 1976 Act and include kangaroos, monkeys, camels, ostriches, crocodiles and a number of spiders together with a large number of large carnivores such as lions, cheetahs and jaguars. See also *A–Z of Countryside Law second edition*.

2 This does not include any bird that is shown to have been bred in captivity.

3 Rising to £5,000 in the case of a bird included in Sch.1 to the 1981 Act.

4 Police and Criminal Evidence Act 1984 s.24(2)(s) as amended by the Countryside and Rights of Way Act 2000.

5 A person shall not be guilty of an offence under s.1(2) if he shows that (a) the bird or egg had not been killed or taken, or had been killed or taken otherwise than in contravention of the relevant provisions; or (b) the bird, egg or other thing in his possession or control had been sold (whether to him or any other person) otherwise than in contravention of those provisions, and 'the relevant provisions' means the provisions of the 1981 Act and the provisions of the Protection of Birds Acts 1954 to 1967. Exceptions to s.1 include birds taken lawfully outside the close season for that bird; that is, game birds, and birds taken or killed by other authorised persons, for example, authorised by the Department for Environment, Food and Rural Affairs. No offences will be committed where a disabled bird is taken for the purposes of tending and releasing it or for killing a bird so disabled there is no reasonable chance of its recovery.

6   Police and Criminal Evidence Act 1984 s.24(2)(s) as amended.

7   Police and Criminal Evidence Act 1984 s.24(2)(t) as amended.

8   No offence is committed if the person is registered in accordance with regulations made by the Secretary of State.

9   Other than a bird included in Part I of Sch.3 to the 1981 Act which refers to birds alive, ringed and bred in captivity.

10   Other than a bird included in Part II or III of Sch.3 which refer to, at all times, dead woodpigeon and, outside the close season, dead birds which may be lawfully taken, for example, duck, teal, widgeon and woodcock.

11   Police and Criminal Evidence Act 1984 s.24(2)(s) as amended by the Countryside and Rights of Way Act 2000.

12   No offence is committed in respect of poultry or to the keeping or confining of any bird while in the course of conveyance; while that bird is being shown for the purposes of any public exhibition or competition if the time does not exceed 72 hours or while the bird is undergoing examination or treatment by a vet.

13   No offences are committed under s.9(1)–(5) if authorised by the Department for Environment, Food and Rural Affiars or in pursuance of an order under the Animal Health Act 1981. Nor shall an offence be committed if the taking or killing is done in the interests of the animal concerned, see note 5. Other exceptions include the protection of crops where a licence has been obtained or sought.

14   Schedule 5 to the Wildlife and Countryside Act 1981 includes 92 animals including the adder, the typical bat, 7 types of beetle, the wild cat, the common frog, the grasshopper, 7 types of moth, the common otter, 4 types of snail, 2 types of spider and the red squirrel. The list also includes 25 varieties of butterfly although these are subject to the restrictions of s.9(5) only.

15   Police and Criminal Evidence Act 1984 s.24(2)(t) as amended.

16   A person shall not be guilty of an offence under s.9(2) if he shows that:

   (a)   the animal had not been taken or killed, or had been taken or killed otherwise than in contravention of the relevant provisions; or

   (b)   the animal or other thing in his possession or control had been sold (whether to him or to any other person) otherwise than in contravention of those provisions; and the 'relevant provisions' means the provisions of the Conservation of Wild Creatures and Wild Plants Act 1975.

17   Police and Criminal Evidence Act 1984 s.24(2)(t) as amended.

18   No offence is committed under this section within a dwelling-house.

19   Police and Criminal Evidence Act 1984 s.24(2)(t) as amended.

20   In any proceedings for an offence under s.9(1), (2) or (5)(a), the animal in question shall be presumed to have been wild unless the contrary is shown.

21 Police and Criminal Evidence Act 1984 s.24(2)(t) as amended.

22 That is, badgers, typical and horseshoe bats, wild cats, bottle-nosed dolphins, common dolphins, hedgehogs, pine martens, otters, polecats, harbour porpoises, shrews and red squirrels.

23 It is a defence to show that the article was set in position in the interests of public health, agriculture, forestry, fisheries or nature conservation and all reasonable steps to prevent injury were taken.

24 A person shall not be guilty of an offence under this section if he shows that the act was an incidental result of a lawful operation and could not easily have been avoided.

25 In Sch.8 to the 1981 Act ,168 species of plant are listed. Full details are contained in *A–Z of Countryside Law second edition*.

26 Police and Criminal Evidence Act 1984 s.24(2)(t) as amended.

27 Ibid.

28 Ibid.

28 Police and Criminal Evidence Act 1984 s.24(2)(t) as amended.

29 It is permitted to take a disabled badger for the purposes of tending it, killing it where such would be an act of mercy or to prevent serious damage to land, crops, property or poultry.

30 Exceptions to this offence include the blocking of a sett by a recognised hunt for the purposes of hunting foxes.

31 Exceptions include an act of mercy, in pursuit of lawful hunting, authorisation under any enactment, the lawful use of snares, traps, dogs or poisons.

32 Defined as any mammal which is not a domestic or captive animal within the meaning of the Protection of Animals Act 1911.

33 There are 278 listed sites.

34 That is, ducks, geese, coots, moorhens, snipe or golden plovers.

35 Wildlife and Countryside Act 1981 s.19(1).

WOUNDING AND GRIEVOUS BODILY HARM

See also Assaults, Burglary, PACE – Arrest, Racial Hatred, Robbery

Offence: It is an offence for a person, unlawfully and maliciously[1] by any means whatsoever, to:

(a)   wound,[2] or

(b)   cause grievous bodily harm[3]

to any person with intent to do some grievous bodily harm to any person, or with intent to resist or prevent the lawful apprehension or detainer of any person.

Contrary to: Offences Against the Person Act 1861 s.18

Max. sentence: Crown Court: life imprisonment / unlimited fine.

Power: Arrestable Offence

Offence:

It is an offence for a person to unlawfully and maliciously:

(a) wound; or

(b) inflict any grievous bodily harm[4]

upon any other person, either with or without any weapon or instrument.

Contrary to: Offences Against the Person Act 1861 s.20

Max. sentence: Magistrates' Court: 6 months' imprisonment / £5,000 fine.

Crown Court: 5 years' imprisonment / unlimited fine.

Power: Arrestable Offence

Offence:

It is an offence for a person to unlawfully and maliciously administer to, or cause to be administered to, or be taken by, any other person, any poison, or other destructive or noxious thing, so as thereby to inflict upon any such person any grievous bodily harm.

Contrary to: Offences Against the Person Act 1861 s.23

Max. sentence: Crown Court: 10 years' imprisonment / unlimited fine.

Power: Arrestable Offence

Offence:

It is an offence for a person to unlawfully and maliciously administer to, or cause to be administered to or taken by any other person, any poison or destructive or noxious thing with intent to injure, aggrieve or annoy.

Contrary to:	Offences Against the Person Act 1861 s.24
Max. sentence:	Magistrates' Court: 6 months' imprisonment / £5,000 fine.
	Crown Court: 5 years' imprisonment / unlimited fine.
Power:	Arrestable Offence

Notes

1 'Maliciously' involves an intention to do the harm that was done, or a recklessness as to whether such harm would occur.

2 Requires a break through all the layers of the skin.

3 That is, really serious bodily harm.

4 May include psychiatric injury [*R* v *Ireland* (1997)].

ZEBRA, PELICAN AND PUFFIN PEDESTRIAN CROSSINGS

See also Drivers and Riders, Highways and Roads, Road Traffic Collisions, Schools, Traffic Signs and Directions

Offence: It is an offence for a person to contravene any regulations made with respect to the precedence of vehicles and pedestrians respectively, and generally with respect to the movement of traffic (including pedestrians), at and in the vicinity of crossings.

Contrary to:	Road Traffic Regulation Act 1984 s.25(3)
Max. sentence:	Magistrates' Court: £1,000 fine.
Power:	Report / s.25 PACE

Offence: It is an offence for the driver of a vehicle to cause the vehicle or any part of it to stop within the limits of a crossing unless he is prevented from proceeding by circumstances beyond his control or it is necessary for him to stop to avoid injury or damage to persons or property.

Contrary to: Zebra, Pelican and Puffin Crossings Regulations and General Directions 1997 r.18

Max. sentence: Magistrates' Court: £1,000 fine.

Power: Report / s.25 PACE

Offence: It is an offence for a pedestrian to remain on the carriageway within the limits of a crossing longer than is necessary for that pedestrian to pass over the crossing with reasonable dispatch.

Contrary to: Zebra, Pelican and Puffin Crossings Regulations and General Directions 1997 r.19

Max. sentence: Magistrates' Court: £1,000 fine.

Power: Report / s.25 PACE

Offence: It is an offence for the driver of a vehicle[1] to cause it, or any part of it, to stop in a controlled area.

Contrary to: Zebra, Pelican and Puffin Crossings Regulations and General Directions 1997 r.20(2)

Max. sentence: Magistrates' Court: £1,000 fine.

Power: Report / s.25 PACE

Offence: It is an offence for the driver of a vehicle to cause it to contravene a prohibition given by a red light signal at a Pelican or Puffin crossing.

Contrary to: Zebra, Pelican and Puffin Crossings Regulations and General Directions 1997 r.23

Max. sentence: Magistrates' Court: £1,000 fine.

Power: Report / s.25 PACE

Offence: It is an offence for the driver of a motor vehicle proceeding towards a crossing to cause it, or any part of it:

(a) to pass ahead of the foremost part of any other motor vehicle proceeding in the same direction; or

(b) to pass ahead of the foremost part of a vehicle which is stationary for the purpose of according precedence to pedestrians or as required by a red light signal.[2]

Contrary to:	Zebra, Pelican and Puffin Crossings Regulations and General Directions 1997 r.24(1)
Max. sentence:	Magistrates' Court: £1,000 fine.
Power:	Report / s.25 PACE

Offence:

It is an offence for the driver of a vehicle to fail to accord precedence to any pedestrian[3] on the carriageway within the limits of a Zebra crossing.[4]

Contrary to:	Zebra, Pelican and Puffin Crossings Regulations and General Directions 1997 r.25
Max. sentence:	Magistrates' Court: £1,000 fine.
Power:	Report / s.25 PACE

Offence:

It is an offence for the driver of a vehicle to fail to accord precedence to any pedestrian[5] when the vehicular light signals at a Pelican are showing the flashing amber signal.

Contrary to:	Zebra, Pelican and Puffin Crossings Regulations and General Directions 1997 r.26
Max. sentence:	Magistrates' Court: £1,000 fine.
Power:	Report / s.25 PACE

Notes

1   Does not include a pedal bicycle not having a side-car attached to it, whether or not additional means of propulsion by mechanical power are attached to the bicycle. Other exceptions include according precedence to pedestrians; where the driver is prevented from proceeding by circumstances beyond his control or it is necessary for him to stop to avoid

injury or damage to persons or property or where the vehicle is being used for police, fire brigade or ambulance purposes. Further exceptions apply to building operations, demolitions and evacuations, the removal of obstructions, road maintenance or improvement as well as to the laying of pipes and mains.

2   In both (a) and (b) this refers to the vehicle nearest the crossing if there is more than one.

3   Where he has entered onto the carriageway before any part of the vehicle has entered those limits.

4   Where there is a refuge for pedestrians or central reservation on a Zebra crossing, the parts of the crossing situated on each side of the refuge or central reservation shall be treated as separate crossings.

5   If he is on the carriageway or a central reservation within the limits of the crossing (but not if he is on a central reservation which forms part of a system of staggered crossings), before any part of the vehicle has entered those limits.

INDEX